THE MAKING OF THE "RAPE OF NANKING"

Studies of the Weatherhead East Asian Institute, Columbia University

The Weatherhead East Asian Institute is Columbia University's center for research, publication, and teaching on the modern East Asia.

The Studies of the Weatherhead East Asian Institute were inaugurated in 1962 to bring to a wider public the results of significant new research on modern and contemporary East Asian affairs.

THE MAKING OF THE "RAPE OF NANKING"

*History and Memory in Japan, China,
and the United States*

Takashi Yoshida

*A Study of the Weatherhead East Asian Institute,
Columbia University*

OXFORD
UNIVERSITY PRESS

2006

OXFORD
UNIVERSITY PRESS

Oxford University Press, Inc., publishes works that further
Oxford University's objective of excellence
in research, scholarship, and education.

Oxford   New York
Auckland   Cape Town   Dar es Salaam   Hong Kong   Karachi
Kuala Lumpur   Madrid   Melbourne   Mexico City   Nairobi
New Delhi   Shanghai   Taipei   Toronto

With offices in
Argentina   Austria   Brazil   Chile   Czech Republic   France   Greece
Guatemala   Hungary   Italy   Japan   Poland   Portugal   Singapore
South Korea   Switzerland   Thailand   Turkey   Ukraine   Vietnam

Published by Oxford University Press, Inc.
198 Madison Avenue, New York, New York 10016

www.oup.com

Oxford is a registered trademark of Oxford University Press

Library of Congress Cataloging-in-Publication Data
Yoshida, Takashi.
The making of the "Rape of Nanking": history and memory in Japan, China,
and the United States / Takashi Yoshida
    p. cm.—(A study of the Weatherhead East Asian Institute, Columbia University)
Includes bibliographical references and index.
ISBN-13 978-0-19-518096-1
ISBN 0-19-518096-8
1. Nanking Massacre, Nanjing, Jiangsu Sheng, China, 1937. 2. Nanjing (Jiangsu Sheng,
China)—History—20th century. I. Title: History and memory in Japan, China,
and the United States. II. Title. III. Studies of the Weatherhead East Asian
Institute, Columbia University.
DS796.N2Y63 2006
951.04′2—dc22   2005052316

9 8 7 6 5 4 3 2 1

Printed in the United States of America
on acid-free paper

To Tomoko and Yoji Yoshida

ACKNOWLEDGMENTS

This project began while I was a first-year Ph.D. student at Columbia University in 1995. Without the encouragement and help of various people, this work would never have been completed. I would first like to thank Carol Gluck of Columbia University for accepting me to the doctoral program, developing my intellectual capability, and training me to be a historian. Her encouragement, patience, suggestions, and critical comments on my work on Nanjing throughout the lengthy stages of the project were simply indispensable.

I would also like to thank Michael Barnhart of the State University of New York at Stony Brook, Alan Brinkley of Columbia University, Joshua Fogel of York University, Laura Hein of Northwestern University, Andrew Nathan of Columbia University, Henry Smith of Columbia University, Bob Wakabayashi of York University, Louise Young of the University of Wisconsin at Madison, and Madeleine Zelin of Columbia University, all of whom read the entire manuscript and gave me thoughtful comments. In addition, I presented some of the chapters at workshops and received valuable suggestions from the audiences. I also have benefited enormously from the stimulating and helpful responses of the participants in Benkyōkai (Columbia University, April 2000), as well as members of my Dissertation Workshop (Columbia University, 2000), and Modern Japan Seminar (Columbia University, October 2000). Special thanks are due to Barbara Brooks of the City College of New York, Theodore Cook of William Paterson University, Edna Ehrlich of Ehrlich International Consulting, Darryl Flaherty of the University of Delaware, Marlene Mayo of the University of Maryland, Laura Neitzel of Brookdale Community College, Suzanne O'Brien of Loyola Marymount University, and Aaron Skabelund of Brigham Young University. In addition, I would like to thank the two anonymous reviewers who were engaged by Oxford University Press to read the earlier version of the manuscript and provided substantive reports, which I found enormously helpful during the final revision. As to the editing of the manuscript, I am grateful to John Matteson of John Jay College, Madge Huntington of the Weatherhead East Asian Institute at Columbia University, and Susan Ferber of Oxford University Press for their illuminating comments and suggestions. I am also indebted to Norma McLemore for painstaking copyediting and the refining touches she added to the manuscript and to Linda Donnelly of Oxford University Press for coordination and editing.

Since the project started I have occasionally traveled to Japan. There I have met a number of activists, journalists, lawyers, scholars, students, and teachers who have supported my work and generously refined my perceptions with their questions and observations. In particular, I am grateful to Awaya Kentarō of Rikkyō University, Kasahara Tokushi of Tsuru University, and Yoshida Yutaka of Hitotsubashi University for their time and assistance.

The history department of Western Michigan University has provided me with a supportive and reassuring working environment. I am particularly grateful to Robert Berkhofer, Joe Brandão, Linda Borish, Juanita De Baross, Nora Faires, Marion Gray, Catherine Julien, Carolyn Podruchny, Jim Palmitessa, and Judy Stone for their friendship and inspiration, particularly when the task seemed so much greater than I believed my talents and endurance to be.

Funding for this study was provided by a Fulbright-Hays Doctoral Dissertation Research Abroad Training Grant (U.S. Department of Education), a Toyota Foundation Research Grant (Toyota Foundation), a Junior Fellowship in Japan Studies (Weatherhead East Asian Institute, Columbia University), and support from the Final Preparation and Publication of Papers, and Exhibition of Creative Works Fund (Western Michigan University). I am profoundly grateful for their generous financial assistance.

For whatever is good in these pages, many may justly claim credit; everything else is mine alone. Although this study would not have been completed without financial, intellectual, and emotional support from various individuals and institutions, I bear all responsibility for errors and interpretations herein.

Throughout the volume, the names of those who live or lived primarily in China, Japan, or Taiwan are written with the surname preceding the given name. For the spellings of Chinese names and places, the Pinyin system is mainly used, though the Wade-Giles system is also adopted for words still commonly used such as "Chiang Kai-shek" instead of "Jiang Jieshi."

CONTENTS

Introduction: The Greater East Asian War, 3

Part I. Allies and Enemies in the Asia-Pacific War (1937–45)

1. Japan: Mobilizing the Nation, Sanitizing Aggression, 11
2. China: Intolerable Atrocities, 27
3. United States: The "Rape of Nanking," 37

Part II. The Storm of Postwar and Cold War Politics (1945–71)

4. Japan: Confronting the Nanjing Massacre, 45
5. China: In Times of Civil and Cold War, 62
6. United States: Rebuilding Japan, 71

Part III. Bringing the Nanjing Massacre into Print (1971–89)

7. Japan: From "Victim Consciousness" to "Victimizer Consciousness," 81
8. China: Nationalizing Memory of the Nanjing Massacre, 102
9. United States: Focus on Japanese Denials of the Past, 114

Part IV. The Internationalization of the Nanjing Massacre (1989 to Present)

10. Japan: A War over History and Memory, 129
11. China: The Nanjing Massacre and Patriotic Education, 154
12. United States: Rediscovery of the Nanjing Massacre, 165

Conclusion, 180
Notes, 185
Bibliography, 237
Index, 259
Studies of the Weatherhead Institute, Columbia University, 267

THE MAKING OF THE "RAPE OF NANKING"

Introduction

The Greater East Asian War (Daitō-A Sensō)

n a 1943 history text, Japan's Ministry of Education presented the following account of the Asia-Pacific War, which dealt *inter alia* with the capture of Nanjing:

> Our nation united Korea and the Japanese mainland and contributed to the foundation of peace in the East. In addition, [our nation] has adhered to the policy that Japan and Manchukuo are indivisible and has given East Asia the strength needed to defend itself. It is absolutely necessary for Japan, Manchukuo, and China to have the most cordial diplomatic relations. Our nation has explained this necessity to China and has repeatedly asked China to cooperate [with our nation]. Nevertheless, not only has the Chinese government failed to understand our sincere wishes, but it has also persisted in anti-Japanese activities. With the support of Europe and the United States, it has vigorously reinforced its military capability and has tried to bring pressure to bear both on Japan and Manchukuo.
>
> Finally, on July 7, 1937, at Marco Polo Bridge near Beijing, Chinese soldiers confronted and began shooting toward our army, which was engaged in maneuvers. Furthermore, [some] even went too far by harming our settlers.
>
> Our nation tried to persuade China to cease its lawlessness and to stem the disturbance; however, [the Chinese government] not only continued, but also increased its unjust activities. Thus, [our nation] dispatched the army to punish China for its violence, and the war expanded from northern China to central and southern China.
>
> During the war unswervingly loyal, brave, and courageous Imperial officers and soldiers traveled to different regions and conquered the enemy's bases one after another. On December 13, soon after [the war began], [they] conquered the capital, Nanjing, and planted the rising-sun flag atop of the walls of Nanjing. By October of the following year, or 1938, [they] had captured crucial places such as Guangdong, Wuchang, and

3

Hankou. As the Navy blockaded the coast and the Army and Navy planes brought the skies under their control, the enemy's government, which had fled to Chongqing, nearly fell apart.

His Imperial Majesty established the headquarters inside the Imperial Palace and worked on military matters day and night. On the first year anniversary of the [China] Incident, [he] issued an imperial rescript and expressed his appreciation for the strenuous efforts of the officers and soldiers and for the support and sacrifices that had been offered on the home front. [He] also encouraged [every Japanese] to [work hard] in order to establish peace in East Asia by cooperating with China as soon as possible. Inspired by the sacred words of His Majesty, our government declared on the Birthday of the Late Emperor Meiji [November 3rd] in 1938 that the goal of the war was to awaken China and to establish new order in East Asia.

Those Chinese who were impressed with our sincere wish founded some new governments in China. This contributed to the eventual establishment of the new Nationalist Government in Nanjing, led by Wang Jingwei. In November, our nation concluded a treaty with the new government and, thereafter, began to work together with Manchuria and China in order to build a new order in East Asia. The Chongqing government, however, survived because of American and British assistance and continued to resist our nation.[1]

In the more than six decades since its occurrence, the Nanjing Massacre has undergone continuous redefinition and reinterpretation in Japan, China, and the United States. Today it is easy to assume that the massacre was always viewed in the three nations as an emblem of Japan's wartime aggression in China and that it has always inspired revulsion like that associated with the Holocaust or Hiroshima. In truth, however, the image of Nanjing as the site of particularly brutal atrocities is a more recent construction. The massacre as it is discussed today did not exist in either national or international awareness until decades after the event. Certainly, Japanese atrocities in Nanjing were reported widely in China and the United States immediately after the fall of Nanjing, and such information, albeit on a limited basis, was available even in wartime Japan. Yet wartime understandings and contemporary reports as to the scale and duration of the atrocities were far less controversial than they later became. In the decades following the Asia-Pacific War (1937–45), the politics of the Cold War dominated historical discourse in East Asia, and the memory of Nanjing was pushed into the background. Throughout the 1950s and 1960s, disputes over the facts and significance of Nanjing were virtually nonexistent. It was only after the early 1980s that Nanjing attained a prominent position in the history and memory of the Asia-Pacific War and attracted the attention of a wide range of commentators.

This book demonstrates the shifting understandings of the Nanjing Massacre. It examines how the history of Nanjing has been constructed in Japan, China (including Taiwan), and the United States from 1937 to the present. Both as a historical topic and as an emblem of countless conflicting emotions and ideas, the Nanjing Massacre has touched these three countries in a startling variety of ways. Nanjing has figured in the attempts of all three nations to preserve and redefine national and ethnic pride and identity, assuming different kinds of significance based on each country's changing internal and external enemies. It has influenced—and in turn been influenced by—foreign policy and diplomatic relations among the four governments considered in this study. Perceptions of it have been used as a barometer of patriotic loyalty, and its memory has been manipulated in order to galvanize such loyalties. It has left its mark on journalism, film, painting, fiction, and museum displays. It has triggered acute controversies among individuals and groups of various political values. It has haunted and influenced the conscience of the world.

Initially an event with primarily local repercussions, the Nanjing Massacre has evolved over decades into a matter of extraordinary international significance. The process of the internationalization occurred in four distinct phases, each of which is treated in a separate three-chapter section. In each of the four phases of this study, one entire chapter is devoted to the history and memory of Nanjing in Japan, China, and the United States, respectively, during the period in question. Part I examines the history and memory of the Nanjing Massacre during the Sino-Japanese and the Pacific Wars (1937–45). Part II discusses the perceptions of Nanjing during the years following World War II, a period dominated by the politics of the earlier phases of the Cold War (1945–71). Part III analyzes the accounts of the massacre between 1971 and 1989, a period when literature concerning Nanjing appeared more frequently than in the previous years. Part IV traces the history and memory of Nanjing during the post–Cold War period, or from 1989 to the present.

Japan, China, and the United States have been studied to the exclusion of other nations. These three nations and their citizens have always taken the lead in internationalizing Nanjing, and memories and histories of Nanjing have influenced the national consciousness of these countries more than they have affected the public awareness of any other nation. For the countries in this study, the question of how to treat the legacy of Nanjing—whether to deplore it, sanitize it, rationalize it, or even ignore it—has mattered most intensely, for that question has touched upon closely held notions of ethics, nationality, and historical identity.

Japanese revisionists, that is, those commentators who have downplayed, excused, or even denied the atrocities in Nanjing, have performed a pivotal role in publicizing Nanjing beyond national boundaries. Had there not been intense challenges from the revisionists, the history and memory of the Nanjing Massacre might have remained a domestic issue rather than becoming an international symbol of Japan's wartime aggression. Vigorous disputes over Nanjing first arose in Japan in the early 1970s. As the revisionists became more visible in the 1980s, their adversaries expanded in number and inspired an increase in commemorative activities in Japan. Toward the mid-1980s, Chinese commentators joined the dispute and condemned the revisionists for their denial of the massacre. Finally, by the early 1990s, Chinese-American organizations had begun to protest vocally against the claims of the Japanese revisionists.

The story of Nanjing in historic memory only begins with an understanding of chronology. What must also be recognized is the immense variety of interpretations that the event has inspired, as well as the strident disagreements about how the massacre should be remembered. Almost everyone who has attempted to retell or reinterpret the story of Nanjing has wished for her or his version to be accepted as authoritative, and the battle for acceptance has led not only to intense public debate, but also to a seemingly endless generation of written narratives and visual materials. No single account or interpretation of the massacre has emerged as dominant, in part because there is no agreement even as to the basic terms of the debate. Commentators have been unable to agree on the very definitions of the matters they are discussing. They differ as to the proper meaning of words like "victim," "perpetrator," "atrocity," and "civilian." The number of victims at Nanjing largely depends on how one has defined "victims," "perpetrators," "atrocities," and "Nanjing," and accordingly, the estimate can go up and down. One may even be able to deny the event altogether by using definitions that serve one's belief and political motive. Since people have disputed the very boundaries of the victimized city, even the meaning of the word "Nanjing" has sparked dissent.

As the result of the decades-long dispute, numerous accounts on Nanjing are now available not only in Japanese, but also in Chinese and English. Some are analytical and scholarly, while others are emotional and polemical. Some provide complex pictures of the massacre; others present simple, black-and-white depictions of Nanjing. These competing accounts by both scholars and nonscholars, especially those who base their positions on ethnocentric arguments, have tended to speak of the massacre in broadly nationalistic terms, reducing the participants to monolithic words such as "the Chinese" and "the Japanese."

Yet national consciousness and character are never monolithic. Nations always contain individuals who speak, think, and act contrarily to the majority of their fellow citizens. In keeping with this philosophy, I prefer to avoid using collective nouns like "the Japanese" or "the Chinese," which tend to reinforce facile generalizations and to obscure the fact that national histories are intrinsically contentious and never garner strict unanimity of opinion or action. Nevertheless, because these collective nouns are rooted in the vocabulary of history, I have been compelled to use them from time to time. My occasional use of this kind of collective noun stems not from my preference, but from a combination of convenience and convention. In historical terms, the various "we's" and "they's" have been defined and redefined throughout the six decades analyzed in this work. Those lives regarded as belonging to "us" have often been treated differently from those regarded as belonging to "them." Similarly, the definition of "atrocity" has also altered since World War II, and the international community today is perhaps less tolerant of gross human rights violations than it was sixty years ago. During the war, killings of enemy soldiers and civilians alike were probably more acceptable among the belligerents in order to defeat the perceived enemies. The history of the "Greater East Asian War," quoted at the beginning of this introduction, comes from a 1943 textbook that sixth-graders in Japan were encouraged to regard as an authentic version of contemporary events. It is only one example of the kind of story that a nation could legitimately tell its children at the time of the war.

Though I begin my analysis from the 1930s, I attempt throughout this volume to provide context and to explain why the intensive disputes about the massacre began in the early 1970s and intensified across national boundaries, particularly since 1989. In trying to sift through the complexities of the history and memory of the Nanjing Massacre, one inevitably discovers that these complexities derive not only from the enormity of the event itself, but also from the political, social, and psychological forces that have molded the perceptions of a given commentator. The goal of this study is to demonstrate how and why each individual came to a particular understanding of Nanjing, rather than to judge who or what is right and wrong or true and untrue based on my personal politics and interpretations. The core of the dispute over Nanjing can be largely attributed to the individual predispositions of the participants in the debate. Without an understanding of the varying motives and politics, it is hardly possible to understand why the dispute over Nanjing has lasted more than three decades and is not likely to end in the immediate future.

Throughout this monograph, although individual names are mentioned when possible, I have loosely used the terms "revisionists" and "progressives" to describe the two opposing camps in Japan that have participated in the dispute over Nanjing. The former has tended to reject the history of the Nanjing Atrocities officially introduced to Japan during the American occupation and has attempted to revise or delete it from modern Japanese history. In contrast, the latter faction disapproves the values of Imperial Japan, including its colonialism and aggression. Progressives may or may not endorse the procedures of the International Military Tribunal for the Far East, but they tend to see the tribunal as possessing factual merit, and they generally accept its findings with regard to the Nanjing Massacre. In reality, however, individuals within both schools of opinion more or less differ as to the particulars of their positions and views, and the coarse division of the disputants into two opposing camps inevitably ignores existing diversities and complexities among them. Nevertheless, such categorization is useful as it allows us to highlight the very essence of the dispute of Nanjing Massacre and its process of the internationalization.

In this study, I try to include the experiences and ideas of the numerous authors, critics, correspondents, curators, filmmakers, lawyers, politicians, veterans, and victims. It has been my intention to treat all points of view with fairness and respect, even when I strongly disagree with them. Nevertheless, my writing cannot be entirely free from my personal politics, either. I have a high regard for activists, historians, lawyers, schoolteachers, and university professors in Japan and elsewhere who have ceaselessly worked to preserve and publicize the history and memory of Nanjing as well as other Japanese wartime atrocities. I am critical of nationalists and ethnocentrists in China, Japan, and the United States, who have intentionally or unintentionally based their judgments of history on the supposition that one's nation or ethnicity determines one's value as a human being. I have written this book as a modest protest against those whose views of the world are imprisoned by concepts of nation and ethnicity.

Finally, as to the sources, this study is heavily based on newspapers from the various countries. They offer some of the traceable footprints that one may follow in an effort to understand the memory and history of the Nanjing Massacre across national boundaries. The role of mass media in nationalizing and internationalizing Nanjing is indisputable, and this study intends to demonstrate the way in which these news reports contributed to the making of the "Rape of Nanking."

I

ALLIES AND ENEMIES IN THE ASIA-PACIFIC WAR (1937–45)

1

Japan: Mobilizing the Nation, Sanitizing Aggression

I n the immediate aftermath of the fall of Nanjing on December 13, 1937, and the subjugation of Chinese forces, the atrocities in Nanjing did not exist in official Japanese accounts, nor did most Japanese learn of these atrocities which had destroyed hundreds of thousands of lives. Authorized newspaper reports, magazine articles, radio programs, textbooks, and even cartoons all supported the war effort and denounced Chinese leaders who, it was said, were promoting the anti-Japanese movement in China. These accounts emphasized Chinese atrocities in sensational reporting designed to stir public antagonism toward the enemy nation and its people.

In order to control the media and public opinion, the government made full use of its police power. It censored the press and even eavesdropped on street conversations between ordinary citizens. It arrested people who challenged its policies and spied on those whom it regarded as potentially harmful to the government. Especially suspect were Communists, liberals, ethnic minorities, and members of religious organizations.

Even during this period of suppression, however, Japanese society was neither monolithic nor perfectly united. Accounts that escaped censorship—the so-called "rumors and lies," banned writings, smuggled publications, and personal diaries—did record and condemn the random killings, looting, and rape in Nanjing. Communists and their sympathizers in China and the United States sent their publications to friends in Japan. Missionaries smuggled in written accounts of Japanese atrocities in China. Japanese soldiers recorded their experience in Nanjing in their field diaries. Yet, at the height of hostilities with China, such brutalities seemed almost indistinct from the rest of the fabric of enmity, nationalism, and war. Thus, in the immediate aftermath of the outrages at Nanjing, only the most attentive observers in Japan were aware that they had even happened.

From the beginning of the armed conflict in July 1937, the Japanese government and its supporters, including the mass media, stressed that Chiang Kai-
shek had planned and initiated armed struggle. According to the official view,
Japan had been seeking peace in Asia, only to be dragged into an unwanted
military conflict with China. Prime Minister Konoe Fumimaro's decision to dispatch additional forces to China received enthusiastic support from the large
national newspaper *Tōkyō asahi shinbun*. In an article titled "Obviously Planned
Anti-Japanese Armed Conflict; Firmly Decided to Dispatch to Northern China;
Determined Statement by the Government to China and Other Countries," the
editor used boldface to emphasize that "this incident was no doubt an anti-
Japanese armed conflict that was carefully planned by China" and "[the Japanese government] sincerely hopes that the Chinese side will immediately reflect
on its attitude and that peaceful negotiations [will be instituted] in order not to
worsen the circumstance."[1]

The media stressed that the Chinese soldiers and guerrillas were recklessly
killing innocent Japanese civilians as well as combatants. Japanese casualties
inflicted by "unlawful" Chinese shootings at the Marco Polo Bridge and other
places were widely reported in the *Asahi*.[2] When approximately 3,000 Chinese
troops in Tongzhou attacked Japanese forces as well as civilians and killed some
200 Japanese and Korean residents, the Japanese war correspondents of *Dōmei*,
Ōsaka mainchi shinbun, *Tōkyō nichi nichi shinbun*, *Tōkyō asahi shinbun*, and other
papers described the event in detail and expressed outrage.[3] The *Asahi*, for example, detailed Chinese looting and destruction in the Japanese community as
well as the stabbing and killing of women, children, and infants.[4] In another
article on the same page, the *Asahi* correspondent Tanaka, who had met survivors of the incident, described his feelings of unprecedented fury and declared
that "July 29th must not be forgotten."[5]

On August 10, 1937, *Asahi* readers learned the details of another atrocity by
the Chinese peace preservation force in Shanghai. Ōyama Isao, a 27-year-old
first lieutenant of the Imperial Navy, was surrounded by Chinese forces and rid-
dled with dozens of bullets.[6] According to those war correspondents who could
express their opinions without police suppression, the Japanese forces were, as
the government insisted, merely responding to Chinese aggression, and it was
the Chinese troops who should be blamed.[7] Typical was the reaction of the war
correspondent Itō when Japanese soldiers burned a farmer's house and opened
fire on fleeing Chinese guerrillas who had been hiding inside it. Itō observed
that the soldiers had done so to avenge Lieutenant Ōyama.[8] In the eyes of many
Japanese war correspondents, the Chinese military in Shanghai were merely vi-
cious. "Blood-thirsty" Chinese fighters had dropped bombs and killed not only

Japanese civilians, but also unarmed American, British, Chinese, and French residents in the city.[9]

Even liberal journalists of the time such as Kiyosawa Kiyoshi and Baba Tsunego stood by the government after the so-called China Incident (*Shina jihen*)—the name officially given to the undeclared war between China and Japan—that began at the Marco Polo Bridge in July 1937.[10] At the meeting of the International Association of Poets, Playwrights, Editors, Essayists, and Novelists (PEN) in London in November 1937, Kiyosawa opposed the Chinese request that the association condemn Japanese attacks on hospitals, schools, and museums. Instead, he advocated that PEN should protest Chinese fortifications of these buildings, the action that had incited the Japanese military to attack. As Kiyosawa explained to a Norwegian colleague, the China Incident was the result of Japan's struggle for survival. The United States and Southeast Asia, he argued, were rejecting Japanese immigrants; moreover, Japanese exports were being excluded by high tariff barriers. Other members of PEN, all of whom supported the Chinese request, might have had a hard time understanding Kiyosawa's Japan-centered explanation, but, to Kiyosawa, Japanese nationals were fighting for international justice, and members of the association were unfairly criticizing Japan.[11]

The liberal journalist Baba Tsunego shared the view that Japan was fighting for international justice. Ordinary Japanese, he argued, never expected to fight such a great war against China, and the people of China were, in fact, not the enemy of the Japanese. He rationalized that Japan was fighting out of an obligation to protect Asia from Western aggression. During the Tokugawa period (1600–1868), when the Western powers were expanding their territories, Japan had isolated itself on small islands and immersed itself in martial arts and tea ceremonies. When Japan awoke, all of the prominent lands around the world had already been occupied, and Japan was itself almost swallowed up by these other powers. Russia, he argued, was pressuring China to fight against Japan in order to exhaust Japanese national strength, so that Russia might expand its own influence into China. Baba, who believed in "Asia for Asia," could not tolerate the possibility of China as a Russian proxy.[12]

The official view of the time was clearly stated in elementary school textbooks. In the fifth-year geography textbook, written for 10- and 11-year-old children, that came into use in 1936, Japan was defined as consisting of the Japanese islands—mainland (Honshū), Hokkaidō, South Sakhalin, Shikoku, Kyushu, Taiwan, Ryukyu islands, the Kurils—and the Korean peninsula.[13] In the sixth-year geography textbook available in 1936, a description of Manchukuo was added in the chapter on Asia. The textbook stressed that relations between Manchukuo and Japan were extremely close and that Manchukuo was Japan's lifeline. According to the textbook explanation, "Our country endorsed Manchukuo's independence as soon as it became independent, then withdrew from the League of Nations, and has been making a substantial effort to develop this nation [Manchukuo] and to maintain peace in Asia."[14] After the China Incident in 1937, the textbook was again revised. The 1939 sixth-year geography textbook emphasized that Japanese efforts to preserve coexistence and co-prosperity with China, as well as Japanese development and sacrifice, were contributing to the development of Chinese transportation and foreign trade. In addition, the textbook blamed Chinese leaders for their "incorrect attitude" (*ayamatta kangae*) and for their provocative anti-Japanese ideology, both of which had led to the China Incident. Japan, according to the textbook, "has been urging China to reflect on [its mistaken policy toward Japan] and continually carrying out its mission of eternal peace in Asia."[15]

Just like the geography textbook, national history textbooks were also revised after Japan went to war against China. A 400-word paragraph in the text issued to sixth graders in 1941 offered the following summary:

> After the Manchurian Incident was settled, our country (*waga kuni*) concluded a cease-fire agreement with China. Moreover, [our country] pursued the establishment of eternal peace in the East based on the co-operation of Japan, Manchukuo, and China. However, the Chinese government, assisted both by European countries and the United States, did not understand our sincerity and persistently tried to exclude our country. Furthermore, [it] also dispatched troops [to the north] and tried to disrupt the development of Manchukuo. In July 1937, at the Marco Polo Bridge near Beijing, Chinese troops fired on our army, which was conducting maneuvers. In addition, some even assaulted our residents. Therefore, in the interest of justice, our country decided to send the military to rectify China's mistaken ideas and to establish eternal peace in the East. Since then our military, both navy and army, has accomplished significant achievements. The people on the home front have sincerely been giving solid support to this campaign and are rushing forward in order to carry out this great mission. The foundation for eternal peace in Asia is gradually being laid.[16]

Also reflecting the trends of the time were readers used in Japanese class in the 1930s. In volume 1 of the newly revised reader issued in 1933, first-year pupils learned to read by mastering phrases like "Forward, forward, soldiers forward" (*susume susume heitai susume*) and "The flag of the rising sun, banzai, banzai" (*hinomaru no hata banzai banzai*), neither of which had been included in the textbooks used during the previous 15 years.[17] In the second-year reader (vol. 2), stories about the navy and army were introduced: "Elder Brother in the Navy" (Kaigun no nīsan) and "Enlistment of Elder Brother" (Nīsan no nyūei).[18] "Elder Brother in the Navy" glorified military technology, with Isamu's elder brother serving as a sailor on a heavily armed, high-tech aircraft carrier. In "Enlistment of Elder Brother," family members and neighbors congratulate the elder brother on enlisting, but the story does not tell whether he comes back alive. Other new readings in the revised textbooks included "Submarine" (Sensuikan) and "Admiral Tōgō" (Tōgō gensui) in the third-year reader; "Great Maneuvers" (Daienshū) in the fourth year; "Riding the Asia Express"

('Ajia' ni norite) in the fifth year; and "Dogfight" (Kūchūsen), "Japanese Sword" (Nihontō), and "Mechanized Unit" (Kikaika butai) in the sixth year.[19]

Revised editions of ethics textbooks in the 1930s superficially resembled the textbooks in geography, history, and language, in that they were aimed at strengthening loyalty to the emperor and promoting patriotism. However, they continued to stress such universal concepts as benevolence, courage, honesty, international peace, public welfare, and the rule of law. They also included stories of nonmilitary figures as well as Western role models. The sixth-year ethics textbook that became available in 1939, for example, contained a brief biography of Benjamin Franklin and stressed friendship between nations in order to maintain international peace. Loyalty to the throne, the development of the nation, the obligations of the people, and Confucian principles were also emphasized.[20] The fifth-year textbook issued in 1938 featured such historical models as Socrates, Nogi Maresuke (a general who achieved fame in the Russo-Japanese war and later committed suicide in order to follow the Meiji emperor into death), Christopher Columbus, Katsu Kaishū (a Shogunal official and master of Western naval science), and Yoshida Shōin (an imperial loyalist before the Restoration).[21] In the fifth-year ethics textbook, the last chapter, titled "Good Japanese" (Yoi Nihonjin), stated that "it [is] our duty not to forget the kindness of others and to be benevolent and generous to everyone."[22]

Popular magazines, including comic books, also encouraged their young readers to believe in Japan's mission in Asia and fostered the desire of male children to become generals or admirals. One of the most popular cartoons among children in the 1930s was Tagawa Suihō's "Stray Dog, Norakuro" (Nora-kuro), published serially in the monthly magazine Boy's Club (Shōnen kurabu) from 1931 to 1941 and in book form by Dai Nihon Yūbenkai Kōdansha (Kōdansha).[23] The protagonist was a homeless orphan dog, Straydog Kurokichi (Norainu Kurokichi), or Nora-kuro for short, who joined the Regiment of Brave Dogs (Mōken rentai) as a second-class private and received a promotion each year. He battled bears, mountain monkeys, pigs, gorillas, chimpanzees, mythic river monsters (kappa), and dinosaurs. The humorous cartoon was an allegory of Japanese foreign affairs and spread a positive image of the military among children. In "Nora-Kuro," dogs were depicted as brave, strong, righteous, and merciful, whereas their enemies were not. In Norakuro's Charge (Norakuro sōkōgeki), the seventh volume of the series, published in December 1937, dogs fought against the nation of pigs, led by the general called Fried-Pork Cutlet (Tonkatsu), who held power by suppressing and exploiting a nation of powerless sheep.[24] The model for General Fried-Pork Cutlet seemed to be Chiang Kai-shek. At the end of the volume, Norakuro, who had now risen to the rank of lieutenant, cried out: "If you want to fight back, go ahead! I will always fight for peace in order to maintain peace in great Asia."[25]

By December 1937, cartoons and other authorized mass media had immersed the ordinary public in narratives intended to mobilize the war effort and to legitimize Japan's aggression in China. Accounts of the Battle of Nanjing were no exception.

VICTORIOUS NEWS REPORTS OF
THE CONQUEST OF NANJING

In the final weeks before the fall of Nanjing, newspapers enthusiastically predicted an imminent, dramatic victory and sought to inspire their readers with
national gratitude toward the Japanese military. On November 30, December 4,
and December 6, 1937, *Tōkyō nichi nichi shinbun* carried reports of a "killing contest" between two second lieutenants, who were trying to outdo each other in
obliterating the Chinese enemy.[26] On December 8, 1937, *Yomiuri shinbun* reported that the Japanese national flag was now waving atop Zijin Mountain and
that the capture of Nanjing, which "the entire nation" had passionately awaited,
would soon be a reality.[27] The same day the Nihon Hōsō Kyōkai (NHK), Japan
Broadcasting Corporation, broadcast a special radio music program "Evening of
the Prelude to the Capture of Nanjing" (Nankin kōryaku zensō no yū) to celebrate the Japanese victory.[28] By this date the Japanese Army had completely surrounded Nanjing, and Matsui Iwane, commander in chief of the Central China
Area Army, had ordered his pilots to drop leaflets containing an open letter to
Tang Shengzhi, the Chinese commander in chief, advising surrender so that the
historical buildings of Nanjing might be saved from destruction. However, as
Japanese media described it, Tang "ignored Matsui's generous *bushidō* attitude in
a rude manner," forcing the Japanese troops to attack Nanjing.[29]

Around 9 P.M. on December 10, *Tōkyō asahi shinbun* issued an extra edition of
the newspaper announcing that the military had seized all the entrances into the
city. With a clever eye to marketing, *Asahi* had the extra distributed among the
crowds at a dance hall in Akasaka. An *Asahi* reporter then recorded the ecstatic
reactions of the 300 dancers for inclusion in the next day's paper. *Asahi* also reported festive lantern parades in Tokyo.[30] Newspapers reported that elementary,
secondary, and college students and prisoners, too, applauded the capture of the
capital and the punishment of Chiang Kai-shek's anti-Japanese government.[31]

After the fall of the city, these newspapers jubilantly announced the annihilation of the enemy.[32] On December 16, 1937, for example, the press reported
that "the Imperial Army [was] now conducting mopping-up operations against
stragglers. . . . Reporters estimated that Matsui's army had captured or killed
approximately 60,000."[33] Two days later, the papers were filled with accounts
of the triumphant entry of Japanese troops into Nanjing. As *Tōkyō nichi nichi
shinbun* observed, the Japanese flag was now raised over Nanjing, a former capital of the enemy, and "all, officers and soldiers alike, were deeply moved to
tears."[34] In a record-breaking three and a quarter hours, spectacular photographs of the ceremony were carried to Japan in *Asahi*'s own airplane and were
printed in the extra of the *Asahi* on the same day.[35]

Longer stories by war correspondents that detailed the capture of Nanjing
also appeared in the large-circulation general magazines in early 1938. These
included not only the simple "you-savage, we-hero" writings often found in the
newspapers, but also narratives that informed readers about the battle in Nan-

jing.[36] Like all other authorized reports at the time, these accounts supported the war effort and the fighting in Nanjing. *Bungei shunjū* correspondent Kosaka Eiichi, for example, rushed from Shanghai to Nanjing on December 8, hoping to witness the dramatic fall of Nanjing. Kosaka vividly described the detritus of battle that he saw on the way from Shanghai to Nanjing. He wrote of the trenches, bullet holes, destroyed houses, exploded bunkers, and countless dead bodies of horses and Chinese soldiers on the side of the road. All attested to the bitterness of the fighting. Kosaka seemed to be embarrassed by what he saw, especially the numerous dead on the road, although he did not comment further on his feelings. Instead, he stated, as if trying to convince himself, that the corpses would later be buried with care by the Japanese troops.[37]

When Kosaka arrived in Nanjing, war fever overtook him. After all, he wrote, if the Japanese troops had dealt a bitter blow to the Chinese defense forces in Nanjing, the defenders had brought this treatment on themselves by ignoring Matsui's ultimatum. Death was the order of the day on the battlefield, and Kosaka himself had almost been killed by Chinese machine-gun fire. He had also observed dead Japanese soldiers being cremated even though there was no Japanese military monk to chant the proper ceremonial sutra. When Nanjing fell, Kosaka was moved to tears of joy, along with many of the soldiers, as he watched the Japanese national flag flying high on the wall.[38]

Ōya Sōichi, a critic and writer who was also in Nanjing at the time, was a more analytical and ironic observer. Whereas Kosaka was merely outraged by anti-Japanese slogans on walls between Shanghai and Nanjing, Ōya was amused to see red posters written in Japanese announcing: "Welcome Imperial Japanese Army" (*kōgun kangei*) and "Welcome Great General of the Land of Rising Sun" (*tōyō dai shōgun kangei*). These posters hung at the entrance of the houses in Wuxi, even though the walls had previously been painted with anti-Japanese slogans. Ōya concluded that residents in Wuxi had tried to appease first the Chinese and then the Japanese troops. As he noticed, these residents, who had suffered a great deal from the turmoil of war, treated the Japanese army just as they might have received another group of Chinese warlords. People in the town were rarely seen because they were hiding, and those who did appear were mostly elderly men with armbands bearing clumsy handmade insignias of the rising sun.[39]

When Ōya examined fortified bunkers immediately after the Japanese military had seized the area around Nanjing, he sometimes smelled perfume and saw women's hair oil and underwear left behind. These items made him imagine young, patriotic Chinese women who did not mind risking their lives to encourage soldiers at the front and who sometimes took up guns themselves. Although he did not see any dead bodies of women in uniform, he found a large white flag stained with blood belonging to "School for Orphaned Daughters" (joshi izoku gakkō), which he assumed the women had used to cover the wounded. These abandoned articles, highlighting the tragic situation of Chinese women, moved him very much.[40]

Like Kosaka, Ōya witnessed many unburied corpses of Chinese soldiers between Kushan and Suzhou. Because of inadequate road conditions near Changzhou, he was forced to leave his car and walk. He soon found that he had to be careful not to step on dead Chinese soldiers. He sometimes had to eat strangely colored rice steamed in water from a creek where dead bodies were floating. As he approached Nanjing, he spent a night on a straw bed that smelled of dung and twice was almost killed, once by land mines and once by a falling artillery shell.[41]

On the night of December 12, Ōya was too excited to sleep because of the expected capture of Nanjing, which he predicted would make a permanent mark in world history. Just after 3 o'clock in the morning, he heard news that Zhongshan Gate had been seized. Immediately after dawn, he entered the walled city, where he saw excited Japanese soldiers dancing and singing. Walking around the city the next day, he felt pity for its impoverished residents who had no place to go and for the Chinese nation, which had the misfortune to be led by such blundering and error-prone government leaders.[42]

Accounts published in widely circulated newspapers and popular journals, such as Kosaka's and Ōya's, celebrated the Japanese conquest of Nanjing, but rarely mourned the devastation of the city and its people. They seemed to regard the war with China as a good war. Although they occasionally expressed some sympathy toward their enemy, for the most part they held Chiang Kai-shek and his "anti-Japanese" movement responsible for the war and its destructive consequences. Wartime narratives emphasized the idea that the state owns its citizens and that public well-being depended on the state and its leaders. In these pro-war narratives, the concept of inviolable individual human rights was largely missing.

"LIARS AND TRAITORS": THE SHACKLING OF OPINION

Undeniably, wartime Japan had capable leaders, practiced in controlling the media and education, in using the police to suppress views that challenged those of the government, and in promoting the ideology of a united Japanese empire fighting for international justice. Measured according to the swelling tide of nationalism and the silencing of criticism they were able to achieve, these leaders were indeed successful.

In order to control public opinion, newspapers, periodicals, and books were censored.[43] Radio programs were also directed to contribute to national war efforts.[44] In addition, the Special Higher Police (Tokkō) maintained a steady surveillance of potentially antigovernment Buddhist, Chinese, Christian, civil rights, Communist, Korean, labor, right-wing, and socialist organizations. The police monitored private conversations, rumors, and even lavatory graffiti, all in the name of maintaining "public order." Liberals and democrats who criticized the government policies or provoked antiwar movements were dismissed from their jobs and sometimes arrested. By the end of 1937, writers and speakers who protested Japanese aggression in China had no place to publicly express their views. In 1937, 529 alleged leftists were arrested, and 210 were indicted for violations of the Peace Preservation Law.[45] In addition, 254 cases of rumors considered harmful to the society were investigated in 1937, and 107 people were prosecuted.[46]

In the three days of the fall of Nanjing, the following examples of repression occurred. Wada Mutsurō, 26-year-old manager of a café in Tokyo, who had told a taxi driver that it was quite natural for Chinese to become anti-Japanese since their nation had been invaded by Japan, was sentenced to three years' probation, violation of which could have led to eight months in prison.[47] Ozawa Nobuo, a 22-year-old student suspected of Communist sympathies, stated in a Tokyo restaurant that Japan was waging an aggressive war against China and that he, who loved China, would not change his ideas even if he were to be killed by the police. He was sentenced to two years' probation with the possibility of ten months in prison.[48] The police found an antiwar slogan in a public toilet at Shinjuku Station and searched for the person who had written in pencil "War does not save poor proletarian farmers. Chinese people, stand up against fascism!"[49]

Police also targeted intellectuals. On December 1, 1937, the Library Bureau of the Ministry of Home Affairs declared that *People and Peace* (Minzoku to heiwa), written by Yanaihara Tadao, a liberal professor of economics at the University of Tokyo, violated Article Nine of the Press Code because the book would provoke antiwar sentiment and disturb peace in society.[50] Yanaihara decided to submit his resignation to the university. At the end of his last lecture there, he said, "I believe that a university is responsible for maintaining a critical mind. A university should be a place where social phenomena are analyzed and criticized from a viewpoint above the fray. Based on true national interests, true should be regarded as true, wrong should be regarded as wrong." He concluded his lecture with an old saying: "Even if your flesh withers, do not kill your spirit" (*nikutai wa horobiru mo seishin o korosu nakare*).[51]

Yanaihara was fortunate compared to the approximately 400 members of the Labor-Farmer faction (*rōnōha*). Even though this faction had earlier seceded from the Communist Party, the authorities were not interested in making formal distinctions. On December 15, 1937, the government declared that the *rōnōha* organization was in violation of the Peace Preservation law. Shortly thereafter, the police rounded up its members.[52] The government and the police accused the *rōnōha* organizations of fomenting antiwar ideology and plotting Communist revolution under Soviet auspices. A monthly report by the Tokkō police urged that overtly Communist activities had to be thoroughly controlled, and any liberal organization was suspect as a breeding ground for Communism.[53]

The government was also anxious to control ethnic minorities within its territory. According to the census, the empire in 1935 encompassed 97.7 million people on Japanese islands (*naichi*), the Korean peninsula, Taiwan, the Kuril islands, and other places.[54] Of these, approximately 626,000 were Koreans.[55] By December 1936, more than 40,000 ethnic minorities, of whom some 29,000 were from China and Manchukuo, lived within this territory.[56] By the end of 1940, according to the Tokyo Metropolitan Police, 7,632 Taiwanese were living in Tokyo.[57] The police considered these new Japanese every bit as dangerous as native-born leftists, and their fears increased after Japan went to war with China. From the outset of the war in 1937, many members of suspect racial and national categories received sentences for allegedly spreading lies and rumors.

For example, on November 22, 1937, Liu Hanfu, a 38-year-old building superintendent from Manchukuo, was sentenced to six months in prison because he publicly stated that Japan would lose the war with China because the Soviets would intervene. On December 10, 1937, Choe Wan-Seok, a 26-year-old student from Korea, was sentenced to eight months in prison because, as an alleged Communist, he asserted that the China Incident was an act of Japanese imperialist aggression and that the long war with China would touch off a civil war in Japan, which would in turn result in Japan's becoming a socialist nation. On April 1, 1938, a 26-year-old refugee from Russia, Alexander Tethler, was sentenced to three years' probation with the possibility of four months in prison because he had commented that Chinese had welcomed Japanese forces by waving the Japanese flag only because they were afraid of being shot.[58]

Although the police considered convicted liars and their rumors dangerous and traitorous, it was these so-called lies and rumors that often offered the most candid criticisms of the government's war effort. Almost by definition, it was only these supposedly dangerous dissenters who expressed profound sensitivity and sorrow for the sufferings of the nation's perceived enemy and its citizens. And, of course, the reports and articles that fell under the wartime censorship would have provided a more diverse perspective of the war than the authorized accounts, which blamed China for disturbing international justice and whitewashed atrocities committed by the Japanese military.

BANNED ACCOUNTS

Although contemporary reportage rarely mentioned the brutalities in Nanjing, unauthorized documents revealed what approved accounts could not. The massacre received rather frank treatment in a number of banned writings. Though these accounts remained suppressed and unavailable to the public during the war, they recorded the Japanese atrocities in Nanjing at the time and later became valuable sources for historians such as Hora Tomio in refuting claims that the Nanjing Massacre was an illusion.

One of these sources was *Living Soldiers* (Ikiteiru heitai), a graphic, thoughtful, and detailed narrative of the atrocities written by Ishikawa Tatsuzō in 1938.[59] After the fall of Nanjing, *Chūō kōron*, a leading monthly magazine, sent Ishikawa to the city with the assignment of writing a novel about the battle. Had the authorities not banned his novel from publication, readers would at least have had the chance to learn of Japanese soldiers mercilessly killing Chinese soldiers and civilians while shedding bitter tears for their own dead countrymen. The manuscript also described Japanese soldiers engaged in looting Chinese homes and businesses for food, bedding, and other goods. Others were shown searching for women. Although Ishikawa's novel also portrayed patriotic soldiers eager to fight to the death, it was no shallow tribute to the glory of war. He described the military brothels and sex slavery in Nanjing and did not gloss over the beheadings of suspected Chinese guerrillas or the Japanese policy of taking no prisoners. Hatred of "the Chinese," the sufferings of those who sought refuge in the safety zone, and the mass killings of Chinese soldiers by Japanese destroyers on the Xiaguang River all received frank treatment, bearing testimony to the inhumanity of the war.[60]

Living Soldiers also tried to explain why Japanese troops had been transformed into something akin to armed bandits. In the novel, the troops supported and fed themselves by systematic larceny. Such looting became an excuse among Japanese soldiers to leave their camps, and soon this pretext began to provide an opportunity to look for women in the villages. Yet few soldiers were able to find young women, since so many, guessing their probable fate from their previous experiences of civil war, had fled. Disappointed in their searches, these soldiers instead brought back such articles as women's handkerchiefs and shoes to show off to fellow soldiers in their units.[61]

Suspicion of civilians seemed to transform soldiers into brutes. When one second lieutenant passed by an 11- or 12-year-old girl on the street, she shot him in the back and killed him. The troops who heard the gunshot surrounded the house where she was hiding, broke into it, and shot rounds of bullets into the girl, who was hiding behind the bed. An old man in the house was also shot to death. Such incidents were used to rationalize the killing of Chinese noncombatants. As the troops approached Nanjing, they were also frightened by the anti-Japanese hostility of the people. Immediately after the incident of the girl's shooting, the troops received a directive allowing them to kill resisting civilians.[62]

In Ishikawa's novel, the killing of prisoners of war resulted from military expediency as well as from the laxness of the Japanese commanding officers. Taking prisoners required extra manpower and police effort, and the troops chose to kill instead. Ishikawa wrote: "To Corporal Kasahara, killing the enemy is like killing fish. He kills the enemy without remorse. Only his instinctive love of his fellow soldiers moves his feelings. He is an impressively excellent soldier, and nothing but a soldier."[63] Although there was no official order from the top to do so, killing surrendered troops was in fact a widespread practice during the Japanese military advance to Nanjing.

In another scene, Katayama, a Buddhist monk who mourned the dead Japanese soldiers, disappointed Nishizawa, a commander who wanted to believe in religion as a unifying force. Ishikawa's commentary following a dialogue between the two characters reflected his concern for the way war changes human beings. The monk, as Ishikawa wrote, "believed that Buddhism would transcend national borders when he was practicing asceticism in Japan. . . . When he volunteered for military service, he thought he would be willing to pray for the Chinese dead. But he could not do so after he actually came to the battlefield." Ishikawa continued: "The battlefield seems to have a strong, mysterious power that can transform combatants into a mass that shares the same characteristics, thinks in the same manner, and has the same desire. As Private Kondō, a graduate of a medical school, lost his intelligence, Katayama Gensen [the monk] seems to have lost his religion, too. The only reminder that he was a monk is that he knows Buddhist sutras and how to conduct funeral ceremonies. As soon as he puts on the uniform after removing his clerical robe, his mind is transformed from that of a Buddhist monk to a soldier's. . . . Yet Katayama is not necessarily solely responsible for this. During peace time, his religion is expansive enough to transcend national borders. The reason he can no longer do so is not that religion has become powerless, but that the hurdle of national boundaries has risen too high to surmount."[64]

Ishikawa's monk, who had begun with compassionate intentions but whom war quickly converted to an ideology of race and nation, is a poignant emblem of psychology that made the Nanjing atrocities possible. Ishikawa's novel was not available to the public until the end of the war, but even if it had been, it probably would have had little effect.[65] A work of fiction, however realistic in its tone and subject matter, was unlikely to persuade ordinary Japanese to confront the military and the government or to hold the military accountable for the atrocities. It was one thing to describe the monk's attitude; it would have been quite another, in the midst of war, to persuade readers to purge similar feelings from their own hearts.

"COMMUNIST PROPAGANDA"

While Buddhism in Ishikawa's novel failed to establish understanding across ethnic or national borders, communism was one ideology that did succeed in crossing these boundaries in wartime Japan and uniting peoples of various ethnicity and nationalities. Although banned writings were generally not circulated in Japan, the police continued to find dissenting publications, both smuggled across and printed within the nation's borders. Ranging in kind from flyers to books, "Communist propaganda," as the police called it, addressed various issues. Stressing Japanese atrocities, emphasizing heavy casualties suffered by the Japanese military, and appealing to the antiwar sentiments of readers, the texts were brought into Japan not only by antiwar activists, but also by Japanese soldiers who picked up the publications in China. Between July and November 1937, the police across Japan confiscated 20 different flyers brought from China. Some consisted only of simple slogans such as "Japan and China are brothers: Why are we fighting?" and "The real enemy is the Japanese military that plagues you." Others were longer essays, like an 800-word piece brought from the Shanghai area.[66]

Among the publications seized by the police, two focused on the violence in Nanjing: "Japan under the Threat of Fascism" (Fassho kyōi no Nihon) in *Far-Eastern War News* (Kyokutō sensō nyūsu), no. 4 (January 10, 1938), and *What War Is* (Sensō to wa). *Far-Eastern War News* was a community newspaper, or rather a flyer, seemingly intended to inform the Japanese community in Seattle, Washington, of what was going on in Asia. According to the Tokkō's monthly report in February 1938, which included excerpts from the flyer, the newspaper's editor of the *Far-Eastern War News*, who learned of the massacre from a *New York Times* article, briefly informed the readers about violence committed by the Japanese military after the capture of the city. In an item titled "A Matter for Great Regret," he wrote:

> At the time the Japanese military captured Nanjing, there were wide-scale looting, rape, and atrocities, which had not been seen in the past. Foreign witnesses were very surprised and expressed the opinion that "the battle of Nanjing would remain not as a brilliant victory in Japanese war history, but as a shameful incident that would ruin national dignity." It is concluded that the large-scale atrocities that took place in Nanjing can be attributed to a deterioration in military discipline among ordinary soldiers influenced by fascist officers, such as Colonel Hashimoto [Kingorō], all of whom indulged in *gekokujō* [insubordination] without severe punishment.
>
> It is also said that military discipline has been lax because this war does not have a noble cause. In either case, an alarming situation was reported in the news.[67]

What War Is, on the other hand, was a Japanese translation of Harold Timperley's *What War Means: Japanese Terror in China*, published in 1938. Although Timperley, a correspondent for the *Manchester Guardian*, did not explain why the Japanese military committed atrocities in Nanjing, his book presented these atrocities based on statements, documents, and correspondence supplied by American and European witnesses who had remained in the city. In the Japanese translation, Kaji Wataru and Aoyama Kazuo, both of whom helped the Guomindang fight against Japanese militarism, wrote introductions for the book. Kaji expressed that he was not surprised to learn of mass Japanese atrocities around Nanjing, having heard other inhumane stories earlier.

During his imprisonment for violation of the Peace Preservation Law in the mid-1930s, Kaji was regaled by his cellmate with stories of life in the military. The inmate boasted to Kaji that he had performed beheadings and committed rape during his service in the military in 1932. What made Kaji furious was the prisoner's emotionless and guiltless manner of talking about his crimes. Kaji heard a similar story in Shanghai in 1936 from a "rogue journalist" who himself bragged of killing civilians during the Shanghai Incident of 1932. Kaji argued that Japanese national ethics had been corrupted by the aggressive war in China and stressed that Japan could be saved only by aborting its aggressive foreign policy.[68] Similarly, Aoyama emphasized the corruption of the morale among the Japanese military, especially after the Manchurian Incident, the popular name for the military confrontation between Japan and China that occurred in 1931. He argued that this corruption was attributable to the structure of the Japanese military as well as to the domestic social system. He urged readers to join the struggle against fascism, militarism, and aggression in order to abolish the fundamental causes of Japan's international shame.[69]

Although the exact number of copies of "Japan under the Threat of Fascism" and *What War Is* was unknown to the police, it is clear that only a few people in Japan had an opportunity to read them. The police confiscated a total of 3 copies of "Japan under the Threat of Fascism" in February 1938 (1 each in Osaka, Hyōgo, and Hiroshima); 10 copies in March 1938 (2 each in Hyōgo and Osaka; 1 each in Kochi, Fukushima, and Fukuoka); and 3 copies in Aichi from April through June 1938.[70] As to *What War Is*, 11 copies, among other antiwar publications, were confiscated from an American missionary in Shanghai named Luther Tucker, who had been distributing this work as well as other "Communist propaganda" in Osaka, Shizuoka, and Tokyo in February 1939.[71]

Although the circulation of these accounts of the Nanjing atrocities was negligible, Japanese authorities were extremely anxious lest such arguments interfere with mobilization and incite criticism against the government. The effort and concern the government devoted to suppressing antagonistic views were demonstrated by its reaction to the Chinese "paper bombing." At dawn on May 20, 1938, two Chinese airplanes scattered thousands of flyers and pamphlets in southern Kyūshū. Although these "paper bombs" fell over a mountainous area inhabited by few people, police officers and firefighters in Miyazaki and Kumamoto were immediately mobilized to protect the people from their "harmful influence."[72] The Chinese propaganda was presented in five different versions: one pamphlet addressed to "the people in Japan" and four flyers addressed to "tradesmen and artisans," "laborers," "farmers," and "members of various political parties."[73] All called on Japanese to stop the aggression and to fight against the military clique. The pamphlet urged the people to follow Mr. and Mrs. Kaji Wataru, Japanese nationals who had rejected the policy of the Japanese government and were supporting China.[74] Despite the mountainous terrain, the searchers collected 1,520 pieces of paper bombs. The chemical composition of the paper was even tested in order to pinpoint where these flyers had been printed. The authorities learned that the paper had probably been produced between 12 and 18 months earlier by a paper mill on the Pacific coast of Canada.[75] Although a few people, mostly farmers, picked up paper bombs that eluded the authorities, they did not show any interest in them. In the report, the Tokkō concluded that there was no evidence of public unrest resulting from the incident.[76]

PERSONAL ACCOUNTS

Smuggled publications were not the only sources of information. Soldiers recorded their experiences of the attack on Nanjing in their field diaries. Their accounts included stories of rape, looting, burning, and killings of civilians. Although they were made available only much later, these diaries provide a contemporary glimpse of the soldiers' lives. In essence, the soldiers recounted stories that paralleled the experience of the characters in Ishikawa's novel. Those written by infantrymen and artillerymen of the Yamada Unit, the Thirteenth Division, demonstrated how ordinary men in their thirties with children back home in Japan were transformed into cold-hearted soldiers capable of killing captured women and children. The diaries described widespread looting in the military, soldiers in constant fear of guerrilla reprisals, and the systematic killing of thousands of prisoners at Mufu Mountain outside the walled city.[77]

Occasionally, the writers, whose real identities were usually concealed during the postwar editing, expressed personal sympathies for Chinese orphans, prisoners, women, or farmers. "Saitō Jirō" wrote of his compassion for a girl who was staring blankly at a burning house next door to her own. Moved by pity, he gave her all the sweets he had in his pocket.[78] "Miyamoto Shōgo" felt sorry for surrendered soldiers who were not adequately fed.[79] "Kondō Eishirō" disclosed his feelings for the wretched survivors he encountered in a village: mothers holding their babies, elders praying for mercy, and children crying from fear. He also gave sweets to a child.[80] "Meguro Fukuharu" discussed his feelings for a Chinese person who was forced to give up his hen.[81] Yet "Saitō," "Miyamoto," "Kondō," and "Meguro" were also the emperor's soldiers, who followed orders and killed prisoners, seemingly without great remorse. "Meguro" confessed his lack of discomfort in beheading Chinese guerrillas and disclosed that at one time he delighted in killing stragglers.[82]

A diary written by Ohara Kōtarō, a transport soldier of the Sixteenth Regiment, Sixteenth Division, was slightly different, in that it was more detailed in its observation of daily activities and also less violent. The content may have been more moderate because Ohara, like other members of his unarmed transport corps, was not involved in combat and also because he was an idealistic and well-educated elementary school teacher. Evidently a popular instructor, Ohara continued to receive letters from his former students and their parents during his two years of service.[83] Like other Japanese soldiers advancing to Nanjing, he and his fellow soldiers supported themselves by looting, though he often expressed his guilt as he plundered cattle and crops and devastated farmlands.[84] Yet when Nanjing was seized, he, too, expressed his gratitude.[85] While Ohara himself never participated in acts of random execution or manslaughter, he did not evince as much remorse with respect to Chinese soldiers and prisoners as he did to the civilians in the villages.[86]

CONCLUSION

By the late 1930s, although the authorities had succeeded in suppressing perceived leftist and democratic organizations, members of which were generally sympathetic toward Chinese victims of the war, they were not so successful in controlling right-wing organizations. As stated in a confidential report in 1941 by a judge of the Kumamoto District Court, ultranationalist movements increased rapidly in Japanese society after the Manchurian Incident in 1931, in contrast to the decline of leftist movements.[87] Despite the fact that these right-wing organizations and their supporters often opposed the government and resorted to terrorist acts, such as the assassinations of the May 15 Incident of 1932 and the attempted military coup of the February 26 Incident of 1936, they were generally supportive of the war effort between July 1937 and the spring of 1939.[88] As the undeclared war between China and Japan bogged down, these ultranationalist organizations aggressively demanded the destruction of the anti-Japanese government in China and the elimination of British, Soviet, and American assistance to Chiang Kai-shek. They also denounced existing political parties and what they called weak-kneed diplomacy (*nanjaku gaikō*), calling instead for the spread of the Imperial Way (*kōdō*), or emperor worship, around the world.[89]

Under such domestic circumstances, the Nanjing atrocities existed neither in official Japanese records nor in general public awareness. Many Japanese were caught up in war fever. Rumors and smuggled documents about the atrocities in Nanjing were introduced to Japan from China and the United States in spite of strict censorship. However, a wartime history of the Nanjing atrocities failed to develop, not merely or even primarily because people in Japan were prevented from telling the story, but rather because the nation as a whole was largely unwilling to hear it.

Nevertheless, careful readers were able to read between the lines of authorized accounts and learn about the atrocities. For example, Hora Tomio, a historian born in 1906 who later became a renowned chronicler of the Nanjing atrocities, always tried to read newspapers critically during the war in search of truth. Although Hora's searches sometimes came up empty, he occasionally felt confident that the censored newspapers had communicated more than the government desired to be known.[90] Certainly, newspaper reports of the "killing contest" and the virtual annihilation of enemy units exposed some of the realities of war, but the tone of the reports also gave attentive readers a strong sense of the generally unbridled violence of the campaign.[91] By and large, however, perpetrators and eyewitnesses of the massacre stored their experiences in private memories and memoirs, planting the seeds of the subsequent controversy over the Nanjing Massacre in Japan.

2

China: Intolerable Atrocities

From 1937 to 1945, the atrocities in Nanjing were by no means the main symbol of Japanese aggression. The international and domestic political realities of the time tended to divert attention elsewhere. People in China experienced indiscriminate bombings, violence against women, chemical and biological warfare, and other atrocities of war. The rape of Nanjing was not an isolated incident of Japanese violence, either in the eyes of most Chinese or in the opinion of the government. The Nanjing atrocities were more prominent in local than national awareness.

Although the Nationalist leaders did not ignore the atrocities in Nanjing, they needed to consider what kind of appeals would produce the most powerful international effect. While desperately seeking military and economic assistance as well as campaigning to have punitive measures instituted against Japan, the Nationalist government found Japan's chemical warfare more politically useful than Nanjing to stir international outrage against Japan and to persuade the international community to take measures to stop Japanese aggression in China.

Though the massacre was not the government's preferred propaganda tool, many individuals and groups did use print media to communicate the atrocities in Nanjing to the world public. These writers included Kaji Wataru, a Japanese national who fled to China and organized the Japanese People's Antiwar Alliance (Nihonjin hansen dōmei) in order to confront Japan's militarism. At the same time that the Nationalist government protested Japanese violence to the leaders of the League of Nations, concerned individuals, both Chinese and non-Chinese, reached out to their counterparts around the world in order to stop Japanese violence in China.

GOVERNMENT APPEAL TO THE LEAGUE
OF NATIONS

The Chinese government first condemned the massacre on the international stage on February 2, 1938, at the sixth meeting at the 100th Session of the Council of the League of Nations in Geneva. On that date, Wellington Koo, first delegate of the Republic of China, reported to the other 15 members of the council about the atrocities that had occurred in China since the Eighteenth Assembly in September 1937, when Koo had made an earlier appeal against Japanese aggression.[1] To Koo and other government leaders, the sack of Nanjing was one of many atrocities perpetrated by the Japanese military. At this meeting, as at the previous one, he first highlighted the indiscriminate bombardment of open towns, which had resulted in the mass killings of Chinese civilians. He stressed that 17 provinces had been bombed and that the victims were mostly women and children.[2]

He then went on to describe the atrocities in Nanjing:

> In addition, the cruel and barbarous conduct in the occupied areas of Japanese soldiery, which used to pride itself on its good discipline, has added to the sufferings and hardships of a war-stricken people and has shocked the sense of decency and humanity. So many cases of it have been reported by neutral eyewitnesses and published in the foreign press that it is hardly necessary to cite evidence here. Suffice it, as an illustration, to quote a description by the correspondent of the *New York Times*, reported in *The Times* of London of December 20, 1937, of the scene of horror in Nanking following the capture of the city by the Japanese; these are his succinct words: "Wholesale looting, violation of women, murder of civilians, eviction of Chinese from their homes, mass executions of war prisoners, and the impressing of able-bodied men."
>
> Another authentic account of the atrocities perpetrated by Japanese soldiers at Nanking and Hangchow, based on the reports and letters of American professors and missionaries, is to be found in the *Daily Telegraph and Morning Post* of January 28, 1938. The number of Chinese civilians slaughtered at Nanking by Japanese was estimated at 20,000, while thousands of women, including young girls, were outraged. The American Chairman of the Emergency Committee of Nanking University, writing to the Japanese Embassy on December 14, 1937, stated in part: "We urge you, for the sake of the reputation of the Japanese Army and Empire, and for the sake of your own wives, daughters and sisters, to protect the families of Nanking from the violence of your soldiers." The correspondent added that "in spite of this appeal, the atrocities continued unchecked."[3]

Koo urged the league to take action to stop Japanese aggression by explaining its threats to vital European and American interests in China. He then alluded to the so-called Tanaka Memorial, a forged petition allegedly presented by Prime Minister Tanaka Giichi to the emperor in July 1927, which purported to outline Japan's plan for world domination, beginning with the subjugation of China and other parts of Asia. Koo argued that the trajectory of Japan's aggression since the Manchurian Incident had conformed to, and therefore established the authenticity of, the Tanaka Memorial.[4]

At the May meeting of the council, after chiding the member states of the league for having done little to aid China, Koo again protested Japanese atrocities against his country. He did not mention Nanjing in this session. He first condemned the killing of civilians by indiscriminate bombing and then disclosed the use of poison gas by the Japanese military in its efforts to break through the Shantung front. He continued to stress that the Sino-Japanese conflict was not a bilateral but an international problem. The league adopted a resolution, similar to previous ones but with a new paragraph requesting that member states submit information concerning Japanese use of toxic gases.[5] Although the British representative voted in favor of the resolution, he predicted that the claim would be proved baseless.[6]

In September, Koo made a much stronger appeal against Japanese chemical warfare and indiscriminate bombing to the representatives of the league. Although he mentioned the terrors in Nanjing reported in the European and American press, he focused his protest on the general methods of the Japanese army: "Of all the methods of warfare which the Japanese forces have employed against my country, the gas attacks and the air bombings are the most inhuman in character."[7] He estimated the number of victims of Japan's indiscriminate bombardments as 10,500 civilians killed and 13,300 wounded between August 1937 and May 1938.

This emphasis on Japanese chemical warfare and indiscriminate bombardments came at the behest of Chiang Kai-shek. Koo, as well as Quo Taichi, ambassador at London, and Tsien Tie, ambassador at Brussels, received a telegram from the diplomatic section of the Guomindang government on September 3, 1938, requesting that they emphasize "Japan's inhumane methods [of] warfare particularly frequent use [of] poison gas."[8]

Indeed, the Nationalist government in Chongqing frequently sent letters to the secretary general of the league informing him of Japanese chemical warfare and other actions. A letter dated August 5, 1938, included a report signed by Dr. H. Talbot, a British surgeon in the Nanchang General Hospital, who concluded that 19 men examined on July 10 and 11, 1938, at the hospital had been poisoned by a type of mustard or chlorine gas.[9] In a letter dated August 24, 1938, Hoo Chitsai, director of the Permanent Office of the Chinese Delegation to the League of Nations, reported the use of asphyxiating gas on August 22, causing the deaths of two battalions of men.[10] A letter dated September 5, 1938, provided further information on Japanese chemical warfare in China, documenting 11 gassings by Japanese troops between May and September 1938.[11]

Although Chinese claims of Japanese chemical warfare in China may have confused mustard gas (blister gas), asphyxiating gas (choking gas), vomiting gas, tear gas, and smoke, they were not unfounded. The chief of the general staff in Tokyo authorized troops in Pingjin to use tear gas as early as July 28,

1937. On April 11, 1938, Tokyo granted troops in Shenxi the authority to use vomiting gas. A month later the government extended this permission to include the use of mustard gas.[12] According to the military statistics describing supplies and actual expenditure on ammunition between July 1937 and November 1938, the Japanese troops in China used 2,588 canisters of tear gas and 14,271 canisters of vomiting gas from a supply of 92,000 and 80,000 cans respectively.[13]

Nearly a year after Koo first sought active support from the members of the league and secured the adoption of three resolutions, the Chinese government was still not satisfied with the situation. On September 19, 1938, Koo made a fourth appeal to the league, urging member states to carry out the previously adopted resolutions to recommend an embargo against Japan of war supplies such as oil and raw materials and to supply financial and material aid to China.[14] However, the president of the council proposed only to invite Japan to discuss ongoing Sino-Japanese disputes. Further Chinese complaints to the league aimed at securing aid in resisting Japanese aggression proved equally useless.

Yet Koo never gave up. In September, Koo forwarded a statement to the secretary general titled "Some Recent Data Concerning Japan's Invasion of China and Her Conduct of Warfare."[15] It comprised five sections: (1) The Names of the Invaded Provinces; (2) Railways Seized by Japan; (3) The Outrage at Nanking; (4) Japan's Method of Aerial Warfare; (5) Japanese Gas Attacks. The section dealing with Nanjing mentioned specific figures based largely on a survey conducted by the Nanjing International Relief Committee. It stated that 74 percent of the 3,250 Chinese killed at Nanjing and 98 percent of the wounded had been victims of deliberate acts of violence. The statement continued: "The total number of civilians killed, including those cases not yet verified, was estimated at 20,000; 4,200 Chinese were forcibly taken away under military arrest, most of whom are believed to have been killed. The number of people thus affected by Japanese acts of massacre and violence represents 1 person in every 23 or one in every five families."[16] In addition, it was estimated that 88 percent of the buildings in the city had experienced some form of material loss, although only 2 percent of this damage had been caused by military operations. By contrast, 24 percent of the damage had resulted from fire, 63 percent from looting, and 11 percent from forcible entry. The report also stated that thousands of women and girls between the ages of 14 and 50 had been sexually abused.[17]

Although not mentioning its sources, "Some Recent Data Concerning Japan's Invasion of China and Her Conduct of Warfare" depended heavily on a survey organized by Lewis Smythe, an American professor of sociology at Nanking University and a member of the Nanking International Relief Committee, a charity organization that succeeded the International Committee for the Nanjing Safety Zone.[18] His survey, titled *War Damage in the Nanking Area* and completed in June 1938, was printed by the Mercury Press of Shanghai in the fall of 1938 and included a foreword by Miner Searle Bates, an American professor of history at Nanking University. In his foreword, Bates expressed his views on the significance of the devastation in the Nanjing area. He stressed that Japanese documents and publications were likely to blame the Chinese for the burning and looting that took place in the city, whereas Chinese documents would likewise blame the Japanese for the damages there. The committee, therefore, considered it necessary to conduct a factual survey concerning the damages in and around Nanjing.[19] The pamphlet was not printed for profit; the committee's goal was to supply copies of the pamphlet to relief committees abroad.[20]

In the survey, Smythe estimated that 12,000 civilians had been killed by violence in the city and in areas adjacent to its walls.[21] Moreover, he reported 30,950 deaths—excluding those of soldiers—in the four and a half counties adjacent to Nanjing.[22] Of these, the violence accounted for the deaths of 22,490 males, mostly able-bodied men up to their mid-40s, and 4,380 females, mostly elderly women.[23] According to Smythe, the counties had a population of 1.2 million to 1.3 million before the war, and that figure had decreased to 1.08 million by the time of the survey. Each family lost an average of 220 Chinese dollars, during a time when approximate annual income of a farming family was 289 Chinese dollars.[24] In addition, 16 percent of the draft animals in the region had been lost during the war.[25]

AMERICAN AND EUROPEAN HUMANITARIANS IN NANJING

Numbers, however, do not fully attest to the experience of the residents of Nanjing and its environs, though many did not remain long enough to witness the full extent of the suffering. The Chinese Nationalist leaders fled from Nanjing to Chongqing in early December 1937, but the devastation in Nanjing continued even after February 1938.[26] The foreigners who stayed in Nanjing sought to rescue its residents and to win international support for their efforts by publicizing their devastation and suffering. Smythe's survey in particular was aimed at achieving this objective. The Nanjing International Relief Committee sponsored two more surveys after Smythe's in order to provide accurate information on the violence and its aftermath: *Crop Investigation in the Nanking Area and Sundry Economic Data* and *The Nanking Population: Employment, Earnings and Expenditures.* The former, a brief survey conducted by six investigators in the summer and autumn of 1938, was a systematic study of the conditions of crops. The latter discussed family conditions in Nanjing during the winter of 1938–39. It concluded that 16 percent of all families in Nanjing had no male head (as compared with 8 percent in the prewar period) and that the employment rate was only 27 percent. As the study stressed, most of the people in Nanjing continued to suffer from poverty more than a year after the fall of Nanjing.[27]

John Rabe, a German who was the chairman of the International Committee for the Nanjing Safety Zone, provided a shelter for hundreds of refugees in his own garden in Nanjing and made every effort to save people during the weeks after the fall of the city. After returning to Germany, he tried to publicize the situation in China. In May 1938 he gave five lectures about the sufferings of the people in Nanjing and showed a film by John Magee, chairman of the Nanjing Branch of the International Red Cross, which documented Japanese atrocities. Believing that German leaders would offer their help if only they knew what was going on in Nanjing, he sent a copy of his lecture to Hitler in hopes that something would be done to save the people of China. But Nazi authorities soon prohibited Rabe's lectures and confiscated the film, presumably because they did not want to jeopardize their relations with Imperial Japan.[28]

George Fitch, associate general secretary of the Foreign YMCA of Nanjing, circulated a 9,500-word letter to his friends in Shanghai and abroad that detailed his observations in Nanjing between December 10 and December 31, 1937.[29] The letter began:

> What I am about to relate is anything but a pleasant story; in fact, it is so very unpleasant that I cannot recommend anyone without a strong stomach to read it. For it is a story of such crime and horror as to be almost unbelievable, the story of the depredations of a horde of degraded criminals of incredible bestiality, who have been, and now are, working their will, unrestrained, on a peaceful, kindly, law-abiding people. Yet it is a story which I feel must be told, even if it is seen by only a few. I cannot rest until I have told it, and perhaps fortunately, I am one of a very few who are in a position to tell it. It is not complete—only a small part of the whole; and God alone knows when it will be finished. I pray it may be soon—but I am afraid it is going to go on for many months to come, not just here but in other parts of China. I believe it has no parallel in modern history.[30]

Fitch's letter is strongly worded and emotionally powerful. Whether or not the events it describes are truly without parallel in modern history, there is no questioning that Fitch himself believed that what he had seen was uniquely horrible. With the highest urgency, he appealed to his friends to help save the residents of Nanjing.

NANJING VERSUS CHINA

Fitch's letter was included in *What War Means: Japanese Terror in China* written by Harold Timperley, a correspondent for the *Manchester Guardian* in China, who was also active in publicizing Japanese atrocities in China to the world. The book was circulated in China, England, France, Japan, and the United States.[31] Timperley cited Fitch's letter virtually in its entirety, deleting only the names of informants, including Fitch's own.[32] In addition to the detailed description of the Nanjing atrocities, which comprised nearly half of the book, he also discussed terrors in North China (Beijing and Tianjin), Shanghai, and the Yangtze Delta (Suzhou, Wuhu, Hangzhou, and Wuxi), from the beginning of the Sino-Japanese hostilities in July 1937 to February 1938.

Timperley provided estimates of casualties, but his report was rather confusing. At the beginning of the book, he stated that "at least 300,000 Chinese military casualties for the Central China campaign alone and a like number of civilian casualties were suffered."[33] At another point, he insisted that more than 300,000 Chinese civilians were killed in the Yangtze Delta, part of Central China, between August and November 1937.[34] Even if its figures were not perfectly accurate, the book provided vivid narratives of suffering in Japanese-occupied areas, quoting personal letters, newspaper reports, and eyewitness accounts written by local and foreign residents. Timperley differed with members of the International Relief Committee and International Committee for the Safety Zone in that his most pressing goal was to elicit financial and military assistance for China as a whole rather than for Nanjing in particular.

Shuhsi Hsu also aimed to bring international assistance to China by exposing readers to sufferings in Central and North China in English-language books. In the *Documents of the Nanking Safety Zone* he compiled, he presented his readers with nearly 70 pleas and protests made by the International Committee for the Nanjing Safety Zone to the Japanese authorities between December 14, 1937, and February 19, 1938.[35] The book, which consisted of letters and reports written by the members, illustrated the efforts of the members of the committee to save lives of the people in Nanjing. Hsu also wrote *Japan and Shanghai, The War Conduct of the Japanese, Three Weeks of Canton Bombing, A Digest of Japanese War Conduct*, and *A New Digest of Japanese War Conduct*.[36] Through these English-language books, he informed readers of sufferings in Central and North China.

Similarly, Wellington Koo and other Chinese leaders were more concerned about the situation in China overall rather than in Nanjing alone. Soon after the seizure of Nanjing, they learned of the atrocities there: on December 23, 1937, Koo received a telegram from his government informing him of the systematic killing of 50,000 people in four days.[37] A second telegram reached him on December 26, 1937, stating that the Japanese atrocities in Nanjing "stagger[ed] human imagination." The report confirmed to Koo's satisfaction the authenticity of a story printed in the *New York Times*.[38] Because the military struggle against Japan continued after the fall of Nanjing, Koo's main concern was to stop the aggressor and to stir world public opinion against Japanese invasion. After receiving a copy of Timperley's book from the author, Koo had his counselor write him a letter congratulating him on his work to "further enlighten world opinion on Japanese ruthlessness and enable it to take more concrete measures to outlaw the aggressor."[39]

Kaji Wataru, the Japanese proletarian writer who wrote the foreword to the Japanese edition of Timperley's *What War Means*, confessed in his introduction that he was not too surprised to learn of the Japanese atrocities in Nanjing. Kaji regarded the bloodshed as an unavoidable consequence of Japan's aggressive foreign policies since the early 1930s. Unless Japanese imperial policies were crushed, the moral values of the nation would never be redeemed from corruption.[40] Unlike so many other Japanese, Kaji never yielded in his resistance against the Japanese imperialism despite intense hardships.

CHINA AND KAJI WATARU

After spending two years in a Japanese prison for violation of the Peace Preservation Law, Kaji was released on bail in 1935. When he emerged from confinement, he found that his leftist friends had mysteriously disappeared and that articles in the press were grotesque distortions of the true political situation. Although he was not sure what he could do in China, he could not bear merely to observe Japan's war preparations and not act.[41] In 1936, he fled to Shanghai, where he met Chinese intellectuals, many of whom had studied in Japan, including Lu Xun. In mid-August 1937, when Japanese and Chinese forces collided in Shanghai, Kaji requested Song Qingling (the widow of Sun Yat-sen) to ask Chiang Kai-shek if he could work for the Chinese Nationalist government.[42] The Nanjing government made no reply for more than three months, during which time Kaji and his wife were hiding in Shanghai, trying to elude both the hostile Chinese public and the Japanese military police and its local collaborators. Spurned by Chiang, the Kajis depended on American, Chinese, and New Zealander friends for their daily survival.[43]

In November, after Kaji and his wife escaped to Hong Kong, where he contributed articles opposing Japanese aggression in China to leftist media outlets such as *Xinhua ribao*, *Jiuwang ribao*, and *Qiyue*. Chen Cheng, who learned about Kaji's articles from Zhou Enlai and Guo Moruo, invited Kaji to Wuhan.[44] He arrived in Wuhan in March 1938 and delivered a speech to the Association for Chinese Anti-Imperialist Literary Artists (Zhongguo Kangdi Wenyuijia Xiehui) in which he declared that the day would come when Japanese and Chinese people together would fight against Japan's despotic militarism.[45]

In Wuhan, Kaji began to carry out his long-deferred plan of reeducating Japanese prisoners of war in China and organizing a group of them to confront Japanese militarism. In the beginning, his task was very challenging. Kaji observed that few Chinese leaders believed that Japanese soldiers could be reeducated. Japanese soldiers, who thought that their lives would be finished if they became prisoners, tended to fight to the death. These soldiers knew that the Japanese government as well as Japanese society would treat prisoners as "social outcasts" (*hikagemono*) and that they and their family members and relatives would be persecuted. In addition, the Chinese general public, given their hatred toward "Japanese devils," often beat Japanese prisoners to death.[46]

The Nationalist government finally ratified Kaji's plan in May 1939, and a POW camp was built in Guilin in July. Kaji selected 11 Japanese prisoners out of some fifty inmates, with whom he lived and studied for about a month. On December 25, 1939, the group established the Japanese People's Antiwar Alliance (Nihonjin hansen dōmei) and left for Kunlunguan in the northern part of Nanning. During the night of December 29, facing Japanese troops about 300 meters away, they sent their first antiwar message through a loudspeaker. Kaji knew that these troops had not returned to Japan since July 1937 and that, by 1939, most of the original members of the units had been killed and replaced. Therefore, the speaker focused on the wastefulness of Japan's military leaders and their needless sacrifice of the nation's soldiers. He reminded the troops of their families back home, eagerly waiting their safe return. He asked the troops whether it was their will to impose suffering on the Chinese people. The Japanese troops at first responded with machine-gun fire, but soon they stopped firing and listened. The alliance concluded that its efforts had significantly damaged morale among the Japanese troops.[47]

As Guomindang-Communist relations deteriorated, the Nationalist government ordered Kaji to dissolve the group on August 25, 1941. Fearing that members of the alliance were overly sympathetic to communism, the government demanded that they be "reeducated." All the members except Kaji and his wife were transported to a POW camp in Zhenyuan. Kaji and his wife were ordered to reside in Chongqing, where an office was provided to them.[48] Kaji's goal of destroying Japanese militarism, however, was carried on by his allies and followers. Nosaka Sanzō (Okano Susumu), a Japanese Communist sent from Moscow to Yenan in 1941, was still leading branches of the alliance in North China, and the Chinese Communists continued their support of the alliance. In North China, some 200 members under Nosaka actively engaged in antiwar operations against the Japanese military. They broke into communication lines among the Japanese troops; scattered antiwar leaflets; appealed to the soldiers' homesickness and sympathy through loudspeakers; and sent "comfort bags" containing soap, underwear, and antigovernment and pacifist messages to the soldiers.[49] In North China, an ally of the alliance known as the Korean Voluntary Army also actively fought against the Japanese military to gain Korean independence.[50]

CONCLUSION

As the Japanese military faced increasing opposition from guerrilla forces in China, it employed more violence to suppress this resistance. From 1940 on, the Japanese army in northern China implemented the so-called "Three-Alls Operation"—burn all, kill all, and loot all—an operation that reached its peak in 1942–43.[51] While many observers in Nanjing would have agreed that the atrocities there were a prime example of wartime brutality of the Japanese military in China, the Chiang Kai-shek government at the time regarded Nanjing as only one of many such outrages visited on the nation by the Imperial Japanese Army. As in 1938, the government leaders felt that Japan's most inhumane actions were its gas attacks and aerial bombings.

It was only after the war, when atrocities against civilians received much more international attention, that Nanjing became the principal emblem of atrocities committed in China. In the late 1930s, before the full fury of the Nazi

Holocaust and the bombings of Hiroshima and Nagasaki, outrages against civilian populations were not generally regarded as the most heinous acts of war. Therefore, the Chinese government saw little point in exploiting memories of Nanjing. Because China's principal appeal at the League of Nations was to European powers that could recall gas and air attacks from World War I, it made sense to emphasize similar current assaults by the Japanese military.

3

United States: The "Rape of Nanking"

After the Manchurian Incident of 1931, Japan's popularity among the American public declined rapidly. When Americans learned about the brutal Japanese attack on Shanghai in January 1932, a movement to boycott Japanese goods gained support, even though the proposed ban was never instituted.[1] When the undeclared war began in July 1937, American and European correspondents relayed detailed reports of the situation in China. Although pro-Japanese accounts were also circulated, those that stressed Japanese atrocities in China were much more popular in the United States. By the summer of 1939, the sympathies of those Americans who paid attention to such matters lay with China rather than Japan.

After the bombing of Pearl Harbor, the brutalities in Nanjing symbolized for Americans the cruelty and barbarism not just of the Japanese military, but of the Japanese people as a whole. Unlike in Japan or China, the "Rape of Nanking," as Americans labeled it, was already recognized by many in the United States as a symbol of Japanese cruelty. Although Japanese military atrocities of all kinds may have inflamed the American public, the images of executions and random killings of Chinese civilians and soldiers alike with bayonets and swords seem to have supplied a particularly volatile fuel for the anti-Japanese imagination, perhaps because they called to mind stereotypical images of the feudal and barbaric Japanese samurai warrior. When China became America's ally and Japan became its enemy, the definition of "Japanese atrocities" applied inclusively to acts perpetrated against Chinese as well as Americans. Indeed, any Japanese display of force in Asia was seen as illegitimate, and casualties inflicted on Americans and Chinese populations, regardless of the circumstances, were likely to be viewed as atrocities.

37

In the United States, the atrocities in Nanjing were reported firsthand in newspapers such as the *New York Times*, the *New York Post*, the *Washington Post*, and the *Chicago Daily News*.[2] Tilman Durdin, a *New York Times* correspondent who was in Nanjing, reported the fall of the city and the killings of civilians in the December 18, 1937, edition of the newspaper. In the article, he insisted that Japan had lost a rare opportunity to gain Chinese support and respect when it committed wholesale atrocities and vandalism. He wrote of mass executions of Chinese soldiers, possibly including civilians, of streets scattered with the dead bodies of women, elderly men, and children, and of citywide looting by the Japanese military.[3]

Durdin's second detailed report appeared on January 9, 1938. He included vivid day-by-day descriptions of events from December 6 to December 13, 1937, and found "little glory for either side in the battle of Nanking." On the one hand, he condemned the arson by the retreating Chinese military and denounced General Tang Shengzhi and his aides, who fled on December 12 and left their subordinates trapped within the walled city.[4] On the other hand, he protested the many incidents of killing, looting, rape, and arson by the Japanese military during and after the seizure of the city.[5]

Archibald T. Steele, a *Chicago Daily News* correspondent who was also in Nanjing, offered his account of the atrocities in the newspaper's editions of December 15, 17, and 18, 1937. Like Durdin, Steele emphasized that Japan had lost an opportunity by failing to win support from the residents in the captured capital. He also reported executions of hundreds of Chinese by the Japanese military; dead bodies piled up almost five feet high at the Xiaguang Gate; Japanese looting of American properties and destruction of American flags; Japanese bayonetings of innocent civilians; and the bravery of American missionaries who stayed in Nanjing to help the Chinese residents.[6] Steele acknowledged that he had observed only a fraction of the army's depredations; nevertheless, he had seen enough to be filled with a sense of sadness, cruelty, horror, and pain.[7]

Durdin estimated that at least 33,000 Chinese were killed, whereas Steele estimated that between 5,000 and 20,000 people were killed in Nanjing.[8] In these articles, the duration of the Nanjing atrocities was a week or less, and the scope of the reports confined to the area inside and around the walled city. To Durdin, unrestrained brutalities and cruelties in Nanjing could be "compared only with the vandalism in the Dark Ages in Europe or the medieval Asiatic conquerors."[9]

These newspaper articles are examples of the media coverage of atrocities in Nanjing available to the American public. In addition, Timperley's *What War Means: Japanese Terror in China*, Smythe's *War Damage in the Nanking Area*, and Shuhsi Hsu's *Documents of the Nanking Safety Zone* were also circulated in the United States.[10] Numerous publications, from *Reader's Digest* to *Life* magazine, informed the American public of Japanese atrocities in Nanjing and other parts of China. By mid-1939 a majority of the American public favored China over Japan in the conflict. According to a Gallup Poll, 43 percent of respondents answered that their sympathies lay with China in August 1937, a figure that rose to 74 percent in May 1939.[11] Sympathy for Japan remained unchanged at 2 percent from August 1937 to May 1939.[12]

UNDECLARED WAR OVER PUBLIC OPINION

In the United States, China and Japan waged an undeclared war for American public support. Although they failed to gain significant support, Japanese propagandists as well as Japan sympathizers publicized their views in the United States. The Foreign Affairs Association of Japan published pamphlets that underscored the supposed legitimacy of Japan's struggle against China. After the military conflict began between the two nations, accounts of Chinese atrocities came forth from the association's presses.[13] For example, its *What Happened at Tunchow [Tongzhou]?* included photographs of destroyed buildings and dead bodies as well as newspaper reports that condemned Chinese atrocities against civilians.[14] Hino Ashihei's *Wheat and Soldiers* (Mugi to heitai), a 1938 bestseller in Japan which described lives of soldiers who participated in the Battle of Xuzhou, was published in English in 1939.[15] Hokuseido press printed books that insisted that Japan had behaved justly and that China itself was responsible for any injustices in the region.[16] People such as A. F. Thomas, an Englishman who sympathized with the Japanese government, gave lectures in the United States and England for five months in 1937–38, arguing that many were prejudiced against Japan.[17]

None of these pro-Japanese works had wide currency in the United States. In contrast, mass media (such as *Time*, *Life*, and *Fortune*), humanitarian organizations (such as the American Committee in Aid of Chinese Industrial Cooperatives, the China Aid Council, and the Church Committee for China Relief), and public figures—such as Madame Chiang Kai-shek (Song Meiling), Pearl Buck, and Henry Luce—all argued the righteousness of the Chinese position. Luce's magazines, *Time*, *Life*, and *Fortune*, together had approximately 3.8 million subscribers in 1941. The United China Relief, which was founded in 1941 and absorbed eight existing independent relief organizations, succeeded in raising $3.25 million in 1941. And Song Meiling became the first Chinese citizen and the second woman to speak before Congress when she traveled in the United States in 1943.[18]

NANJING AFTER PEARL HARBOR

After the Pearl Harbor attack, authors who emphasized alleged Japanese racial characteristics and natural "uniqueness" began to flourish. One example is Harold Timperley's *Japan: A World Problem*, published in 1942. Timperley insisted that "megalomaniacal ideas have been working in the blood of the Japanese, not merely for generations, but for centuries."[19] He believed that the ongoing military conflict between Japan and the West was irreconcilable and that few were paying attention to the psychological forces that were driving the Japanese to world domination. He stressed that a feudal *bushidō* mentality, which prevented Japan from accepting Christian values and Western democracy, remained strong in Japan.[20]

In 1942, a 120-page paperback titled *Our Enemy* was published by James Young, who had been imprisoned in Japan for two months in 1940. He emphasized that the Japanese "duplicat[ed] all Nazi brutalities, exceed[ed] them, and add[ed] a whole satanic range of their own peculiar cruelties."[21] According to Young, among the many Japanese mass atrocities (from the indiscriminate bombings in China, to Pearl Harbor, to atrocities in Manila), those committed against Nanjing were the worst. In addition, he warned that Japan had long planned this war and that Japanese-Americans were agents of Japan whose task was to aid in a Japanese invasion of the United States. He claimed that no matter where they lived, the Japanese were nationalistic and followed instructions from Tokyo. He not only supported the internment of Japanese descendants in California, but also advocated a tougher policy toward all Japanese in American territories.[22]

Academics also interpreted matters from a standpoint of ethnicity. Some stressed the uniqueness of Japanese culture and character and tried to understand Japanese atrocities from this perspective. In April 1942, "Japan: Beauty and the Beast" appeared in *Amerasia*, a left liberal scholarly journal for specialists of Asian studies in the United States, Great Britain, Japan, and the Soviet Union.[23] In the article, Bradford Smith, who taught at Rikkyō University and Imperial University of Tokyo between 1931 and 1936, attempted to explain how the Japanese could at the same time be both gentle, family-loving people and the inhuman barbarians who had assaulted Nanjing.[24] To him, the typical Japanese married man—whom he called "Watanabe-san" for the purpose of the article—would be "loyal to his family, fond of his home, sensitive to art and nature, clean, patient, enduring, [and] courteous" at home.[25] Yet, he argued, the same person could commit atrocities.[26] According to Smith, nine factors in the Japanese "racial" background combined to explain the behavior of "Watanabe-san":

> (1) moral training restricted to family and national loyalty; (2) the notion of their unique divinity setting them apart from the rest of mankind; (3) the inferiority psychosis; (4) fear and hatred of individualism; (5) disregard for the value of human life; (6) unbridled sexuality; (7) the background of head-hunting; (8) the release from cramping social restrictions; (9) the lack of a religious literature based upon ethical and spiritual principles worthy of respect.[27]

Other scholars, however, found Smith's approach unenlightening. In the June 1942 issue of *Amerasia*, Smith's viewpoint was assailed by two articles, one of which was "Japan: Neither Beauty nor Beast," written by A. Grajdanzev, a research associate of the Institute of Pacific Relations.[28] Although Grajdanzev agreed that Smith's points were true for a certain group in Japan then in power, he found none of Smith's nine factors specifically Japanese or connected to Japanese heredity.[29] To Grajdanzev, the issue was not a racial question, but a social phenomenon that could be altered by a change of social forces inside Japan; otherwise, there would be no hope of future peace with Japan.[30]

In the other article contesting Smith's claims, William Holland, international research secretary of the Institute of Pacific Relations, also underscored that many of the Japanese attitudes and habits described by Smith were not racially inherited.[31] Afraid that Smith's article would lead readers to conclude that Japanese were intractable by nature, Holland argued that the current Japanese attitudes and habits were systematically inculcated. The principal source of this indoctrination had been the educational system, which could be changed.[32] As for the Japanese atrocities in Nanjing and elsewhere, Holland argued that one should not seek explanations in the Japanese character and that a small group of leaders were responsible since the atrocities were mostly organized and deliberate.[33]

In contrast to the many emotional and simplistic publications in circulation, editors of *Amerasia* challenged the myth of "Japaneseness" and emphasized pluralism in Japanese society. As the war deepened, the tone of *Amerasia's* antiracist message became increasingly firm. In the issue of April 1, 1943, the journal raised the question of whether there was another Japan that bore no resemblance to the imperialist monolith that haunted the Western imagination. In a review of seven books about Japanese social structure, an anonymous author expressed disbelief in the argument, advanced in most of the books, that all Japanese thought and acted alike and differed as a group from all other peoples.[34] The writer singled out John Embree's *The Japanese* as providing authoritative evidence refuting Japanese uniqueness.[35] In November 1943, the anonymous editor of the journal again raised the question of whether there was another Japan. In the issue, the editor strongly objected to the theories of John Goette, the author of *Japan Fights for Asia*, and Sydney Greenbie, the author of *Asia Unbound*, both of whom emphasized Japanese racial uniqueness.[36] In order to challenge the racial theory, the editor this time called attention to Japanese Americans fighting for the United States on the Italian front. He also introduced Yashima Taro's *The New Sun*, in which the author described his prison life in Japan and friendship with his cellmates, many of whom were also being held as political prisoners.[37]

CONCLUSION

The views advocated by *Amerasia* did not succeed in slowing the overwhelming current of anti-Japanese emotion in the United States. The Japanese atrocities in Nanjing contributed to the image of inherent Japanese cruelty, as the stories about Nanjing were coupled with information about other atrocities. During World War II many Americans supported this monolithic perception of the Japanese, and opinion polls consistently showed that 10 to 13 percent of respondents desired the extermination of the Japanese as a people.[38]

In both Japan and China, the enormity of the Asia-Pacific War as a whole and expediencies of wartime domestic politics contributed to the general exclusion of the Nanjing atrocities from national memory. Ironically, it was in the United States that the atrocities had the greatest initial influence on popular perceptions. The same events that triggered relatively little immediate outcry in Asia resounded more loudly on the other side of the world; they not only inflamed public opinion against Japan, but also proved useful to those who chose to highlight the alleged Japanese psyche and its supposedly unique capacity for cruelty.

These understandings of Nanjing that were publicized through the mass media in the United States during the war played a central role in establishing an American orthodoxy on the subject of Nanjing. When the war ended and Americans arrived in Japan as the liberators of the Japanese people from their oppressive leaders, the American interpretation of Nanjing was exported to Japan and contributed to educating Japanese. In wartime America, literature on Nanjing emphasized the unique cruelty of the entire Japanese population, but in occupied Japan, this literature served to enlighten its citizens about the practices of their military. As in the wartime United States, a substantial role in spreading awareness of the Nanjing Massacre among the Japanese public was played by the media.

II

THE STORM OF POSTWAR AND COLD WAR POLITICS (1945–71)

4

Japan: Confronting the Nanjing Massacre

I n the years that immediately followed the Asia-Pacific War, Japanese awareness of the Nanjing atrocities was deeply influenced by external forces, principally the social and political reforms imposed by the American occupation,
and the geopolitical tensions of the nascent Cold War. Whereas American policy
early in the period called for the condemnation of wartime Japanese leaders,
mounting fears of socialism and communism later impelled the United States to
ally itself with the same conservative forces it had initially sought to discredit. As
American foreign policy followed this so-called reverse course, a parallel reversal
became visible in the history and memory of the Nanjing Massacre.

Unlike in the period prior to 1945, the Nanjing Massacre became a subject of
broad discussion in Japan once the occupation began. When the occupational
forces arrived, they brought with them American perceptions of Japan's conduct
during the war. Images of scenes like the atrocities in Nanjing quickly became
part of a public Japanese understanding of history. The Supreme Commander for
Allied Powers (SCAP) fostered the integration of Nanjing into Japan's official history and, along with its exposure of Japan's other wartime actions, actively disclosed the facts of the outrage in Nanjing. Public awareness spread among Japanese through newspapers, radio programs, textbooks, and the International
Military Tribunal for the Far East, better known as the Tokyo Trial. The war-weary
people accepted these narratives of wartime brutality, and issues of war responsibility were publicly debated in the period immediately following the defeat.

GREATER FREEDOM THROUGH CENSORSHIP

Within two weeks after Emperor Hirohito's message of surrender was announced, American troops landed in Japan. Because of occupation initiatives,

Japanese gained a freedom that stood in stark contrast to their wartime experience. This freedom nonetheless remained a limited, supervised one. In mid-September 1945, the occupations' Civil Censorship Detachment (CCD) issued a press code, ostensibly intended to educate the Japanese media in the responsibilities and meaning of a free press. The code required the Japanese press to meet 10 strict guidelines to adhere to "the truth." Just as the Japanese government had strictly prohibited news media from criticizing its war effort, the CCD ordered journalists not to mention "false or destructive criticism" of the Allied Powers, their wartime policies, or the American occupational policies. In the eyes of the CCD, no piece that included such material could be considered a "true" news story.[1]

On the same day the code was issued, *Asahi shinbun*, which had denounced the use of atomic bombs against civilians and crimes by American soldiers after their arrival in Japan, was ordered to suspend publication for 48 hours.[2] The CCD maintained that the *Asahi* articles would disturb the public tranquility and could be categorized as false or destructive criticism of the Allied Powers.[3] It was, however, acceptable for Japanese media to be critical of Japan, the war, and Japanese wartime military leaders. On September 17, 1945, after the Allies released stories of Japanese atrocities in the Philippines to the Japanese media, the *Asahi* editorial commented that the war had been shameful and blamed military leaders, particularly Tōjō Hideki, for dictatorial wartime politics.[4] The *Asahi* editorial on December 7, 1945, the fourth anniversary of Pearl Harbor, suggested that Japanese policies since the Manchurian Incident had been entirely mistaken and that the devastation and suffering inflicted on the nation were inevitable outcomes of Japan's wartime acts.[5] A week later, the editor urged every Japanese to be critical of the war and to recognize the domestic and international crimes that the nation had committed. It also stressed that Japan must be reborn and make its best efforts to rid the world of war.[6]

Asahi's newly self-critical attitude should not be read as insincere. A survey conducted by the United States Strategic Bombing Survey between November 10 and December 29, 1945, found that an overwhelming number of the Japanese interviewed for the survey answered that they were better off currently than during the war and reacted favorably to the occupation.[7] The survey also discovered that the most frequent suggestion received from participants was to change Japan into a peaceful, more democratic nation, free at last from militarism.[8] A majority of the Japanese citizens indeed supported the occupation and its reforms. Yet American reformers carefully directed the news media to inform the public of the evils of wartime militarism while suppressing criticisms against the occupation.

REVISIONS AND BLACKENED TEXTBOOKS

Japanese government organs such as the Ministry of Education also came under occupation authority. On September 20, 1945, less than a month after

Gen. Douglas MacArthur arrived in Japan to assume leadership of the occupation, the ministry issued an order to delete or revise certain sections in textbooks, especially in ethics, national history, and geography. Materials that emphasized arms and defense, that intended to stir patriotism, that might disturb international cooperation and friendly relations, or that significantly misrepresented the current situation under the occupation were subject to deletion or revision.[9] In classrooms, the same teachers who once had demanded that their students become loyal patriots now made their students either black out sentences or tear out pages based on the ministry's new guidelines.[10]

On December 31, 1945, SCAP prohibited the teaching of ethics, national history, and geography altogether. By November 1946, geography and national history were again allowed in schools, and a two-volume national history textbook for elementary schools, *The Course of the Nation* (Kuni no ayumi), which had been approved by SCAP, was published in September 1946.[11] Because national history, geography, and ethics were combined into social studies from April 1947, *The Course of the Nation* was only used for a short period.[12] Nonetheless, the second volume of *The Course of the Nation*, which covered events from the Tokugawa period to the end of the Asia-Pacific War, presented Japanese wartime history quite differently from previous national history textbooks. Concerning the China Incident, it stated:

> Six years after the Manchurian Incident, the China Incident occurred. In July 1937, at the Marco Polo Bridge near Beijing, a fight between Japanese and Chinese forces suddenly began. Our army immediately advanced its forces and occupied Beijing. Then, [the army] took Qingdao and Shanghai as well as ravaging Nanjing. [The Japanese forces] occupied such important places as Guangdong, Wuchang, and Hankou.[13]

According to the textbook, it was the military that had dragged Japan into an unwanted war. "Although the government made every effort to end the incident and to maintain friendly relations with China, the military rapidly enlarged the fighting. Like a stone gathering momentum as it rolls down a slope, the incident got out of hand."[14] On the subject of the defeat, the text stated:

> Our country was defeated. Japanese people suffered greatly during the war. The military, which suppressed the people and waged reckless war, caused this unhappiness. . . .
> Under General MacArthur, the Allied Powers occupied Japan. This occupation was aimed at establishing public order in Japan, destroying the military, completely overthrowing militarist ideologies, giving freedom to the people, and rebuilding Japan into a democracy. . . .
> The government and the people have been working together to build a peaceful Japan in order to carry out the goal set by SCAP. . . .
> A new politics has begun. Now, truly, the people must combine their efforts in order to make Japan a democratic nation.[15]

Although the discussion was very brief, this textbook explained for the first time that Japanese troops had ravaged (*arasu*) Nanjing. History books for junior high school and high school students published by the Ministry of Education in 1946 stated: "Atrocities in Nanjing, committed by our military when it occupied the city in December, served to stiffen the resistance of the Chinese people."[16] Written in an elliptical style that characterizes schoolbooks the world over, these texts did not contain extensive discussions of the massacre and other Japanese wartime atrocities. However, even these brief treatments revealed the desire, shared by SCAP and the Japanese authors of the textbooks, to educate the people about these atrocities and to inculcate the occupation's perspective on the war.

ENLIGHTENING THE PUBLIC: THE NANJING MASSACRE IN THE PRESS

While censoring the press, the American authorities also initiated an effort to educate the Japanese people about their version of the history of the Pacific War. Beginning on December 8, 1945, four years to the day (local time) after the Japanese attack on Pearl Harbor, the first installment of "The History of the Pacific War" (Taiheiyō sensō shi) appeared in all national newspapers. The articles, written by Bradford Smith, author of "Japan: Beauty and the Beast" (1942) who was then working for the U.S. Office of War Information, was serialized for 10 days.[17] NHK Radio also broadcast a serial program on the history of the Pacific War titled "Now It Can Be Told" (Shinsō wa kōda) from December 9, 1945, to February 10, 1946.[18] According to "The History of the Pacific War," neither Hirohito nor the ordinary public bore any blame for the war. Rather, the military leaders were solely responsible for the abuses of power, the deprivations of the people's freedom, the inhumane treatments of civilians and prisoners of war, and other violence that had occurred during the war. Of all the crimes that the military leaders committed, the worst had been the suppression of truth that had followed the enforcement of the Peace Preservation Law in 1925. According to Smith's history, it was against Hirohito's will to launch a surprise attack on Pearl Harbor.[19] In short, the facile script approved by the Civil Information and Education (CIE) emphasized that both innocent ordinary people and Hirohito had been deceived by the military leaders. Tōjō and his allies bore the blame for establishing despotism and dragging Japan into a devastating defeat.[20]

Although Smith's series never criticized Allied wartime policies and actions, it offered a critical view of the Japanese wartime policies and atrocities that the people in Japan could never have read in authorized publications during the war. The articles included descriptions of such atrocities as the Nanjing Massacre and the Bataan Death March. In "The History of the Pacific War," the atrocities in Nanjing (*Nankin ni okeru akugyaku*) were described as follows:

> On December 7, the Japanese army began its attack on the outlying vicinities of Nanjing. One week later, prompted by fierce Chinese resistance in Shanghai, the anger of the Japanese army exploded in Nanjing, and the

soldiers committed horrible atrocities. According to witnesses who insisted that the atrocities in Nanjing were the worst in modern history, more than 20,000 men, women, children were confirmed to have been murdered. For four weeks, Nanjing was a city drenched in blood, and human bodies lay scattered on the streets. Under such conditions, the Japanese army became still more brutal and inflicted a variety of sufferings upon civilians, committing murder and other atrocities.[21]

The description given in "The History of the Pacific War" thus reflected an American understanding of the Nanjing Massacre, and this is what was disseminated in the mass media to educate the Japanese populace.

ATROCITIES IN THE "SACRED WAR": THE TOKYO TRIAL AND THE NANJING MASSACRE

Through national and local mass media, the citizens learned for the first time the details of Japan's wartime atrocities, including the Nanjing Massacre. The International Military Tribunal for the Far East (1946–48), which tried 28 Japanese wartime leaders, significantly contributed to publicizing the gruesome stories of Nanjing. On July 25, 1946, one of the nine prosecution witnesses in regard to the Nanjing atrocities, Dr. Robert Wilson of the University of the Nanjing Hospital, testified before the court. Newspaper articles offered detailed accounts of these witnesses, often with stunning headlines such as "Children Also Brutalized; Dr. Wilson Discloses the Nanjing Atrocities"; "Women and Children Also Perished; Atrocities in Nanjing Revealed"; and "Shoot to Kill If You See Them; Mr. Xu Chuanyin Testifies."[22]

On July 30, 1946, the press reported the testimony of Miner Bates, a professor of history at Nanking University, who estimated that 12,000 noncombatants were slaughtered within the walled city alone and some 20,000 rapes occurred in the month after Japanese troops seized Nanjing.[23] On the following day, reflecting on the massacre, *Yomiuri shinbun*'s editorial stated:

> Newspaper correspondents accompanying the army that captured Nanjing were more or less aware of the atrocities by the army. They witnessed innumerable atrocities during the so-called "sacred war," which was in fact a war of aggression. Yet they dared not remonstrate to the military, deeming it wiser to shut their eyes and to excuse the brutality as an unavoidable wartime evil. The irresponsibility of war correspondents, ourselves included, is reprehensible in its disregard of humanity.
>
> Despite the fact that the military committed unspeakable brutalities, the government issued a statement declaring that Japan would consider Chinese people its friends. Such contradictory actions were characteristic of all Japanese policies on China, resulting in spreading hostility toward Japanese among Chinese people. This hostility remains the bitterest in the more than one-thousand-year history of relations between China and Japan. We must acknowledge the crimes committed by the militarists, epitomized by the Nanjing Massacre, as an ineradicable blot on our history.[24]

On August 8, 1946, in its letters section titled "Voices" (Koe), *Asahi shinbun* printed an emotional letter from Hanaki Sankichi, a farmer in Chiba who had been shocked to learn about the massacre. Hanaki wondered how the Japanese could purge the hereditary evil from their blood and insisted that the sobs of Nanjing must cause every single Japanese person to tremble. He wished that all of the Japanese would reflect on these things and admonish themselves. He wondered when and how the world would trust Japanese as peace-seeking nationals and stated that he would be glad to write with his own hand a nonaggression covenant for the Japanese people to sign.[25]

Unlike Hanaki, who wholeheartedly believed the court testimony, Radhabinod Pal, a justice from India who served at the Tokyo Trial, was much more skeptical. Although Pal believed that there was "no doubt that the conduct of the Japanese soldiers at Nanking [had been] brutal and that such atrocities [had been] intense for nearly three weeks and continued to be serious to a total of six weeks," he found some difficulty in accepting the prosecution's account of the Nanjing Massacre in its entirety.[26] In his 1,235–page dissenting opinion, Pal contended that some testimonies regarding the massacre must be exaggerated and sometimes even distorted.[27] One of the testimonies whose authenticity Pal particularly questioned was one made by Chen Fubao (Ch'en Fu-pao), an 18-year-old Nanjing resident at the time of the massacre.[28] Chen testified on July 26, 1946, before the court as follows:

> On the second day the Japanese were in Nanking, 14 December, they took thirty-nine from the Refugee Area. They were civilian men. They examined them, and those that had a hat mark on the forehead, or a callous spot on hands caused by handling a gun, were brought to a little pond, and taken out on the other side. I and another were put to one side, and the Japanese used light machine guns to kill the rest. There were thirty-seven who were killed in this way, and I saw this. . . .
>
> On the 16th of December I was taken by Japanese soldiers again, and also a lot of healthy young men and they put them in a crowd and Japanese soldiers wrestled with them and those that the Japanese could not defeat wrestling, they killed with the bayonet. I saw them kill one man for this reason. On the same day in the afternoon I was taken to Tai Ping road and saw three Japanese set a fire to two buildings, which were: one, a hotel, the other, a store or furniture shop. The names of the Japanese soldiers who set the fire are: UMAYAHARA and MURAKAMI of the Kuwata Regiment of the Mukai Unit.[29]

Pal found it extraordinary that Japanese soldiers seemed "to have taken such a special fancy of him [Chen] as to take him to various places to witness their various misdeeds and yet spare him unharmed."[30] In addition, the very certitude of Chen's statement regarding the precise numbers of the dead, dates of atrocities, and names of Japanese soldiers raised Pal's doubts as to the authenticity of the young man's testimony.[31] The justice was not claiming that Chen or any other witnesses had intentionally lied before the court; rather, he suggested that it is a normal emotional reaction for victims of injury to uncritically accept the kinds of rumors and speculations that they would ordinarily dismiss as fantastic. These same emotions could easily prompt survivors to exaggerate their accounts.[32]

Although the defense requested that dissenting opinions be read before the court, this request was denied.[33] Nonetheless, albeit briefly, newspapers such as *Asahi shinbun* reported the four minority opinions, including Justice Pal's. "Indian Justice Votes Not Guilty" (Indo hanji muzairon), which appeared on November 13, 1948, was very short, containing only some 400 Japanese characters, and nearly hidden at the bottom of the newspaper page. Only careful readers would learn that Pal's dissenting opinion was nearly 1,300 pages long and that he declared that all of the defendants were innocent and should be freed immediately. Also noted was Justice Pal's belief that the tribunal must not subordinate justice to carrying out any political goal.[34]

The Tokyo Trial sentenced seven of the accused to death. One of the seven was Matsui Iwane, the commander of Central China forces at the time of the massacre, for not taking any effective action to halt the wholesale atrocities. The court ruled that Japanese soldiers killed 200,000 civilians and prisoners of war in six weeks of the occupation and that approximately 20,000 cases of rape occurred during the first month of the occupation.[35] This judgment of the Nanjing Massacre set in place the standard understanding of the event in Japanese postwar historiography, and SCAP prohibited any harsh criticisms of that judgment during the occupation. But immediately after the occupation was over, those whose voices had been silenced during the occupation began to challenge the established account of Japan's wartime history.

RETURN OF THE PREWAR ELITES

Because it suspected that Pal's statements would undermine the policies of the occupation government, SCAP prohibited the publication of Pal's critical dissent during the occupation.[36] It is important to note that Pal was not trying to excuse the alleged behavior of Japanese troops in Nanjing; to the contrary, he was merely questioning the defendants' legal responsibility under international law. Nevertheless, given SCAP censorship as well as the general public support of the trial, even a recklessly nationalistic editor would have paused before printing even a legalistic defense of the atrocities. The more right-wing view that the war was a sacred crusade, fought for the benefit of Asia, was even less likely to appear in print.[37]

On April 29, 1952, one day after Japan's independence, *On Japan's Innocence: The Truth on Trial* (Nihon muzai ron: shinri no sabaki), was printed. Its author, Tanaka Masaaki, had traveled in China with Matsui Iwane and attended Matsui's funeral after the latter was hanged in 1948. At the funeral, Itō Kiyoshi, chief Japanese defense counsel for Matsui, shocked Tanaka by informing him that Pal's dissenting opinion existed. Tanaka told of his own attempts, through Japanese publishers and politicians, to obtain the permission of the occupation authorities to publish Pal's opinion. However, his efforts came to nothing. He then borrowed a copy of Pal's opinion that had been distributed to Japanese defense lawyers and hired three part-time translators to render the document into Japanese. Since Tanaka and his publisher believed that they would be arrested if they published the document immediately, they prepared Pal's dissent so that it could be published as soon as the occupation ended.[38]

Tanaka's book reflected his deep frustration over the Tokyo Trial, his anger toward the Allied forces, and his disappointment with his countrymen. In his introduction, he condemned the trial for failing to punish war crimes by the Allies. He deplored the American dropping of atomic bombs on Hiroshima and Nagasaki. In addition, he pointed an accusing finger at "white people," who discriminated against "colored people" and excluded Asians from their lands. Tanaka was convinced that European and American racial discrimination had been responsible for causing the war between Japan and the Allied powers.[39] He argued strenuously that Japan was innocent and that it was the Allied countries that were responsible for war crimes. Intentionally or not, Tanaka distorted the essence of Pal's arguments to support his thesis. In his separate opinion, Pal did not claim that Japan was innocent, nor did he examine whether or not Japan's actions and policies in China and elsewhere were justifiable in law or morality.[40] Pal had stressed that he had simply found the evidence insufficient to convict the 28 defendants on any of the counts charged in the indictment.[41]

Moreover, Tanaka's understanding of Pal's opinion regarding the Nanjing Massacre was imperfect, to say the least. Tanaka condemned three witnesses who testified for the prosecution—Magee, Xu, and Chen—as propagandists and misleadingly suggested that Pal had entirely rejected their testimony.[42] On the contrary, Pal never argued that these three witnesses intentionally exaggerated or distorted the evidence, nor did he discount their entire testimony.[43] In addition, by not mentioning other witnesses and evidence submitted to the court, Tanaka created the false impression that Magee, Xu, and Chen were the only witnesses who testified to Japanese atrocities in Nanjing before the court, when in fact Pal had evidence from nine witnesses and more than 20 statements.[44]

Tanaka's book conveys his deep personal embarrassment over the Japanese nation's submissive behavior following its defeat. Tanaka stressed that, because of the defeat, Japanese had lost their self-confidence and ethnic pride. He insisted that the people had taken to heart the bitter accusations made by the prosecution without judging them true or false. He was deeply disappointed that intellectuals, critics, scholars, wartime political leaders, and ordinary people all excused themselves from taking any responsibility for the acts of the state. He even declared that he was ashamed of the Japanese as a people. As Tanaka observed, the people (kokumin) claimed that they had been deceived by the wartime leaders, while their apologetic leaders emphasized that they had opposed the war, that they had done their best to avoid the war, or that they had always searched for ways of ending the war.[45]

By the time the occupation was over, the United States had radically revised its ideas of what leadership was best for Japan, and center stage had been reclaimed by old-time political elites who felt no further need to apologize for their wartime behavior. Impelled by the spirit of the Cold War, SCAP indulged in its own form of McCarthyism in the form of the Red Purge. Whereas it had once purged more than 200,000 wartime political, economic, and social leaders, it now restored many of them to favor, including former suspected war criminals. Simultaneously, SCAP purged more than 10,000 Communist Party members and party sympathizers, eliminating them from positions in both the government and private sectors.[46] In November 1954, Hatoyama Ichirō, who was rehabilitated from the original purge in 1951, formed Japan's Democratic Party (Minshutō), which included Kishi Nobusuke, who spent the first three years after the war awaiting trial for alleged Class A war crimes. According to a survey conducted in 1952 by the Prime Minister's Office, 58 percent of 480 male and 48 percent of 120 female respondents voiced concern lest Japan's militarism return, now that the purge was being lifted from the wartime leaders.[47]

In 1955, the Democratic Party published a report titled *The Problem of Deplorable Textbooks* (Ureubeki kyōkasho no mondai). The report warned its readers that Japanese education was facing great danger because "red textbooks" (*akai kyōkasho*), mostly written by members of the Japan Teachers Union (Nikkyōso), had been indoctrinating schoolchildren with leftist biases. According to the report, these red textbooks were aimed at either promoting the political activities of the Japan Teachers Union; mobilizing radical and destructive labor movements; substantially denouncing (*kokiorosu*) the mother country of Japan; romanticizing the Soviet Union and Communist China; or spreading Marxism-Leninism among schoolchildren.[48] For example, *Bright Society* (Akarui shakai), a social studies text edited by Takahashi Shin'ichi and Hidaka Rokurō, greatly disturbed Democratic Party members. *The Problem of Deplorable Textbooks* claimed that the latter part of the textbook was filled with the "history of Japan's invasion of China" and quoted a passage that the Democratic Party considered infuriating: "The Kwantung Army in Manchuria was believed to be by far the strongest army among the Japanese military. Yet the Russian army defeated it easily."[49] To the party, it was unbelievable that the textbook seemed to applaud the Russian victory over Japan's Kwantung Army. The author concluded the report by calling for action to prevent the spread of the evil communist influence. He urged other politicians to join the movement initiated by the Democratic Party.[50]

From the mid-1950s on, as conservatives returned to positions of political influence and as the Cold War progressed, textbooks toned down their discussions of Japanese aggression in Asia. Descriptions of the Nanjing Massacre, which had never been discussed in detail, now disappeared almost completely from history textbooks.[51] The first task of the conservative survivors of the initial postwar purge was to reeducate the hostile public, most of whom supported the postwar educational system and opposed the social values that had prevailed in wartime, such as the emphasis on ethics and loyalty to the throne. A survey conducted in 1950 disclosed that 64 percent of 2,000 people interviewed considered postwar education to be better than what had been offered during or prior to the war, and only 6 percent wanted schools to revive the wartime emphasis on emperor worship.[52] The battle between the old-time ideologues and the so-called progressives was more general than specific.[53] In the 1950s, would-be Nanjing Massacre revisionists, such as Tanaka, never focused their attack solely on representations of the massacre. Those who idealized Japan's part in the war were never forced to confront these progressives over the Nanjing Massacre proper, because no detailed study of the massacre was conducted by journalists, activists, or scholars during the 1950s.[54]

PROGRESSIVES IN THE OCCUPATION PERIOD

The Tokyo Trial and news articles on Japanese atrocities, including the Nanjing Massacre, caused progressive intellectuals to ponder issues of war guilt and the future role of a new Japan. However, few prominent figures limited their attention solely to the Nanjing Massacre, for their concerns were much broader. They asked questions such as who had been responsible for the war. Unlike the majority of the public, who saw neither the emperor nor the people as responsible for Japan's aggression, these progressives emphasized that the public as well as the emperor must share the responsibility.

Masaki Hiroshi, a lawyer who had continually challenged the government in his private journal *Up Close* (Chikaki yori) throughout the war, concluded in early 1946 that overthrowing the emperor system (*tennōsei*) was an essential first step toward taking responsibility for Japan's wartime misconduct, both toward non-Japanese and the nation's own citizens. In his postwar writing, Masaki stressed that thrusting the responsibility for the war upon a small circle of military leaders was immoral and irresponsible. He felt that the emperor and the public were both trying their best to avoid their responsibilities. Although Masaki, who identified himself not as a communist but a humanist, was aware that people overwhelmingly supported the emperor system, he felt responsible for enlightening them as to the real cause of Japan's wartime misdeeds and for increasing the number of people who shared his view. Masaki argued that the essential system of the postwar government was no different from what it had been in wartime. Therefore, left to its own devices, the government was fated to repeat the errors of the past. The only hope for avoiding such tragic repetitions lay with the people. Japanese must realize the institutional causes of the war and assume responsibility for changing the system. Otherwise, Masaki insisted, Japan would never make positive contributions to the future of humankind.[55]

Similarly, Hani Gorō, a renowned Marxist historian who was elected to the Upper House in 1947, strongly advocated in 1949 that Japan must overthrow the emperor system and become a republic. He argued that all of Japan's wartime atrocities were in essence committed in the name of the emperor and that the issue of *tennōsei* was not only domestic, but also international. He stressed that Japan's ability to contribute to world peace would depend on its transformation into a republican government. Otherwise, large corporations (*zaibatsu*), the military, bureaucrats, or crime syndicates would always be able to use the current system in order to achieve their goals. In the eyes of Hani, *tennōsei* was nothing but a potential means to revive ultranationalism and endanger international humanity.[56]

Just as Masaki and Hani faced war responsibility, so did many educators. An overwhelming number of teachers felt responsible for having imparted an education that had romanticized the war and contributed to Japan's war mobilization. Many felt that their own hands had been stained with blood.[57] Members of the Historical Science Society of Japan (Rekken) in Tokyo agreed in 1945 that history textbooks must be based on scientific truth.[58] In 1949, history teachers founded the Association for History Educators (Rekishi kyōikusha kyōgikai) and pledged themselves to the doctrine that "history education must be based on historical studies as well as pedagogical theories and must be independent from everything but truth."[59]

In the late 1940s and 1950s, neither Japanese progressives nor ethnic minorities within Japan had forgotten the devastation inflicted on other countries by Japan's war effort. However, faced with a series of domestic and international "reactionary movements," including the Red Purge, Japan's rearmament, and the Korean War, they failed in their efforts to convince the public that Japan had played a predatory role in the Asia-Pacific War. Despite this failure to spread "victimizer consciousness," namely the acknowledgment of Japan's victimization of neighboring nations during the war, the progressives did succeed in organizing mass peace movements by appealing to antiwar emotion among the public.[60] For example, the Association for Preserving Peace, Japan (Nihon heiwa o mamoru kai) collected more than 6.5 million signatures nationwide in 1950 supporting the so-called Stockholm Appeal, which demanded an absolute ban on nuclear weapons, the establishment of strict international weapons controls, and the classification of the use of nuclear weapons as a war crime.[61]

In coming to terms with the aftermath of the war, many Japanese were more likely to embrace the notion of "victim consciousness" than "victimizer consciousness." This "victim consciousness" (*higaisha ishiki*) gained a firmer foothold among the public following an atomic bomb test on the Bikini atoll carried out by the United States in March 1954. The test killed one of the 23 fishermen exposed to radiation and also led to atomic poisoning that contaminated food supplies and the environment. By the time the first international conference on the banning of atomic weapons was held in Hiroshima in August 1955, more than 30 million persons worldwide had signed a petition demanding a global ban of atomic weapons. After the conference, the organizers of the conference continued to strengthen antinuclear opinion by educating the public about what had happened in Hiroshima and Nagasaki.[62] Public awareness of the war found a symbol in the slogan "Never Send Our Students to the Battlefield" (*os-hiego o futatabi senjō ni okuruna*), a phrase adopted by the Japan Teachers Union at the 18th meeting of its Central Committee in January 1951. Although the antiwar climate of the 1950s did not evolve beyond the level of "victim consciousness," the new Japan did contain voices dedicated to reminding the nation of its past aggressions.[63] Even during the years of conservative reaction, antiwar activists devoted themselves to reminding the nation of the suffering it had inflicted on other peoples.

ROCKING THE BOAT: 1950S ANTIWAR ACTIVISTS CONFRONT THE PAST

These antiwar activists never gained the support of a popular majority, however. Although the Nanjing Massacre received little attention, a handful of devoted antiwar activists persistently challenged the public to remember Japan's wartime atrocities. After the People's Republic of China (PRC) was established in October 1949, Chinese, Japanese, and Taiwanese who celebrated the creation of the new government agreed to found the Association for Japan-China Friendship (Nit-Chū yūkō kyōkai). The association was formally founded on October 1, 1950, and included some 180 representatives of various political and ethnic groups. Uchiyama Kanzō, who owned Uchiyama Bookstore and had helped proletarian writers such as Lu Xun and Kaji Wataru in Shanghai during the war, became the first chairman of the trustees.[64]

The association organized various projects to inspire reflection on Japan's wartime misdeeds against China. In the late 1950s, it sponsored a memorial service commemorating the deaths of Chinese and Korean slave laborers in Hanaoka, Akita (known as the Hanaoka Incident). In February 1953, with the help of Buddhist, labor, and humanitarian organizations, the association founded the Committee for Mourning the Dead Chinese Prisoners (Chūgokujin horyo junnansha irei jikkō iinkai). The committee researched more than 130 forced labor sites and excavated remains of the laborers. It sponsored memorial services for the laborers, sent the remains of approximately 3,000 victims back to China, and sought to hold the government legally responsible for the killing of slave laborers.[65]

In summer 1956, some 1,000 war criminals, who had been detained in a special prison in Fushun, China, returned to Japan. While they were incarcerated, some of these prisoners wrote narratives of their wartime experiences. The resulting book, published in March 1957, was titled *Three Alls* (sankō) in reference to a Chinese word that means kill-all, burn-all, and loot-all. Because of pressure from right-wing extremists, the publisher suspended the sale of the book for three months.[66] Refusing to give in to this pressure, the authors, who had organized the Group of Returnees from China (Chūgoku kikansha renrakukai), published another, more extended book of confessions with a different publisher. The group gave this volume a different title, *Invasion: Confessions of Japanese War Crimes in China* (Shinryaku: Chūgoku ni okeru Nihon senpan no kokuhaku), and added four new confessions to the text.[67] Just like *Three Alls*, *Invasion* included photographs of such subjects as skeletons, dead infants, and people being buried alive. The pages of *Invasion* are filled with confessions to acts that included arson, looting, the use of toxic gas, and the killing of women and infants.[68] Readers of the book were exposed to tales of unimaginably inhumane conduct committed by writers like Suzuki Yoshio.

Suzuki, a newly recruited private at the time, volunteered to burn houses in a village in order to impress his commander. An elderly woman, who lived there, begged him not to set a fire, pointing to her little granddaughter. He pushed her away with his rifle. The child, who was helping her grandmother, stared at him with sorrowful eyes, but even her silent pleading did not stop him. Suzuki set a fire, which soon spread to neighboring houses. He then went into the next house. A woman who had just given birth was lying on the bed. For a moment the sight reminded him of his sister and her baby in Japan, but this did not stop him. Another elderly woman begged him with tears in her eyes not to burn her house. He kicked her away and set the fire. The woman went into the house, and screams and the cries of a baby came from inside. Not wanting to hear them, Suzuki threw another bundle of flaming straw into the house.[69]

In the afterword to *Invasion*, the Group of Returnees from China expressed concern about how their family members would react to the book; they were quite aware that their stories were horrific and shameful. Despite their shame and their rudimentary writing abilities, they felt responsible for recording their honest confessions and enlightening the public about the reality of the war in order to atone for the sins that they had committed. Just as the members of the group had once believed in Japan's aggression as a sacred cause and had been ready to give their lives for it, they now staked their lives to acknowledge their wartime crimes. According to the book, their motive for disclosing their wartime inhumane acts was that they wished never again to see young people of Japan murder innocent people in Asia.[70] Although these returnees have often been accused of being brainwashed by the Communists, they now had a new mission to educate their fellow Japanese citizens about the reality of the war and to remind the nation of Japan's wartime atrocities. Surviving members continue to pursue this mission to this day.

"I WILL NOT LET IT HAPPEN AGAIN": PROGRESSIVES STRIKE BACK

A lesson that progressives learned from the war was to act before it was too late. Unlike during wartime, when no organized resistance succeeded against the state, progressives banded together in the postwar period and fought against the state when necessary. Antinuclear movements in the 1950s were one example. Another example was the anti-Japan U.S. Security Treaty movements that mobilized more than 5 million people nationwide and forced Kishi Nobusuke, then the prime minister, to resign from the office in 1960.[71] Liberal activism was also reflected in countless protests against the Vietnam War and meetings held during the 1960s.[72] The first Ienaga textbook lawsuit also demonstrated such atmosphere of the time.

In June 1965, Ienaga Saburō, a history professor at Tokyo University of Education, began legal proceedings against the government, which had "requested" that he revise and rewrite descriptions in his *New Japanese History* (Shin Nihonshi), a high school history textbook. The government's "request" was accompanied by a threat to withhold authorization to publish the book until Ienaga complied. Ienaga, who had been writing and revising the textbook since the early 1950s, had nearly a decade of experience with the textbook authorization system. As the government tried to promote nationalism among youth via textbooks starting in the mid-1950s, Ienaga began to experience stronger official opposition. After examining the 1964 textbook, the government told the publisher that 323 items would have to be revised in order to pass the authorization, among them Ienaga's description of the Pacific War. Government inspectors would not allow Ienaga to characterize the war as "reckless" (*mubō*) and found his description of the war too negative (*kurai*). By the mid-1960s, Ienaga was well prepared to confront the government.[73]

Ienaga explained to a reporter his reasons for suing the government:

> In the prewar period, although I disagreed with the war, I never spoke up and could not prevent that idiotic [*bakageta*] war. As a result, I was forced to see the motherland ruined. I was teaching at Niigata High School from 1941 till 1943 and at Tokyo Teachers College from 1944. I sent my students off for the battlefront. I regret this deeply. I feel a certain responsibility for the war. I will not let it happen again. The basis of my motive is this feeling of responsibility for the war. [The inspectors] claimed that illustrations and descriptions of the war were too negative, and this outraged me. I can no longer bear it.[74]

Ienaga was not sure how he would pay his potentially enormous legal fees. However, as soon as news reports publicized the lawsuit, Ienaga received anonymous donations daily, and supporting organizations were founded nationwide.[75]

Backed by his supporters, who ranged from teachers and lawyers to homemakers, Ienaga filed another lawsuit against the government in 1967. This time Ienaga and his lawyers strategically narrowed their demands. In the 1966 edition Ienaga had reinstated six of the 323 items that the government had demanded to have stricken. These six changes, the ones Ienaga considered most important, included the use of the term "reckless" to characterize the war. Despite these fairly modest revisions, the 1966 edition failed the government's inspection. Ienaga's second suit concerned only these half-dozen changes. Perhaps because the issues had been so drastically narrowed, the judgment of Ienaga's second lawsuit of 1967 was rendered before his first lawsuit of 1965 could come to an end. In 1970, the Tokyo District Court ruled in favor of Ienaga in his second suit, though the government immediately appealed.

In Ienaga's first and second lawsuits, the representation of the Nanjing Massacre did not become an issue because there was no specific discussion of it in the versions of his textbook under scrutiny. Although he was certainly aware of Nanjing, perhaps he did not feel compelled to mention the incident in a textbook that had to cover Japanese history from the Stone Age through the postwar period in fewer than 300 pages. The massacre was not yet a contested issue in Japanese historiography, and few authors had extensively written about it. Moreover, Ienaga's concern extended beyond Nanjing: he denounced all aspects of the "Fifteen-Year War" (*jūgonen sensō*) that was waged from 1931 to 1945.[76]

BEGINNINGS OF NANJING MASSACRE HISTORIOGRAPHY

The Nanjing Massacre remained largely outside common awareness in Japan throughout the 1950s and the 1960s. For practical purposes, the 1960s may be considered as marking the beginning of the historiography of Nanjing. In 1965, veterans of the Kumamoto Units published their military history and included a brief discussion of the "Nanjing Incident" (*Nankin jiken*). Its editor agreed that Japanese must reflect on the Nanjing Incident and accept responsibility for the killing of innocent civilians. Nonetheless, he expressed astonishment at the claim that the Kumamoto Sixth Division was responsible for inflicting 230,000 casualties during the atrocities. This statistic, which had been claimed by the Chinese military tribunal that pronounced the death sentence on Tani Hisao, the division's commander, had infuriated veterans of the division, who considered it an irresponsible exaggeration. The editor defined the incident as including only those atrocities that took place between December 12 and December 17, 1937. Although he admitted a fraction of the alleged atrocities that resulted in the deaths of civilian Chinese, the editor did not find any veterans who witnessed the gigantic scale of atrocities that the Chinese side claimed. In addition, the editor argued that, unlike the Ninth and Sixteen Divisions, the Kumamoto units entered the city on December 14 to join the mopping-up operation and had maintained their discipline. The editor concluded that the trial was politically motivated and that the court had executed Tani because it was not politically expedient to prosecute imperial family members like Prince Asaka, the army commander in Central China during the war. The editor further suggested that Tani had been made a scapegoat for other responsible high-ranking generals, most of whom had already been killed in action or executed.[77]

In 1966, Gotō Kōsaku, a war correspondent who advanced to Nanjing with the Kumamoto Sixth Division, edited a book titled *The Truth of the Nanjing Operation* (Nankin sakusen no shinsō). Gotō's single motive in publishing the book was to clear the Kumamoto Sixth Division of the charge of the Nanjing Massacre. Gotō, together with Shimono Ikkaku, the chief of staff of the Kumamoto Sixth Division at the time of the incident, discovered a number of living witnesses among Japanese soldiers, whose stories Gotō included in the book along with the division's military history. The book also contained Tani's diary and testimony, in which Tani insisted upon his innocence, and letters written by veterans and bereaved family members of the division, expressing their gratitude for Gotō's and Shimono's efforts to exonerate the division.[78]

The first detailed study of the Nanjing Massacre by a historian also appeared in the 1960s. In 1967, Hora Tomio, a history professor at Waseda University, published *Riddles of Modern War History* (Kindai senshi no nazo), in which he examined the Nanjing Massacre (1937), the Marco Polo Bridge Incident (1937), the Nomonhan Incident (1939), and the Korean War (1950–53).[79] American atrocities in Vietnam led him to think comparatively about Japanese atrocities during the wars in East Asia and to analyze them more fully than newspaper reports had. In his section on the Nanjing Massacre, Hora examined documents submitted by both the defense and prosecution to the Tokyo Trial, Pal's dissenting opinion, newspaper and periodical reports at the time of the massacre, and accounts written by Smythe and Timperley. After discussing atrocities against prisoners of war, plainclothes guerrillas, and civilians, Hora estimated that some 100,000 combatants were killed while fighting and that 100,000 civilians were killed during and after the battle. Using this method of analysis, he concluded that the death toll of the massacre was considerably more than the figures originally assessed by American and European witnesses. Hora also wrote that he tended to agree with Timperley's estimate that the Japanese invasion from Shanghai to Nanjing took the lives of approximately 300,000 Chinese, many of whom were noncombatants.[80]

CONCLUSION

After Japan was defeated in World War II, a new consensus committed to preserving peace emerged among the people. Later, during the height of the Cold War, this consensus was generally linked to antiwar and antinuclear weapons sentiment and took firm root in postwar Japanese society. This peace activism often disregarded Japanese wartime aggression and atrocities, however, and it tended not to touch upon issues regarding war responsibility. Although some Japanese and others tried to promote public awareness of the devastations inflicted on other Asian peoples by the Japanese military, they achieved little success. Under these conditions, Nanjing and other Japanese atrocities, which had been given nationwide publicity by the occupational authorities, were gradually overshadowed by the new pacifist sentiment.

Moreover, between 1945 and 1971, both those who disputed the credibility of the Nanjing Massacre and those who fully acknowledged the event were less aggressive and more benign in their writings than in the post-1971 period. During this period, neither side took particular notice of the other, nor did either side regard the other as its opponent. Revisionists did not feel compelled to place the massacre in the context of other mass atrocities in order to make it seem less terrible. Nor, on the other hand, did progressives feel obliged to emphasize the inhumanity or scale of the massacre in order to refute the denials that emanated from revisionist writers. In general, revisionists were primarily concerned not with refuting specific individual atrocities committed by the Japanese military, but with resisting the wholesale demonization of Imperial Japan in postwar Japanese society. Similarly, progressives were more concerned with analyzing the fundamental cause of the war and its relation to the emperor system. Both the tone and the stakes of the debate over Nanjing were soon to change.

5

China: In Times of Civil and Cold War

After Japan's defeat, relations between the Nationalist Chinese government and the Communist Party deteriorated, and the United States took an increasingly active role in Asia. Under such domestic and international circumstances, political considerations affected the Nationalists' and Communists' definition of Chinese patriots as well as their respective images of Japanese war criminals. For the Nationalist government, collaborators and Communists became the most reviled enemies, while Nationalist supporters and sympathizers as well as American imperialists with their nuclear weapons became the most threatening enemies of the Communist government.

From 1945 through the 1960s, influenced by domestic and international politics, neither the Nationalist nor the Communist government emphasized the uniqueness of the Nanjing Massacre among other atrocities committed by Japanese troops during the war. Both governments continued to view the Japanese people as victims of their own military leaders, just as they had during wartime. During the civil war, the main focus of both Nationalist and Communist governments was on defeating their current enemies rather than remembering the war against Japan of the 1930s and 1940s. Even after the victory of the People's Republic of China (PRC), the massacre did not become a symbol of Japan's wartime aggression in PRC's official historiography.

In the 1950s, the Communist government instead used the memory of the massacre to denounce American imperialism and to oppose the rearmament of Japan. According to the official interpretation, Americans had conspired with Japanese imperialists to make the massacre possible. In the 1950s and '60s, the PRC government was not eager to preserve memories of the massacre because it feared they might contradict the image of national strength among the Chinese public. Nonetheless, without challenging the official interpretation, locals in Nanjing preserved their personal memories and the history of the massacre by initiating detailed studies of the event within the framework of the official narrative.

GUOMINDANG POLICY TOWARD JAPANESE WAR CRIMINALS AND CHINESE COLLABORATORS

On August 15, 1945, following the Japanese acceptance of the Potsdam Declaration, which outlined the terms of surrender, Chiang Kai-shek broadcast a speech in which he appealed to the people not to seek retaliation against the Japanese people. He stated:

> We have . . . repeatedly declared that we were only opposed to the Japanese militarists and harbored no enmity for the Japanese people. . . . While we must insist on the strict compliance with the term of the surrender, we must not look forward to retaliation, and much less shall we impose insults on the innocent civilians. We can only sympathize with their plight—coerced and misled as they have been by their Fascist and Nazi leaders, and hope that they will repent of their mistake and sins. If, on the other hand, we attempt to retaliate with atrocity for the past atrocities of the enemy, and repay with insult their mistaken superiority complex in the past, then the spirit of revenge shall be interminably perpetuated—a development far from the intentions of our righteousness-loving Army.[1]

This rule did not, however, apply to Chinese collaborators. Immediately after Japan's China Expeditionary Army officially surrendered to the Guomindang government on September 9, 1945, the authorities began to arrest those whom they regarded as traitors, including intellectuals, celebrities, businesspeople, and former personnel of the puppet Nanjing government.[2] According to *China Year Book* 1948 (Zhonghua nianjian 1948), 30,185 people were indicted in high courts (*gaodeng fayuan*) nationwide. Of these, 369 were sentenced to death, and 979 were sentenced to life imprisonment. Another statistical study concluded that the high court in Nanjing alone sentenced at least 17 Chinese to death and 38 Chinese to life imprisonment between April 1946 and August 1947.[3]

On April 12, 1946, a week after the first hearing, Chen Gongbo, the head of the Nanjing puppet government, was sentenced to death by the High Court in Jiangsu. The Supreme Court (*zuigao fayuan*) in Nanjing upheld the decision, and Chen was executed on June 3, 1946. Although the court held that Chen had collaborated with the Japanese militarists, established a puppet government in Nanjing, and exploited the Chinese people, Chen insisted that he decided to cooperate with the militarists because he believed that his countrymen stood to lose more by resisting the invaders than by cooperating with them. Admitting he had been incorrect, Chen testified that he thought he could achieve a reasonable compromise with Japanese authorities.[4]

A comparison of the sentences of Chinese collaborators and Japanese war criminals is revealing. Overall, the Guomindang authorities arrested more than

30 times as many Chinese collaborators as Japanese war crime suspects. Chinese collaborators were condemned to death nearly two and a half times more often than Japanese defendants, and they were more than 10 times more likely to receive life sentences. While asking the public to treat Japanese generously, the Nationalist government treated its own nationals whom it regarded as traitors with little benevolence. Immediately after the surrender of the Japanese military in China, the Guomindang made suspected traitors figures onto whom the public could release its anger.

THE GUOMINDANG AND THE NANJING MASSACRE:
THE MILITARY TRIBUNAL IN NANJING

Whereas Class A war criminals accused of committing crimes against peace and humanity were tried in Tokyo, Japanese, Koreans, and Taiwanese accused of conventional offenses, that is, Class B and Class C defendants, were tried in various Allied nations. The Guomindang government held its first trial of Japanese war crime suspects in Beijing on April 16, 1946. Military tribunals were held in 10 cities in China, including Nanjing. These trials resulted in fewer executions than did the trials held in other Allied nations.[5] Tani Hisao (the division commander of the Kumamoto Sixth Division) and Tanaka Gunkichi (a company commander of the Kumamoto Sixth Division) were executed for committing wholesale atrocities in Nanjing. The two participants in the alleged "killing contest," Noda Tsuyoshi and Mukai Toshiaki, were given the same sentence.

Unlike many of those who concealed themselves for fear of execution or lesser punishments, Tani, Tanaka, Noda, and Mukai, who believed themselves innocent, did not try to flee and were arrested between February 1946 and September 1947.[6] In court, all four emphatically proclaimed their innocence, and they also declared in their wills that they did not commit the alleged atrocities. All accepted execution as their fate, and each believed he died for upholding his values rather than as a punishment for his alleged crimes. Tani convinced himself that he would die for his motherland.[7] Tanaka believed that his soul would be with the emperor after his death.[8] Mukai and Noda fervently hoped their deaths would establish a stronger bond between China and Japan.[9]

In the minds of Tani, Tanaka, Mukai, and Noda, all of whom were graduates of either the Military Staff College or the Military Academy, the military tribunal in Nanjing had misunderstood the function of military justice. As Mukai protested in his will, the killings that the army committed during combat were, to his mind, not crimes, but justified acts.[10] The defendants' definition of "atrocity" differed from that of Chinese prosecutors, who regarded killings of Chinese people, whether combatants or civilians, as "atrocities." In the eyes of the tribunal judges, news reports of such phenomena as the "killing contest" proved that the Japanese military had amused themselves by murdering innocent Chinese people. The tribunal did not regard these deeds as acts of combat. The judges concluded on March 10, 1947, that the Japanese military killed more than 300,000 Chinese between December 12 and 21, 1937. This judgment was based on the conclusion that 190,000 victims were put to death in mass executions, and their bodies were destroyed without a trace, whereas another 150,000 were interred by volunteer burial societies.[11] The judgment also seems to have involved some strange arithmetic, since adding these two numbers yields a number greater than 300,000. There is evidently no way to explain the discrepancy.

Moreover, the court could not understand why criminals like Tani Hisao claimed innocence. It insisted that Japanese commanders, including Tani, were all responsible for the organized and wholesale murder, arson, rape, and looting. Although Tani stressed that Chinese victims could not identify any specific Japanese division as the perpetrators, the court condemned Tani for evading his responsibility. Though Tani moved to introduce testimony from Shimono Ikkaku and other members of his staff during the Nanjing campaign, the court declined to hear these witnesses because it considered them accomplices in the atrocities. Because of the unimaginable cruelty of the crimes, the judges concluded that Tani deserved a public execution.[12] Although tribunals in China as a whole acquitted 350 of the 883 indicted Japanese (including 16 Korean-born and 41 Taiwanese-born Japanese), the tribunal in Nanjing had no mercy for these four defendants who symbolized the Nanjing atrocities.[13]

Because of the civil war, the Guomindang government closed military tribunals in nine cities in 1947. A tribunal in Shanghai was still operating, but it issued its last judgment on January 26, 1949.[14] As Wellington Koo, a Chinese diplomat, later recollected, because of the civil war and Chiang Kai-shek's presumption that Japan would be an important Asian ally for China, the Nationalist government supported a generous policy toward Japan even during this period, when the people still vividly remembered Japanese atrocities.[15] Meanwhile, the communist People's Liberation Army (PLA) seized Shenyang on November 2, 1948, conquered Beijing on January 31, 1949, and captured Nanjing on April 23, 1949. On October 1, 1949, the PRC was established.

WAR CRIMINALS AND THE CHINESE COMMUNIST PARTY

From 1945 to the mid-1950s, three turning points in international affairs in Asia influenced the Chinese Communist Party (CCP) in its definition of "war criminals": Japan's defeat, the civil war in China, and the CCP's participation in the Korean War. On September 14, 1945, an editorial in the Communist Party's newspaper *Jiefang Ribao* named suspected war criminals for whom the editor urged punishment. The newspaper demanded that the Allied Powers mete out stern justice to the alleged offenders, including military personnel, politicians, imperial family members, bureaucrats, and business leaders in both Japan and occupied areas. The party declared such military leaders as Tōjō Hideki, Araki Sadao, and Okamura Yasuji the leading war criminals who were most responsible for preparing and waging an aggressive war against China. The second tier of war criminals were those who had abetted the most wanted military leaders: namely, Emperor Hirohito and other imperial family members, such as Prince Asaka; bureaucrats like Aoki Kazuo; *zaibatsu* leaders including Furuta Toshinosuke; reactionary politicians such as Shigemitsu Mamoru; and propagandists of ultranationalist groups like Tokutomi Sohō. The editorial warned that many Japanese war criminals were pretending to have been pacifists and were planning future revenge against the Allied Powers. In addition, it underscored that the Chinese people should be especially concerned about war criminals because China had experienced the longest period of occupation and the most prolonged suffering. The editors insisted that stern justice was required not in the name of retaliation but of eternal peace. Although the party included Matsui Iwane in the list of second-tier war criminals, it held Matsui responsible for being a propagandist of an ultranationalist group rather than for the Nanjing Massacre.[16]

The term "war criminals" acquired additional meanings as the civil war progressed. On July 7, 1947, the Central Committee of the Communist Party declared 16 slogans to guide the revolutionary movement. The first slogan exhorted the people to win the defensive war and to annihilate Chiang Kai-shek's invading army. The second one urged them to oppose the traitor Chiang Kai-shek, and the third one vowed to bring to justice all the Nationalist war criminals being harbored within Chiang's forces and to confiscate all the assets they had stolen from the people. In the eighth and ninth slogans, the committee expressed its gratitude to the PLA and the people for supporting the party's war efforts. The twelfth and thirteenth slogans appealed to the Nationalists and their supporters to give up their reactionary resistance and to unify the nation under the banner of democracy. The seventh slogan mentioned punishment for Japanese war criminals, but it also stressed the need to punish Chinese collaborators and to prevent Chiang from using reparations from Japan to fight the civil war.[17] These slogans suggest that the CCP's primary concern was no longer Japan's war crimes, but the present war crimes of the Nationalists during the ongoing civil war.

On November 1, 1948, the General Headquarters of the PLA issued an order to prosecute Nationalist war criminals for certain actions during the civil war. It strongly condemned the Nationalist forces that, according to the order, were deploying chemical weapons and were murdering people, looting, and indiscriminately bombing cities.[18] On January 14, 1949, Mao Zedong, the chairman of the Central Committee of the CCP, responded to a peace proposal offered by Chiang Kai-shek by accusing him of concluding unpatriotic treaties with the United States, committing wholesale atrocities, and impoverishing the people. Mao called Chiang the most prominent of all war criminals and declared that the PRC would not conclude a peace treaty unless the Nationalist government agreed to eight conditions, which included punishing war criminals as well as abolishing the unpatriotic treaties.[19]

After the outbreak of the Korean War and the entry of China into the war, the PRC government added American servicemen to its lists of war criminals. In November 1950, it sent Wu Xiuquan to the United Nations as chief of the PRC delegation to protest U.S. imperialism and aggression. In the speech he prepared—but was not permitted to give because of alleged American objections—Wu blamed American imperialists for 150 consecutive years of aggression against China. According to Wu, in the 1830s, American merchants had helped Britain introduce opium into China and had supported British troops during the Opium Wars; in the 1930s, the U.S. government had exported massive military supplies to Japan as the latter nation was invading China; and after Japan's defeat, the U.S. government tried to transform China into an American colony. Wu insisted that American cultural and humanitarian efforts in China were a form of invasion and that American friends in China such as Chiang Kai-shek and other reactionaries had all been proxies in America's invasion of China.[20] On March 8, 1952, Zhou Enlai, premier and foreign minister of the PRC, accused American invading forces of conducting biological warfare and declared that if any American pilots were captured while dropping biological agents over China, they would be prosecuted as war criminals.[21]

As the term "war criminals" expanded to include Chinese Nationalists and American servicemen, the CCP's policy toward Japanese war criminals also changed, shifting from punitive to nonpunitive. When military tribunals were held in Shenyang and Taiyuan in June and July 1956, only 45 military personnel and civilian officials out of 1,108 Japanese detainees were indicted. Neither the death penalty nor life imprisonment was recommended for any of these defendants. Although the prosecution had intended to indict 180 detainees and to demand the death penalty for 70 of them, their plans were thwarted by Zhou Enlai, who disagreed with the charges, ordered the prosecution to indict fewer Japanese, and forbade the prosecution from recommending either the death penalty or life imprisonment. In July 1956, the PRC allowed those Japanese who were not prosecuted to return home, and all 45 of those indicted had been repatriated by mid-1964.[22]

All of those indicted, including army generals, admitted the charges against them before the court, whose proceedings were public. Some even requested that the court impose the death penalty upon them for their wartime conduct. By the time tribunals were held, the 45 defendants, as well as many of the other detainees, had confessed their wartime atrocities as war crimes and acknowledged responsibility for their acts. The PRC's treatment of the detainees, which was astonishingly lenient, was calculated to persuade the prisoners of the humanity of their captors and to inspire heartfelt repentance. The detainees were served Japanese-style cuisine three times a day, while the guards who fed them ate only two meals a day, and they were given expensive foreign medicines when ill. Furthermore, the guards were forbidden from using violence against the detainees under any circumstance. In contrast to prevailing practices in the Soviet Union, the detainees had no obligation to work. Instead, they were given time to think, study, and discuss what they had done to Chinese victims.[23] The humane treatment the detainees received served to intensify their shame. As the nameless Chinese whom the detainees had killed during the war were transformed from subhuman to human in their minds, their definitions of "military justice" and "atrocity" also changed. Whereas they may once have thought of their wartime killings of Chinese as a service to the nation, they now saw their deeds as crimes. Their former triumphs became painful psychological wounds, deeply etched in their memories. These memories later propelled these Japanese to become diehard antiwar activists and advocates of establishing diplomatic relations with the PRC after their repatriation to Japan. The strategy that the PRC government followed was reminiscent of the work of Kaji Wataru, whose reeducation of Japanese soldiers led to the Japanese People's Antiwar Alliance.

THE NANJING MASSACRE IN THE PEOPLE'S REPUBLIC OF CHINA

Among the 45 Japanese indicted in 1956, none was charged with the atrocities in Nanjing. The charges against them mirrored official understandings at the time of leading war crimes. The prosecution condemned such crimes as the Japanese policy of Three-Alls (burn all, kill all, and loot all) in North China; the arrest, torture, and murder of civilians; chemical and biological warfare; the production and sale of opium; the political, economic, and cultural aggression in Manchuria; the postwar assistance given to the Nationalist army; and the transportation of human "guinea pigs" to Unit 731, Japan's chemical and biological unit.[24] These charges did not tend to include atrocities that occurred in Nanjing and other Nationalist-occupied areas.

As the United States became more threatening to China, the PRC government began to use the Nanjing Massacre as a political tool against the United States.[25] In March 1951, *Xinhua Yuebao*, a monthly journal published in Beijing, reprinted an article from the Nanjing daily *Xinhua Ribao* titled "Recollections of the Great Japanese Massacre in Nanjing" (Zuiyi Rikou zai Nanjing datusha). The anonymous reporter accused American missionaries in Nanjing, such as Miner Searle Bates, of being more concerned with preserving American property than with saving Chinese lives. According to the writer, the creation of the Nanjing safety zone was a covert plot between American and Japanese devils to destroy Chinese patriotic resistance, which had inflicted severe casualties on Japanese invading forces. The reporter claimed that the safety zone had become a convenient slaughtering pen, drawing the Chinese patriots into a single location and enabling the Japanese invaders to kill them more efficiently. According to the article, an American devil deceived Chinese women and gathered them in one place so that Japanese soldiers could kidnap young and beautiful Chinese girls in order to gratify their sexual desires.[26] To stir readers' emotions, the photograph section of the monthly journal included two pages of photographs of

Japanese atrocities in Nanjing and elsewhere with the slogan "Remember the Japanese Atrocities; We Must Firmly Protest the Remilitarization of Japan!" (Jiqile Rikou baoxing, women jiuyao jianjue fandui Meidi chongxin wuzhuang Riben!).[27] Overall, the article portrayed American humanitarians as being as evil as, if not more so than, invading Japanese troops.

Nevertheless, the PRC government did not emphasize the uniqueness in scale and brutality of the massacre. Typical was a journal article by the famous scholar Guo Moruo, a delegate of the PRC who opposed the American invasion of Korea and the remilitarization of Japan.[28] Although Guo mentioned the unprecedented devastation that Japan's militarism had inflicted on Asian countries and their people, he neither referred to Nanjing nor distinguished it from Chinese sufferings at other scenes of mass atrocity. Rather, Guo placed Chinese casualties within the larger framework of atrocities in Asia, noting that Japanese militarism had led to the deaths of more than 10 million people in China; 2 million slave laborers in Indonesia; 1 million Filipinos; 2 million Vietnamese; and 3.5 million Indians. As for the damages that Japanese militarism inflicted on Japan itself, he argued that it had resulted in more than 2 million orphans, 1.83 million war widows, and the dropping of atom bombs on two open cities.[29] Among the nations that Guo excluded from his statistics were South Korea, Taiwan, and the United States, though all three nations had also lost hundreds of thousands of lives because of Japan's wartime aggression.

In addition, in the view of the PRC in the 1950s, the Nanjing Massacre never came close to Hiroshima and Nagasaki in terms of its scale and brutality. Faced with an American nuclear threat, the PRC directed its sympathies toward atomic bomb victims in Japan. In an article in *Renmin ribao* in August 1955, Mei Ruao, a justice from China at the Tokyo Trial, who had visited Hiroshima six months after the explosion, strongly condemned the American killing of innocent civilians in the two cities. Although Mei acknowledged that Japan's militarism had wrought damage in China since the Sino-Japanese War of 1894–95, he argued that dropping atomic bombs on civilians, most of whom were old people, women, and children, outweighed these acts and was an unprecedented atrocity in world military history.[30] The PRC sent delegates to the first World Rally against Atomic and Hydrogen Bombs, held in Hiroshima in August 1955, and donated 7.2 million yen to help finance the event.[31]

Although the PRC leaders apparently did not depend on the Nanjing Massacre to remind the Japanese government of its wartime atrocities in the 1950s, this policy was not observed by all Chinese commentators. For example, Xu Dunzhang, a professor at Beijing Institute of Law and Politics (Beijing fazheng xueyuan), singled out the Nanjing Massacre in order to remind the Japanese government of its wartime aggression in China and its annihilation of more than 10 million lives in eight years.[32]

Moreover, the massacre remained a topic of strong interest among local residents of Nanjing. In 1960, the Department of History at Nanjing University began conducting two years of interviews with survivors of the massacre, resulting in an eight-chapter manuscript with collected statistics and photographs.[33] Although the manuscript followed the PRC's official line—that the American missionaries were responsible for the Japanese atrocities in Nanjing—the Chinese government classified the document instead of allowing its publication. As Mark Eykholt argued in his study of the Chinese historiography of the massacre, the PRC government did not welcome public focus on wartime weakness at a time when it was trying to build up national pride and strength among the people.[34] The manuscript was turned over to the city government in Nanjing, which made the study available to interested Japanese visitors.[35]

CONCLUSION

From 1945 to 1971 the Nanjing Massacre was not a popular emblem of the sufferings of people in China. The Nationalist government, which was preoccupied with its internal enemy and sought an alliance with Japan, did not publicize Japanese wartime atrocities to a global audience as it had done during the war. Similarly, the Communist government, which sought to foster an image of national pride and strength among its people, perceived no advantage in preserving the massacre in Chinese national memory. Locals in Nanjing preserved their memories and history of the massacre within the official narrative approved by the central government. During this period, few Japanese, if any, openly denied the existence of the massacre or challenged the death tolls recognized by the Tokyo Trial (200,000) or by the military tribunal in Nanjing (300,000). Thus the PRC government found it unnecessary to underscore the wholesale horrors of Nanjing or the death count in order to teach Japanese revisionists the lessons of its wartime aggression.

6

United States: Rebuilding Japan

Because new foreign enemies of the United States emerged after Japan's defeat, the Nanjing atrocities received scant attention from the American public in the aftermath of the war. The Allied occupation brought some 465,000 American troops to Japan in 1946.[1] American correspondents followed them. At the same time that it closely monitored the Japanese press, Douglas MacArthur, the Supreme Commander for Allied Powers (SCAP), tried to control the American news media, though with far less success. On October 12, 1945, MacArthur announced his intention to restrict the American press in its coverage of occupied Japan. An official quota, effective October 27, allowed 53 American news agency and radio personnel to stay in Japan.[2] To those back home, the American troops, correspondents, and their family members contributed to spreading SCAP-sponsored narratives regarding Emperor Hirohito and Tōjō Hideki, and they portrayed Japanese in a more complex way than the caricatures widely held during the war. After Japan's defeat, the previously monolithic image of the fanatical Japanese began to acquire more diverse and human faces. Particularly influential was John Hersey's "Hiroshima," published in the *New Yorker* in 1946, which emphasized individual suffering. His work helped the public to see Japanese not as the enemy but as people.

Tracing the American press reports of the time reveals a revised version of wartime Japanese history. Hirohito was not just humanized—he was no longer held responsible for the war. Instead, Tōjō Hideki and his company became solely responsible for the war. Japanese wartime atrocities, including the Nanjing Massacre, were not given heavy emphasis in these accounts, perhaps because they had been so extensively reported during the war. Instead, the newspapers gave greater coverage to the sufferings of the Japanese people and the human dignity of the once-reviled Son of Heaven, Hirohito.

"THE NECESSARY CHANGES": SHIFTING THE MANTLE
OF BLAME FROM HIROHITO TO TŌJŌ

When Japan announced its surrender on August 14, 1945, the editors of the *New York Times* were skeptical. An editorial titled "Only Temporary Surrender?" probably represented the mood of many readers who believed that the aim of Japan was to conquer the world; that the Japanese people were natural war-mongers; and that the Japanese as a people must be punished severely.[3] The editorial argued:

> While preparing them [the Japanese people] for defeat in the present con-flict they [the Japanese leaders] also have been sowing the seed they hope will sprout into another holy war for conquest of the world. . . .
> The strictest control of the Japanese people, even for a hundred years, would not be enough. It has been truly said that you cannot shoot an idea. The only answer to the Japanese belief that their emperor is a god, and that they have a divine mission to bring under his control all the other peoples of the world, is the inculcation in them of a better idea, the idea of liberty, fraternity and equality. That will take more doing than the fabrica-tion of an atomic bomb. And it is not something that can be done in a few years. But it is a task that must be undertaken if we are to win the peace, as we have won the war. . . . There is no hope for continuing peace until it [the Japanese belief] is dead. Everyone must hope that it can be killed. The effort must be made and it must be continued far into the future. We can set no limitation on the winning of the peace.[4]

By the time the Pacific War was over, Emperor Hirohito's name was well known in the United States. Thirty-three percent of respondents in a June 1945 poll wanted him to be executed.[5] Like many Japanese who worshiped the em-peror during the war, many Americans viewed Hirohito as "the only Japanese god" rather than a dictator.[6] After the war, the American public was also ex-posed to a SCAP narrative that contradicted the wartime image of the emperor and spread a more positive image of him. Taking Hirohito's place as the man most responsible for the war was Tōjō.

On September 25, 1945, the *New York Times* printed two articles about the emperor. The front page announced "Hirohito in Interview Puts Blame on Tojo in Sneak Raid; Says He Now Opposes War." Frank Kluckhohn, a *Times* corre-spondent in Tokyo, reported on his meeting with Hirohito, which was author-ized by both MacArthur and Hirohito. Although he claimed to be the first non-Japanese since Japan's surrender to interview Hirohito, Kluckhohn was in fact instructed not to ask any spontaneous questions. He was required to submit written questions in advance, and Hirohito's written answers were handed down to Kluckhohn afterward. During the meeting, the emperor asked ques-tions of the correspondent, to which Kluckhohn gave brief replies.[7]

Although the meeting was just 10 minutes long, Kluckhohn seemed to be quite impressed with Hirohito. He had come to the interview with the belief, in-stilled by previous media accounts, that the emperor "had the power of life and death over the entire Japanese nation." However, when he met the emperor face to face, Kluckhohn saw a man who behaved much like any other person. He was impressive not in a sense of superhuman majesty, but in his very human honesty and dignity. Unlike Hirohito's servants, Kluckhohn never bowed to the emperor from the waist. Instead, he nodded to the emperor, and Hirohito nodded back. Then they shook hands. While Hirohito was talking, he looked directly into Kluckhohn's eyes, which impressed Kluckhohn as a sign of sincerity and openness.[8]

Asked whether he intended that his war rescript should be used as Tōjō Hideki had used it to launch the attack on Pearl Harbor, Hirohito answered, to the contrary, that he "expected Tojo to declare war in the usual, formal manner, if necessary." When asked whether he felt or hoped that the Japanese people themselves could make necessary changes to bring a peaceful and cooperative Japan, Hirohito assured Kluckhohn that "his people would prove themselves capable of making the necessary changes to bring Japan into the concert of nations again and eliminate the possibility of future wars."[9]

A shorter article in the same paper contained remarks made by Kido Kōichi, one of Hirohito's closest advisors during the war. It addressed the emperor's reaction to the so-called Hull Note, a 10-point proposal issued by the U.S. State Department on November 26, 1941, which demanded complete evacuation of China and Indochina as well as the abandonment of the puppet regime in Manchuria. According to Kido, the emperor ignored the proposal on the advice of government leaders. Kido also stated his belief that Tōjō delivered Franklin Roosevelt's personal appeal for peace, but that Hirohito was advised to ignore it by Tōjō. Moreover, Kido's article emphasized that the emperor "knew nothing in advance about the Pearl Harbor attack, learning about it later from the palace radio."[10]

Kluckhohn's article disturbed officials of Japan's Home Ministry, the existing Japanese civil administration during the occupation. The ministry promptly seized all available copies of Japanese newspapers that mentioned the article and prohibited the distribution of any copies that had evaded seizure.[11] Within a few hours, SCAP ordered the Japanese government to "render inoperative procedures for enforcement of peacetime and wartime restrictions of freedom of press and communication." According to MacArthur, censorship was permitted only when undertaken by SCAP.[12]

As the American authorities in Japan probably wished, Tōjō, not Hirohito, was depicted in the American media as the real dictator responsible for the Pearl Harbor attack and the Pacific War. Throughout the occupation, SCAP never confronted Hirohito, seeing his cooperation as essential to the efficient introduction of reforms. By contrast, one of SCAP's first official acts upon its arrival in Japan in September 11, 1945, was to issue an arrest warrant for Tōjō and 38 other suspected war criminals. Moreover, the Tokyo Trial helped to promote the simplified view of Tōjō as a dictator, an image popularized in the American mass media.

DEMONIZING TŌJŌ, HUMANIZING "THE JAPANESE," AND OVERLOOKING THE NANJING MASSACRE

Compared with the coverage in the Japanese press, articles regarding the Tokyo Trial in American newspapers and periodicals were shorter and less frequent. They featured few photographs of the defendants except Tōjō. In the eyes of correspondents like Lindesay Parrott of the *New York Times*, Tōjō represented "Japan's first group of top-flight war criminal suspects," while the other 27 defendants tried in Tokyo were scarcely identified by name.[13] The *Christian Science Monitor* even failed to print an accurate head count in its May 2, 1946, edition, reporting that Tōjō and "25 others accused as co-conspirators" would stand trial.[14] On May 3, 1946, when the *New York Times* covered in detail the opening of the trial, it referred to Tōjō more frequently than to the other 27 defendants combined.[15] On May 6, 1946, the *Times* and *The Chicago Daily Tribune* included an article about 27 accused who were pleading not guilty (before he could enter a plea, Ōkawa Shūmei had been removed from the courtroom on grounds of mental instability).[16] Although both newspaper articles described Tōjō's demeanor in the court and his denial of the charges, the other 26 suspects who pleaded not guilty remained nameless.[17]

The focus remained on Tōjō until the end of the trial when the 25 remaining defendants received their sentences (Matsuoka Yōsuke and Nagano Osami died during the trial, and charges against Ōkawa were dropped). Typical was the *Times'* discussion of the sentencing on November 12 and 13, 1946. It devoted a portion of a page to the trial and supplemented its report with a photograph measuring about 4 by 6 1/2 inches of Tōjō wearing a headset and listening as his sentence was read.[18] The others, including the six other war criminals who received the death penalty, were not given detailed treatment.[19] Although the *Washington Post* article on November 13, 1948, did include photographs of the seven condemned war criminals, the focus of the article was on Tōjō.[20]

The Nanjing Massacre was likewise given short shrift during the Tokyo Trial. In July 1946, when Robert Wilson, a surgeon who had remained at the University of the Nanjing Hospital during the assault on the city, testified before the court regarding atrocities in Nanjing, the same testimony that produced a strong reaction in the Japanese press made little impression in American newspaper accounts. The *New York Times*, *Newsweek*, and *Time* magazine made no mention of Wilson's testimony. The *Chicago Daily Tribune* and the *Washington Post* carried only brief articles about the massacre. The former was a 130-word article, headlined "200,000 Killed in Nanking Rape, Professor Says," which reported on the testimony given by Wilson and Xu Chuanyin, a deputy head of the Red Cross Society in Nanjing.[21] The latter, headlined "Rape of Nanking Witness Recalls 40,000 Bodies," was about 150 words in length and briefly reported Xu's eyewitness account.[22] Matsui Iwane, the defendant who had commanded the Japanese troops during the battle of Nanjing, was not mentioned in either article and rarely received any notice from the American media.

In contrast to their practice during the war years, American media during the occupation no longer energetically depicted the entire Japanese people as demonic. As early as August 26, 1945, the *New York Times Magazine* included two full pages of photographs under the title "These Are the Japanese." Each of the 20 photographs showed a different representative of Japanese society: politician, schoolgirl, schoolboy, old woman, craftsman, young mother, peasant, girl worker, soldier, dancer, artist, peasant woman, skilled worker, peasant girl, general, homemaker, businessman, working woman, shopkeeper, and schoolteacher.[23] At the same time that the Japanese public were observing Americans in Japan and discovering that all Americans were not the same, United States servicemen, correspondents, and their family members were learning through personal experience about Japanese diversity. Day by day, they acquired the ability to see the Japanese as a mosaic of different individuals, from Class A war criminals, to conservative government officials, to ordinary war-weary people on the street. As the occupation went on, newspaper articles embraced an ever broader range of topics and viewpoints in regard to Japan.

HIROSHIMA IN AMERICAN MEDIA

As the occupation went on, the image of Hiroshima, especially as set forth by John Hersey's article in the *New Yorker*, also helped Americans to develop a more sensitive understanding of the people in Japan. According to a Gallup Poll, an overwhelming number of respondents (85 percent) interviewed between August 10 and 15, 1945, approved of using the atomic bomb on Japanese cities. As time went by, this approval rating remained virtually constant, but it became qualified by ambivalence. Although most Americans continued to see the use of the bomb as a legitimate means to end the war, they could not ignore the horrors the bombs had inflicted.[24] As they became aware of the suffering of the victims of nuclear warfare in Japan, the American public was also compelled to imagine what it might be like to be on the receiving end of nuclear force.

On August 23, 1945, the *New York Times* published a report of the Japanese government's estimate of casualties of the nuclear attack on Hiroshima and Nagasaki. The government estimated that 70,000 persons (60,000 in Hiroshima and 10,000 in Nagasaki) had been killed outright, 120,000 persons had been wounded (100,000 in Hiroshima and 20,000 in Nagasaki), and 290,000 had been made homeless (200,000 in Hiroshima and 90,000 in Nagasaki).[25] Two days later, the newspaper also included a Japanese radio report that, during the first two weeks following the explosion over Hiroshima, 30,000 had been killed by radiation or ultraviolet rays. To many Americans, such numbers were incredible and untrustworthy. According to the same article, American experts on Japanese propaganda emphasized that "the Japanese may be attempting to capitalize on the horror of atomic bombing in an effort to win sympathy from their conquerors and to play on possibly divided opinion among the

Allies." In addition, Robert Oppenheimer, director of the atomic bomb research project, denounced as impossible the kind of aftereffects that Japanese radio insisted had occurred.[26]

Nevertheless, more detailed studies and reports by American officials and correspondents in Japan began to appear in 1946. In early February, SCAP announced that 78,150 persons had been killed in Hiroshima alone, 13,983 persons were still missing, 9,428 persons had been seriously injured, and 27,997 persons had been slightly injured.[27] In its February 11, 1946, issue, *Time* magazine included the first detailed account by a Hiroshima survivor. Father John A. Siemes, professor of modern philosophy at Tokyo's Catholic University, described his observations of the city and rescue work following the blast.[28]

Yet these accounts did not affect the American public as much as John Hersey's book-length report, which originally appeared in the *New Yorker* on August 31, 1946. Hersey told in detail the stories of Ms. Sasaki Toshiko, Dr. Sasaki Terufumi, Dr. Fujii Masakazu, Ms. Nakamura Hatsuyo, Father Wilhelm Kleinsorge, and Reverend Tanimoto Kiyoshi, all of whom survived the Hiroshima bombing.[29] A *New York Times* editorial praised Hersey's work highly:

> What happened to about 100,000 is clear. They died. What happened to the lucky six is an example of what human beings can endure and not die. . . . We have had pictures of what an atom bomb, or many atom bombs, could do to an American city. Naturally they have appalled us. We might also ask ourselves if we could endure the burden of conscience if it ever again seemed necessary to us to drop atomic bombs, and we did drop atomic bombs, on a foreign city.
>
> We believe millions of Americans have already asked themselves this question. We believe their answer has been reflected in the Lilienthal report and the Baruch proposals for the control of atomic energy. We wish our friends in Russia and elsewhere could know how strong the dominant American emotion in this matter is; we hope those Americans who do not yet feel it will read Mr. Hersey. For the death and destruction not merely of people but of the human conscience is clearly involved.[30]

Other institutions and individuals also held Hersey's work in high regard. The U.S. Army wanted copies of the *New Yorker* issue for its education service; the Belgian Chamber of Commerce requested 500 copies; and Albert Einstein asked for 1,000 copies. Newspapers from Boston to California asked the *New Yorker* for permission to reprint "Hiroshima." All of these requests were granted on condition that it be reprinted in full and that all profits go to the Red Cross. The American Broadcasting Company canceled its regular 8:30 to 9 o'clock programs on four successive evenings to read the text aloud to more than 1 million radio listeners.[31] When republished as a book, Hersey's work appeared on the *New York Times* best-seller list for five weeks.[32]

Although most Americans approved of the use of the atom bomb on Hiroshima and were not necessarily sympathetic to the people who died there, Hersey enlightened his readers and listeners about what these six survivors saw, what they did, and what they felt.[33] In this way, they were able to experience the Hiroshima bombing from the viewpoints of ordinary people in the city, each of whom was very different from the stereotypical idea of "the Japanese" that the American public had been accustomed to during the wartime years. According to anthropologist Sheila Johnson, author of *The Japanese through American Eyes*, Hersey's report on Hiroshima was the first postwar account that restored a sense of the Japanese people as human beings.[34] The change in the image of the Japanese people was noticeable in the polls as well. By May 1946, those who stated that the Japanese people "will always want war" declined to 37 percent (from 56 percent in July 1945), while those who considered the Japanese people "potential good citizens" increased to 21 percent (from 13 percent in July 1945).[35]

CONCLUSION

As the U.S.-Soviet rivalry intensified, SCAP was no longer vigorous in its pursuit of Japan's wartime criminals for fear that such inquiries might embarrass Japanese political and economic leaders in power under the U.S. occupation. As early as May 1946, Mark Gayn, Japanese correspondent for the *Chicago Sun*, observed that reform-minded American planners who had directed purges of Japanese wartime leaders and planned the democratization of Japan were being removed from their positions one by one.[36] In addition, the American press was not as concerned with Japan's atrocities as it had been during the war. Although Tōjō Hideki, who was regarded as responsible for the Pearl Harbor attack and the Pacific War, often appeared in articles regarding the Tokyo Trial, his colleagues were not known among the general public in the United States. With regard to ordinary Japanese, there was no further need for the American media to stress their racial particularity. Hiroshima gave the American public an opportunity to restore human faces to the Japanese people. Moreover, a series of crises in international relations after World War II—the Soviet invasion of Iran (1946), the establishment of East and West Germany (1949), the Korean War (1950–53), the Chinese Communist attacks on Quemoy and Matsu (1955, 1958), the Cuban missile crisis (1962), and the Vietnam War (1965–73)—all contributed to turning American attention away from the memory of Japan's wartime atrocities against peoples in Asia, atrocities that included the Nanjing Massacre. Nevertheless, these same international crises, particularly the Vietnam War, functioned in Japan as a reminder of Japanese wartime atrocities.

III

BRINGING THE NANJING MASSACRE INTO PRINT (1971–89)

7

Japan: From "Victim Consciousness" to "Victimizer Consciousness"

International media coverage of the Vietnam War and domestic attempts by the Japanese government to influence the official public understanding and teaching of the Nanjing Massacre gave rise to two highly significant turning points in the literature of Nanjing atrocities: Honda Katsuichi's serialized reports in *Asahi shinbun* in 1971 and the textbook controversy of 1982. Dominated by a handful of social critics, journalists, and historians, the debate of the 1970s focused almost exclusively on the "killing contest" originally reported in 1937. Particularly after the 1982 textbook controversy, new voices emerged, as veterans, politicians, schoolteachers, lawyers, and government officials published their own views of the Nanjing Massacre. These included scholarly work which detailed and analyzed the atrocities in Nanjing, accounts responding to and refuting the revisionists, Japanese translations of Chinese works on the Nanjing Massacre, pedagogical essays on how to teach accounts of wartime atrocities to Japanese pupils, and confessions and memoirs written by veterans who had participated in the atrocities in Nanjing. At the same time, accounts denying what had happened in Nanjing increased dramatically, both in number and in vigor.[1]

During the 1970s and 1980s, the dispute over Nanjing became publicized in mass media, and the participants of the debate were now all aware of their allies and enemies. Whether they were eager to admit or deny the atrocities in Nanjing, these participants confronted one another openly and sought to thoroughly discredit the arguments with which they disagreed. The urgency with which each side pressed its claims incited more opposition. For decades, some Japanese had maintained the importance of acknowledging Japan's victimization of other Asian peoples, even to the extent of elevating these experiences over Japan's own suffering. The impassioned denials of Japan's war crimes only raised awareness of Japan's atrocities to a higher level. Conversely, this growing sense of "victimizer consciousness" prompted even fiercer denials.

REMINDING SOCIETY OF PAST ATROCITIES

First appearing in August 1971, Honda's "Travels in China" (Chūgoku no tabi) stirred controversy that lasted well beyond *Asahi shinbun*'s final installment in December. After traveling in China for nearly two months and interviewing more than 100 Chinese survivors of the war, Honda reported Japan's atrocities in China, supplementing his work with photographs. Part I detailed the Pingdingshan Incident of August 16, 1932, in which Japanese troops, responding in anger to the resistance of Chinese guerrilla forces, destroyed an entire village and killed as many as 3,000 residents.[2] Part II described *manninkō*, a dumping ground where thousands (some said tens of thousands) of Chinese forced laborers lay buried.[3] In Part III, Honda recounted stories of the Nanjing Massacre.[4] In Part IV, he examined the Three-Alls Operation (burn all, kill all, loot all), which the Japanese army conducted from the early 1940s as a means of coping with Communist guerrilla forces.[5]

Honda reported what the Chinese survivors had seen, heard, and remembered. Jiang Genfu, a survivor of the Nanjing Massacre, tearfully recounted how he had watched Japanese soldiers kill his parents, one of his sisters, and a baby. Even after Jiang (9 years old at the time) and his surviving sister (11 years old) and two brothers (ages 7 and 5) escaped from Japanese invaders, their fates were dire. Chinese collaborators sold his sister and 5-year-old brother into slave labor. Jiang and his 7-year-old brother survived by begging until they were adopted by a man who became their stepfather. When Jiang was 13, the Japanese authorities drafted him and his stepfather into forced labor. Not until after the civil war was Jiang finally reunited with his brother and sister.[6]

Jiang also told Honda of killing contests between two Japanese soldiers, Second Lieutenants Mukai Toshiaki and Noda Tsuyoshi, although Honda's article identified them only as "A" and "B." According to Jiang, "A" and "B" competed to see who would be the first to kill 100 Chinese as the army conquered the 10 kilometers between Jurong and Tangshan. When neither lieutenant reached the goal ("A" killed 89, and "B" killed 78), the commander, who offered a prize, ordered them to start over. This time, the field of contest lay in the 15 kilometers between Tangshan and Zijin Mountain. "A" killed 106, and "B" killed 105, but the commander was not sure who had been first to reach 100, so a third contest was set for the first to kill 150, between Zijin Mountain and the Nanjing castle, 8 kilometers apart.[7]

Compared with previous accounts of Nanjing, Honda's serialized articles in the *Asahi*, whose evening edition was delivered to approximately 4 million subscribers, reached a much larger audience.[8] In his summary of readers' reactions he noted that 80 percent of the letters expressed approval. Honda was pleasantly surprised to receive more favorable letters from veterans and bereaved families than he had expected.[9] One such letter, published on the editorial page of the *Asahi*, came from Uno Shintarō, a veteran. Uno wrote that he was deeply moved by the articles and urged *Asahi*'s readers to face Japan's war responsibility in order to normalize relations with China.[10] Shirasawa Yuriko, a high school student, wrote that the articles taught the reality of war that textbooks never touched, and Tsubaki Yoshiko, a 48-year-old homemaker, urged the public to reconsider Japan's wartime past from the viewpoint of a perpetrator.[11]

The remaining 20 percent, however, were incredulous or accusatory. Two of the most common criticisms insisted that there was nothing to gain from reopening the wounds of the past and that Japanese experience was not unique since war is brutal by nature. Responding to such refutations, Honda emphasized that the Japanese media had published few in-depth treatments of wartime Japanese atrocities and that the Japanese public must learn what Japan did to China and its people during the war. He also urged readers not to excuse Japan's wartime atrocities in the name of war, but to learn what the Japanese military did in China and how it was now perceived there. He stressed that this acknowledgment would be the first step toward mutual understanding between the two nations.[12]

Honda's articles appeared just as public attention was focused on China's changing perception in international relations. In July 1971, U.S. president Richard Nixon's announcement that he would visit China shocked many Japanese, particularly the pro-American, pro-Taiwan politicians who had been reluctant to normalize relations with Communist China.[13] In addition, many Japanese became anxious at the prospect of the PRC's joining the United Nations. In 1971, *Asahi shinbun* received 1,605 letters from readers on issues related to China, making it the second most popular topic of reader commentary that year.[14]

Honda wrote the article not in response to these changes in Sino-Japanese relations, but because of his experiences in reporting the Vietnam War.[15] As a war correspondent in 1967, Honda had reported the experiences of ordinary Vietnamese, including a family with seven children with whom he stayed in Saigon.[16] He was present when American troops destroyed a village suspected of being a base of Communist guerrilla forces, and he afterward wrote about the sorrows of the people whose properties were burned and destroyed. At one point he infiltrated a village of guerrillas and described their daily lives. Honda himself experienced machine-gun and rocket attacks during his stay. In his reports, he was severely critical not only of American involvement in Vietnam, but also of Japan's support of the war, revealing how Japanese-made products such as tank landing ships had contributed to the killing in Vietnam.[17]

Honda's sympathy for the powerless, ordinary Vietnamese led him to wonder what had happened to the ordinary people in China during Japan's invasion decades before. He believed that, although tales of Japanese victims after the bombing of Hiroshima and Nagasaki had been widely publicized, few had told the other side of the story. As a journalist, he felt obliged to enlighten his audience from the viewpoint of the Chinese people who had experienced Japan's wartime atrocities.[18]

REPERCUSSIONS OF "TRAVELS IN CHINA"

Not surprisingly, Honda's accounts disturbed some Japanese and prompted them to challenge his work. Among them was Yamamoto Shichihei, known as a translator of best-selling novels by Isaiah Ben-Dasan. Unknown to his readers, Yamamoto had invented the fictitious "Ben-Dasan," using him as a persona through whom he could publish his own critiques of Japanese society from a Jewish point of view.[19] In the January issue of *Shokun!*, a conservative monthly magazine, Yamamoto "translated" Ben-Dasan's "'Apology' from *Asahi shinbun*" (Asahi shinbun no 'gomen nasai'). In the article, Yamamoto pointed out what he saw as a disingenuous motive behind Honda's prose. A mere verbal apology, Yamamoto suggested, does more to soothe the psyche of the guilty party than to improve the situation of the victim. Indeed, such apologies are self-serving because they appear to absolve the apologizer from assuming more concrete responsibility, whether in the form of compensating the victim or sincerely resolving to reform one's conduct. It was wrong, Yamamoto implied, to suppose that a few self-critical newspaper pieces would suffice to put to rest the wrongs of the past. On the contrary, Honda's work would have the opposite effect. It would be received not as an apology, but as an insult, resulting in further distrust and anger between the two nations.[20]

In the February issue of *Shokun!*, Honda responded to Yamamoto. Strongly suspecting that Ben-Dasan was the alter ego of Yamamoto, Honda cynically asked if Yamamoto was willing to share the original manuscript of Ben-Dasan's article, which had supposedly been written in English. Refuting Yamamoto's indictment of his motives, Honda referred to his speech to Chinese survivors of the Nanjing Massacre whom he interviewed:

> During the massacre I was still a little boy. As you said, I was not directly responsible for this crime as a member of "the general public" because I was probably too young. In essence, I believe that ordinary Japanese people were victims like ordinary Chinese people. The crime was committed by Japanese. Nonetheless, I do not think my verbal apology would mean much to you. What is important is the present rather than the past. Even more than twenty years after the defeat, the Japanese public was not informed of what Japan did in China during the war. I am afraid that Japan is walking the same path as it did before the war. This time, though, if we do nothing and become bystanders, we would be directly responsible [for the act of the state]. Apologizing for Japan's wartime militarism is meaningless. The real apology would lie in preventing Japan from reviving its wartime militarism. I believe that my report of Japan's wartime militarism and its consequences can contribute to preventing the nation from reverting to militarism in the future. I greatly appreciate your help.[21]

In addition, Honda challenged Yamamoto's understanding of Hirohito and *tennōsei* (the emperor system). To Honda, Hirohito was the ultimate untried war criminal, and overthrowing the emperor system was indispensable in extirpating the roots of Japan's militarism. Honda was puzzled as to why "Ben-Dasan" had never written about Hirohito and his responsibility for the Asia-Pacific War. He wondered what justice Jews would have demanded for Hirohito if China had been a Jewish nation, hypothesizing that if the emperor had been tried by the same law applied to Adolf Eichmann, the Nazi administrator of the concentration camps, he would have received the death sentence.[22]

In the March issue of *Shokun!*, Yamamoto again "translated" an English response from "Ben-Dasan," who was supposedly living abroad. Yamamoto avoided answering issues that Honda had raised in the previous issue and played contemptuously with Honda's words while mounting an ad hominem counterattack. He did not discuss his opinion of Hirohito's responsibility for the war or whether *tennōsei* was the foundation of Japan's militarism. Instead he accused Honda of being a Nazi for arrogantly deciding what ideologies should be eliminated and what preserved. Yamamoto taunted Honda to send a letter to Hirohito accusing him directly rather than through the media.[23]

Yamamoto also claimed that Jiang's story of the killing contests was nothing but hearsay. Dismissing the story as rumor, he accused Honda of intentionally using it to accomplish his political goals. Yamamoto understood Jiang to be claiming that the Japanese soldiers had been able to advance 10 kilometers in 150 minutes, a pace that he derided as impossible. (In fact, the advance took days because of fierce Chinese resistance.) Using his condensed time line, Yamamoto concluded that "A" must have killed one Chinese person every 1 minute and 36 seconds, a feat he considered physically impossible. Yamamoto also denounced Honda for concealing the identity of the two second lieutenants and demanded their names.[24]

In the April issue of *Shokun!*, Honda replied again. In order to refute Yamamoto's challenge, Honda cited articles on the killing contest printed in *Tōkyō nichi nichi shinbun* in 1937 and explained the editorial policy of the *Asahi*, which compelled him to protect the identities of the two lieutenants. Moreover, having no doubt that "Ben-Dasan" was Yamamoto, Honda made his reply even blunter. If "Ben-Dasan" were real, then he was a disgrace (*tsurayogoshi*) to Jews because his views lacked the compassion of those held by Jewish people whom Honda knew and respected. Honda stressed that he had learned important things from people who had a long history of persecution, including Vietnamese, African Americans, Koreans, and Jews. In the article, Honda underscored two primary reasons why he decided to confront "Ben-Dasan." First, Yamamoto's *The Japanese and The Jews* (Nihonjin to Yudayajin) had sold more than 1.2 million copies, a publishing record at the time, and Honda was therefore concerned about the extent of "Ben-Dasan's" influence. Second, Honda wanted to unmask the core of Yamamoto's reactionary thesis, which supported the emperor system and legitimized Japan's wartime aggression.[25]

The April issue included not only Honda's article, but two hostile responses as well. One was "Postscript to Mr. Honda Katsuichi" (Honda Katsuichi sama e no tsuishin) written by "Ben-Dasan," in which he reiterated that Honda's logic was the same as the Nazis'.[26] The other was "The Illusion of the 'Nanjing Massacre'" ("Nankin daigyakusatsu" no maboroshi), written by Suzuki Akira, a critic who identified himself as a nonfiction writer. Although the title suggests a wholesale refutation of the massacre, Suzuki's argument merely denied the accuracy of Jiang's recollections of the Nanjing Massacre, especially his testimony as to the killing contests. Like Yamamoto, Suzuki had not been particularly interested in the Nanjing Massacre until he read Honda's "Travels in China." After he read about the killing contests, Suzuki did some research on the Nanjing Massacre, which led him to the original source of Jiang's story.[27]

Referring to the articles on the killing contest in *Tōkyō nichi nichi shinbun* published at the time, Suzuki pointed out differences between Jiang's and the original versions: Although Jiang stated that the contest was repeated three times, the earlier articles had described only one incident, in which the goal was initially 100 but later extended to 50 more. According to Jiang, it was not clear whether the two second lieutenants conducted the contests during or outside combat, whereas the earlier articles made clear that they were competing during the battle; finally, Jiang told Honda that a superior ordered the two soldiers to compete, but no such superior was mentioned in the articles.[28]

Suzuki contended that Japan's atrocities in Nanjing had been exaggerated or distorted among the people in Nanjing in the intervening 34 years. Although Suzuki claimed no intention of arguing that the Japanese military did not commit atrocities in Nanjing, he was skeptical that 430,000 Chinese were killed, the figure cited by Honda in a footnote as the estimate by the Nationalist government at the end of the war.[29] Suzuki admitted that some atrocities occurred in Nanjing, but he argued that what was now being remembered as the Nanjing Massacre—that is, the great historic atrocity in which the Japanese military murdered 430,000 Chinese—was the product of rumors and exaggerations handed down by the Chinese people.[30] To Suzuki, Jiang's version of the killing contests, as reported in Honda's article, was an example of such exaggeration.

Suzuki continued to write articles challenging Honda. Among them was "Why Was Second Lieutenant Mukai Executed?" (Mukai shōi wa naze korosaretaka). Unlike Honda, who wrote his articles from the viewpoint of survivors of the Japanese atrocities, Suzuki presented Mukai's point of view, based on his interviews with Mukai's widow, daughter, comrades, and the *Tōkyō nichi nichi shinbun* reporter who had written the articles on the killing contest in the 1930s. Both Honda and Suzuki claimed to be writing in the name of international understanding, though they proposed two very different paths. While Honda sought mutual understanding by urging readers to realize what the Japanese military did in China and how it was viewed by Chinese, Suzuki insisted that readers who desired an accurate understanding of events must comprehend the viewpoint of the two second lieutenants and their bereaved families.[31]

Yamamoto's work in *Shokun!* also continued its attempt to discredit Honda's report on the killing contest.[32] In addition, Bungei shunjū, the publisher of the journal, published both Yamamoto's and Suzuki's work in book form.[33] Others, such as Ishihara Shintarō, the Liberal Democratic Party politician, and Tanaka Masaaki, the same veteran who had written *On Japan's Innocence: The Truth on Trial* 20 years earlier, also expressed their displeasure with Honda's articles. In one round-table discussion, Ishihara insisted that China was trying to stir up Japan's war guilt and that the *Asahi* had taken up the Nanjing Massacre to serve its own perverse political agenda.[34] Similarly, in his *Thesis of Japan's Innocence* (Nihon muzairon), published in July 1972, Tanaka denounced the mass media and so-called progressive intellectuals for exaggerating the atrocities in Nanjing.[35]

While some challenged Honda, others enthusiastically supported him. The publisher of the *Asahi* released Honda's serial articles as a book in March 1972.[36] That same year, another publisher printed a similar book by Honda titled *The Japanese Army in China* (Chūgoku no Nihongun), which included an extensive array of photographs documenting scenes of Japanese atrocities.[37] Also in 1972, Hora Tomio, a historian, published *The Nanjing Incident* (Nankin jiken), a revised edition of his 1967 *Kindai senshi no nazo* (Riddles of Modern War History).

Honda's widely read "Travels in China" set off a chain reaction, spreading knowledge of the Nanjing Massacre among the Japanese public. It stirred those who objected to Honda's view to refute it, and these responses in turn inspired Honda and his supporters to meet the challenge. Each outraged by the other, the two camps continued to exchange fire, and every new round of controversy stimulated greater public interest in the massacre. The editors of *Shokun!* expressed their gratitude for the increase of letters from the readers prompted by the disputes between Yamamoto and Honda.[38] In the journal's four years of publication, no topic had ever elicited such a strong response from readers.[39]

By sponsoring Yamamoto's and Suzuki's challenges, the editors of *Shokun!* and their publisher, Bungei shunjū, were probably most concerned with boosting the circulation of the journal. But they contributed nonetheless to enriching the study of the Nanjing atrocities. In 1973, Hora Tomio edited collections of documents, including translations of lengthy testimonies of massacre survivors before the Tokyo Tribunal.[40] In 1975, Hora published *The Nanjing Massacre: Criticism of the Making of an Illusion* (Nankin daigyakusatsu: "maboroshi" ka kōsaku hihan), in which he made use of his rich knowledge of historical documents to refute Yamamoto and Suzuki. In the introduction, he stressed that he could not ignore "those who relied on unscientific intuition to turn the gears of history counterclockwise." He also felt responsible both for rebutting those who claimed that the Nanjing Massacre was an illusion and for clarifying the historical facts of the event.[41]

SOWING THE SEEDS OF "VICTIMIZER CONSCIOUSNESS"

The year 1971 proved to be a turning point in the historiography of what became known as "victimizer consciousness" (*kagaisha ishiki*)—a term that stands for the acknowledgment that Japan was also an aggressor and bore responsibility for the Asia-Pacific War. Honda's article was not alone in reminding the nation of its wartime conduct. Others, like the members of the Group of Returnees from China, held similar positions. The gradual rise of "victimizer consciousness" was the consequence of the international and domestic climate of the time, fueled by growing awareness of the Vietnam War, the PRC's entry into the United Nations, and the recovery and growth of the Japanese economy.

In the 1970s, many began to share Honda's views. They realized with regret that Japan had inflicted tremendous sufferings on other Asian countries and peoples. In 1971, Maruki Toshi and Maruki Iri, acclaimed painters of the murals of the horrors of the atomic bombings, completed *Crows* (Karasu), the fourteenth painting in their series *Hiroshima Panels*. It depicted Korean residents of Hiroshima who, because of their ethnic origin, received inferior medical treatment after the blast. In 1975, the Marukis completed their painting titled *The Rape of Nanking* (Nankin daigyakusatsu no zu), in which they underscored the horrors inflicted on the people of Nanjing.[42] Only occasionally have these paintings been exhibited outside their permanent home at the Maruki Gallery for Hiroshima Panels in Saitama. Ever since its opening in 1967, the Maruki Gallery has played an important role in enlightening visitors about the cruelty of the war and the significance of peace.[43]

During the 1970s, schoolteachers began presenting Japan's wartime history with an emphasis on the devastations in Asia. The December 1973 issue of *Rekishi chiri kyōiku*, a monthly education magazine, published an article by Oda Baku, a high school teacher and a member of the Association for History Educators (Rekishi kyōikusha kyōgikai) founded in 1949. Oda urged his fellow educators to understand that Japan had been a perpetrator during the Fifteen-Year War. He argued that if teachers emphasized the devastation inflicted on Japan and its people when they taught about the war, students would learn to hate war, but they would do so only as an unthinking reflex. They would avoid asking more challenging questions about who was responsible for the aggression and why Japan had been unable to avoid the war.[44] In winter 1973, Yoneda Shinji, a high school teacher who also belonged to the association, had his students read Honda's *Travels in China* and write a paper in response, assignments that he hoped would give his students a more complicated view of Japan's role than that presented in history textbooks. He also required his students to interview a person who had lived through the period of the Japan-China War (1937–45).[45]

Such changes in public consciousness began to appear in the school textbooks of the time. Whereas history textbooks still generally did not detail

Japan's wartime atrocities, descriptions of the Nanjing Massacre reemerged in at least four junior high school and four high school Japanese history textbooks in the 1970s, although the matter was usually addressed in footnotes rather than in the main text. A footnote to the 1975 edition of Nihon shoseki's and Kyōiku shuppan's junior-high-school history textbooks defined the Nanjing atrocities as an event in which the Japanese military killed approximately 42,000 civilians, including women and children. In its 1978 edition, Tōkyō shoseki's junior high school history textbook stated in a footnote that, after the seizure of the city, the Japanese Army killed a vast number of (*obitadashii*) Chinese people, including POWs, stragglers, women, and children. The author of Jikkyō shuppan's high school Japanese history book, published in 1977, defined the atrocities in the footnote as the incident in which the military massacred (*gyakusatsu*) a vast number of (*obitadashii*) people in Nanjing. Although the Ministry of Education prohibited authors of textbooks from citing death tolls in the range of 200,000 or 300,000, they were able to keep references to the massacre by replacing numbers with vague words such as "a vast number of" (*obitadashii*).[46] These descriptions of the massacre may seem modest, but compared to the silence of the previous two decades, these references signaled an important reversal.

As more people began to see wartime Japan not as a victim, but a victimizer, others responded by defending Japan's war efforts and its alleged contribution to freeing Asia from Western domination. The Nanjing Massacre was one of the points at issue in this debate. While some, like Honda, informed the public of the Nanjing Massacre and sufferings of the Chinese people, others, like Yamamoto, promoted different versions. But these controversies of the 1970s were limited compared to the textbook controversy in 1982, which erupted into a fierce international debate.

JAPAN'S WARTIME HISTORY INTERNATIONALIZED

In late June 1982, national newspapers reported that the recently approved history textbooks were choosing to take less notice of the negative aspects of Japan's war record than their previous editions. Although not entirely correct, these reports prompted protests from other Asian nations, while provoking domestic disputes over their accuracy. *Asahi shinbun* criticized the Ministry of Education for its deemphasis of Japan's wartime aggression and its attempt to justify the actions of wartime and prewar Japan.[47] The *Asahi* included a "before-and-after" table that showed the modifications in the new history textbooks. According to the article, censors altered descriptions of such topics as the March First Independence Movement in Korea in 1919, Japan's aggression (*shinryaku*) in northern China, the so-called Three Alls, and the emperor-centered Meiji Constitution.[48]

On July 26, 1982, the PRC government officially protested the Japanese government's decision to revise the textbooks. Basing his remarks on Japanese press reports, a Chinese official denounced the Ministry of Education's effort to distort the historical facts of Japan's wartime aggression. He gave four examples: (1) the ministry changed Japan's "invasion (*shinryaku*) of northern China" to "advance (*shinshutsu*) into northern China"; (2) it altered "full-scale aggression (*shinryaku*) against China" to "full-scale advance (*shinshutsu*) on China"; (3) the 9.18 Incident of 1931 (i.e., Japan's seizure of Manchuria) was no longer described as an invasion, but as a mere incident in which "the Japanese military bombed the South Manchurian Railway"; (4) the Nanjing Massacre was justified as a reaction to the fierce resistance of the Chinese military.[49]

In a similar vein, on July 31, the Taiwanese government sent a memorandum to the de facto Japanese embassy to Taiwan, urging the Japanese government to deal with the issue appropriately.[50] On August 3, the South Korean government followed suit, lodging an official protest. In response, Korean communities in the United States boycotted Japanese products.[51] That same month, Hong Kong's labor unions and their allies hand-delivered a letter of protest to the envoy at the Japanese Consulate.[52] And in Geneva, the British representative to the United Nation's subcommittee on human rights addressed the Japanese delegate, criticizing the Japanese government for its textbook policies.[53]

These international criticisms and denunciations, particularly the government protests, upset the administration of Prime Minister Suzuki Zenkō. On July 28, the Japanese ambassador to the PRC in Beijing visited the Chinese foreign ministry and explained the government policies regarding textbook authorization. The ambassador assured him that the government's understanding of the war had not changed and that the government felt its responsibility for having caused significant damage to the people of China.[54] The Ministry of Education completed its research and issued a report on the textbook authorization. It found that, out of the 20 different Japanese and world history textbooks examined that year, 4 passages in three Japanese history textbooks and 10 passages in six world history textbooks used "invasion" (*shinryaku*) with regard to the Japan-China War. Pursuant to the inspector's "recommendation," 1 passage in one Japanese history textbook and 3 passages in two world history textbooks had been amended, either eliminating or replacing the word with "advance" (*shinshutsu*). The others continued to use the word "*shinryaku*." The ministry announced that it would deliver its findings to its Chinese counterpart.[55]

On July 29, Ogawa Heiji, the minister of education, appeared before the Committee on Education of the Upper House of the Japanese Parliament to explain the reason for the changes. Ogawa argued that the goal of history education was to help students improve their objective analytical skills based on historical facts. Because the term "invasion" (*shinryaku*) had previously been used only to describe Japan's wartime expansion, whereas the term "advance" (*shinshutsu*) had been used to illustrate the wartime and postwar maneuvers of Western powers, the ministry recommended that authors apply the same standard to both sides and use "advance" in both cases. Ogawa stressed that the Japanese government never forced any publishers to eliminate the term "invasion" and that many books were still using it. He argued that anyone who read the texts would understand that the war was not justifiable. Speaking before the same committee, Suzuki Isao, a bureau chief of elementary and junior high school education, implied that the press reports had been erroneous to begin with; he emphasized that the ministry had not found any case of "Japan's aggression (*shinryaku*) against northern China" being altered to "Japan's advance (*shinshutsu*) into northern China" in high school history textbooks during this cycle.[56]

On August 25, expecting an official announcement from the Japanese government, *Asahi shinbun* published its own findings on whether "invasion" had been replaced with "advance." It confirmed that, in 1982, there was no case in which "Japan's aggression against northern China" had been replaced with "Japan's advance into northern China" in high school history textbooks. On this point, the *Asahi* concluded that the Chinese government had been mistaken. It also confirmed that two high school Japanese history textbooks and four high school world history textbooks continued to use the term "invasion" with regard to the Japan-China War. But the article also pointed out that, in general, the ministry had been discouraging writers of textbooks from using the term "invasion" and requesting the use of "advance" since the mid-1950s. In the 1982 inspection, "Japan's invasion (*shinryaku*) of South East Asia" had been changed to "Japan's advance (*shinshutsu*) into South East Asia" in two high school world history textbooks published by Teikoku shoin. The article also revealed that, in the widely used junior high school history textbooks published by Chūkyō shuppan, the sentence "Japan regarded Manchuria as a lifeline and pursued aggression against China with military might" had been altered to read, "Japan tried to advance into the mainland with military might in order to protect its rights in Manchuria."[57]

The next day Miyazawa Kiichi, the chief cabinet secretary, announced the government's position on history textbooks, stressing in his remarks Japan's wish to maintain friendship with other Asian nations:

> Japan and its nationals have deeply reflected on Japan's past infliction of tremendous sufferings and damage on peoples in Asia, including China. Being very much aware of this historical fact, [they] have made efforts to pursue peace. . . . Today descriptions of textbooks in our country have been criticized by nations such as Korea and China. Our nation shall sincerely listen to these criticisms in order to maintain friendships with neighboring nations in Asia and shall take responsibility for rectifying [such descriptions]. . . . [A]s to future textbook authorization, [the government] with the approval of the Council of Inspecting Textbook Authorization (Kyōkayō tosho kentei chōsa shingikai) will promulgate a new standard of authorization. [It will also] take careful considerations to accomplish this. . . . Our nation shall continue to make every effort to facilitate mutual understandings and develop friendships with neighboring countries, sincerely hoping that [our nation] will contribute not only to peace in Asia, but also to world peace.[58]

This statement, as well as the international protests, angered those who believed that textbook issues were an internal matter and that patriotism should be emphasized in school education. They alleged that the government had given in to "foreign intervention" and that the entire incident had arisen from inaccurate news reports. For example, in the October issue of *Shokun!*, Watanabe Shōichi, professor of English at Sophia University, accused *Asahi shinbun* and other newspapers of intentionally fabricating reports that he believed had triggered the official protests from China and Korea. He denounced the Japanese mass media as dominated by sympathizers with China's Cultural Revolution and condemned them for trying to force the Japanese government into an embarrassingly abject apology.[59] Throughout the article, Watanabe repeatedly and decisively stated that there had been no case in which "invasion" was replaced with "advance."

Watanabe's assertion was based on the explanation that the Ministry of Education made in late July, but it was not entirely faithful to that statement. The ministry claimed that in no case had "invasion" been altered to "advance" in the context of *the Japan-China War* in *high school* Japanese and world history textbooks inspected *in 1982*.[60] This qualification perhaps suggested the government's awareness that the ministry had sought to suppress the use of *"shinryaku"* since the mid-1950s and had long used its powers of authorization to tone down textbook descriptions of Japan's wartime aggression. Nevertheless, Watanabe concluded that news reports on textbook authorization were misrepresentations, calculated to provoke foreign intervention into Japan's domestic affairs.

This facile viewpoint was shared by the conservative allies of Watanabe. *Sankei shinbun*, a national newspaper, and *Seiron*, a monthly magazine published by *Sankei*, took up the cry that news reports of the replacement of "invasion" with "advance" were completely erroneous.[61] According to the editors of *Sankei*, the ministry had suggested the use of "advance" instead of "invasion" more than 20 years before, and this year's inspection had done nothing to hasten a change. They found it irrational for China to accuse Japan of trying to revive militarism through its textbooks, since, in *Sankei*'s view, the books had not changed significantly from previous years.[62]

For Watanabe and his allies, the major concern was whether "invasion" was replaced with "advance." However, news reports of textbook authorization and the ensuing disputes raised difficult issues among progressive intellectuals. For Hidaka Rokurō, a professor of sociology at Kyōto Seika University, the significance of this single choice of word extended beyond mere semantics. It represented arguments over historical accuracy that had changed the path of his career. In the mid-1950s, Hidaka had given up writing textbooks because the ministry demanded that he replace "invasion" with "advance." From that point on, he had been a vocal critic of textbooks. To Hidaka, the remarks of the government officials were nonsense. He argued that they simply revealed that

Japan's "reflection on the war," as expressed to Chinese and Korean governments during normalization of relations in the 1960s and 1970s, meant nothing. He stressed that the issue was not merely the substitution of terms, but Japan's foreign policy toward Asia in general.[63]

Hidaka also condemned the Liberal Democratic Party for its arrogance, saying it had intentionally distorted Japan's wartime history and ignored domestic criticisms of its control over textbooks. Hidaka warned "powerless people" not to expect that the government would reflect thoroughly on its past deeds and urged them to think over what reflection on the past really meant. In addition, Hidaka noted that, like China and South Korea, Okinawa had protested the ministry's removal of passages describing atrocities against its people. Unlike the complaints of the two Asian nations, however, the Okinawan outcry had received little official acknowledgment. Hidaka demanded it be accorded appropriate attention and respect.[64]

Similarly, Dai Guohui, a professor of Chinese history at Rikkyō University in Tokyo, suggested that the real issue was not as simple as reinstating the term "invasion." Dai was born in Taiwan in 1931. The Japanese military had conscripted his two brothers and an uncle, and his uncle died fighting for Japan. Dai argued that diplomatic platitudes would not solve the fundamental problem, which was the lack of concern among the majority of ordinary Japanese about Japan's wartime colonialism and aggression. He urged the public to acquire knowledge of all aspects of Japan's modernization: its expansionism, its colonialism, the Manchurian Incident, and the Nanjing Massacre.[65]

The textbook controversy provoked Kim Hak Hyon, a Korean professor at Momoyama Gakuin University, to think not only of his wartime experience under Japanese rule, but also about international politics. During the war Kim had been forced to worship the emperor, speak Japanese instead of Korean, and sing patriotic Japanese songs. Although the ministry's efforts to tone down Japan's colonial policies in Korea disturbed him, Kim saw the event as a natural consequence of collusive postwar relations between Japan and Korea. Japan was still controlled by politicians who were the successors of Kishi Nobusuke and Kaya Okinori, champions of Japanese colonialism, and South Korea was led by figures who had collaborated in Japan's colonialism during the war. To Kim, this configuration of power explained why the South Korean government did not lodge protests against the Japanese government except when under intense pressure from the opposition parties.[66]

As Hidaka, Dai, and Kim wisely observed, the textbook controversy was not merely the fight over the usage of the term "shinryaku" or "shinshutsu." The real issue at stake in this dispute was whether or not modern Japanese history should include sufferings inflicted on other Asians by the nation during the war. The textbook controversy provoked concerned individuals to write their ideal history of wartime Japan, and in this context the dispute over Nanjing again rose to the surface.

REVIVAL OF THE DISPUTE OVER THE NANJING MASSACRE

In the wake of China's denunciation of the textbook descriptions of the Nanjing Massacre, the topic again became a public issue. This time disputes were much more intense, and the number of participants increased significantly. In general, those who claimed to be outraged by China's intervention in Japan's domestic affairs were likely to challenge the authenticity of the Nanjing Massacre. For example, Watanabe Shōichi advocated that scholars of neighboring nations must objectively consider Suzuki Akira's The Illusion of the "Nanjing Massacre" and Maeda Yūji's In the Course of War (Sensō no nagare no nakani). Watanabe believed that both of these books convincingly showed that the killing of 300,000 civilians after the occupation of Nanjing could never have happened.[67] Maeda was a wartime correspondent who had accompanied the Sixteenth Division in China. Published in 1982, his book argued that most of the deaths occurred during the battle and that the death toll could have reached 300,000 only if the entire Chinese population, both troops and civilians, had been killed.[68] Although Watanabe conceded that the Japanese military committed a certain number of atrocities in Nanjing, he emphasized that the scale and the degree of the atrocities in Nanjing were far less terrible than the crimes at Auschwitz and that the death toll of 260,000 or 300,000 was highly inflated.[69]

Uno Seiichi, a professor of Chinese philosophy at Keiō University, shared Watanabe's view. Citing both Suzuki and Maeda, Uno condemned the alleged toll of 200,000 as fabrication. To Uno, the term "advance" (shinshutsu) was an objective term. He emphasized that it should not be Japan's concern whether other nations would consider Japan's wartime conduct a matter of "aggression" (shinryaku). He also denounced history textbooks as dominated by leftists who exaggerated the government's control of textbooks and used foreign pressure to achieve their political objectives.[70]

Similarly, Mayuzumi Toshirō, a classical composer, insisted that the progressives were plotting to destroy the textbook authorization system, which had, in his eyes, succeeded in producing better books. He stressed that no country should be allowed to influence another nation's pedagogical principles; the task of educating the children of "our" nation should be Japan's alone, he argued. To Mayuzumi, such interference was a violation of national sovereignty. He was deeply disappointed with the government for bowing to China's and South Korea's protests. Mayuzumi argued that if the PRC and South Korean governments were so deeply offended by the term "invasion" (shinryaku), they should consider, from a foreign policy perspective, why the invasion had occurred. In Mayuzumi's view, the war was indeed reckless, but it had been Japan's only viable choice. Thus, China and South Korea were wrong simply to understand the Japanese expansion as a result of militaristic expansionist policies. He was also dismayed with the Japanese media, which, he said, unfairly and sensationally exploited Japan's past atrocities. To Mayuzumi, the Japanese government was simply trying to foster a more objective view of Japan's wartime history.[71]

Unlike Mayuzumi and other supporters of textbook authorization, Ienaga Saburō, who wrote Sanseidō's *New Japanese History* (Shin Nihon shi), took offense at the changes that he had been forced to make in order to gain authorization. To his chagrin, the ministry had presented him with more than 400 "suggested" revisions. The textbook inspector had specifically requested that Ienaga alter his original manuscript because students might conclude that the Japanese military committed systematic atrocities in Nanjing.[72] Because of the government's public promise to correct the descriptions in the textbooks, Ienaga submitted a request to have his original sentences reinstated, including those regarding the massacre, but the government rejected it. In January 1984, Ienaga instituted his third lawsuit seeking damages against the government.[73] At this trial, Ienaga focused his challenge on the ministry's suggestions regarding the use of "*shinryaku*," Japan's chemical and biological warfare, and atrocities against Okinawans inflicted by the Japanese military, as well as those pertaining to the Nanjing Massacre.[74]

Although the ministry did not accept Ienaga's request, changes in the descriptions of Japan's wartime history could be seen in other books after the textbook controversy. For example, writers of the textbooks were now free to use the term "invasion" (*shinryaku*).[75] As to the descriptions of the massacre, a higher estimate of the death toll began to appear in the high school and junior high school history textbooks authorized by the ministry in 1983. For example, a footnote in Tōkyō shoseki's junior high school history textbook described the massacre as follows:

> Within a few weeks after the occupation of Nanjing the Japanese military killed many Chinese in and around the city. It is said that 70,000–80,000 residents alone were killed, including women and children. If surrendered soldiers are included, it is said that more than 200,000 Chinese were killed. By contrast, China claims that the number of victims, including those killed in combat, exceeded 300,000. This incident was known as the Nanjing Massacre, and foreign countries blamed Japan for it. Nonetheless, the ordinary people in Japan were not informed of the facts.[76]

Similarly, Jiyū shobō's high school history textbook, *New Japanese History* (Shin Nihonshi), revised and expanded its footnote on the Nanjing atrocities. Like Tōkyō shoseki's textbook, it estimated that the Japanese military altogether killed more than 200,000 Chinese soldiers and civilians. The text also alluded to the Chinese estimate of 300,000.[77]

However, such revisions disturbed army veterans such as Tanaka Masaaki and Unemoto Masami. On March 13, 1984, Tanaka, Unemoto, and five other veterans filed a lawsuit against the Ministry of Education claiming that it allowed textbooks to include misrepresentations of the incident based on hearsay and other unreliable sources. Tanaka demanded 7 million yen in compensation, as well as the deletion of textbook allusions to "the Nanjing Massacre" and its significance.[78] Tanaka insisted that textbooks made newly available in 1984 unfairly exaggerated the cruelty of the Japanese military in Nanjing. Moreover, he argued, the authors of these textbooks defined Japan's wartime expansion as "an aggressive war," while Soviet, European, and American invasions in Asia throughout history were described as either "advances," "invasions," or "the sending of troops." He denounced the texts as being tainted by biased historical views that neglected the pride and distrusted the motives of the mother nation, besmirching it with a large number of flawed descriptions.[79]

To further publicize his argument, in June 1984, Tanaka published *The Illusion of "the Nanjing Massacre"* ("Nankin gyakusatsu" no kyokō). In the afterword, he stated:

> The world first learned of the Nanjing incident at the Tokyo War Crimes Trial. Without a doubt the Tokyo Trial was a tribunal at which victors unilaterally punished a defeated Japan. Thus [the victors] concluded that the defeated nation must take all the responsibility for the war. They demonized Japan and propagandized Japan's alleged crimes through the tribunal. [The victors] fabricated the Nanjing incident, inventing atrocities committed by the Japanese military in order to create a counterpart to the Nazi crimes at Auschwitz. Therefore, in my view, the key to understanding the incident depends on revising our understanding of the Tokyo Trial. Unmasking the trial and revealing its fabrications and errors would result in exposing the truth of the Nanjing incident. As long as "the Tokyo Trial's historical view" (*Tōkyō saiban shikan*) has not been refuted, neither the textbook accounts of Nanjing nor larger problems regarding the textbooks will be corrected. We must see things with Japanese eyes. We must analyze things the Japanese way. I believe that the time has come no longer to be held hostage by the "Tokyo Trial's historical view." It is time to search for the truth of history from a broader viewpoint.[80]

Tanaka labeled writers such as Hora Tomio and Honda Katsuichi, who argued that large-scale atrocities had occurred in Nanjing, as "the great massacre faction" (*daigyakusatsuha*). According to Tanaka, they were fundamentally wrong for placing their complete trust in documents and testimonies put forward by the Chinese side and by prosecutors at the Tokyo Trial. In addition, they disregarded even the possibility that the incident was artificially contrived by the victors at the time of the trial. They ignored the live-or-die situation on the battlefield and the great losses sustained by Japan's military, overlooked the fact that Chinese plainclothes guerrilla forces had inflicted substantial casualties on the Japanese military, and dismissed Chinese atrocities during the incident.[81]

Those who believed that the Nanjing Massacre had been fabricated by the Tokyo Trial and the Chinese government applauded Tanaka's work. Watanabe Shōichi wrote a foreword for the book, praising it for confronting "the great massacre faction," which had disgraced Japan and the Japanese.[82] About 100 veterans and journalists, including Gotō Kōsaku, Maeda Yūji, and Unemoto Masami, who either fought at the battle or witnessed the occupation of Nanjing, supported Tanaka's claim that there had been no great massacre in Nanjing. They offered him their versions of events and lent him photographs as well as other historical materials. For example, Unemoto, a leader of a tank section at the time, wrote Tanaka that his men had been fighting against fierce resistance and that Chinese guerrillas had concealed weapons under their clothes. Unemoto stressed that there had been no formal surrender and that he and his company were afraid of being attacked. Thus they killed without taking prisoners. Tanaka referred to Unemoto's confession in order to highlight the psychology and motives of soldiers during the battle.[83]

Tanaka repeatedly challenged the statistic of 200,000 or 300,000 deaths throughout the book. He argued that the prosecutors of the Tokyo Trial and the Japanese writers who insisted that a huge massacre had happened in Nanjing had made no attempt to address Lewis Smythe's far lower casualties estimates; in his *War Damage in the Nanking Area* (1938), Smythe stated that 2,136 people were killed, 2,745 were injured, and 4,200 were taken away by the Japanese military between the fall of Nanjing and March 15, 1938. Tanaka also stressed that the atomic bomb that exploded over Hiroshima killed 140,000, but that Hiroshima was 17 times larger than Nanjing in area and contained half again as many people. Thus, he argued, the killing of 200,000 or 300,000 in Nanjing was quite unlikely. In addition, Tanaka emphasized that approximately 200,000 civilians sought refuge in the safety zone protected by the military. He wondered where the other 200,000 or 300,000 civilians whom the military allegedly "massacred" could have come from. As to the burial records that documented 155,337 dead bodies, he questioned how many of these casualties were actually "massacred." Not only did Tanaka believe that the figure itself was untrustworthy, but he also suspected that many of the dead were killed in combat and were not the victims of atrocities.[84]

THE FLOWERING OF NANJING MASSACRE LITERATURE

In March 1984, the same month Tanaka and other veterans filed their lawsuit, some 20 people—historians, journalists, lawyers, teachers, workers, and others—established the Research Committee on the Nanjing Incident (Nankin jiken chōsa kenkyūkai). Outraged by claims that the Nanjing Massacre was an illusion, they met (and still continue to meet) every month or two to discuss issues relating to the massacre. Among the committee's founders were historians Fujiwara Akira, Hora Tomio, Kasahara Tokushi, and Yoshida Yutaka; journalist Honda Katsuichi; attorney Watanabe Harumi; and factory worker Ono Kenji.[85] These men have continued to publish books and articles in order to confront the revisionists.

In 1985, Hora published a revised version of his two-volume work, *A Collection of Historical Materials on the Japan-China War*, originally published in 1973.[86] In 1986, he refuted Tanaka and his allies in a new book titled *The Proof of the Nanjing Massacre* (Nankin daigyakusatsu no shōmei). Hora had at first felt it was fruitless to respond to what he regarded as the baseless and poorly researched claims of the revisionists. Over time, however, he felt that a response was necessary as Tanaka and newcomers to the revisionists' camp, such as Itakura Yoshiaki, a business owner who identified himself as a Nanjing Massacre scholar, continued to denounce the massacre as a fabrication in popular monthly magazines like *Bungei shunjū*.[87]

In his book, Hora pointed out that he, as a historian, had always been careful to take a critical view of historical documents and materials and had always tried to collect a wide variety of sources even if they contradicted his viewpoint. He also responded forcefully to the claim, made by both Tanaka and Itakura, that those writers who had called attention to mass atrocities in Nanjing had ignored Smythe's survey. He noted that his document collection included the very translation of Smythe's document that both Tanaka and Itakura had consulted.[88]

In Hora's view, it was Tanaka and his supporters who uncritically accepted materials that would support their claim, while unfairly ignoring contradictory sources. They had even manipulated documents in order to support their claims. He argued that Tanaka had distorted General Matsui's field diary in more than 900 places by adding, deleting, and replacing words and sentences.[89] For example, Tanaka changed "a few tens of thousands of stragglers" (*sūman*) to "a few thousand stragglers" (*sūsen*) in order to lessen the apparent number of victims. He deleted part of his journal entry dated February 6, 1938, where Matsui deplored the low morale in the military, which was causing Chinese civilians to be frightened of the Japanese military and nervous about what the army might do. As to Itakura, Hora was puzzled why he often came to conclusions heavily based on intuition and suspicion. For example, when Itakura found that Hora had misidentified Fitch's diary as Magee's, Itakura seized on this mistake as proof that Hora had intentionally and manipulatively hidden Fitch's identity in order to support the Tokyo Trial's fabrications. Hora repeatedly urged "the negationists of the Nanjing Massacre" (*daigyakusatsu hiteiha*) to consult historical documents as well as his own work carefully and thoroughly and to make arguments based on what he had actually written.[90]

In addition, Hora emphasized that he had never insisted that 200,000 or 300,000 civilians were "massacred" in Nanjing. His understanding of the scale of the killing in Nanjing was that approximately 200,000 soldiers and civilians were killed in and around Nanjing during the event. He said that he was certainly aware that the number included those who were killed in combat, and he condemned Tanaka's attack on his methodology. (Tanaka had claimed that Hora simply summed up available Chinese and Tokyo Trial figures in order to arrive at the 200,000 figure.) In the book, Hora highlighted Japan's wartime military documents that reported the execution of approximately 114,000 alleged Chinese stragglers and prisoners as "achievements."[91] To Hora, the killing of nonresistant stragglers and prisoners, many of whom were civilians, was not a legitimate military action, as Tanaka and his supporters claimed.

Nonetheless, Hora's refutation produced little, if any effect among what he called "the negationists of the Nanjing Massacre." One example of the negationists' continued intransigence was *An Outline of the Nanjing Incident: Fifteen Grounds for the Denial of the Massacre*, published by Tanaka Masaaki in 1987. Tanaka restated views similar to those expressed in his *The Illusion of the "Nanjing Massacre"* and *Thesis of Japan's Innocence* (Nihon muzairon). In his new book, he explained that the adding, dropping, and replacing of words and sentences in Matsui's field diary had resulted from mere carelessness, and he denounced as slanders those who claimed he had intentionally distorted the text. He insisted that Matsui never discussed in his diary whether the Nanjing Massacre had occurred or not. He condemned *Asahi shinbun*, textbooks, historians such as Hora Tomio, and the Nanjing Massacre Memorial Hall, on whose walls the death figure of 300,000 was inscribed. He also alleged that Han Chinese, as a race, were congenitally and uniquely brutal, emphasized Chinese atrocities of Japanese nationals, and highlighted General Matsui Iwane's benevolence and his love of China.[92] In its foreword, written in the seldom-used classical Japanese style, Kobori Keiichirō, a professor of comparative literature at Tokyo University, praised the solidity, fairness, and objectivity of Tanaka's study. Kobori characterized Tanaka as a dutiful and passionate person who had devoted his life to researching the truth of the Greater East Asian War and destroying the fabrication of the Nanjing incident.[93]

In 1987, members of the Research Committee on the Nanjing Incident published another book on the Nanjing Massacre titled *Consideration of the Nanjing Massacre*, to which Hora contributed an article refuting Tanaka's latest book. Instead of raising more persuasive arguments, Tanaka, Hora argued, had just shamelessly repeated his erroneous and emotional views, and Kobori had done nothing more than to praise Tanaka's assertions. Hora sarcastically remarked that both men seemed to be living in another world.[94] Throughout the 1980s, Hora and other members of the Research Committee were motivated to produce their work in order to refute the revisionists, stimulating Tanaka and his supporters to respond to both domestic and foreign accounts that highlighted atrocities in Nanjing.

Eventually and perhaps inevitably, the battle between these two camps expanded to affect others who were not allied with either faction. In 1986, Hata Ikuhiko, a history professor at Takushoku University, published *The Nanjing Incident: The Structure of the "Atrocities"* (Nankin jiken: "gyakusatsu" no kōzō). Placing himself in a different faction, Hata argued that, whereas earlier scholars had tried conscientiously to weigh the testimonies and claims of the massacre's survivors, the current attempts to deny the wholesale atrocities in Nanjing were the work of "inconsiderate people" (*kokoronai hitobito*). He tried to position Nanjing in a larger framework by using a rich variety of primary and secondary sources in Chinese, English, and Japanese. Unlike other scholarly materials on Nanjing in the previous years, Hata's book attempted to answer why such gigantic atrocities took place in the city. His reasons included the following combination of factors: (1) reckless local officers who ignored the government order to limit the war in Shanghai and instead advanced to Nanjing; (2) the lack of military police and facilities to detain prisoners of war; (3) the blockaded thick walls that trapped Chinese soldiers inside the wall; (4) Tang Shengzhi's refusal to surrender and his irresponsible escape from the city while leaving his troops without any command structure; (5) ignorance of the international law and human rights among the Japanese soldiers; and (6) the overly zealous Japanese mopping-up operation of Chinese guerrilla soldiers.[95]

Despite his extensive critique of Tanaka's work, Hata stopped far short of endorsing the conclusions of the Nanjing Research Committee. Although he acknowledged that wholesale atrocities had taken place in Nanjing, he disagreed with Hora and other members of the Research Committee regarding the death toll, concluding that between 38,000 and 42,000 civilians and surrendered soldiers were the victims of the atrocities. Unlike Hora's calculations, his estimate excluded Chinese soldiers killed in action from the headcount. While Hata was rather sympathetic to the victims of Nanjing and critical of the Japanese invading troops, he regarded the Chinese estimate of 300,000 deaths as exaggerated. He considered it likely that the larger figure had been based on the anecdotal testimony of a few survivors.[96] Hora, although disagreeing with Hata's definition of "atrocity" and the number of victims, welcomed Hata's contribution to the scholarship on Nanjing.[97]

CONCLUSION

The explosion of literature on the Nanjing Massacre in the 1980s was not an isolated event. Prompted by the textbook controversy, accounts of Japanese abuses inflicted on other Asian peoples also increased. Historical investigations were moving in other directions as well. For example, in the early 1980s, the Association for History Educators enjoined its members to "research the war from a local point of view" (chiiki kara sensō o kangaeru) and urged them to examine topics dealing with the home front: local cooperation or resistance to the national war effort; mobilization of slave laborers and their lives in military factories across the nation; and damage caused by fire bombings in their regions.[98]

The flourishing literature on Nanjing reflected the increasing awareness of wartime Japanese atrocities and the growing "victimizer consciousness" in Japan. Many more progressive scholars began to reexamine wartime Japanese history from an angle that had largely been overlooked. Their newly revised writings of wartime Japanese history tended to illuminate how Imperial Japan had victimized its neighbors and their peoples.

Nevertheless, in correspondence with the growth of these self-critical histories, accounts that denied or legitimized Japan's wartime expansion also became more visible. Whatever their political stances, all these writers who churned out contradictory narratives on the Asia-Pacific War were concerned with the question of what should be remembered. Consensus even on seemingly trivial points became impossible, as each contributor insisted on her or his own absolute correctness. The 1982 textbook controversy internationalized Japan's wartime history and ignited an apparently never-ending dispute. Nanjing had once again become a battleground, this time in an intractable war of words.

8

China: Nationalizing Memory of the Nanjing Massacre

I n 1972, the Japanese government normalized diplomatic relations with mainland China and recognized the People's Republic of China as China's sole legitimate government. The main objective of the PRC's policy toward Japan since 1972 has been to maintain friendly relations. Even after the textbook controversy of 1982, this policy did not essentially change. Nonetheless, 1982 was a turning point in the history and memory of the Nanjing Massacre in China, as fears of so-called spiritual pollution by Western influences prompted the PRC government to stress the teaching of the history of the Anti-Japanese War (1937–45), including Nanjing, in order to promote patriotism and nationalism among the youth who had not experienced the PRC's liberation of China from Japanese militarism.

The nationalization of memory of Nanjing occurred within this framework. From 1982 on, testimonies and eyewitness accounts of Japanese wartime atrocities began to appear frequently in the Chinese press such as *Renmin ribao*. A museum to commemorate victims of the atrocities in Nanjing was opened in 1985. New statements about the massacre no longer featured Americans and Nationalists as villains. "We" began to include Chinese both on the mainland and on the Taiwanese islands. In the 1980s, Nanjing Massacre literature in China tended to underline the horrors and the uniqueness of the massacre, centering on Japanese soldiers who committed genocidal atrocities in Nanjing. The challenge that the government faced was to promote patriotism among the youth without undermining its diplomatic relations with Japan.

DIPLOMATIC NORMALIZATION AND FRIENDSHIP

On September 29, 1972, the PRC and Japanese governments issued a joint statement normalizing relations. The Japanese government acknowledged that it was responsible for causing great damage to the Chinese people during the war, recognized the PRC government as the only legal government of China, and declared that Taiwan was an indispensable part of China's territory. The PRC government renounced its claim to war reparations from the Japanese government in exchange for friendship between Chinese and Japanese peoples.[1] An editorial in *Renmin ribao* observed:

> Diplomatic normalization between China and Japan has finally been accomplished, as the result of long-term efforts by both the Chinese and Japanese peoples. Both the Chinese and Japanese peoples have been connected by a long history of friendship. In the past, the intrusion of Japanese militarists into China brought tremendous sufferings not only to the Chinese people, but also to the Japanese people. The Chinese people respect the teaching of Mao Zedong, which strictly distinguishes a majority of the Japanese people from a handful of militarists and which extends deep sympathies for sufferings inflicted on the Japanese people. Since the establishment of our nation, we have cultivated friendly relations with the Japanese people, while the Japanese people have always desired friendship with the Chinese people.[2]

In December, the Japanese embassy opened in Beijing. The PRC government stressed friendship between the two nations and even celebrated Hirohito's birthday. On April 28, 1973, Ogawa Heishirō, Japan's ambassador to China, hosted a party to celebrate the emperor's birthday, and it was attended by nearly 40 Chinese officials.[3] Although the PRC government occasionally criticized the Japanese government and LDP politicians for their views of Japan's wartime history in the 1970s and '80s, it never attacked the emperor. Indeed, every year until Hirohito's death in 1989, the PRC sent birthday congratulations to the emperor, routinely wishing him a long life.[4]

After diplomatic normalization, maintenance of friendship became a linchpin in China's policy toward Japan. As Allen Whiting, a political scientist, observed, economic and strategic concerns caused Beijing to value friendly relations with Japan, though it often communicated with its own citizens in a different tone to inspire nationalism.[5] Even during the Chinese protest over the reports of the revisions of history textbooks in 1982, the policy of maintaining friendship remained paramount, as highlighted by the carefully chosen words of Xiao Xiangqian, the director of the First Asian Bureau of the Ministry of Foreign Affairs, in his protest to the Japanese ambassador in Beijing:

> The Chinese government has always held the opinion that Japanese militarists provoked and carried out Japan's aggression in China. This aggressive war brought tremendous sufferings to the Chinese people, but a majority of the Japanese people, too, experienced substantial damage. We must learn lessons from history and must not repeat it. Both governments are responsible for this goal, which offers substantial fundamental benefits to both peoples. The Japanese government stressed in the 1972 joint statement that "Japan is deeply aware that it brought great damage to Chinese people during the war and expresses its deepest regret." We believe that only if our offspring remember these lessons from wartime history will

friendship between the Chinese and Japanese peoples be possible, now and for generations to come.[6]

Moreover, Chinese media often distinguished ordinary Japanese from the "few militarists" whom it held solely responsible for the war. On June 30, about a month before the official protest over the textbooks, *Renmin ribao* emphasized that the Japanese public deplored the attempts of the Ministry of Education to romanticize Japan's wartime aggression. The article cited editorials of *Yomiuri shinbun* and *Mainichi shinbun* as examples of the voices of ordinary Japanese.[7] On July 30, *Renmin ribao* denounced the "tiny elites" in the Japanese administration who supported the Ministry of Education and rejected foreign advice on "internal affairs." The article urged these elites to follow the sincere attitudes of Japanese intellectuals who stressed that the regrets expressed during normalization must be mirrored in school education. The editors emphasized that their intention was to prevent "a few Japanese" from disrupting friendship between the Chinese and Japanese peoples and that they found it uncomfortable to remind not only Chinese, but also Japanese of sorrowful memories.[8]

In August 1982, Chinese mass media intensified their protests against the revisions of history textbooks in Japan. Related articles appeared in *Renmin ribao* almost daily.[9] Testimonies of survivors of the war, including the Nanjing Massacre, were publicized through newspapers and radio broadcasts.[10] Chinese scholars organized symposia and protested against Japan's Ministry of Education.[11] Nonetheless, separating the "tiny elites" from the ordinary Japanese people remained a touchstone of the campaign. For example, *Renmin ribao* devoted considerable attention to Japanese visitors in China—professors, members of Japan Teachers Union, businessmen, and others—who harshly denounced the Ministry of Education for its distortion of history in school textbooks.[12] Mitsuhashi Atsuko, a representative of the Japan Teachers Union, promised a Beijing audience that she and other members would teach historical truth to Japan's future generations.[13]

Chinese mass media such as *Renmin ribao* also kept close watch on views and voices in Japan that challenged the Ministry of Education and its attempts to revise textbooks. The official newspaper not only informed Chinese readers of articles and editorials that appeared in Japanese national newspapers, but also reported the activities of members of the Diet, grass-roots citizen's groups, and religious organizations that demanded that the government correct school textbooks.[14]

Renmin ribao continued to include articles and criticisms of the Japanese government regarding these subjects until September 10, 1982, when the editors praised the efforts of Prime Minister Suzuki Zenkō and other government officials in correcting textbook distortions of Japan's wartime aggression.[15] The editors hoped that the Japanese government would immediately carry out the necessary measures and win the trust of Chinese, Japanese, and other Asian peoples. Moreover, they wished that Suzuki's visit to China might contribute to the further development of friendly relations between China and Japan.[16] When Suzuki arrived in China in late September to celebrate the tenth anniversary of Chinese-Japanese normalization, the editorial page of *Renmin ribao* responded with these sentiments:

> We wish to take this opportunity to extend a warm welcome to Prime Minister Suzuki and to extend our heartfelt greetings to the Chinese and Japanese people and to all official personages and other public figures in the two countries who exerted themselves to achieve the normalization of Sino-Japanese diplomatic relations.
>
> China and Japan are close neighbors separated only by a strip of water, and the people of the two countries have a traditional friendship.[17]

The article stressed the longevity of the friendship between the two countries, and said that the duty of China and Japan to maintain friendship and cooperation was dictated not only by history, but also by the demands of the present day. At the same time the editorial expressed concern that a Japanese minority was trying to revive militarism and to prevent the development of friendly relations between the two nations. It urged both China and Japan to be frank and sincere with each other in order to deepen mutual understanding and overcome the disturbance created by the small militarist faction so that friendly relations between both peoples would be maintained for generations to come.[18]

"A RESISTANCE BY ALL THE PEOPLE": TEACHING THE ANTI-JAPANESE WAR

To maintain friendship between Chinese and Japanese peoples was one thing; to teach Chinese people about the Anti-Japanese War was another. News reports of the textbook revisions outraged many Chinese officials and prompted them to explore new ways of teaching the history of the Anti-Japanese War to the people.[19] Moreover, in the post-Mao period, the teaching of the war was linked with the political goal of promoting patriotism and loyalty to the party, a party now eager to encourage the creation of more literature and memorials regarding the Anti-Japanese War. Newly empowered reformers such as Vice Premier Deng Xiaoping, Secretary General Hu Yaobang, and Premier Zhao Ziyang needed to adopt a nationalistic posture in order to prevent opposition forces such as the People's Liberation Army from achieving greater popularity.[20]

On July 2, 1983, the Propaganda Department of the CCP Central Committee and the Research Office of the Secretariat of the CCP Central Committee issued a joint statement calling for a strengthening of patriotic education. The spokesperson argued that patriotism had been a superb tradition among ethnic Chinese for thousands of years and that this spirit had always driven the society forward. The government was concerned that a few comrades, particularly the youth, had lost faith in the party because of errors such as the Cultural Revolution (1966–76), which imposed tremendous suffering on tens of millions of Chinese people. They stressed that patriotism tended to be easily accepted by people regardless of social status, occupation, ethnicity, age, culture, and ideology. In order to achieve a higher standard of Communism, they advocated strengthening ideological and political education by mobilizing the patriotic energies of the people.[21]

On October 12 and 13, 1983, Deng Xiaoping, Zhao Ziyang, Hu Yaobang, and other members of the Standing Committee of the Political Bureau presided over the Second Plenary Session of the Twelfth Central Committee of the Communist Party. At the session, they decided to confront "spiritual pollution" (*jingshen wuran*) in order to purify the party.[22] Thereafter, frequent articles urging readers to fight against spiritual pollution appeared in Chinese media.[23]

In honor of the fortieth anniversary of China's victory in the Anti-Japanese War on September 3, 1985, the government began widely and deliberately publicizing the history and memory of the war. On July 1, 1985, the Chinese Museum of Art in Beijing opened a photo exhibition on the Anti-Japanese War, which displayed some 280 photographs. These photographs would subsequently travel through provinces and cities in the eastern region. On the same day, 100 women who fought against the Japanese military during the war held a symposium in Beijing. On July 6, a memorial service for patriots who died during the war was held at the Marco Polo Bridge in Beijing. Tan Xunzhi, who had come to the mainland from Taiwan a few years earlier, emphasized that China had won the Anti-Japanese War because of multilateral cooperation among all peoples within the nation and between the Nationalist and Communist Parties. Wenshi ziliao chubanshe, a publisher, announced its intention to publish a 12-volume collection of memoirs by former Nationalist officers, including those who lived in Taiwan and elsewhere, by the end of 1985.[24]

On August 11, the Committee for Repairing Historical Sites at the Marco Polo Bridge (Lugouqiao lishi wenwu xiuli weiyuanhui) was established, and the Beijing city government appropriated 100,000 yuan for the committee's budget. The committee was in charge of building the Museum of the War of Chinese People's Resistance against Japan (completed in July 1987) and repairing other historical monuments in the area. On August 13, 1985, Gao Liang, director of the Propaganda Department of the CCP Central Committee, informed correspondents of numerous forthcoming events in August and September to commemorate the Anti-Japanese War:

> China's victory in the Anti-Japanese War was an event of great historical significance, made possible by the unified front proposed by the Chinese Communist Party. Each and every ethnic group, anti-Japanese organizations, patriots in every social class, overseas Chinese, and others joined the war under the united front between Nationalist and Communist parties. It was a resistance by all the people. It was a war of liberation in which the Chinese people achieved a perfect victory, putting an end to foreign invasions that had begun some one hundred years earlier. The victory wiped away one hundred years of disgrace endured by the Chinese people and was a brilliant example of a quasi-colonized nation's triumph over an imperial power. The victory contributed to the awakening of Chinese people

and showed that the ethnic Chinese, when they are united, are enormously strong.[25]

Gao highlighted that the mission of these celebrations would be to mobilize youth in order to strengthen their patriotism and internationalism as well as to honor the nation's tradition of revolution. He announced that Beijing and other provinces would sponsor commemorative events such as pilgrimages to memorial sites, including the graves of Anti-Japanese War patriots. Government leaders also planned to open the nation's doors to visits from participants in the war who did not reside in mainland China, welcoming former comrades-in-arms from Taiwan, Macao, and other places. In Beijing, between September 2 and 4, 1985, approximately 10,000 boys and girls were scheduled to assemble in Tiananmen Square to commemorate officers and soldiers who died during the war. Gao also gave notice of a number of scholarly meetings as well as publications, films, videos, television programs, radio broadcasts, and special commemorative stamps dealing with the Anti-Japanese War. Organizers of one symposium planned to invite Chinese patriots from Hong Kong, Macao, Taiwan, and elsewhere.[26]

From 1985 on, a number of Anti-Japanese War museums and memorials were established. On August 13, 1985, the newly renovated Chinese People's Revolutionary Military Museum in Tiananmen Square opened to the public. On August 15, 40 years to the day after Hirohito announced Japan's intention to surrender, the Memorial for Compatriot Victims of the Japanese Military's Nanjing Massacre (the Nanjing Massacre Memorial Hall) was opened in Nanjing. On the same day, 11 historical sites that had been operated by Unit 731, Japan's chemical and biological warfare unit, were opened in Harbin, including an exhibition that displayed approximately 100 artifacts.[27] In July 1986, the Chinese government appropriated special funds for repairing the Fushun War Criminal Prison, where members of Returnees from China (Chūgoku Kikansha Renrakukai) were subjected to reeducation, and the exhibition hall was planned to open by the end of the year.[28] In September 1986, Xinhua News Agency reported that a camp of Japanese prisoners in Zhenyuan—a base of the Japanese People's Liberation Alliance—would be opened in the early 1987.[29] On the eve of the fiftieth anniversary of the July 7 Incident of 1937, the completion of the Memorial Museum of the Chinese People's War of Resistance against Japan was celebrated.[30]

"LESSONS OF THE BLOOD": THE ROLE OF THE NANJING MASSACRE IN PATRIOTIC EDUCATION

Amid these events, several books on the Nanjing Massacre appeared in the 1980s. In August 1983, the Research Committee on Historical Materials of the City of Nanjing, Jiangsu Province, Chinese People's Political Consultative Conference, published an 85-page booklet titled *Historical Sources: Materials on the*

Nanjing Massacre Committed by the Japanese Army of Invasion (Shiliao xuanji Qin-Hua Rijun Nanjing datusha shiliao zhuanji). Classified for internal circulation only, this booklet was not intended for a broad audience. Yet the fact that it was published at all indicated a shift in government attitudes toward the massacre. In the afterword, the editors outlined their objectives as follows:

> Our goal is not only to offer a comparative analysis of the history of the Nanjing Massacre perpetrated by the Japanese military and to preserve this history systematically. We also desire to conduct patriotic education by using true historical facts in order to protect the nation. By raising public awareness, we want to encourage our countrymen to pledge to maintain peace.
>
> The Chinese government and its people both insist upon friendship between China and Japan. However, [we must] learn lessons of the blood from the history of the Japanese militarists' invasion of China. We must always be vigilant against the possible resurrection from the ashes of Japan's militarism. Undeniably, Japan's aggressive war inflicted deep and severe misfortunes upon the peoples of China and other invaded nations. It also forced the Japanese people to suffer similar misfortunes. Understanding the reactionary essence of militarism will prevent its revival and thus will also serve the fundamental interests of the Japanese people. [31]

Despite the editors' emphasis on friendship, all the Japanese soldiers in the book were described as villains who committed preplanned, organized atrocities in Nanjing. The accusations expressed in the booklet are indeed sweeping, as the following passage illustrates:

> After entering the city, the Japanese military killed every person they saw, raped and killed every woman they encountered, looted valuables wherever they found them, and burned houses indiscriminately. The Japanese military employed various methods of killing: beheading; the smashing of skulls; disembowelment; and live burial. Hands and legs were mutilated, sexual organs were cut off, and sticks were rammed into vaginas and anuses. People were drowned, machine-gunned, and burned alive. The ferocious atrocity of these acts is unique in human history. [32]

The book omitted mention of American devils, evil Nationalists, or Chinese collaborators and held the Japanese military solely responsible for the destruction in Nanjing as well as the sufferings of the people. The editors based their account of the atrocities in Nanjing on a variety of testimonies by survivors, all of whom underscored the unimaginable horrors that the Japanese military committed in Nanjing. One of them was Li Xiuying, who was stabbed nearly 40 times by three Japanese soldiers in an attack that killed her unborn child.

> Around 9 o'clock in the morning [on December 19], six armed Japanese soldiers broke into the basement and took away some ten young women. I was one of them. Then I thought. I decided in my mind not to be disgraced even if I must die and resolved to resist [against the Japanese military] even at the cost of my life. I hit my head hard against the wall. Blood flowed from my head, and I fainted. When I regained consciousness, the Japanese devils were gone. . . .

Around eleven o'clock, three Japanese soldiers came into the basement again. . . . Then I was wearing a one-piece dress, and this devil [a Japanese soldier] tried to unhook my buttons. I saw this devil was carrying a knife at his waist. I recognized this kind of knife because my uncle wore one. The knife is kept in a case, and it is not easy to pull out. I knew something about how to use one, so I tried to unbutton the case immediately, hoping to grab the knife, get up from the bed, and fight against the devil! The devil was quite surprised at this and tried to release my hand from the knife. At the same time, he held my hand, and we struggled for the knife. A desperate fight had begun. At this time I did not much care about my life. I kicked him, butted him, and bit him. Because of my biting, he screamed. Two devils came from the next room as soon as they heard the scream. Thus, the six or seven women they had been holding captive were able to escape. I fought against three devils. I desperately tried to take the knife, and the devil did so, too. We rolled on the ground struggling for the knife. In a fit of rage, the other two devils stabbed and cut me. My legs were stabbed many times, and blood ran freely. Yet I did not feel any pain. My face was stabbed several times, too, and blood stained my clothes red. But I continued to fight desperately.[33]

Li was presented as a traditional Chinese woman with a patriotic spirit who was not at all afraid of violence. Throughout the book, the editors praised such patriotic women and men who resisted the invaders, to the death if necessary.[34] Their main themes were that the people in Nanjing were united as one, regardless of ethnicity or ideology, that they suffered unspeakable violence at the hands of the Japanese military, and that the people in China and elsewhere around the globe defeated Japanese invaders and forced them to surrender unconditionally.[35] The book took no account of Chinese collaborators, of Japanese suffering, or of any detail that would complicate the image of a pure struggle of good against evil.

In July 1985, as the fortieth anniversary of the victory approached, a number of books appeared that included historical documents and eyewitness accounts. The Committee for the Compilation of Sources on the Nanjing Massacre published *Historical Materials on the Nanjing Massacre Committed by the Japanese Army of Invasion* (Qin-Hua Rijun Nanjing datusha shiliao).[36] It printed eyewitness reports published in Chinese newspapers, contemporary diaries by soldiers and residents, the translation of Smythe's *War Damage in the Nanking Area*, and testimonies of survivors of Japanese atrocities.[37] In the same year, Gao Xingzu, a professor at Nanjing University, published *Japanese War Atrocities: The Nanjing Massacre* (Rijun qin-Hua baoxing: Nanjing datusha).[38] In July 1987, on the fiftieth anniversary of the July 7 Incident, *The Fall of Nanjing* (Nanjing de xianluo) became available to the public. In November, *Archival Materials on the Nanjing Massacre Committed by the Japanese Army of Invasion* (Qin-Hua rijun Nanjing datusha dang'an) was published.[39] This included many declassified documents such as official records that indicated various atrocities in Nanjing, burial records written between 1938 and 1947, and court documents on the postwar military tribunal in Nanjing.[40] No interviews with survivors were included in the volume.

Though these writings on the Nanjing Massacre can be seen as state propaganda or as the products of narrow-minded bias, they still vividly present the recollections of men and women who had experienced grief and pain. The editors attempted to preserve the memories of Nanjing within the limiting framework of the imperfect political freedom that existed at the time. After all, the government strictly monitored classified documents maintained by the Number Two China Historical Archives and the Nanjing City Archives, both of which preserved unknown quantities of related documents.[41] The politically correct version of the massacre maintained by the government in these documents seemed to have four consistent characteristics: photographs must show Japanese brutalities only; Japanese villains must not have human faces; it must be accepted that the Japanese military ferociously killed at least 300,000 innocent Chinese after the fall of Nanjing; and the literature must contribute to stirring patriotism and loyalty to the party among the people in China, including Taiwan.

The PRC government wished to promote patriotism and loyalty, but not necessarily at the cost of stirring hatred toward postwar Japan or Japanese. Endangering diplomatic relations with the Japanese state was not an option. Nonetheless, patriotic education that underlined Japanese evil and inhumanity in Nanjing and elsewhere in China ignited anti-Japanese movements and criticisms directed by Chinese students toward their government. For example, in September 1985, a visit by Prime Minister Nakasone Yasuhiro to Yasukuni Shrine, which honors Japan's war dead, including Class A war criminals, sparked a demonstration by approximately 1,000 students at Beijing and Qinghua Universities. The protest, which took place without official approval, condemned Nakasone's visit to the shrine, the perceived revival of Japanese militarism, and Japan's economic penetration of China with the acquiescence of the PRC government. Such protests occurred in other cities and often expressed criticisms against the Chinese government for allowing this economic invasion.[42]

Whether the government was concerned with the double-edged potential of patriotic education, it continued to stress both patriotic education about the Anti-Japanese war and the friendship between Japan and China, both on the government and popular levels. By July 1987, according to China National Radio, approximately 400,000 people, including Japanese, had visited the Nanjing Massacre Memorial Hall.[43] This figure included a visit by Nakano Ryōko, an actress, and 59 other Japanese to the Memorial Hall to pay tribute to the victims of Japanese atrocities in Nanjing. They viewed exhibits and a documentary film at the Memorial Hall and mourned the dead by planting trees in the yard of the Memorial Hall and other places in the city.[44] The head of the group, Kikuchi Yoshitaka, emphasized in his greeting speech that they had come to Nanjing in order to pray for eternal peace between China and Japan and to remember the tremendous damage and suffering inflicted on Chinese people by imperial Japan.[45]

Though the PRC government had incorporated the Nanjing Massacre into its national history by the late 1980s, the memory of the Nanjing Massacre was never institutionalized in Taiwan. Nevertheless, the accounts of Nanjing that reemerged in the 1970s served to remind the Japanese of their wartime atrocities in a different context.

As the PRC government was moving to normalize its relations with Japan in 1972, Ho Ying-chin (He Yingchin), the supreme commander of the China Theater who accepted the unconditional surrender of the Japanese forces in China in 1945, expressed his fury over the PRC's attempt to take credit for the Nationalist government's wartime accomplishments. In two separate speeches given in July 1972, Ho argued that the PRC was trying to discredit the Nationalist efforts during the war and to deceive international public opinion.[46] On the thirty-fifth anniversary of the Marco Polo Bridge Incident on July 7, 1972, Ho stressed that it was the Nationalist Army who fought against the Japanese Army, that the Japanese military surrendered to the Nationalist government, not to the PRC, and that the Communist forces occasionally attacked the Nationalist troops and disturbed the war effort by the Nationalist government.[47]

On the same day, the editorial of *Zhongyang Ribao* expressed its concern over Japan-PRC relations. The editor argued that Japan's postwar prosperity would have never been accomplished had it not been for the nonpunitive policies adopted by the Nationalist government, to say nothing of American support. The newspaper insisted that Japan's normalization with the PRC would not only harm Japan, but also lead to chaos throughout Asia. It warned that the ultimate goal of the PRC would be an international communist revolution and the destruction of the capitalist camp.[48]

In 1979, four years after the death of Chiang Kai-shek, Guo Qi, a battalion commander of the Nationalist Army during the Battle of Nanjing who survived the atrocities, published *Nanjing datusha* (The Nanjing Massacre) in Taipei. In 1938, in the direct aftermath of the massacre, Guo had published a series of articles collectively titled "Xiandu xielei ji" (Record of Blood and Tears of the Fallen Capital) in *Xijing pinbao*.[49] As he explained in his introduction to *Nanjing datusha*, Guo had initially intended to publish a book on the massacre soon after the war but had abandoned this plan after the execution of General Tani Hisao in 1947 and in deference to Chiang Kai-shek's generous nonpunitive policy toward Japan (*yide baoyuan*). However, as Guo put it, "the Tanaka Kakuei administration forgot a debt of gratitude and returned evil for good, and unilaterally abandoned the treaty between China [Taiwan] and Japan." Such Japanese betrayals infuriated him and motivated him to write an extended account of Nanjing. Guo stressed the inhumanity of the Japanese military that committed slaughters, rape, and destruction, and he included in his account a number of graphic and horrific photographs of Japanese atrocities. He held Tani accountable for slaughtering more than 100,000 of his fellow Chinese.[50] Guo's book was very similar to his earlier "Record of Blood and Tears of the Fallen Capital."

In the years that followed Japan's recognition of the PRC, reevaluations of Nanjing occurred continually in Taiwan. For example, the Institute of Modern History, Academia Sinica, organized a three-day conference on the Sino-Japanese War of 1937–45 from August 2 to August 4, 1985. At the first panel on the first day, Li Yunhan, vice chairman of the Guomindang Party History Commission (Zhongguo Guomindang dangshi weiyuanhui), presented a paper that examined Chinese-, English-, and Japanese-language materials on the Nanjing atrocities. Li argued that neither Chinese nor English sources that he examined denied the atrocities in Nanjing, whereas a few Japanese authors such as Tanaka Masaaki claimed that the Nanjing Massacre was an illusion.[51] Responding to questions from the floor, Li affirmed his belief that the death toll in Nanjing amounted to 300,000, the figure confirmed not only at the Nanjing trial in 1947, but also materials on Nanjing published in the mainland. At a second panel at the conference, Li was critical of the practice of history in the PRC, going so far as to suggest a Communist conspiracy to rewrite the history of the war. Nevertheless, when it came to the casualty figures in Nanjing, Li did not challenge the findings of the same Communist historians whom he otherwise distrusted.[52]

In the 1980s, Taiwan saw the publication of two major collections of materials on Nanjing originally written in Chinese, English, and Japanese: Hong Guiji's "Nanjing datusha" (The Nanjing Massacre) appeared as part of his more than 1,000-page-long *Riben zai Hua baoxing lu* (Account of the Atrocities Committed by Japan in China), published in 1985; and Guomindang Party History Commission's two-volume *Rijun zai Hua baoxing: Nanjing datusha* (Atrocities Committed by the Japanese Army: The Nanjing Massacre), released in 1987.[53] In his anthology, Hong included Harold Timperley's *What War Means: Japanese Terror in China*, Guo Qi's *The Nanjing Massacre* and excerpts written by the Japanese authors such as Hora Tomio and Honda Katsuichi. The History Commission's publication also anthologized Timperley's and Guo's work, as well as Lewis Smythe's *War Damage in the Nanking Area* and Li Yunhan's "Youguan 'Nanjing da tu sha' Zhongwai shiliao de pingshu" (In Regard to Chinese and Foreign Discussions of the Historical Materials on the Nanjing Massacre).[54] Neither, however, included any account written by an author from the PRC.

As on the mainland, government officials in Taiwan often celebrated Chinese victory over Imperial Japan during the period from 1972 to 1989, and Nanjing literature became available to the public.[55] However, the Taiwanese government did not sponsor the construction of any war museums that highlighted Japanese wartime atrocities or used Nanjing to provoke nationalism among its citizens. The government had no wish to offend its conservative friends in the Japanese LDP, such as Kishi Nobusuke, a former Class A war crimes suspect, and Fujio Masayuki, who in 1986 denied Nanjing and refused to admit the evil aspects of Imperial Japan. These Japanese politicians occasionally visited Taiwan and publicly expressed gratitude for Chiang's extremely generous postwar policy toward Japan. They also affirmed that the policy had not only saved Japan from destruction, but also contributed to postwar economic growth.[56] Moreover, nationalist feeling in Taiwan tended to define and express itself in terms of anticommunism and opposition to the PRC, not in terms of memories of the Asia-Pacific War. Therefore, resurrecting the ghosts of Nanjing has been a matter of small importance to the government in Taipei.

CONCLUSION

On December 13, 1987, on the fiftieth anniversary of the beginning of the massacre, some 400 PRC government officials and bereaved family members attended a commemorative ceremony at the Nanjing Massacre Memorial Hall in Nanjing. By the time of the ceremony, a renovation of the memorial hall had been completed. It now housed not only artifacts reminding visitors of Japanese atrocities—such items as a gasoline tank allegedly used to burn innocent civilians and a wooden box allegedly broken by the bayonet of a Japanese soldier—but also books, articles, news reports, and never-again promises written and contributed by Japanese visitors. In addition, major displays now had captions in Japanese and English in addition to Chinese. Other commemorative events included a ceremony in which students and faculty from Hehai University placed floral tributes at the sites of Japanese atrocities.[57]

By 1987, the Nanjing Massacre had become a part of Chinese national memory and a symbol of Japan's wartime atrocities and cruelty in China. The Sino-American normalization, the textbook controversy, and the internal struggle against unwanted Western influences all contributed to embedding the massacre in public memory on a national level. However, the history of Nanjing weighed less heavily on the island of Taiwan, where political ties to conservative elements in Japan and animosity toward the Communist government made the commemoration of the massacre a more delicate issue.

9

United States: Focus on Japanese Denials of the Past

Before the United States normalized its relations with China in 1979, the Nanjing Massacre received scant attention in the United States, either from news media or other sources. From 1982 on, events in Japan led American correspondents to turn their attention to the topic of war and memory in Japan, including the Nanjing Massacre. In the 1980s, discussions of the massacre appeared frequently in the press. The majority of these discussions did not place Nanjing at a focal point of wartime memory, but used references to it merely to contextualize events that stood prominently in American memory, such as Pearl Harbor and Hiroshima.

In the 1980s, these American news reports often stressed the dominant sense of victimization among the Japanese public. Although some articles acknowledged the intense disputes within Japan over how to remember the Asia-Pacific War, most made the blanket assessment that Japanese were trying to forget the past and that most Japanese were ignorant of the nation's wartime atrocities. Chinese Americans who accepted these reports at face value were outraged, and groups dedicated to preserving the memory of Japan as perpetrator began to form. In 1987, the Chinese Alliance for Memorial and Justice was founded in New York and staged its first public event to commemorate the victims of the Nanjing Massacre. Since then, the alliance and its supporters have held a commemorative event every December and have played a major role in enlightening the public.

Between 1971 and 1989, American media rediscovered the Nanjing Massacre, but the number of journalists and other writers who participated in this revival of interest was still quite small, and their treatment of the issue was often simplistic and one-sided. Ironically, by condemning Japan for presenting only one view of the massacre—an accusation that ignored the intense debate among Japanese commentators over Nanjing—many American accounts committed the same error of one-sidedness. This misleading information in the American press led some concerned individuals to investigate the past for themselves and to gain a new level of awareness of wartime Japanese atrocities in China.

1970S: BERGAMINI CHARGES HIROHITO WITH RESPONSIBILITY

Although few authors underscored Nanjing before the 1982 textbook controversy in general, David Bergamini included a substantial discussion of Nanjing in his *Japan's Imperial Conspiracy* (1971), a book whose introduction was written by William Webb, the former presiding judge of the Tokyo Trial. Bergamini was born the son of American missionary parents in Japan in 1928 and spent the first eight years of his life there. Then he and his family moved to China, where he saw exchanges of violence between Japanese and Chinese: Japanese troops raided a Chinese farm village and bayoneted inhabitants, and the following day Chinese guerrillas attacked Japanese troops and brought back Japanese heads on bamboo poles. After two years in China, Bergamini was no longer a Japanese sympathizer. He felt that "the gentle, thoughtful, courteous, good-natured" Japanese, whom he had known throughout his boyhood, were "now transformed, hideously and most puzzlingly." Japanese soldiers resorted to unnecessary violence toward noncombatants, raped women, murdered infants, and believed Chinese confessions only if they were made under torture.[1]

By Christmas 1941, Bergamini and his family were in the Philippines, where Japanese soldiers interned him and his family members in a concentration camp. Bergamini found the conditions in the camp were not as cruel as his experience in China had led him to expect. He also encountered a few humane Japanese individuals such as "Mazaki," a benefactor of the prisoners who was killed by the time American troops arrived and liberated the Bergaminis and other prisoners. The rescue occurred only 24 hours before Bergamini and others were scheduled to be executed.[2]

In the book, Bergamini insisted that Hirohito was a formidable war leader who eliminated political opponents through ruthless tactics like assassination. The emperor, he argued, led Japanese people into war in order to accomplish a mission, inherited from Emperor Meiji, to liberate Asia from white people. Bergamini wrote that "all Japanese" worshiped Hirohito as a god between 1926 and 1945, and that Hirohito was able to manipulate the entire people and had been preparing them for the sacred mission for 29 years before the Pacific War. Bergamini found Hirohito personally responsible for the killing of an anarchist named Ōsugi Sakae, his wife, and his nephew (1923); Zhang Zuolin, a Manchurian warlord (1928); prime ministers Hamaguchi Osachi (1931) and Inukai Tsuyoshi (1932); and others.[3]

In his first chapter, titled "Rape of Nanking," he argued that Yasuhiko

(Prince Asaka), Empress Nagako's uncle, delivered an order to kill all captives in Nanjing.[4] Bergamini claimed that General Matsui Iwane was trying to occupy Nanjing with a few well-disciplined troops in order to win support from Chinese residents. Nonetheless, Yasuhiko and his two helpmates let Japanese troops loose in Nanjing. They ordered their soldiers to loot and then burn shops and home industries. According to Bergamini, it was not until after Yasuhiko left for Tokyo in February 1938 that the systematic terror finally ended.[5]

In his second chapter, which dealt with the atomic bombings, Bergamini alleged that Hirohito, who understood the significance of the bomb, felt it necessary to end the war after the bomb was dropped on Hiroshima and summoned his foreign minister to advise him of his wish to surrender. Bergamini claimed that War Minister Anami Korechika and his fellow generals planned a fake coup in order to convince Americans that Hirohito was a victim rather than a ringleader of Japan's wartime aggression. Bergamini argued that the atomic bombs created an opportunity for the Allies to reconstruct Japan without vengeance because the revenge had already been accomplished: "The 140,000 corpses of Hiroshima and Nagasaki had paid for Nanking, and the 166,000 killed in the fire raids on Tokyo had more than paid for American, Australian, and British war prisoners who had been starved and beaten to death in Japanese concentration camps."[6]

Although William Webb was convinced by Bergamini's general thesis that Hirohito had initiated both domestic and international violence to carry out his inherited mission of liberation of Asia, scholars of Japanese studies were not similarly persuaded. Herbert Bix, Alvin Coox, James Crowley, Okamoto Shumpei, Herschel Webb, among others, wrote critical reviews of *Japan's Imperial Conspiracy*.[7] James Crowley pointed out Bergamini's misuses of the *Sugiyama Memoranda*, a key piece of evidence, while Okamoto Shumpei detailed the errors in Bergamini's translation of Kido Kōichi's diary, another central text underpinning his argument.[8] Alvin Coox was also dissatisfied with numerous factual mistakes that appeared throughout the book: He found 21 errors in the section on Zhanggufeng, a Soviet-Japanese skirmish in 1938.[9]

In his review article, Herbert Bix identified errors in Bergamini's book and also deplored Bergamini's skewed moral arithmetic, which Bix regarded as a salient flaw in the work. He was particularly disturbed by Bergamini's balancing of war atrocities. He condemned the book for its lack of moral values and denounced Bergamini as applying a double standard. To Bix, if Bergamini were really appalled by Japanese atrocities in Nanjing, he would also be appalled by American atrocities in Hiroshima and Nagasaki.[10]

Nevertheless, Bix gave credit to Bergamini for performing a necessary service; the book, however erroneous and prejudiced, reminded his readers of sufferings that Japanese inflicted on other peoples during the war. Bix argued that people in the United States who measured a country by its industrial vitality would be inclined to glorify the Japanese experience of economic growth after the war, while minimizing the wartime sufferings of both non-Japanese and

Japanese. Rather than labeling the Rape of Nanking as Hirohito's conspiracy, Bix argued, Bergamini would have been better advised to discuss the causes of the wholesale atrocities in Nanjing by employing transcultural concepts such as racism, dehumanization, and educational indoctrination. This approach would have allowed readers to compare Japan's conduct with American racism and war atrocities in Indochina.[11]

Although Bergamini's work stirred critical responses from academics, American mass media in general paid little attention throughout the 1970s to disagreements about Japan's wartime aggression or to disputes within Japan over the Nanjing Massacre. However, American media eventually began to reconsider these issues, prompted first by America's official recognition of the PRC government in 1979 and then, much more noticeably, by the textbook controversy in 1982. Some news reports of the controversy displayed an awareness that there had been a number of Japanese who called for a direct and candid discussion of Nanjing and its legacy. Too often, however, many reporters made the facile assumption that Japan as a nation wanted to expunge Nanjing from the public memory. Indeed, those who reported the controversy in terms of misleading simplifications contributed to rekindling and preserving memories of Nanjing and other Japanese wartime atrocities in the minds of Americans.

IN THE 1980S: WWII MEMORIES REVIVED

After China's official protest of the descriptions of Japanese wartime history in school textbooks, news reports about the controversy appeared frequently in the American press. On July 28, 1982, the *New York Times* informed its readers of complaints that had appeared in Chinese newspapers such as *Renmin ribao*. The *Times* underscored China's concern with the censorship of textbooks by Japan's Ministry of Education and the suspicion that people in Japan were dreaming again of aggression.[12] On August 11, 1982, the paper informed its readers of the disagreement between the Ministry of Education, which insisted no revision of the textbooks was necessary, and the Ministry of Foreign Affairs, which urged corrections.[13] Three days later the *Times* reported President Ronald Reagan's statements of foreign and domestic policy at the press conference, which included his view on the textbook controversy:

REPORTER Mr. President, what is your personal view on Japan's revision of history and the rationale regarding Japan's invasion of China and oppression of Korea, and also attack on [*sic*] to justify the Japanese military actions elsewhere?

REAGAN Well, I think we would be going into past history there. And, of course, those were tragic times. And we think there was a different philosophy than is governing Japan today. And I think the fact that we have been able to forget, or forgive— whichever you want to use—that period, and become the good friends that we are today I think is what we should be more interested in. I would rather not rehash the war feelings that I am sure were felt on both sides, and that led to that tragedy.[14]

On the one hand, President Reagan was right. Japan in 1982 was different from Imperial Japan. Unlike the wartime period, the government had a difficult task in confronting Marxists and Marxist-influenced educators who often wrote the history textbooks. As Henry Stokes of the *New York Times* observed, the *bête noire* of the right-wing politicians of the Liberal Democratic Party, which won majorities in both houses of Parliament in June 1980, was the Japan Teachers Union. Stokes argued that the right-wing extremists of the party felt "the best way to control the 'red' teachers union [was] to hamstring its members in the classrooms with textbooks that [gave] the teachers no scope for 'inoculating'— a favorite verb with right-wingers—the young with left-wing ideals."[15]

On the other hand, President Reagan seemed not to recognize that not all people in the United States were as forgetful, or forgiving, as he was. On September 18, 1982, more than 500 people, most of them Americans of Chinese and Korean descent, demonstrated in Washington, D.C., to protest revisions of wartime Japanese aggression in Japanese school textbooks. Although the Chinese and Korean governments had accepted the Japanese government's pledge to amend the controversial passages a week earlier, Kyo R. Jhin, one of the organizers, stressed that their decision to drop the dispute had been for economic reasons. Similarly, Jane Hu, chairperson of the Alliance against Japanese Distortion of History, emphasized that the objective of the protest was "to preserve true history" and that she and other members would not "want the Japanese to forget," in order that similar historical tragedies might be avoided in the future.[16]

ANNIVERSARY JOURNALISM, 1985: REMINDING THE LIVING OF THE DEAD

In the years between 1982 and 1984, few if any journalists in the mainstream American press wrote detailed articles on the disputes over the Nanjing Massacre in Japan. In 1985, however, prompted by the dramatic rise in publications on Nanjing in Japan, John Burgess of the *Washington Post* recounted them, summarizing the viewpoint of Tanaka Masaaki, author of *The Illusion of "the Nanjing Massacre"* ("Nankin gyakusatsu" no kyokō). Although he acknowledged that Tanaka and his supporters spoke for a relatively small group of people and organizations, Burgess argued that "the Japanese [were] gradually dropping taboos against questioning the victors' account of Japan's conduct in the war."[17]

Not only did Burgess give voice to the views of Tanaka and other revisionists who claimed the civilian death toll in Nanjing was a mere 2,000 or so, but he informed readers of the existence of another camp, which he called the liberal camp, that denounced Tanaka and his allies. Burgess emphasized that nine such scholars, including Fujiwara Akira and Hora Tomio, had spent a week conducting research in Nanjing in December 1984 and had rejected the revisionist view. According to Hora, Burgess wrote, a total of about 200,000 people, soldiers and civilians, were killed in the city of Nanjing. In addition, Burgess pointed out that revisionist articles tended to appear in periodicals published by Bungei shunjū, whereas refutations of the revisionist position were more likely to appear in newspapers and journals published by *Asahi shinbun*.[18] Burgess's article was not entirely accurate because it failed to recognize that Tanaka and his supporters had continually challenged the narratives of victors' justice since 1952. Nevertheless, his article represented the two opposing camps with little bias and gave much-deserved credit to historians who had been fighting against the revisionist position for more than a decade.

In the latter part of the year 1985, Nakasone's controversial visit to Yasukuni Shrine, China's celebration of the fortieth anniversary of the victory of the Anti-Japanese War, and the fortieth anniversary of Hiroshima and Nagasaki gave rise to articles in American newspapers that illuminated Japanese remembrance of the Asia-Pacific War. Some of these articles were as illuminating and informative as Burgess' article, among them that of James Reston Jr., "How Japan Teaches Its Own History," in the *New York Times*.[19] In the article, Reston detailed intense disputes in Japan over how to teach Japan's wartime history as well as problems with so-called peace education in Japan.

In order to understand the disputes, Reston interviewed a number of teachers, writers, and government officials. He discussed Kobayashi Kunio, a professor in Hiroshima, who emphasized Japan's role as a victimizer in his lectures and who took students to Nanjing in order to visit a historical site where 10,000 Chinese had reportedly been slaughtered. Reston also cited the views of Satō Teiichi, the former head of the textbook division at the Ministry of Education, who expressed his frustration with Chinese and Korean protests over the textbooks as well as the revisions made after the protests.[20]

In addition, Reston pointed out that many Japanese students had virtually no notion of how their country became involved in the Asia-Pacific War, the names of the leaders responsible for the war, or whether Japan's cause was righteous or not. Yet he also underlined a general, intuitive repugnance toward war among the students and many others, an attitude that existed regardless of the lack of understanding of the causes of war. Reston cited a social psychologist at Keiō University who argued that platitudes like "war must never happen again" would quickly fade from a student's memory unless they were reinforced by a factual understanding of the causes of war. Reston observed that many high-school students were not being taught the details of wartime history such as the Nanjing Massacre, Pearl Harbor, the colonization of Korea, and the atomic bombings. He also pointed out that government officials would prefer students to remember the roots of Japan's modernization (or history of early modern Japan) rather than Japan's wartime aggression abroad and devastation at home. Even when these topics were covered, Reston indicated, students tended to learn about them as if they had been natural disasters that no one could be blamed for failing to anticipate and avoid. Moreover, Japan's peace education had tended to focus on devastations in Japan without supplying much historical context.[21]

Departing from Burgess's and Reston's analytical approaches, James Bailey, a freelance writer based in Tokyo, wrote a more cynical and one-sided report on Japanese society based on the war films released between 1981 and 1985. Examining eight war films from this period, such as *The Harp of Burma* (Biruma no tategoto), *The Burning of a Zero Fighter* (Zerosen moyu), and *The Great Empire of Japan* (Dai-Nippon teikoku), Bailey concluded that these films presented Japanese soldiers and civilians during the war years as misunderstood victims. He claimed that Japan's "cultural uniqueness, reinforced by centuries of isolation . . . contributed to a widespread feeling [among Japanese] that they [were] easily misunderstood by the outside world." While his observations possessed some merit, Bailey weakened his own credibility by rather hastily dismissing films whose messages did not fit his thesis. For example, although he admitted that two of the films he addressed—*The Unfinished Game of Go* (Mikan no taikyoku) and *Welcome to Shanghai* (Shanhai Bansukingu)—condemned Japan's wartime actions, Bailey speculated that the producers had adopted this perspective in order to get permission from the Chinese government to shoot the films in China.[22]

Similarly, on December 7, 1985, Susan Chira of the *New York Times* stressed the prevalence of victim consciousness and the general ignorance of wartime history among most Japanese. Focusing on Japan's fortieth-anniversary commemorations of the end of the war, Chira complained that the only notes of mourning had been sounded for Japanese soldiers killed in battle. Apparently unaware of the fierce historical debates within Japan, Chira also claimed that, during the anniversary, there was little public discussion of Japan's role as a victimizer. Drawing on the arguments of scholars such as Takeda Kiyoko, a professor of Japanese intellectual and social history at International Christian University, Chira concluded that "Japanese tend to forget the past" and that Pearl Harbor as well as other wartime history did not mean much to most Japanese.[23]

In the view of a number of veterans and their supporters, it was ordinary Americans who had forgotten the significance of Pearl Harbor. A. J. Smith, a reader of the *San Diego Union-Tribune*, blamed American mass media for failing to give decent coverage to the anniversary of Japan's attack. On the op-ed page on December 16, 1985, Smith wondered why the media published few special reports on Pearl Harbor and interviews with survivors of the attack.[24] Nearly four months earlier, similar views appeared in the same paper. Frank Peters wrote:

> I am awfully tired of having the ultra-liberal element in this country beat me over the head with Hiroshima and Nagasaki.
> They ignore the fact that Japan started that war with a sneak attack

on Pearl Harbor that left several thousand Americans dead. They also ignore the millions of Chinese killed by the Japanese, the slaughter of thousands of Filipinos and the destruction of Manila on the approach of MacArthur, to name only a handful of the hundreds of atrocities committed by the Japanese.

Do the churches that memorialize the bombing of Hiroshima also memorialize the Rape of Nanking, the slaughter of the Filipinos and the deaths of the Americans at Pearl Harbor? If not, they are hypocrites.[25]

Likewise, Stan Steenbock, a WWII veteran who was disappointed with the lack of media coverage on the anniversary of V-J Day, voiced his annoyance in an op-ed in the *Los Angeles Times* on August 24, 1985. Steenbock had spent an hour examining every item in the principal news sections of the paper, and he found only a brief description of the coming ceremonies to mark the fortieth anniversary of Japan's surrender. He asked:

> After the reams of copy that only a few days previously had agonizingly, and in many cases accompanied by abject wringing of hands, analyzed Harry Truman's decision to drop atomic bombs on Hiroshima and Nagasaki 40 years ago, why could not there have been space for one story on the anniversary of the final chapter of history's bloodiest war? Have we become ashamed of our triumph, uneasy about calling attention to it? . . .
>
> I wonder what I could possibly say tonight to those who sleep in poncho shrouds on some forgotten island or lie entombed in the rusting hulk of the Arizona beneath the sparkling waters of Pearl Harbor?
>
> Could I face those with whom I had shared the long convoys, the K and C rations, the wrath of the enemy, the loneliness and separation from what we loved and knew best? How could they be told that 40 years after the victory they had helped win by freely spending the gift of life, their sacrifice had become virtually a non-event in the judgment of some of the nation's most influential media?[26]

Although it is difficult to state which event was most frequently mentioned in American media, the anniversary journalism of 1985 certainly reminded readers and viewers of such historical events as Pearl Harbor, the Nanjing Massacre, and Hiroshima and Nagasaki. As often highlighted in the op-ed articles, the central issue at stake was a question of national identity. In any case, from the early 1980s on, the mass media provided a diverse American public with ample occasion to consider whose history and memory it needed to remember.

DELETIONS AND DENUNCIATIONS: AMERICAN OPINION IN THE LATE 1980S

In the latter half of the 1980s, as Japanese mass media chronicled the debates over public memory of the war, American newspapers had many opportunities to highlight the views and frustrations of senior LDP politicians, college professors, and critics in Japan. On June 23, 1986, Daniel Sneider of the *Christian Science Monitor* reported Chinese and South Korean protests over the Japanese high school history textbook titled *New Edition of Japanese History* (Shinpen Nihonshi), written by the National People's Council to Defend Japan (Nihon o mamoru kokumin kaigi), an organization led by Kase Toshikazu, a former ambassador to the United Nations, and Mayuzumi Toshirō, a renowned classical composer. Founded in 1981, the council called for the revision of Japan's Peace Constitution as well as the restoration of the emperor as the formal head of state. Inspired by the 1982 textbook controversy, the group decided to write its own textbook. Its writers included Kobori Keiichirō, a professor of comparative literature at Tokyo University who later wrote the foreword for Tanaka Masaaki's *An Outline of the Nanjing Incident: Fifteen Grounds for the Denial of the Massacre* (1987). In the article, Sneider cited Mayuzumi's view that Japanese public schools did not teach patriotism at all and that the Pacific War was not a war of aggression.[27]

On June 4, the Chinese government officially protested the Japanese government's approval of the textbook, which asserted that the atrocities in Nanjing were still under debate.[28] Responding to the protests, Prime Minister Nakasone Yasuhiro ordered a review of the textbook even though the ministry had already approved it in principle. As a result, the textbook writers had to make another revision, deleting, among other things, the sentences indicating the event was still under debate.[29]

To Clyde Haberman, a *New York Times* correspondent, this 1986 textbook controversy was another instance of attempts by the Ministry of Education to minimize or gloss over Japan's wartime history. Haberman seemed to assume that the council's textbook was typical of history textbooks in Japan and represented the opinions of the dominant majority of society. Emphasizing that the council's textbook played down Japan's wartime atrocities such as the Nanjing Massacre, Haberman inferred that most Japanese "assumed no moral blame for their country's expansion across Asia in the 1930s."[30] To support his view, he again referred to Takeda Kiyoko of International Christian University, who alleged that Japanese were predisposed to forget their history.[31] When Nakasone Yasuhiro fired Education Minister Fujio Masayuki in September 1986 for his remarks about the legitimacy of Japan's colonization of Korea and dismissal of the Nanjing Massacre, Haberman presumed that Fujio and other conservative LDP politicians' views were typical of Japanese thinking, which he assumed was reflected not only in the council's textbook, but in all others as well.[32]

Sam Jameson, a *Los Angeles Times* correspondent, saw the controversy differently. Probably because he disliked "leftists" as much as the members of the council did, Jameson was at least aware of Fujio and the council's motivations: that is, to respond to "leftists who seek to emphasize the brutality of Japan's militarists and the evils of the capitalist system that they [leftists] say produced it." He argued that the ministry was trying to steer a middle course through the ongoing controversy. In 1982, the ministry had tried to tone down history textbooks "written by authors with a Marxist point of view who attempted to play up Japan's military brutality and aggression." In the case of 1986, however, the ministry instructed the council's textbook "to insert harsher language about

Japan's war role." He insisted that *New Edition of Japanese History* was the first since the end of the war written by "a self-avowed conservative group" and that it was only one of 127 textbooks inspected for use in all subjects in high school in 1987. Citing the opinion of Edwin Reischauer, a professor of Japanese history at Harvard University, Jameson stressed that both education and textbooks had been dominated by Marxists and that Marxist philosophy pervaded "the thinking of the Japanese." Although he conceded that the council's textbook offered too many justifications for aggression, Jameson found the final version of the council's textbook "reasonably objective" in general and "far more objective toward the United States" compared with the views stated in the existing "Marxist" textbooks.[33]

The council set a sales goal of 50,000 copies of the *New Edition*. Once this goal was achieved, the council planned to produce junior high and elementary school textbooks with similar ideological overtones.[34] But sales fell drastically short of the council's expectations, as only 31 of the 5,508 private and public high schools in Japan adopted the text in 1987.[35] The book was by all measures a failure, not only selling poorly but also provoking members of teachers' groups such as the Association for History Educators to widely denounce its "alarming contents" (*kiken na naiyō*) in their communities.[36]

Although 1987 marked the fiftieth anniversary of the Nanjing Massacre, major newspapers in the United States took scant notice of the event. Only the *New York Times* acknowledged it, covering an memorial exhibition of paintings and photographs of the Nanjing Massacre in New York, organized by the newly founded Chinese Alliance for Memorial and Justice. Sam Chen, the organizer of the exhibition, told the reporter of his frustration with the Japanese government, which, in his view, had adopted a more self-justifying attitude in the last few years, as indicated by the textbook controversies. Sixty-four artists who had immigrated to the United States from China, Taiwan, Hong Kong, or Singapore contributed work to the exhibition. C. J. Yao, for example, submitted a painting in hopes that the younger generation would not forget the Nanjing Massacre.[37] Joseph Policano, in a letter to the editor of the *New York Times*, shared a view similar to Yao's. Policano lamented that few commemorative pieces on the massacre had appeared in the press and stressed that the memory of the Nanjing Massacre must be kept alive.[38]

In January 1988, however, the Nanjing Massacre received renewed attention in the American press, reminding American correspondents both of the textbook controversies and of Fujio's denial of the massacre. The Japanese distributor Shōchiku Fuji Co. edited Bernardo Bertolucci's *The Last Emperor* without the director's permission, deleting 30 seconds of newsreel footage depicting Japanese atrocities in Nanjing. Haberman wrote in the *Times* that the deletion was "only the latest incident of many over the years in which the Japanese [had] demonstrated difficulty in coming to grips with the past." In the article, Haberman again alluded to the textbook controversies and the hawkish politicians of the Japanese right wing in order to support his black-and-white viewpoint.[39]

Other correspondents, such as Margaret Shapiro of the *Washington Post*, reminded their readers of the 1982 textbook controversy as well as of the statement of Fujio Masayuki.[40] For their part, the *Los Angeles Times* editorial writers were less sympathetic to Japan's revisions of public record than Jameson had been a year earlier. Commenting on the removal of the newsreel footage from *The Last Emperor*, these editors observed: "Twice in the last six years major controversies have arisen over the rewriting of Japanese textbooks in such a way as to weaken and make ambiguous what until recently had been largely straightforward accounts of World War II and its antecedents."[41]

Another news story in 1988 prompted correspondents to highlight disputes over the memory of the Asia-Pacific War in Japan. In April and May, Okuno Seisuke, director general of Japan's National Land Agency, made a series of candid public declarations that Japan was by no means the aggressor nation in World War II.[42] Okuno first attracted attention to his views at a news conference on April 22, shortly after he visited the controversial Yasukuni Shrine. He urged his fellow politicians not to blindly accept Deng Xiaoping's criticism of Japan's leaders for visiting the shrine.[43] On May 9 and 10, during parliamentary debates, he continued to legitimize Japan's wartime expansion and denounce the Tokyo War Crimes Trial as victors' justice.[44] Okuno, like Fujio Masayuki, preferred rather to give up his political career than to withdraw his controversial statements. On May 13, Prime Minister Takeshita Noboru accepted Okuno's resignation.[45] Nevertheless, the American press hardly questioned why Okuno continued to make provocative statements that would likely cost him his position in the government.

CONCLUSION

Because of the U.S.-Chinese normalization in 1979 and the increasing concern with justifying America's wartime experience, the Nanjing atrocities were frequently referenced in news articles and op-ed articles in the 1980s. Early in the decade, American media coverage of the controversies over war memories was more likely to recognize at least two sides to the debate inside Japan, but over time American media tended to publicize only revisionist efforts to excuse or conceal the actions of the Japanese military. Although the increasing awareness of wartime atrocities within Japan was provoking fierce reaction from those who cherished memories of Imperial Japan, it was this reaction, not the increased sensitivity that had triggered it, that drew attention from American media. It should also be noted that the increased attention to Nanjing came principally from media sources and that those who responded to these reports were mainly immigrants from Asia and their children. As a matter of public discourse in the United States, the Nanjing Massacre remained dormant. When the subject of Nanjing did arise, it was more likely subservient to an argument concerned with national pride. During this period, a number of Chinese and Korean Americans addressed the past with understandable zeal. In trying to publicize the memory of Japanese aggression, they were relying upon American reports that misrepresented the Japanese people as monolithic in their rejection of "victimizer consciousness," a reliance that may help to account for the vigor of their responses. They sought not only to reeducate Japanese observers as to the horrors of the Asia-Pacific War, but also to Americanize the history of the Japanese atrocities so that other Americans, too, would remember this long-neglected history.

IV

THE INTERNATIONALIZATION OF THE NANJING MASSACRE (1989 TO PRESENT)

10

Japan: A War over History and Memory

The end of the Cold War, Hirohito's death, the loss of conservative LDP dominance in domestic politics, the more inclusive textbook descriptions of Japanese wartime atrocities, and the growing awareness of wartime devastations in Asia and the Pacific caused by Imperial Japan all combined to heighten the intensity of the disputes over the Nanjing Massacre throughout the 1990s. In this decade, while public discussions of Japan's war responsibility became more animated, nationalistic narratives also flooded the market. The rift between the progressives and the revisionists remained insuperable. In simplified terms, Nanjing crystallizes a much larger conflict over what should constitute the ideal perception of the nation: Japan, as a nation, acknowledges its past and apologizes for its wartime wrongdoings; or Japan, as a nation, stands firm against foreign pressure and teaches Japanese youth about the benevolent and courageous martyrs who fought a just war to save Asia from the Western aggression. Both positions are, in their own way, an expression of national pride. However, the two factions differ intensely as to their means of defining terms like pride, honor, and shame. Some may feel that being forced to confront the memory of Nanjing stains their sense of national dignity. Others may feel with equal sincerity that they can be proud of the nation only if it candidly acknowledges even the worst episodes of its past.

THE END OF SHŌWA

Late at night on September 19, 1988, Emperor Hirohito vomited blood. From that moment, detailed reports on his health appeared daily in the mass media. Simultaneously, discussions of the emperor's war responsibility gradually appeared in the media. Public lectures and meetings on the Asia-Pacific War and the emperor's responsibility for it were held nationwide. On October 6, 1988, for example, the Group for Constitutional Study (Kenpō o manabu kai) convened a public symposium in Kanagawa on the emperor system.[1] On October 9, the Kyoto Committee against Strengthening the Emperor System (Tennōsei kyōka o yurusanai Kyōto jikkō iinkai), a group that comprised thirty citizens' organizations, met to denounce the mass media for trying to glorify Hirohito.[2] On October 10, Christians who feared that the emperor might once again become a focus of worship organized a meeting to discuss the coming imperial funeral and succession ceremonies and problems under the law.[3]

Between November 28 and December 3, Meiji Gakuin University, a private Protestant university in Tokyo, organized a series of symposia and lectures on issues of the emperor system and related matters. More than 60 faculty members participated in this special project, which included lectures on such topics as "The Emperor System and Japanese Capitalism," "The Emperor System and the Greater East Asian Co-prosperity Sphere," and "China and the Emperor System." Morii Makoto, who was the president of Meiji Gakuin University and had served in the military for two years, emphasized that emperor worship before and during the war had led to the decimation of Asian peoples and strongly objected to the latter-day attempt to mobilize emperor worship. One of the objectives of the weeklong series of special lectures was to discourage a potentially dangerous form of nostalgic romanticism. It was feared that, if people romanticized their memories of Hirohito the person, they were likely to forget the more sobering aspects of the aggression that had been waged in Hirohito's name.[4]

The emperor's war responsibility became a topic of debate in political assemblies as well. Members of the Communist Party often raised the issue. Suzuki Shun'ichi, the governor of Tokyo, came under sharp criticism after delivering a keynote address to the municipal assembly on September 28 in which he stated that he had signed his name to Hirohito's get-well register on behalf of the people of Tokyo. A Communist member of the assembly condemned him for the remark and asked the governor what he thought of bereaved family members who had lost their loved ones in the war fought in the emperor's name. Liberal Democratic Party (LDP) members charged that the question was inappropriate and demanded its withdrawal, and the assembly was forced to adjourn for a few hours.[5]

On December 7, responding to a question regarding Hirohito's responsibility for the war, Motoshima Hitoshi, mayor of Nagasaki, answered:

> Forty-three years after the war, I believe that [I have] reflected enough on the war. Based on the readings of various foreign accounts, Japanese accounts by historians, and my own experience in the military as a teacher [of military science at the military academy], I think that Hirohito was responsible for the war.
>
> However, it was the will of the majority of Japanese, as well as the choice of the Allied Powers, to evade [the issue of Hirohito's war responsibility], and [Hirohito] became a symbol of the new Constitution. Therefore, I understand that we must accept this choice.[6]

At the press conference on the same day, Motoshima further stressed that if the emperor had decided to surrender earlier than he actually did, neither the bloodshed in Okinawa nor the atomic bombings of Hiroshima and Nagasaki would have occurred. For 20 years, Motoshima had served in the prefectural assembly as a member of the LDP and, after being elected mayor of Nagasaki, became an advisor (komon) to the LDP members of the prefectural assembly in that city. Although some LDP assemblymen tried to persuade him to withdraw his statement, Motoshima refused, insisting that he had merely stated his personal belief.[7]

Although Motoshima endured harassments and intimidation from those who disagreed with him, he also earned a great deal of support from people and organizations. The Historical Science Society of Japan (Rekishigaku kenkyūkai) sent a letter to Motoshima, endorsing his view of Hirohito's war responsibility.[8] Many peace activists and survivors of the atomic bomb in Nagasaki also supported his statement.[9] More than 380,000 nationwide signed their names to a manifesto supporting Motoshima's understanding of Hirohito and his responsibility for the war. Some even sent history books to Motoshima to assist him in further investigations. Through reading these books, Motoshima learned more about Japan's wartime atrocities in China, Korea, Singapore, and other Asian nations. He first learned that those who were suffering in Asia regarded the atomic attacks as a relief sent from God. Motoshima's belief seems to be summarized in the concluding sentences of his Statement of the Mayor of Nagasaki (Nagasaki shichō no kotoba): "[We] must not see Japanese only as victims. [Japanese were] perpetrators; therefore, they suffered. Men in power forced Japanese to bear the burdens of victim and victimizer."[10] Motoshima was later shot by an assailant angered by his remarks on Hirohito's war responsibility.[11] Nonetheless, even after the assassination attempt, he continued to espouse his belief that the emperor bore responsibility for the war and that Imperial Japan caused immense suffering in Asia.[12]

On January 7, 1989, Hirohito died, and the period of Shōwa officially ended. But discussions of the war, including Hirohito's responsibility, continued in the media after his death. On the following day, the Asahi printed interviews with politicians, academics, and writers. Although most of the interviewees expressed their regrets at Hirohito's passing, Miyamoto Kenji, chair of the Communist Party, emphasized that Hirohito should have been criticized even during his illness. For his part, Akira Iriye, a professor at Harvard University, urged the public to use the emperor's death as an occasion to debate the issues of war responsibility and the future of the emperor system.[13]

In fact, citizens' groups continued to organize public meetings and lectures in order to discuss issues like the Shōwa emperor's war responsibility and Japanese wartime atrocities in Asia. In the week prior to Hirohito's funeral alone, 12 public protest meetings were organized in the Tokyo area.[14] These meetings were quite small in comparison to the crowds, some larger than 200,000, who lined the streets to witness the funeral procession on February 24.[15] Whether people agreed or disagreed about Hirohito's moral or legal responsibility for the war, the emperor's illness and his death stimulated discussions over his role in the war and his responsibility.

CHANGES IN NATIONAL POLITICS:
THE HOSOKAWA REVOLUTION AND
VICTIMIZER CONSCIOUSNESS

Another epochal moment that raised public consciousness over Japan's wartime past came in August 1993, when Hosokawa Morihiro became the first non-LDP prime minister since 1955. On August 10, 1993, responding to a question about his view of the "past war" (saki no sensō), Hosokawa answered that he himself understood it as an aggressive war (shinryaku sensō) and a morally wrong war (machigatta sensō).[16] Hosokawa did not specify whether he conceived of the "past war" as beginning in 1931 with the conquest of Manchuria, or in 1937 with the Marco Polo Bridge Incident. In either case, however, his statement was significant, since no LDP prime minister had ever fully recognized the war as an act of Japanese aggression. The parties of the coalition government he led agreed on the importance of fostering a new Japan, one whose desire not to repeat the past would inspire it to contribute to peace in Asia.[17]

On August 15, at a government-sponsored memorial service for the war dead, Hosokawa lamented not only the Japanese war dead but also, for the first time, the non-Japanese killed during the war.[18] In addition, Doi Takako, the Socialist Party Speaker of the House of Representatives, condemned the past war as an act of wrongdoing (ayamachi) in history and stressed that Japan had not yet accomplished an amicable settlement (wakai) with the peoples in Asia who had suffered during the conflict.[19] On August 23, at his inaugural address, Hosokawa again highlighted his willingness to see Japan become a responsible member of the international community:

> Forty-eight years [after Japan's surrender], Japan has now become one of the prime beneficiaries of world prosperity and peace. Yet we should never forget that this achievement rests upon the supreme sacrifices made during the war and is the result of the great efforts made by previous generations. I believe it is important at this juncture that we state clearly before all the world our remorse about our past history and our renewed determination to do better. I would thus like to take this opportunity to express anew our profound remorse and apologies for the fact that past Japanese actions, including aggression and colonial rule, caused unbearable suffering and sorrow for so many people and to state that we will demonstrate our new determination by contributing more than ever before to world peace.[20]

Debates concerning whether or not the past war was an act of aggression began to take place in the Diet. On October 4, 1993, at a meeting of the Budget Committee of the House of Representatives, Hashimoto Ryūtarō, a member of the LDP, denounced Hosokawa's view of the war. As chairman of the Association of Bereaved Families, Japan (Nihon izokukai), Hashimoto had received many angry letters from bereaved family members. He urged Hosokawa to listen to the voices of those who lost loved ones during the war. In addition, Hashimoto criticized Hosokawa for reopening issues that had already been resolved internationally.[21]

Etō Takami and Ishihara Shintarō, both LDP politicians, were more aggressive, blunt, and emotional. Speaking before the same budget committee, Etō first asked Hosokawa whether the Russian Army, which invaded Manchuria and the Northern Islands, committed atrocities against civilians, including women and children. When Hosokawa admitted that such violence probably took place, Etō urged Hosokawa to demand an apology from the Russian president. He also accused Hosokawa of being brainwashed by propaganda outlined by MacArthur and carried out by the Japan Teachers Union.[22] When Hosokawa urged Ishihara to remember that the war had also brought unbearable suffering to many people among the Allies, Ishihara declared that Hosokawa's opinions were ludicrous (*kokkei*) and masochistic (*mazohisutikku*), since they showed an inadequate regard for the Japanese who had also suffered horribly. Ishihara stressed that Japan had no obligation to apologize to other colonial powers since they had all been equally aggressive.[23]

Unfortunately for those who appreciated Hosokawa's comments and political ideals, the Hosokawa administration lasted less than a year. Hosokawa was forced to resign when it was learned that he had received an illegal political contribution from the Sagawa Express, an express carrier and package delivery company. Nevertheless, Murayama Tomiichi, the first Socialist prime minister (June 30, 1994–January 11, 1996) in 47 years, continued to follow the same path as Hosokawa despite consistent opposition from the Diet. On June 9, 1995, the House of Representatives adopted the Resolution to Renew Resolve for Peace Based on the Lessons of History (Rekishi o kyōkun ni heiwa e no ketsui o arata ni suru ketsugi).[24] Although the author of the resolution wished to transcend differences over historical views of the war, fewer than half the House members voted for the resolution. Members of the New Frontier Party (Shinshintō), a leading opposition party, boycotted the session because the ruling parties did not accept its proposed amendment, which would have added a pledge that "Japan would never again commit such deeds [aggression-like acts]," while deleting the passage that stressed the need to transcend "differences in historical views of the past war."[25] Communist Party lawmakers voted against the resolution because they thought that it excused Japan's past actions by likening its deeds to those of other powers.[26] Conservative politicians like Okuno Seisuke and his supporters, who believed Japan was neither an aggressor nor a colonizer, also boycotted the session.[27]

On August 15, 1995, the fiftieth anniversary of the end of the Asia-Pacific War, Murayama issued a statement expressing his "deep remorse" (*tsūsetsu na hansei*) and "heartfelt apology" (*kokoro kara no owabi*) for Japan's colonial rule and wartime aggression. He underscored the importance of educating young generations about "the horrors of the war" in order not to "repeat the errors of the past."[28] Murayama emphasized that a mistaken national policy had led Japan to the war and caused tremendous damage and suffering to people at home and abroad. He also urged that self-righteous nationalism in Japan be eliminated and that international cooperation be promoted instead.[29]

As they debated the motivations behind the war and argued over Japan's duty to apologize for the past, the Diet members acted out in microcosm the concerns of Japanese society as a whole during the 1990s, when diverse groups of different political persuasions flourished more than ever. Some stressed the importance of including Asian sufferings in Japanese wartime history, while others denounced such views and defended Japan's wartime behavior.

ACKNOWLEDGING RESPONSIBILITY THROUGH HISTORY

Between December 1991 and June 1995, Japanese lawyers initiated at least 27 lawsuits against the government and corporations to seek compensation for wartime atrocities and misconduct. Plaintiffs included former Dutch and British prisoners of war; Filipino and Korean women who had been forced into sex slavery by the military; non-Japanese slave laborers; and Korean soldiers who fought for Japan and were later convicted as Class B and C war criminals, but who were ignored by the Japanese government after the collapse of the empire.[30]

From August 1995 to September 1997, the Counsel in the Case for Awarding Compensation to Chinese War Victims (Chūgokujin sensō higai baishō seikyū jiken bengodan) filed lawsuits against the government and a number of private companies. More than 200 lawyers nationwide participated in the litigation. The plaintiffs included former "comfort women," survivors of massacres in Nanjing and Pindingshan, victims of indiscriminate bombings and medical experiments, and people injured long after the war by abandoned poison gas canisters. Their lawyers were all volunteers, many of whom conducted research in China at their own expense. Onodera Toshitaka, one of the attorneys, urged that acknowledgment of war responsibility and reparations for wartime damages were indispensable for Japanese to live harmoniously with the rest of the world in the twenty-first century.[31]

In order to support these lawsuits, the Society to Support the Demands of Chinese War Victims (Chūgokujin sensō higaisha no yōkyū o sasaeru kai) was founded in August 1995. Representative committee members included historians Fujiwara Akira and Ienaga Saburō and journalist Honda Katsuichi. The society published newsletters, invited plaintiffs to Japan, organized public meetings to hear plaintiffs' testimonies, and arranged pilgrimages to war memorial sites in China.[32] As of October 1998, the society had approximately 3,000 individual members and 200 group members, including corporations, unions, and other nongovernmental organizations.[33]

In April 1993, the Center for Research and Documentation on Japan's War Responsibility (Nihon no sensō sekinin shiryō sentā) was established. The center organized public lectures, sponsored research projects, and published a quarterly newsletter and journal. In a Statement of Purpose, published in the first issue of its quarterly journal, *The Report on Japan's War Responsibility* (Kikan sensō sekinin kenkyū), Arai Shin'ichi, representing the center, stressed that the center's goals were to research the truth and to clarify who owed what responsibility to whom. Arai also urged that settling issues of war responsibility and postwar compensation was a task not only for the government, but also for ordinary Japanese citizens.[34]

The *Report* provided up-to-date information and analysis on issues such as the Nanjing Massacre, Japan's chemical and biological warfare, military sex slavery, Japan's wartime atrocities in Southeast Asia, ongoing lawsuits demanding compensation, and war memorials and monuments. Contributors to the journal included not only leading scholars in various disciplines, but also lawyers, journalists, and peace activists.[35] In addition to the journal, the center published a newsletter, *Let's*, which informed readers of new publications, the dates of compensation trials and public meetings, and other announcements.

The 1990s witnessed the emergence of private and public museums that commemorated the suffering not only of Japanese, but of non-Japanese as well. Among them were the Osaka International Peace Center (Pīsu Ōsaka, opened in 1991); the Kyoto Museum for World Peace, Ritsumeikan University (Ritsumeikan daigaku kokusai heiwa myūjiamu, 1992); the Kawasaki Peace Museum (Kawasaki-shi heiwakan, 1992); the Peace Museum of Saitama (Saitama-ken heiwa shiryōkan, 1993); and Oka Masaharu Memorial Nagasaki Peace Museum (Oka Masaharu kinen Nagasaki heiwa shiryōkan, 1995). After their renovations in 1994 and 1996, respectively, both the Hiroshima Peace Memorial Museum and the Nagasaki Atomic Bomb Museum included exhibits acknowledging Japanese wartime atrocities in Asia.[36] The degree of emphasis given to Japan's wartime atrocities and aggression varied among the museums, but all shared the belief that the war must be narrated from perspectives more diverse than "victim consciousness."[37]

These exhibits of Japanese wartime atrocities in public museums sometimes provoked protests. For example, the Nagasaki Atomic Bomb Museum endured harsh criticism because it exhibited footage taken from an American wartime propaganda film to demonstrate horror of Japanese aggression. In April 1996, approximately 300 members of right-wing organizations, their trucks mounted with loudspeakers, gathered in Nagasaki to demand the removal of the entire installation, titled "The Japan-China War and the Pacific War," and the resignation of Mayor Itō Kazunaga, who had succeeded Motoshima Hitoshi. Not just extreme rightists, but also some locals who felt that attention to American atomic atrocities was being canceled out by the focus on Japanese atrocities, demanded that the section be closed. Nevertheless, supported by many of the city's residents who wanted a wide spectrum of perspectives to be acknowledged, the museum continued with the exhibit, although it did replace problematic photographs, captions, and video footage with less controversial substitutes.[38]

These museums hosted special exhibits, public lectures, and symposia. In January and February of 1993, for example, the Kyoto Museum for World Peace exhibited a series of large wall panels explaining the role of doctors in wartime Germany and Japan. This special exhibit received 2,601 visitors. On January 16, 1993, the museum organized a discussion group on the same topic, inviting both German and Japanese experts. Before an audience of 150 people, the panelists talked about such issues as medical experiments on human subjects and wartime studies of chemical and biological agents in Germany and Japan.[39] During two weeks in July, the museum exhibited paintings by Dutch prisoners of war, as well as these prisoners' personal belongings. Approximately 1,000 visitors saw this exhibit.[40] From July 22 to August 10, 1994, the museum offered a special display called "War and Children." 6,916 people came to this exhibit, which explored the lives of children under Japanese rule in Korea and Southeast Asia.[41]

This trend toward devoting more attention to Asian victims did not originate from the top down. Grass-roots citizens' groups nationwide organized special exhibitions on the Asia-Pacific War. For example, from July 1993 to December 1994, an exhibition on Unit 731 (731 *butaiten*), the biological warfare unit, toured the nation, attracting approximately 230,000 visitors in 18 months.[42] The exhibition borrowed some artifacts from the Unit 731 Memorial Museum in Harbin, China, and displayed 54 explanatory wall panels. Visitors were invited to try on reproductions of the shackles worn by the unit's "specimens," so that they might imagine what it was like to be human guinea pigs.[43] In August 1995, the War Exhibition for Peace 1995 (Heiwa no tame no sensōten 1995) went on display in Shibuya, Tokyo, and Japanese WWII veterans confessed to having committed war crimes in China.[44] From December 9 to 14, 1996, the Executive Committee of the Nanjing Massacre Art Exhibition (Nankin 1937 kaigaten jikkō iinkai) sponsored an art exhibition of the Nanjing Massacre, consisting of oils and watercolors painted by Chinese artists living in New York.[45]

Moreover, local historians and teachers published studies on the wartime experiences of people in their regions and catalogued local monuments and memorials.[46] The Association for History Educators, Gifu (Gifu-ken Rekishi kyōikusha kyōgikai) published *Cities and Towns Were "Battlefields," Too* (Machi mo mura mo "senjō" datta) in 1995.[47] Ikeda Ichirō and Suzuki Tetsuya explored war memorial sites in Kyoto and outlined their brief history. This study included the wartime facilities of the Twentieth Infantry Regiment, which participated in the atrocities in Nanjing.[48] The Association for History Educators, Mie (Mie-ken Rekishi kyōikusha kyōgikai) discussed its local history, including the history of the Thirty-Third Infantry Regiment, which had witnessed the Nanjing Massacre.[49] These local historians believed that exploring wartime history would shed light on aspects of local history, pointing toward the consciousness of a victim as well as that of a victimizer.

FROM REFUTATION TO EXAMINATION:
DEVELOPMENT OF THE STUDY OF
THE NANJING MASSACRE

In the early and mid-1990s, social and political contexts in Japan produced a highly favorable climate for progressive views on the massacre. As in the 1980s, members of the Research Committee on the Nanjing Incident (Nankin jiken chōsa kenkyūkai) published their studies with continued vigor. These members actively conducted research in China, Japan, and the United States. They published their new findings and sources on the massacre and used different approaches to examine the atrocities in Nanjing. In the 1980s, the work of the Research Committee had been primarily reactive, concerned above all with publishing refutations of the revisionists' claims. During the better part of the 1990s, the Research Committee took greater initiative in shaping the direction of the debate as it examined the event from various viewpoints.

A Collection of Historical Materials on the Nanjing Incident (Nankin jiken shiryōshū) was a two-volume source book on the massacre. Volume 1 included Japanese and American government documents and personal correspondence between American missionaries and their friends and families at home. It also featured articles from American newspapers and periodicals illustrating Japanese atrocities in Nanjing, as well as interviews with Tillman Durdin and Archibald Steele, correspondents for American newspapers who had reported on the Massacre from Nanjing.[50] Volume 2 transcribed reports of Chinese newspapers on the mainland and abroad regarding Japanese atrocities in Nanjing. This volume also contained burial records, survivors' testimonies, Nationalist government documents published in Taiwan during the war, and memoirs of the massacre that had previously appeared in Chinese publications such as *Historical Materials on the Nanjing Massacre Committed by the Japanese Army of Invasion* (Qin-Hua Rijun Nanjing datusha shiliao) and *Archival Materials on the Nanjing Massacre Committed by the Japanese Army of Invasion* (Qin-Hua Rijun Nanjing datusha dang'an).[51]

As Yoshida Yutaka, a Japanese historian, stressed in the foreword of Volume 1, previous works written by the members of the Research Committee had aimed mainly at refuting the denials of the massacre. By contrast, this document collection was an elaborate empirical and academic examination of the massacre. Yoshida underscored that these materials would enable readers to understand how foreigners at the time viewed Japanese aggression in China.[52] In a foreword to Volume 2, Inoue Hisashi, a Japanese scholar of Chinese history, emphasized the importance of subjecting available Chinese, Japanese, and English documents to comparative analysis. He urged readers not to dismiss the emotional testimonies and memoirs of Chinese survivors as exaggerated hearsay because these were part of the entire picture of the atrocities in Nanjing.[53]

In contrast, Kasahara Tokushi, another expert on Chinese history and a member of the Research Committee, invoked oral history in his *One Hundred*

Days in the Nanjing Safety Zone (Nankin nanminku no hyakunichi), in which he detailed the lives of people in Nanjing during Japan's attack and occupation. He consulted Chinese, Japanese, and English sources and narrated the event through the eyes of many different Japanese soldiers, Chinese refugees, and American missionaries. He not only depicted mental and physical sufferings of the people in Nanjing, but also discussed why ordinary Japanese men, with families back home, committed wholesale atrocities in Nanjing. He suggested three main causes of Japanese military violence against women: the general dehumanization of the Chinese; the moral despair that came with life on the battlefield; and the military's use of sex as a tool for managing the aggression of the soldiers. Kasahara implied that the lives of the soldiers, as well as those of the victimized women, had been cheapened and degraded by military superiors, who regarded their men as no more valuable than the other raw materials of war.[54] Kasahara was able to draw a richer and more complex picture of the massacre by combining his knowledge of the events with the practice of oral history.

In the afterword, Kasahara argued that the study of the massacre must not be dominated by disputes over the death toll. He stressed that a fuller understanding of the massacre would lead to a more accurate count of Chinese victims.[55] In 1997, Kasahara published *The Nanjing Incident* (Nankin jiken), in which he employed a different approach to understanding the Nanjing Massacre. In contrast to his earlier book, this study took a broader view of the massacre, arguing that it took place over a longer time and in a larger geographical space. He defined the "Nanjing Massacre" as including atrocities committed by the Japanese Army and Navy during both the battle of Nanjing and the ensuing occupation, namely from December 4, 1937, until March 28, 1938. And he included events not only within the walled city of Nanjing, but also in its six neighboring counties (Gaochun, Jiangning, Jiangpu, Jurong, Lishui, and Liuhe Xian), regions which, in Kasahara's view, had previously been neglected by scholars.[56]

Kasahara admitted that it was almost impossible to determine precisely how many Chinese civilians and military personnel were killed in and around Nanjing. But he denounced the revisionists for their wholesale dismissal of all Japanese atrocities simply because no agreement had been achieved about the death toll. Based on his research, Kasahara concluded that between 100,000 and 200,000 Chinese soldiers and civilians were killed in Nanjing and its six counties between December 4, 1937, and March 28, 1938. He estimated that approximately 80,000 out of the 150,000 Chinese soldiers and support personnel who defended Nanjing were killed during the battle and its aftermath.[57]

Another compilation, *The Imperial Soldiers Who Recorded the Nanjing Massacre* (Nankin daigyakusatsu o kiroku shita kōgun heishi tachi), provided field diaries written by soldiers of the Yamada Unit, which participated in the battle of Nanjing.[58] These diaries enabled readers to understand how ordinary men gradually became less concerned with moral restraints and found it progressively easier to loot rations and other valuables from local Chinese and to kill "the enemy" to avenge their comrades.[59] As time went by, many soldiers who kept diaries became accustomed to seeing human blood and to beheading Chinese.[60] In addition, the editors proved that careful examination of field diaries, which often included records of "military achievements" (that is, killings of Chinese soldiers and prisoners of war), would assist researchers in estimating more accurately the number of lives taken by the Japanese troops.[61]

One more important primary source on Nanjing, *The Diary of John Rabe: The Truth about Nanking* (Rābe nikki: Nankin no shinjitsu), was published in 1997.[62] Arai Shin'ichi, a historian and director of the Center for Research and Documentation on Japan's War Responsibility, found Rabe's diary significant in two respects: it not only recorded his observations of events in Nanjing, but also helped historians corroborate survivors' testimonies. Arai pointed out that the original diary included more than 20 photographs, including a picture of the young woman Li Xiuying, who was 19 at the time of the massacre and who was stabbed nearly 40 times by Japanese soldiers. In February 1997, Li testified in a lawsuit seeking government compensation for the attack. Arai explained that Li's allegations received independent confirmation from entries in Rabe's diary. In the eyes of Arai, the anecdotal evidence of Rabe's diary was a potent weapon for confronting the revisionists, who often attempted to discredit testimonies as hearsay.[63]

TEXTBOOKS IN THE 1990S

In the 1990s, the teaching of history placed increased emphasis on the importance of accepting responsibility for the nation's errors. This trend is evident in the history textbooks of the time, which tended to devote more space to Japan's wartime role as a perpetrator and to deemphasize the image of Japan as victim. This attitude was also evident in the descriptions of the Nanjing Massacre. Many textbooks now stated death tolls of more than 200,000. For example, Tōkyō shoseki's 1997 edition of a junior high school textbook, a book which accounted for more than 41 percent of the market, described the Nanjing Massacre as follows:

> On July 7, 1937, without a declaration of war, the Japan-China War began after an armed clash between the Japanese and the Chinese troops at the Marco Polo Bridge in a suburb of Beijing. The war expanded from North China to Central China. By the end of 1937, the Japanese military occupied the capital, Nanjing. At this time, the Japanese military killed as many as 200,000 Chinese, including women and children.[64]

Overall, six out of seven junior high school history textbooks available in 1997 estimated that between 100,000 and 200,000 Chinese were killed during and after the battle. Four of the seven also included the official Chinese estimate of 300,000 deaths. Authors discovered that, if they mentioned the figure but did not necessarily endorse it, the government would not withhold authorization. A common practice was to relegate the Chinese estimate to a footnote and to present the number more as a matter of opinion than as undisputed fact. For example, Ōsaka shoseki's history textbook for junior high schools, which boasted the second-largest market share, asserted in its main text that the massacre was an atrocity in which the Japanese military killed as many as 200,000, adding the Chinese estimate in a footnote.[65]

Compared with junior high school history textbooks, whose descriptions of the massacre varied little from publisher to publisher, those in high school history textbooks often differed substantially. Two of the most popular texts in use in 1994 explained the atrocities in very different tones. Yamakawa shuppan's *Detailed Japanese History* (Shōsetsu Nihonshi) simply mentioned in a footnote that "At this time [of occupation], the Japanese military killed large numbers of Chinese, including non-combatants, an incident which, after the defeat, became a major issue at the Tokyo Trial (the Nanjing Incident)."[66] Jikkyō shuppan's *Japanese History B* (Nihonshi B), published in 1994, offered more explicit language:

> During the occupation of Nanjing, the Japanese military killed large numbers of Chinese, including those who had surrendered and prisoners of war. The military engaged in looting, arson, and rape. This event received international denunciation as the Nanjing Massacre. The number of Chinese killed during the few weeks before and after the occupation, including combatants, totaled as many as *jūsūman* [130,000–150,000].[67]

In Jikkyō shuppan's *High School Japanese History B* (Kōkō Nihonshi B) and Hitotsubashi shuppan's *World History B* (Sekaishi B), the Nanjing Massacre was presented in greater detail.[68] The main text of the former described the massacre as follows:

> In December 1937, the Japanese army captured Nanjing, the capital of the Nationalist government. Within a few weeks after the fall of the city, the Japanese army killed *jūsūman* [130,000–150,000] Chinese, including prisoners of war, those who had surrendered, and women and children, in and around Nanjing. The army [also] committed looting, arson, and rape. Division Commander Nakajima [Kesago] wrote in his diary on December 13 that he was not going to have prisoners of war and that the Sasaki Unit alone "took care of" [shori] 15,000 Chinese. This incident was not reported in Japan. In Tokyo, Nagoya, and Osaka people celebrated the "fall of Nanjing" and participated in lantern parades. However [while Japanese were celebrating], in Europe and the United States, media such as *The New York Times* reported that "all prisoners were killed," and the incident (called the Nanjing Massacre) was internationally condemned.[69]

In a footnote, the textbook added that the event had been commemorated by the construction of the Nanjing Massacre Memorial Hall in Nanjing, where visitors could observe the remains of victims, as well as photographs of Japanese atrocities. Another footnote mentioned the Chinese estimate of deaths. Hitotsubashi's *World History B* included a section on the massacre written by Kasahara Tokushi. Although Kasahara did not refer to the number of the deaths in Nanjing, he highlighted that the Japanese army had rushed toward Nanjing despite its realization that it lacked sufficient rations to support the campaign. Instead, the army's leaders assumed that their troops would have to feed themselves by looting civilian properties for food. This looting was often accompanied by violence, frequently ending in the deaths of resisting Chinese.[70]

In the 1990s, progressives generally succeeded in including more details of the massacre in school textbooks, a fact that they regarded as a victory over their adversaries who had sought either to downplay or eliminate descriptions of Japan's wartime aggression. Yet the battle over history did not end here. Inclusive descriptions of Nanjing, as well as other Japanese atrocities, infuriated a number of conservative revisionists. To them, such approach was "masochistic" and completely at odds with their ideal Japanese national history, which glorified Japan's wartime sacrifices and achievements.

RESISTING "MASOCHISM": ADVOCATES OF JAPANESE HISTORY FOR "JAPANESE"

On August 23, 1993, outraged by Hosokawa's admissions of Japanese aggression, 105 LDP Diet members joined the Committee to Examine History (Rekishi kentō iinkai).[71] Between October 1993 and February 1995, the committee organized 20 meetings, inviting 19 revisionist speakers. They included Kobori Keiichirō, a professor of comparative literature at Tokyo University; Tanaka Masaaki, a social critic; Satō Kazuo, a professor of international law at Aoyama Gakuin University; and Hasegawa Michiko, a professor of philosophy at Saitama University, all of whom condemned the Tokyo Trial and justified Japan's wartime expansion. The head of the committee, Yamanaka Sadanori, declared that the organization's goal was to absolve the war dead of disgrace and to teach the correct historical view to other Diet members.[72]

Although the leaders of the LDP supported the Diet Resolution of 1995, they were unable to maintain consensus in their ranks. On December 1, 1994, 212 LDP Diet members broke ranks with their leaders and organized the Diet Members' League for the Fiftieth Anniversary of the End of the War (Shūsen gojū shūnen kokkai giin renmei).[73] Okuno Seisuke became the head of the league, whose declared goal was to revise the "masochistic understanding" of wartime and prewar Japanese history "initiated by the American occupation policy as well as left-wing forces in Japan."[74] Similarly, on February 21, 1995, 41 members of the New Frontier Party (Shinshintō) defied the wishes of their leaders by founding Diet Members for the Transmission of a Correct History (Tadashii Rekishi o tsutaeru kokkai giin renmei), under the leadership of Ozawa Tatsuo. Like Okuno's league, Ozawa's faction aimed at blocking the resolution.[75] Members of these two leagues included politicians such as Fujio Masayuki, Nagano Shigeto, Shimamura Yoshinobu, and Etō Takami, all of whom had openly denied or would later deny Japan's responsibility for the war during their tenure as cabinet ministers. Facing the unprecedented surge of movements to acknowledge Japan's war responsibility, it was perfectly understandable that these conservative politicians joined ranks to battle what they regarded as outrageous nonsense.

In March 1995, encouraged by these conservative movements, the National People's Council to Defend Japan (Nihon o mamoru kokumin kaigi), the Japan Association of Bereaved Families (Nihon izokukai), and others formed the National Committee for the Fiftieth Anniversary of the End of World War II.[76] Kase Toshikazu and Mayuzumi Toshirō, who had advocated the restoration of the emperor as the head of the state, became president and vice president of the committee. Between September 1993 and May 1995, the participating organizations mounted a nationwide petitioning effort and collected more than 5 million signatures opposing the 1995 Diet resolution.[77]

On May 29, 1995, the committee hosted "A Celebration of Asian Nations' Symbiosis" (Ajia kyōsei no saiten) at the Japan Hall of Martial Arts. Participating in the gathering of approximately 10,000 people were representatives of Bangladesh, Bhutan, Cambodia, Taiwan, India, Indonesia, Laos, Malaysia, Myanmar, Nepal, Sri Lanka, Thailand, and Tibet. On hand to express their gratitude for Imperial Japan's contribution to Asian independence from the Western rule were speakers Thanat Khoman, former deputy prime minister and foreign minister of the Thailand; Syed Hussein Alatas, vice chancellor of the National University of Malaya; and Sayidiman Suryohadiprojo, ambassador at large to Africa from Indonesia. Kase, Mayuzumi, and Okuno all emphasized the importance of Asian unity and Japan's wartime contributions in greater Asia, as well as denouncing the 1995 Diet resolution.[78] The committee did not invite any of the victims of Japan's wartime aggression. Rather, the celebration's guest list featured a number of those who endorsed a conservative historical narrative; they believed that Imperial Japan had contributed to liberating East Asia from Western colonialism. Essentially, the celebration was a gathering of Asian social and political elites, many of whom did not remember Japanese wartime occupation as being particularly dreadful, and some of whom may even have benefited from the Japanese presence.

The year 1995 marked the emergence of another revisionist group that received significant attention from the media. In January 1995, about four months before the celebration at the Japan Hall of Martial Arts, Fujioka Nobukatsu, a professor of education at Tokyo University, founded the Association for the Advancement of a Liberalist View of History (Jiyūshugi shikan kenkyūkai).[79] In December 1996, Fujioka and his supporters, such as Nishio Kanji, professor at University of Electro-Communications, and Kobayashi Yoshinori, a popular cartoonist, formed the Japanese Society for History Textbook Reform (Atarashii rekishi kyōkasho o tsukuru kai) to eliminate "masochistic historical views" as well as to contribute to a renewed formation of national identity among "Japanese."[80] Although these organizations used terms like "liberalist" and "reform" to characterize their agendas, their objectives were very much similar, if not identical, to Kase and Mayuzumi's National People's Council to Defend Japan as well as Okuno's and Ozawa's leagues of Diet members.

These advocates who attempted to minimize, if not whitewash, Japan's wartime atrocities repelled those whose ideal was to integrate the suffering of other countries into Japanese history. Fujioka and his colleagues condemned peace museums for being masochistic. In their view, other instances of self-abasement included the descriptions of "comfort women" in junior high school textbooks and other criticisms of Japan's wartime actions. Predictably, as Fujioka and others like him strove to propagate their own ideal concept of Japanese history, the Nanjing Massacre became a target once again.

DENIALS OF THE NANJING MASSACRE
IN THE 1990S

As in the previous decades, denials of Nanjing continued. Though little changed among those who had already denied the Nanjing Massacre in their writings and speeches, the second half of the 1990s saw the emergence of new proponents of this view. Whether new or old, they all denounced as impossible the alleged killing of 200,000–300,000 civilians after the fall of the city. They insisted that the Nanjing Massacre, as it had come to be understood in the public imagination, did not exist in reality. In an interview conducted for the October 1990 issue of *Playboy* magazine, the politician Ishihara Shintarō discussed his controversial book *The Japan That Can Say "No"* (1989), coauthored with Morita Akio, the cofounder of SONY. Amid his discussion of a range of other issues such as racism, Lee Iacocca, and the nuclear attacks on Hiroshima and Nagasaki, Ishihara told the interviewer that stories of Japanese atrocities in Nanjing, collectively known as the Nanjing Massacre, were lies fabricated by Chinese for propaganda purposes.[81] This claim sparked the publication of *The Japan That Can Still Say "No"* (1990), which Ishihara coauthored with Watanabe Shōichi, a professor at Sophia University already known for his denial of Nanjing. In the book, Watanabe reiterated his view that atrocities in Nanjing were not uniquely cruel in world history and that the death toll had been inflated by wartime propaganda in the United States. Responding to the international climate of the late 1980s, Watanabe insisted that the practice of Japan bashing had arisen from racialist misunderstandings. Because Americans believed Japanese were innately reckless and predisposed toward cruelty, they imagined that the Japanese were capable of committing the Nanjing Massacre.[82]

In April 1993, Hashimoto Mitsuji sued Azuma Shirō, Shimozato Masaki, and their publisher, Aoki shoten, on grounds of libel. Azuma was the author of *My Platoon in Nanjing: A Conscript Soldier's Experience in the Nanjing Massacre*, from which Shimozato had taken excerpts for inclusion in his own work on the Nanjing Massacre.[83] Although Azuma did not use Hashimoto's real name, his book contained an episode in which a soldier, identifiable as Hashimoto, threw a Chinese person into a mail bag. The soldier then allegedly doused the bag with gasoline and set it on fire. Then, according to Azuma, as the Chinese man writhed inside the burning bag, the soldier attached two hand grenades to the bag, activated them, carried the bag to a pond, and threw it in. Hashimoto insisted that he did not do these things, pointing out that the details of the story were absurd and illogical. Azuma, for his part, could not explain to the court how Hashimoto had obtained and carried gasoline from a car (whether he had used a bucket or pump); how long the bag was burning; and how Hashimoto was able to tie two hand grenades to the flaming, writhing bag. Another mystery was how Hashimoto could have carried the still-burning bag and disposed of it in the seconds before the grenades would have detonated. Though the Tokyo District Court firmly stated that its aim was not to challenge the historical fact of the Nanjing Massacre, the judge ruled against Azuma on April 26, 1996. Itakura Yoshiaki, who initiated the trial, wrote a triumphant two-page article about the lawsuit and falsely claimed that the court had ruled that the entire portion of Azuma's book was a fabrication.[84] Although Azuma, Shimozato, and Aoki shoten appealed, they again lost the case.

On May 5, 1994, the *Mainichi* newspaper published an interview with the new justice minister in the Hata administration (April 28–June 25, 1994). Justice Minister Nagano Shigeto, a WWII veteran, told the reporter of his views of the Asia-Pacific War, claiming that Japan's goal was to liberate Asian colonies and that its objectives were legitimate from the viewpoint of the time. He also commented that he regarded the so-called Nanjing Massacre as a mere fabrication.[85] Facing both domestic and international protests, he withdrew his statements the next day and apologized for his remarks, which he described as careless. Asked for his opinion on the Nanjing Massacre, Nagano answered that he would not deny that atrocities took place in Nanjing and asserted that Japan had to apologize to the Chinese.[86] He resigned the following day.

On May 10, 1994, before an audience of LDP Diet members of the Committee to Examine History (Rekishi kentō iinkai), the 83–year-old Tanaka Masaaki gave a talk titled "The Fabrication of the 'Nanjing Massacre.'" Tanaka reiterated his long-held view that the massacre, as described by progressive commentators, never occurred. During the question-and-answer session, he expressed his profound regret that Nagano Shigeto had withdrawn his denial of the massacre. In addition, Tanaka urged his audience to oppose the forthcoming Diet Resolution, which would, in his view, permanently damage Imperial Japan in world history.[87]

As was his custom, Tanaka condemned postwar educators for demonizing Imperial Japan and "the great massacre faction" for their insistence that wholesale atrocities took place in Nanjing. Tanaka stated that killing enemy guerrillas, stragglers, and deserters was justified in war and thus would not fall within the category of "massacre." He emphasized that surrounding the enemy and annihilating them was the most efficient way to achieve military victory. In contrast, he strongly insisted that American atomic bombings and fire bombings, as well as the mass execution of Polish officers by the Russian army at

Katyn in the spring of 1943, were much more appropriately characterized as "massacres."[88]

In the mid-1990s, hard-line revisionists came together to found the Association for the Advancement of Liberalist View of History and its affiliated organizations. From that moment on, these revisionists, many of them now quite advanced in years, became the visible standard-bearers for the denial movement. Using every medium available, both old and new participants in the revisionist cause enthusiastically challenged the orthodoxy of Nanjing. In September 1995, in the first issue of Fujioka Nobukatsu's *Reforming Instruction in "Modern and Contemporary Japanese History"* ("Kingendaishi" no jugyō kaikaku), Itakura Yoshiaki, who identified himself as a Nanjing Massacre scholar, advanced the thesis that, in the six weeks that followed the fall of Nanjing, approximately 10,000–20,000 Chinese were killed in violation of international law. He argued that there had been no "Nanjing Massacre" as his opponents had described it because a mass murder of more than 200,000 never took place in Nanjing.[89]

In 1996, outraged by the figures of 200,000 and 300,000 mentioned in junior high school history textbooks, Fujioka denied the killing of ordinary citizens in Nanjing by the Japanese military. Instead of blaming the Japanese army, he condemned Chiang Kai-shek and his officers for deserting the city, a withdrawal that resulted in the pointless deaths of their own soldiers. Furthermore, Fujioka justified the Japanese killing of Chinese prisoners of war on the grounds that, by taking prisoners alive, the Japanese soldiers would have endangered their own lives. He claimed that the so-called Nanjing Massacre was a lie and that, by printing the baseless figures, the textbooks made themselves accomplices to a fabrication.[90]

After *The Diary of John Rabe* became available in 1997, Fukuda Kazuya, a self-proclaimed nationalist and a professor at Keiō University, urged young people to read the diary and to learn about Japanese atrocities in Nanjing, where he believed that the military killed some 50,000 Chinese. Fukuda argued that the youth must take seriously the fact that Japanese committed such atrocities in Nanjing. He insisted that the rising generation should not excuse the incident by asserting that war is always inhumane and that similar misdeeds are part of every nation's history. Moreover, it would do no good to blame the Chinese in Nanjing for their own sufferings. Even belated apologies for the army's misconduct did not put an end to Japan's responsibility. Instead, he emphasized, the youth must remember their discomfort in learning about the event and their anger with the soldiers in order to motivate themselves to understand why the people of Japan, who lived in a beautiful land and who had a long history and rich culture, committed such atrocities. In the eyes of Fukuda, a major reason for the Japanese military's atrocities was their loss of a strong sense of morality. Fukuda especially warned against the error of thinking of the Japanese army as a "they," safely sequestered in the past. Rather, the actions of the army were committed by a continuing, still-existing national "we." He stressed that "we" must accept responsibility for Japan's wartime misconduct in order to be proud of "our" national history and characteristics.[91]

Fukuda's reading of Rabe's diary disturbed Kobayashi Yoshinori, an author of the best-selling cartoon *On War* and a member of the Association for the Advancement of Liberalist View of History.[92] Kobayashi, who used his drawings to publicize his distinctive ideology, often appealed to readers by highlighting ethnic nationalism. In "Don't Read *The Truth about Nanjing* as You Did, Fukuda Kazuya!" Kobayashi ridiculed what he saw as Fukuda's blind, naive trust in Rabe's diary. Kobayashi insisted that although Rabe recorded Japanese atrocities in Nanjing, most of his reports were based on hearsay. Kobayashi also claimed that sexual contacts described by Rabe as rape could have been consensual acts of prostitution. From reading Rabe's diary, Kobayashi concluded that fewer than 10,000 Chinese civilians were killed outside combat. Thus, in his eyes, there was no Nanjing Massacre, as that phrase is typically understood. Kobayashi denounced Fukuda, who identified himself as a nationalist, for not dismissing the Chinese government's estimate of 300,000 deaths as a fabrication. To Kobayashi, Fukuda was merely another credulous Japanese brainwashed by the postwar democracy led by the Left.[93]

When critiquing a text that tends to confirm the reality of the massacre, revisionists often used a handful of identifiable textual errors to discredit the entire work. In this way, Iris Chang's *The Rape of Nanking* (1997), a work with numerous errors and inaccuracies, became an opportune target for the revisionists in their campaign to deny the massacre and to arouse ethnic nationalism among their audience. For example, Fujioka Nobukatsu, a founding member of the association, and Higashinakano Osamichi, a professor of intellectual history at Asia University, stressed that Chang's book contained nearly 170 errors, including chronological errors, misspelled names and inaccurate titles of Japanese officers, and incorrect explanations of military technology in the Tokugawa period. In addition, Fujioka and Higashinakano argued that Chang used photographs that had nothing to do with Nanjing in order to fabricate a dreadful image of the atrocities. They emphasized not only that Chang's book was flawed, but also that the Chinese assertion that 300,000 were slaughtered in Nanjing was a mere piece of anti-Japanese propaganda. In the eyes of Fujioka and Higashinakano, Chang's objective was to demonize the Japanese race, culture, history, and nation.[94]

This emotional and facile view was shared by other prominent revisionists such as Ishihara Shintarō and Kobayashi Yoshinori.[95] *Sankei shinbun*, a conservative newspaper, publicized errors and inaccuracies in Chang's book.[96] Popular magazines published special reports, including a feature in *Sapio*, a biweekly magazine, titled "Plotting 'The Nanjing Massacre' Campaign" (Bōryaku no 'Nankin daigyakusatsu' kyanpēn). Arguing that the Chinese government was using the Nanjing Massacre as a political tool, *Sapio* offered its report as an attempt to "analyze the massacre from various perspectives in the intelligence war."[97]

In February 1998, stirred into action by the publication of *The Rape of Nanking* and its uncritical use of wartime photographs, the association held the first meeting of the Study Group on Propaganda Photographs (Puropaganda shashin kenkyūkai), whose objective was to examine "masochistic" photographs, videos, and other visual materials, including those treating the Nanjing Massacre.[98] Based on his findings, Matsuo Ichirō, who was in charge of the group, later wrote *Propaganda War, The "Nanjing Incident": The Truth of the "Nanjing Massacre" as Seen through Secret Photographs* (Puropaganda sen "Nankin jiken": Hiroku shashin de miru "Nankin daigyakusatsu" no shinjitsu).[99] In the same year, Higashinakano Osamichi published *"Nankin gyakusatsu" no tettei kenshō* (Solid Examination of the "Nanjing Massacre"), arguing that no one has been able to prove that 300,000 Chinese were killed in Nanjing in violation of international law. Thus, he concluded, there was no Nanjing Massacre as claimed by the Chinese government.[100]

When the publisher Kashiwa shobō abandoned plans to publish a Japanese translation of *The Rape of Nanking* in 1999, its decision further provoked the imaginations of the revisionists. In the eyes of Fujioka and Higashinakano, the publication of the Japanese version was a part of an international plot to demonize wartime Japan, with the cooperation of the Japanese Left. They expressed the rather self-congratulatory and inaccurate view that the Japanese Left had given up publishing the translation because they had successfully persuaded the public of the book's errors and inaccuracies. Fujioka and Higashinakano emphasized that the goal of the "masochistic faction" (*jigyakuha*) was to publicize the alleged atrocities in Nanjing; however, because of the successful campaign to expose the weaknesses of Chang's work, the "masochistic faction" had been forced to conclude that its efforts to achieve its goal would be impeded by the Japanese version. In order to save face, the two revisionists claimed, this "faction" had used the alleged rightist threat to rationalize the cancellation.[101]

This same year saw additional publications by the revisionist authors, all of whom supported the association's initiative. Suzuki Akira, a journalist who wrote *The Illusion of the "Nanjing Massacre"* in 1973, published a new edition of his earlier work. In the 1970s, Suzuki had stopped short of calling the massacre a fabrication. Now, however, he fiercely denounced the Nanjing Massacre as a piece of foreign-inspired propaganda, citing the manipulation of memory of Nanjing by the Chinese government and the political motivations of American and European accounts that highlighted Japanese atrocities in Nanjing.[102] Kitamura Minoru, a professor in modern Chinese history at Ritsumeikan University, stressed in his three-part serial article "An Introductory Study of the 'Nanjing Massacre'" ("Nankin daigyakusatsu" kenkyū josetsu) (1999–2000) that at the time of the Japanese takeover of Nanjing, no one reported Japanese killings of 300,000 Chinese civilians. Kitamura argued that Harold Timperley was a propaganda agent for the Nationalist government and that his writings very likely included exaggerations and deceptions.[103] In the eyes of Kitamura, the Chinese government and the Allied Powers invented the death estimate of 300,000 after the war in order to blame Japan for war crimes.[104]

In the late 1990s alone, numerous revisionist authors published books on Nanjing, challenging the previously accepted history of the massacre. Nevertheless, the vigorousness of their activity did not necessarily suggest either that they were winning the battle over public memory or that they had succeeded in silencing their adversaries. As the recent episodes discussed below will demonstrate, both sides have experienced gains and losses, and neither side will surrender unconditionally to its opponent in the foreseeable future.

A NANJING QUARTET: FOUR RECENT EPISODES IN AN ONGOING TALE

Episode I: *Pride* versus *Don't Cry, Nanjing*

The film *Pride: The Moment of Destiny* (Puraido: Unmei no toki; 1998) was produced to mark the thirtieth anniversary of the founding of Higashi Nihon House, a company that sells prefabricated housing units. Nakamura Isao, the founder of the company, believed that Japan had fallen under the control of politicians who had forsaken the interests of the nation. He also believed that the country's honor had been blackened by news and entertainment media, as well as by the authors of school textbooks. Born in 1936, Nakamura had read Tanaka Masaaki's *On Japan's Innocence: The Truth on Trial* (1952), when he was in high school and had been impressed by Judge Pal and his minority opinion at the Tokyo Trial. When he retired in 1994, he pursued his long-held goal of rectifying the national understanding of its past. In his view, Japan's existence was in danger because national history merely focused on the dark side.[105] It was no coincidence that members of the production committee for the movie *Pride* included Tanaka Masaaki and Fuji Nobuo, both of whom had argued that the Nanjing Massacre was a fabrication.

Tanaka's and Fuji's views of the Tokyo Trial were readily apparent in the 161-minute film. In the scene in which the defendant Ōkawa Shūmei slaps General Tōjō's bald head and is taken away from the court, he loudly denounces the tribunal as a travesty, screaming in English: "It's comedy." In reality, Ōkawa folded his hands, mumbled something incomprehensible, and slapped Tōjō's head. As he was being taken away, the mentally ill Ōkawa appeared semiconscious and was not able to speak coherently.[106] The film's treatment of the massacre also reflected the beliefs and wishful thinking of the members of the production committee. In the film, Tōjō criticizes his lawyer, Kiyose Ichirō, for his failure to refute the chief prosecutor's attempt to fabricate atrocities in Nanjing. As if to reiterate the points stressed by Tanaka in his work, Tōjō emphasizes that eyewitness accounts presented to the court are exaggerations, hearsay, or outright lies.[107] Tōjō urges Kiyose to do something, saying: "If you fail [to refute the prosecutor], it will leave a root of evil in Japan's future. Japan and the Japanese will be regarded as the most evil nation and race. If this happens, I shall have committed a blunder that our offspring will never forgive."[108]

The members of the production committee also borrowed other characters such as Justice William Webb, president of the tribunal, as mouthpieces for their views. In one scene, the chief prosecutor Joseph Keenan visits Justice Webb's hotel room in order to urge him to conclude the trial as soon as possible. Webb tells Keenan that the pace of the trial depends on the prosecutor's ability to present effective evidence. He complains that witnesses for the prosecution have been worthless, including those who have testified to the reality of the massacre. He urges Keenan to proffer more useful witnesses and evidence. Webb states contemptuously to Keenan: "It is my embarrassment at the world's bar and bench to be responsible for such a trial."[109]

The first Japanese film to portray Tōjō as a hero who fought against the Tokyo prosecution for the sake of Japan's national honor, *Pride* received considerable attention in Japan. Whether it changed a significant number of minds is unclear. For the most part, the film served to assure those who already agreed with its political message and to irritate those who rejected its viewpoint. In the eyes of Honda Katsuichi, the film was a fraud made by "traitors" who threatened to destroy Japanese pride completely.[110] Akazawa Shirō, a professor at Ritsumeikan University, presented various historical documents to show how the Tōjō depicted in the film differed from the actual man.[111] In contrast, Fujioka Nobukatsu, Nakamura Isao, Tanaka Masaaki, and other prominent revisionists praised the film and did their best to promote ticket sales. It was reported that Nakamura required his employees to buy 30 tickets each, and that Fujioka sent two discount coupons to each member of his organization.[112] Although not everyone necessarily agreed with its message, the film succeeded commercially.

In Japan, as elsewhere, a film that appeals to patriotism and nationalism seems much more likely to succeed commercially than does one that focuses on national shame. *Don't Cry, Nanking*, a 1995 film about the Nanjing Massacre directed by Wu Ziniu, was released in Japan at the same time that *Pride* was in national distribution. But Wu's film was unanimously shunned by Japan's major film companies, none of which was willing to risk controversy by purchasing the rights to the film. *Don't Cry, Nanking* might never have gained a wide audience had it not been for the efforts of 15 cinema proprietors, scholars, and other concerned individuals who pooled their resources to purchase the film's distribution rights in August 1997.[113] Activists established screening committees in each region of Japan and showed the film in small theaters and community halls. It was seen in Osaka by some 4,000 people in December 1997. In Nagoya, between December 6, 1997, and January 2, 1998, approximately 2,200 people saw the film.[114] Although *Don't Cry, Nanking* was not a commercial success, it did receive considerable public attention. The ultranationalist organizations that attempted to block the showing of Wu's film merely added to the controversy, thus supplying free publicity for the film.[115]

Episode II: Research Committee on the Nanjing Incident versus Japan Association for "Nanjing" Studies

In 1999, the Research Committee on the Nanjing Incident responded to the recent profusion of revisionist work, publishing *Thirteen Lies by the Deniers of the Nanjing Massacre* (Nankin daigyakusatsu hiteiron 13 no uso). The volume was a manual aimed at refuting 13 of the most common claims advanced by the revisionists of the Nanjing Massacre. *Thirteen Lies* sought an audience among the general public, and contributors used plain language to appeal to their readers. In his introduction, Fujiwara Akira regretted the recrudescence of denials of Nanjing in recent years. Fujiwara argued that these recent denials ignored the written and oral accounts of victims, perpetrators, and witnesses. He alluded to an array of lies that had been used to deceive the popular audience who were unfamiliar with the history and historiography of the Nanjing Massacre.[116]

This volume systematically addressed a series of contentions that the authors exposed as fallacies, for example: "The Tokyo Trial fabricated the Nanjing Massacre"; "No international organization condemned the Japanese atrocities in Nanjing"; "No Chinese sources mentioned Nanjing during the war"; "Because the death count of 300,000 is greatly exaggerated, the Nanjing Massacre was an illusion"; and "Killing guerrillas is a justified act, not a massacre."[117] Fujiwara Akira emphasized that the Tokyo Trial did not invent the massacre because it had already been documented in Chinese and English news reports, letters written by foreign bystanders, Japanese diplomatic documents, and even memoirs written by military personnel.[118] Kasahara Tokushi pointed out that the League of Nations protested the Japanese bombing of Nanjing and that American missionaries and journalists reported the Japanese atrocities there. He also warned that merely debating the total number of the victims was unproductive and would divert attention from the devastation and despair that occurred in Nanjing.[119] Inoue Hisashi presented examples of Communist and Nationalist primary sources that referred to the Japanese atrocities in Nanjing.[120]

Despite such strong argument and evidence, many revisionists were unconvinced. In the firm belief that the historical truth about Nanjing still had yet to be written, Higashinakano Osamichi and Fujioka Nobukatsu founded the Japan Association for "Nanjing" Studies (Nihon "Nankin" gakkai) in October 2000. Within five years, the association has published four volumes on Nanjing, including three annual reports. Contributors included such scholars as Hata Ikuhiko, the author of *The Nanjing Incident* (1986) and Kitamura Minoru. Although Higashinakano, who edited the annual reports, included articles that did not conform to his own point of view, the overall tone of the volume, as well as the chapters written by Higashinakano himself, evinced a clear perspective: the Nanjing Massacre was not historical truth, but an illusion resulting from political manipulation.[121]

The historiography of the Nanjing Massacre has demonstrated how those who have not consulted historical sources or existing scholarship and those who have done so but who also have an agenda can shape public views of a politically charged event. Using an especially amusing analogy, historian Kasahara Tokushi likened the task of responding to poorly informed revisionists to an amusement park game called "Whack-A-Mole" (*mogura tataki*). In this game, the player uses a mallet to strike mechanical moles that rise continually from holes in front of the player. Similarly, the progressive historian finds that, no sooner has he used his mallet of facts and scholarship to "whack" one revisionist than another appears with more ill-founded claims. Kasahara foresees no shortage of "moles" in the future.[122]

Episode III: The Li Xiuying Trial versus the Killing Contest Trial

In 1998, Matsumura Toshio, a retired worker who became interested in Nanjing, wrote *Serious Questions about the "Nanjing Massacre"* (Nankin gyakusatu e no daigimon). Seemingly disturbed by the lawsuit against the Japanese government by Li Xiuying, Matsumura claimed in his book that Li faked her identity and pretended to be a victim of the Nanjing Massacre.[123] In September 1999, Li sued Matsumura and his book's publisher, Tendensha, for defamation. In April 2003, the Tokyo High Court ruled that Matsumura and the publisher must pay 1.5 million yen (approximately US$13,600) to Li. In January 2005, the Supreme Court upheld the trial court's verdict.

In April 2003, immediately after the high court rendered its verdict in favor of Li, bereaved relatives of the two lieutenants who participated in the killing contest in 1937 sued Honda Katsuichi, two newspaper companies, and a publisher, demanding compensation for the damages that the families had incurred because of the reports.[124] The two cases had more than their timing in common. Honda and his lawyer, Watanabe Harumi, had assisted Li in her litigation, while many of the prosecuting lawyers in the killing contest trial had been members of Matsumura's defense team.[125]

Since the lawsuit against Honda was filed, his supporters have found new evidence suggesting that the two lieutenants killed not only combatants, but also noncombatants, during the contest.[126] On August 23, 2005, the Tokyo District Court dismissed the suit. The plaintiffs immediately expressed their intention to appeal, and the case may not be resolved for a few more years. In the interim, at public briefings and seminars, both sides will continue to present their versions of the truth.

Episode IV: *New History Textbook* versus *History That Opens the Future*

In 2001, the Japanese Society for History Textbook Reform finally published its ideal junior high school history textbook, titled *New History Textbook* (Atarashii rekishi kyōkasho). In order to pass textbook authorization, the text included a discussion of the Nanjing Incident, but its description was different from its counterparts:

> In August of the same year [1937], two Japanese officers were killed in Shanghai. This led to a full-scale war between Japan and China. The Japanese military expected that Chang Kai-shek would surrender if the Capital, Nanjing, fell. In December, [the Japanese troops] captured Nanjing. (At this time many civilians were wounded and killed by the Japanese troops. [This event] is known as the Nanjing Incident.) However, Chiang Kai-shek moved the capital to Chongqing and continued to fight.[127]

The textbook held China responsible for the war and indicted Chiang Kai-shek for resisting the will of the empire, an argument almost identical to that of the wartime textbooks. Nonetheless, as had been the case with *New Edition of Japanese History*, a controversial high school textbook printed in the mid-1980s, *New History Textbook* was a complete failure in terms of sales. The authors of the textbook had hoped to garner more than 10 percent of the entire market share. However, as a result of determined opposition both inside and outside Japan, the textbook reached less than 1 percent of Japan's students, selling a mere 543 copies.[128]

Despite the commercial failure of *New History Textbook*, the venture was not a total loss for revisionist interests. The book supplied a rallying point in a campaign of scathing criticism directed at the existing, more progressive junior high school textbooks. Apparently in response to this pressure from the revisionists, the 2002 editions of these more popular textbooks toned down their descriptions of the Nanjing atrocities. Only Nihon shoseki and Shimizu shuppan retained their numerical estimates of the victims, and the other five publishers merely used the term "many" (*tasū, tairyō, ōzei,* or *ōku*) to convey the loss of life.[129]

Another important outcome of the *New History Textbook* controversy was a countermeasure from the progressive side of the debate. The year 2002 saw the establishment of the Committee for Sharing the Same Historical Material in Japan, China, and South Korea. In 2005, this organization published *History That Opens the Future: The Modern History of Three East Asian Nations* (Mirai o hiraku rekishi: higashi Ajia sangoku no kingendaishi). More than 50 scholars, teachers, and members of activist organizations from the three countries joined the committee to write a history of modern East Asia that could be shared among the people of Japan, China, and South Korea. Although the textbook has not been approved for use in Japan, the editors appear to have been striving above all to present a candid version of wartime history that they could agree to endorse, regardless of their personal politics. Its description of Nanjing was far more detailed than that of *New History Textbook*, and it includes discussion of the indiscriminate bombing of Nanjing that started in August 1937. As to the number of victims, *The Modern History* included the estimates introduced by both the Nanjing Trial (340,000) and the Tokyo Trial (200,000).[130] Inclusion of such estimates, however, will no doubt provoke refutations from the revisionists, and more episodes will likely be added in the future.

CONCLUSION

The war of words over Nanjing has already lasted far longer than the military conflict that originated it. Although both progressives and revisionists would dearly love to declare victory in this conflict, the real victory may lie in the discussions themselves. As the memory of Nanjing was internationalized in the 1990s, ethnocentric narratives flooded the market, some of which sold well. But this did not mean that they achieved uncontested dominance over Japanese public opinion. Anecdotes that refute nationalistic accounts have continued to appear one after another.[131] Concerned scholars traveled across the nation giving talks, while activists organized public meetings to battle against revisionists like Fujioka and Kobayashi.[132] As the dispute over Nanjing was popularized, historians' writing changed. For example, *Thirteen Lies by the Deniers of the Nanjing Massacre* (1999) used plain language to appeal to the general public, including Japanese youth, who are not familiar with the long-lasting dispute over the massacre.[133] By the late 1990s, the Nanjing Massacre had no doubt been incorporated into Japanese history, and this is precisely when a number of ferocious, committed, and organized revisionist challenges emerged.

The flood of nationalistic accounts of Nanjing provoked those who disagreed to heighten their efforts to facilitate international cooperation and to organize international symposia. On December 13 and 14, 1997, the Research Committee, the Center for Research and Documentation on Japan's War Responsibility, and seven other citizens organizations conducted an international symposium in Tokyo to commemorate the sixtieth anniversary of the massacre. The gathering welcomed participants from China, Germany, and the United States.[134] Sixty years earlier, the streets of Tokyo had been filled with people carrying lanterns in jubilant celebration of the fall of Nanjing. On December 13, 1997, these streets again witnessed a parade, smaller and less riotous than its predecessor. The leader of this parade quietly carried a special lantern made in Nanjing. The lantern bore the two Chinese characters meaning "to commemorate" (*zhuidao*), and the peaceful crowd marched, not in celebration, but in shared memory of the deaths in Nanjing.

11

China: The Nanjing Massacre and Patriotic Education

Beginning in 1989, when government efforts to suppress pro-democracy movements culminated in the use of military force at Tiananmen Square, the Communist Party strengthened its emphasis on education, especially the study of history, as a source of patriotism. The authorities wanted the people to understand the martyrdom of their forebears who fought hard under socialism and, through ultimate sacrifice, achieved victory over foreign imperialism. The official narrative stressed that the Chinese economy had grown significantly under socialism since the civil war and that socialism was the key to maintaining China's economic development.

In order to accomplish patriotic education even among China's youngest citizens, policymakers employed every available medium, including literature, news reports, films, television programs, music, museums, and monuments. The official position on how to teach the Nanjing Massacre was no exception. Popular accounts of the massacre became widely available to the public, and the Japanese revisionists became notorious among the general public. The authorities strongly condemned these revisionists and warned the public about the rebirth of militarism in Japan. They urged the people to make China strong so that the Chinese people would not suffer a second horror. The official narrative of the massacre gave the Beijing government a powerful story, and the Japanese revisionists supplied a convincing villain.

MASSACRE AT TIANANMEN AND PATRIOTIC EDUCATION

April 15, 1989, marked the death of Hu Yaobang, the former general secretary of the Communist Party. Hu, a leading spokesman for liberalization of the political system, had been ousted from the government in January 1987. Four days after Hu's death, according to Xinhua News Agency, approximately 300 students attempted to break into the Zhongnanhai compound, where Chinese leaders live and work. Their assault on the compound was deflected by the police, four of whom were injured.[1] On April 22, Hu's official public memorial service was held at Tiananmen Square in Beijing. Demonstrations by students occurred in cities such as Xian and Changsha.[2] The editorial of *Renmin ribao* condemned such organized "upheavals" (*dongluan*) as being perpetrated by an "extremely small number of people" (*jishaoshuren*) whose goal was to "sow dissension among the people, plunge the whole country into chaos, and sabotage the political situation of stability and unity." It urged all the peoples in China to put a firm and immediate stop to the upheavals.[3]

On May 19, 1989, Premier Li Peng made a speech at a meeting of the Beijing cadre and called for resolute and powerful measures to curb the turmoil, blaming a handful of agitators for manipulating the masses for their own gain.[4] The following day, Li authorized martial law in some districts of Beijing and prohibited students from boycotting classes, making speeches, circulating leaflets, and resorting to violence.[5] However, the so-called handful proved more stubborn than the government had anticipated. Denouncing the rioters as "inhuman" (*canwu renxing*), the government suppressed them by force, putting down the "counterrevolutionary riot" (*fangeming baoluan*) on June 3 and 4, 1989, in what became known as the "Tiananmen Square Massacre."[6]

According to the official interpretation, the Chinese Communist Party had led the people to yet another historical victory in the name of proletarian political power. It stressed that an "extremely small number of students" (*jishaoshu xuesheng*) had taken an incorrect political stand, become counterrevolutionaries, and manipulated the patriotic enthusiasm of the well-intentioned majority of the students. The analysis of the alleged rebellion carried in *Renmin ribao* urged patriotic students to realize the crime committed by the counterrevolutionaries and to rally in defense of the nation and its Constitution.[7]

These domestic circumstances prompted the government leaders to embark on a further campaign for patriotic education. On June 21, 1989, *Guangming ribao*, a daily newspaper in Beijing, published an article promoting the understanding of correct patriotism among young students who did not fully understand it. The writer defined "patriotism" as the dedication of one's wisdom and talents to the country in order for China to become stronger, more prosperous, and more civilized. The article firmly declared: "History has proved that without the CPC [Communist Party of China], there will not be any New China and that only socialism can save China. This is the irrefutable truth for which countless numbers of our revolutionary martyrs paid a very high price."[8] Teaching narratives of revolutionary martyrs in the battle against Western and Japanese imperialism became increasingly important to the Chinese decision makers in the 1990s in order to unite the nation and firmly associate national identity with loyalty to the Communist Party.

The year 1990 marked the 150th anniversary of the Opium War. In March, the State Education Commission decided to use the war as the basis for an in-depth patriotic education movement in primary and secondary schools as well as in colleges and universities. Teng Teng, vice minister of the commission, stressed that the goal of the education was to teach the history of foreign inva-sions of China, the repulsion of these invaders by a nation united under the Communist Party, and the achievements of New China under socialism. As Teng highlighted, students must understand that only the Communist Party would be able to save and further develop China.[9] In May, institutions of higher learning in Wuhan, Hubei Province, held a series of forums and symposia com-memorating the Opium War, presented British atrocities and crimes to the pub-lic, and stressed the importance of socialism in China.[10] On June 1, 1991, the commission announced that schools nationwide would spend more classroom hours teaching modern Chinese history since the mid-nineteenth century, a pe-riod filled with foreign invasions.[11]

By the mid-1990s, the policymakers had developed an effective strategy to promote patriotic feelings and party loyalty among youth. On April 28 and 29, 1993, the Propaganda Department of the Central Committee held a forum on patriotic education.[12] Sixteen delegates from various party organizations par-ticipated in the forum and suggested effective means of patriotic education. These included the use of mass media such as newspapers, film, and television and radio programs; the establishment of museums and memorial halls; the popularization of patriotic art and literature; and the creation of systematic outlines for the patriotic education in kindergartens, elementary and second-ary schools, and colleges and universities.[13] The government's emphasis on education in patriotism influenced the history and memory of Japanese war-time aggression and atrocities.

In January 1991, the Association for the Study of the Anti-Japanese War (Kang-Ri zhanzhengshi xuehui) was established in Beijing. Some 150 historians across the nation participated in the founding ceremony. Liu Danian, the presi-dent of the association, welcomed the active participation of scholars from Hong Kong, Macao, and Taiwan, as well as Chinese living in other nations.[14] In May 1995, 50 years after the victory in the Anti-Japanese War, a new, larger es-timate of the killed and wounded during the war was introduced. The old figure included only those casualties inflicted from 1937 to 1945 and excluded victims in certain geographic areas, such as Taiwan. By contrast, the new estimate was extended to embrace all the geographic areas that the government claims and to cover the time period between 1931 and 1945. When Japan's Prime Minister, Murayama Tomiichi, visited the Memorial Hall of the War of Resistance against Japanese Aggression (Kang-Ri zhanzheng jinianguan) in Beijing on May 3, 1995, the Memorial Hall had already revised its statement on the casualties from the war, replacing the figure of 21.685 million with 35 million.[15] In the post-Tiananmen years, the Nanjing Massacre did not escape revision either.

FANNING THE FLAMES: THE REVISIONISTS' CONTRIBUTIONS TO THE PATRIOTIC EDUCATION

In the 1990s, Japanese revisionists inadvertently made significant contributions to the promotion of patriotic education among the public in China. After Ishihara Shintarō's denial of the massacre appeared in the October 1990 issue of *Playboy*, Zhang Yijin wrote "Nanjing Massacre: A Historical Fact That Brooks No Denial" (Nanjing datusha shishi bulun fouren) for *Renmin ribao*. In the article, Zhang stressed that Japanese invasion forces used the most barbaric and cruel means to kill more than hundreds of thousands of Chinese. He also pointed to the Nanjing Massacre Memorial Hall in Nanjing, which had educated both Chinese and non-Chinese about the crimes committed by the Japanese military during the war; he considered the evidence housed in the Memorial Hall irrefutable. According to Zhang, who apparently based his understanding on the 1947 judgment of the Nanjing Trial, more than 300,000 innocent civilians and unarmed soldiers became victims of the massacre. Of these, 190,000 were shot to death in mass executions, and their bodies were destroyed without a trace. Moreover, 150,000 corpses were buried by voluntary organizations throughout Nanjing. In addition to the death toll, Zhang briefly summarized the killing contest between Noda Tsuyoshi and Mukai Toshiaki, the International Military Tribunal for the Far East (1946–48), and diaries and confessions of atrocities by Japanese perpetrators.[16]

The article carefully refrained, however, from demonizing the entire Japanese nation. Zhang emphasized that revisionists such as Ishihara belonged to a "very small minority" (*jishaoshu*) in Japan. The article informed readers of "good" Japanese who visited the Memorial Hall in Nanjing, learned historical facts about the Nanjing Massacre, planted symbolic trees of peace, and expressed regret over the atrocities in Nanjing.[17] However, it was the handful of revisionists, not those Japanese who expressed apologies and remorse, who received the greatest attention from the mass media. Nagano Shigeto's denial of the massacre in May 1994, nationalists' challenges over exhibits of the massacre at the Nagasaki Atomic Bomb Museum in 1996, authors of books that justified the Nanjing Massacre, remarks of the supporters of the film *Pride* that humanized Tōjō Hideki, and conservative plaintiffs celebrating their victory in the Azuma Shirō case at the Tokyo High Court in December 1999 were all reported in detail.[18]

Treatments of Japanese attitudes in Chinese media were at times paradoxical. By 1996, although the news reports still drew a sharp distinction between the militarist "handful" and the general masses, they also warned readers of a surge of militarism in Japan. One such warning came on August 14, in response to a visit by Japan's cabinet ministers to the Yasukuni Shrine. Da Jun of the Xinhua News Agency emphasized that the ghost of militarism was still haunting Japan more than 50 years after the defeat. Da claimed that "a handful of people in the Japanese government have never ceased their efforts to cover up Japan's war crimes in textbooks and the media."[19] On August 22, Beijing China Radio International echoed these sentiments and warned the ordinary public that Japan was now one of the most militarily powerful states in the Asia-Pacific region and was being influenced by a small number of politicians who had forgotten the history of wartime aggression, including the massacre.[20] The day before the sixty-fifth anniversary of the September 18 Incident of 1931, generally known in Japan as the Manchurian Incident, Ji Wen of the Xinhua cautioned that some Japanese politicians were dreaming of re-creating the Greater East Asian Sphere. He urged the Chinese public to defend the nation against any possible repeat of past tragedies.[21]

THE NANJING MASSACRE AND THE FIFTIETH ANNIVERSARY OF VICTORY IN THE ANTI-JAPANESE WAR

The Chinese government not only exploited opportunities provided by Japanese revisionists, but it also used other means to promote patriotism and educate the public about the horrors of the massacre. The campaign included films, television documentaries, and photograph albums. On December 13, 1994, 57 years to the day after the Japanese military captured Nanjing, film director Wu Ziniu began shooting his *Don't Cry, Nanking* in China. Substantially completed by the end of March 1995, the film was released in China as *Nanjing datusha* (Nanjing Massacre), as part of the activities to commemorate the fiftieth anniversary of China's victory in the Anti-Japanese War.[22] Politically correct by government standards, the film promoted the official understanding of the massacre and stressed as two of its central themes the unity and ethnic identity of the Chinese people.

Don't Cry, Nanking revolves around a Chinese doctor (Chengshen) who once studied in Japan and has married a Japanese woman (Rieko), who is now pregnant. Both have a child by a previous spouse: Xiaoling is Chengshen's son, while Haruko is Rieko's daughter.[23] Seeking shelter, they have left Shanghai for Nanjing, unaware that the city is soon to be attacked by the Japanese military. The Japanese soldiers in the film are depicted as devils, eager to indulge in slaughter and rape. No humane Japanese soldiers appear in the film, though Rieko and Haruko are given humane characteristics. In the film, Rieko uses her Japanese identity to save her family members from the Japanese troops, while Chengshen protects his wife and daughter from an angry Chinese mob. When the Japanese troops capture the city, the family attempts to evacuate to the safety zone. However, they come across the Japanese soldiers who discover that Chengshen and Xiaoling are Chinese. Chengshen is briefly enslaved by Japanese soldiers but is set free by a Taiwanese soldier named Ishimatsu, whose loyalty to the Japanese army gives way to his sense of Chinese identity. Ishimatsu's reward for this act of courage is to be killed by an enraged Japanese soldier. Chengshen is reunited with his wife and children in the safety zone, but the

Japanese troops break into the safety zone and inflict severe beatings on German and American members of the International Committee for the Safety Zone. The Japanese invaders attempt to rape Haruko, but Rieko rushes toward the soldiers and screams that Haruko is Japanese. The soldiers desist from the sexual assault. However, realizing that Rieko is pregnant, one of Haruko's would-be rapists kicks Rieko in the belly. Nevertheless, Rieko gives birth and begs Chengshen to name their baby Nankin.

Probably because the film had to serve the state's policy of promoting patriotism and national unity, it omitted historical facts that would undermine its objective. For example, it did not mention that General Tang Shengzhi and his close subordinates, who were in charge of defending the city, fled the scene to save their own lives. In addition, the film ignored the plight of many Chinese soldiers who were forcibly conscripted from the countryside and were ordered to fight to the death without adequate training or military gear. Also neglected is the story of the Thirty-Sixth Chinese Division, which opened fire on other Chinese troops to protect Tang and his staff as they fled. Indeed, no atrocities of any kind committed by Chinese are acknowledged.[24]

In the film, Chinese soldiers are united and brave, but when a massacre scene is presented, the soldiers suddenly become obedient and march toward the execution site without any resistance. At the beginning of the film, a subtitle appears on the screen and states that the Japanese military killed more than 300,000 Chinese in cold blood and that the event known as the Nanjing Massacre (*Nanjing datusha*) was as dreadful as Auschwitz and Hiroshima. The film was an enormous success. According to Wu's own estimate in October 2000, as many as 30 million Chinese saw his film.[25]

In further commemoration of the war's end, a mobile exhibition on the Nanjing Massacre was unveiled in Xuzhou, Jiangsu Province, on June 15, 1995.[26] Two hundred eighty photographs illustrating the massacre, as well as two video documentaries, were displayed in the exhibition, which toured 11 cities in Jiangsu in three months. More than 400,000 people in Jiangsu visited the exhibition. In Xuzhou, according to the Xinhua, visitors lined up outside the exhibition center awaiting their turn.[27] In August 1995, after eight months of shooting, the Jiangsu television station completed its commemorative documentary series titled "Nanjing Massacre: Testimony of Survivors." The crews interviewed more than 100 survivors and eyewitnesses to substantiate the official narrative of the massacre.[28]

Another of the commemorative events of 1995 was the publication of a photographic album of the massacre, which contained 800 photographs, captioned with a total of 50,000 Chinese characters. According to Wan Renyuan, deputy curator of the Number Two China Historical Archives, this book was "the first set of systematic historical data on the Nanjing Massacre ever published in China."[29] The editors of the book reconstructed a narrative of the massacre using photographs of Japanese brutalities, many of which were almost too repugnant to look at.[30]

The intended impact of this collection was not necessarily to arouse outrage against either the entire Japanese people or the present-day Japanese state as a perceived enemy. In a departure from the normal practices of propaganda, the last 28 pages of the 295-page volume were mainly devoted to illustrating "good" Japanese in order to underscore that Japanese society was not monolithic. This closing section included photographs of Japanese veterans who had confessed their crimes in Nanjing, of Japanese historians such as Hora Tomio who had studied the massacre for decades, of Japanese visitors to the Nanjing Massacre Memorial Hall praying for peace in front of the skeletons, and of Chinese President Jiang Zemin and Japanese Prime Minister Murayama Tomiichi shaking hands and exchanging smiles. On the other hand, the section also included portraits of Japanese revisionists such as Tanaka Masaaki and Ishihara Shintarō. A caption urged the Chinese people to give serious attention to this "small number of" (shaoshu) revisionists in Japan. As the editors stressed in the introduction, this book was written for the benefit of Chinese youth: to educate them so that they would not forget the shame of the massacre and to inspire them to work for a stronger and more prosperous China.[31]

All of this exposure—the film, the photograph collection, and the post-Tiananmen media blitz for patriotism—made the Nanjing Massacre so important to the Chinese authorities that a new commemorative tradition began in 1996 and has continued to the present. On December 13, 1996, 59 years after the Nanjing Massacre, sirens wailed in Nanjing to commemorate victims of the massacre and to recall the Japanese atrocities. Since that year, sirens have sounded every December 13. Hu Tingjian, a deputy secretary of the city committee of the CCP who participated in the ceremony, stressed that "some" Japanese revisionists were hurting the feelings of the Chinese people and that "we" must not forget the invasion, slaughters, and enslavement that comprise the legacy of Japanese militarism.[32]

THE CASE OF AZUMA SHIRŌ: A POPULAR SYMBOL
OF JAPAN'S WARTIME CRUELTY

Throughout the 1990s, Chinese media consistently described revisionists as few or extremely few in number. Nevertheless, as time went by, the mass media and other literature on the Nanjing Massacre became less tolerant of this alleged minority, perhaps because the writers had become much less concerned with observing a distinction between good Japanese and militarists. The Chinese media stressed that Japan must squarely face the past and learn a lesson from its history of wartime aggression. Indeed, to judge from the increasing stridency of this message, readers might well conclude that the denying few were dominating Japanese society. By the end of the century, authorities in China had become defensive not only when the official version of the massacre was attacked, but also when people criticized unofficial accounts that were generally favorable to the government's position. If one criticized any part of a work that confirmed the massacre, one was likely to be labeled a denier of the event itself.

For example, after Japan's ambassador to the United States, Saitō Kunihiko, denounced Iris Chang's *The Rape of Nanking* as erroneous and one-sided, Yu Shuning, spokesman for the Chinese embassy in the United States, issued a statement on May 8, 1998, emphasizing that the Nanjing Massacre was not a historical fiction. Deliberately or not, Yu had missed Saitō's point. Whereas Saitō had intended only to criticize the accuracy of Chang's work, Yu interpreted his statements as a denial of the massacre *in toto*. In the statement, Yu urged the Japanese side to understand correctly the history of Japan's wartime aggression, and he emphasized that recognition of the past misdeeds was an important foundation of a healthy relationship between China and Japan.[33]

A more publicly notorious case was the December 1998 verdict of the Tokyo High Court in the libel action against Azuma Shirō. On December 24, Zhu Bangzao, China's Foreign Ministry spokesman, condemned the verdict and exhorted the Japanese side to face up to history and respect reality. In the eyes of Zhu, the verdict completely ignored the historical facts of the Nanjing Massacre.[34] On the following day, Su Ru of the Xinhua News Agency denounced the ruling as erroneous and accused the court of ruling in favor of Japanese right-wingers. In the eyes of Su, the diary of Azuma was an irrefutable record of the massacre and a valuable proof of Japanese atrocities. Su suggested that more Japanese people read the diary in order to understand Japan's past crime. He further stated that Japan had not changed since 1945 and that some militarists still persisted in romanticizing Japan's wartime expansion. Su urged the Chinese people to a higher level of vigilance, while calling upon Japan to understand wartime history correctly.[35]

Similarly, on December 26, Beijing China Radio International criticized the Tokyo High Court for ignoring historical facts and giving an unjust ruling. The commentator condemned the verdict for seriously hurting the Chinese people's feelings and exhorted all justice-loving people to denounce it forcefully. The commentator informed listeners that forums to support Azuma were being held in cities such as Shenyang and Nanjing, as well as in Japan. Again, the commentator urged Japan to squarely face the past and learn lessons from it in order to develop healthy Sino-Japanese relations.[36] Two days later, Zhu Bangzao, China's foreign minister, reiterated that the verdict had severely hurt the feelings of the Chinese people. Japan's Ministry of Foreign Affairs had explained that Azuma's case was a civil suit and that its outcome did not reflect the view of the government, which acknowledged that atrocities in Nanjing were an undeniable historical fact. Nevertheless, Zhu insisted that the case was not an ordinary civil suit, but an attempt by Japan's right-wing forces to deny the Massacre. Zhu repeated the sentiments of Yu, Su, and Beijing China Radio, urging Japan to face up to its history.[37]

Although the verdict against Azuma was widely publicized in the Chinese media, little, if any, commentary addressed the inconsistencies of Azuma's statements before the court. Nothing was made, for example, of the impossible story of the Japanese soldier who threw a Chinese person into a mailbag, doused the bag with gasoline, set it on fire, attached two hand grenades to the burning bag, activated them, carried the bag to a pond, and threw it in. Indeed, Chinese officials and media did not refer to the disputes before the court at all. Although the Xinhua issued a report on January 17, 1999, that purported to explain why the Tokyo High Court ruled against Azuma, its report was inaccurate. The report erroneously claimed that the ruling was based on there being no evidence that there was a pond at the site of the alleged killing—an issue not considered by the Tokyo court. The Xinhua stressed that there had been three ponds in the immediate area and condemned the court for not researching historical records.[38]

Because of the media coverage of his lawsuit, Azuma Shirō became a celebrity in China. On April 18 and 25, 1999, he and his Japanese supporters appeared in "Shihua shishuo" (To Tell the Truth), a popular Sunday television program seen by millions across China. On the program, Azuma and his Japanese supporters echoed the statements of Chinese officials and reporters, stating that the verdict was unjust and political. They claimed that the verdict was an outgrowth of the domestic political situation and the current rightward leanings in Japan. Azuma condemned the verdict and warned the audience and viewers that the purpose of the right-wingers at this trial was to deny the massacre.[39]

Mizutani Naoko, a doctoral student of the history of Sino-Japanese relations at Japan Women's University (Nihon joshi daigaku) who was studying at People's University (Renmin daxue) in Beijing, challenged Azuma and his supporters from the floor of the broadcast studio.[40] Mizutani questioned Azuma's assertion that Japanese young people were ignorant about the massacre and that teachers in schools rarely taught the event to their students. In addition, she stressed that the court's decision was not based on the historical facts of the massacre, but rather on Azuma's testimonies before the court. Responding to Mizutani, Azuma reiterated that everything he had recorded in his diary was nothing but the truth, and again blamed the judge for ignoring the truth. Then, an angry Chinese woman stood up, pointing and yelling at Mizutani, demanding to know whether Mizutani believed or disbelieved Azuma's testimony. Another member of the audience joined in the confrontation, declaring in defiant tones that Mizutani must state whether she would accept or reject the Nanjing Massacre as a historical fact. Although it did not really surprise her, the audience's reaction embarrassed Mizutani. She had meant merely to call into question the mistaken belief, seemingly held by many Chinese laypersons, that Azuma was the only Japanese who was fighting a lonely, heroic battle against a nation of revisionists. Nevertheless, as she later acknowledged, her challenge merely provoked anger rather than inspiring fruitful conversation.[41]

Although the massacre at the Tiananmen Square momentarily diminished cultural exchanges between Beijing and Taipei, such exchanges continued and were encouraged under the administration led by Li Tenghui, the first native-born Taiwanese to lead the Taiwan government. The military tension across the Taiwan strait declined, and martial law on Quemoy and Matsu was finally lifted in 1992. The thaw in the political climate was mirrored in the historiography of the Nanjing Massacre in Taiwan. Accounts of Nanjing writers on the mainland became publicly available on the islands. For example, in 1989, Xu Zhigeng's *Nanjing datusha*, originally published in Beijing two years earlier, was published in Taiwan.[42] The newly published photograph collection *Muji kangzhan wushinian: 1895–1945 Zhong-Ri zhanzheng tulu* (Eyewitness to the Fifty-Year Resistance: A Pictorial History of the Sino-Japanese War of 1895–1945) contained photographs of Japanese atrocities in Nanjing, as well as in other places. Significantly, these same images had been exhibited in the Museum of the War of Chinese People's Resistance Against Japan in Beijing.[43] Moreover, the Taiwan-based Long Shong Production was a co-producer of the 1995 film *Don't Cry, Nanking*.[44] The translation of Iris Chang's *The Rape of Nanking* also appeared in Taiwan in 1997.[45]

In the foreword of the translation of Chang's volume, the CEO of the publisher Gao Xijun emphasized the importance of establishing one powerful China. Gao, who was born in Nanjing and left the city only three months before the Japanese attack, stressed that the PRC and the Taiwanese governments must work together for the Chinese people so that the tragedy of the Nanjing Massacre would never be repeated.[46] As social and political exchanges progressed between the two sides of the Taiwan strait, Taiwan toned down its formerly strident accusation that the Communist government had stolen the fruits of the Nationalist victory in the Anti-Japanese War. In the new atmosphere of reconciliation, Nanjing provided a common ground for those who wished the two governments to merge into a single nation for "the Chinese."

CONCLUSION

In the post-Tiananmen period, China's efforts at establishing patriotism led to a reevaluation of war history. Literature on the Nanjing Massacre flourished in China. People were exposed to accounts of the heroic activities of members of the International Committee for the Safety Zone, dreadful stories told by survivors of the massacre, confessions of Japanese perpetrators, and scholarly studies of the massacre.[47] There can be no doubt that these publications, as well as films and other materials, contributed to increased public awareness of Nanjing. They included scholarly articles written by both Chinese and Japanese historians. And yet their contribution was often marred by the presence of an underlying agenda. The numerous accounts of inhumanity and horror in Nanjing that became available to the public were meant to serve the interests of the state in order to promote patriotic education, and denials of the massacre emanating from Japan received a high degree of attention. But in their attempts to highlight Japanese cruelty or Chinese suffering, Chinese treatments of the massacre neglected other sides of the story. They omitted reference to the ordeals of Chinese conscript soldiers and the sufferings of civilians in rural areas who endured atrocities at the hands of both Japanese and Chinese. Also unexamined were the reasons why China's official estimate that more than 300,000 died in Nanjing so greatly exceeded that of Japanese progressive historians such as Kasahara Tokushi (between 100,000 and 200,000).

By the end of the century, the Nanjing Massacre had become one of the best known symbols of Japan's wartime atrocities in China. By then, December 13 had become a significant date in the official and popular history of China. As the massacre grew in symbolic significance, however, it became more elusive as a subject of objective discussion. As most dramatically demonstrated in the Chinese responses to the verdict against Azuma Shirō, opinions about the massacre's definition, scope, and meaning gravitated toward a more rigid orthodoxy, and those who espoused "incorrect" narratives of the event were met with intolerance both from the government and their fellow citizens.

12

United States: Rediscovery of the Nanjing Massacre

n the 1990s, because of the relative decline of Japan's strategic importance in the Pacific and increasing anxiety over the perceived Japanese economic invasion, critical news reports on Japan continued to appear frequently in American media. Through these reports, lay observers had ample opportunities to rediscover the Nanjing Massacre. Moreover, publicity regarding the massacre was fanned by a combination of events and anniversaries, including the dispute over the Enola Gay exhibition at the Smithsonian Institution in 1994–1995; the fiftieth anniversary of the atomic bombings and V-J Day; the 1997 publication of Iris Chang's *The Rape of Nanking* and the cancellation of the Japanese edition of Chang's book in 1999. After decades of indifference, an unprecedented number of individuals in the United States began to take interest in Japan's wartime atrocities in China. Chinese-American activists played a central role in organizing memorial meetings, concerts, symposia, and photographic exhibits. During this time, as indicated by the underlying assumptions in the reports of their news media, Americans tended increasingly to subscribe to a stereotypical collective image of the Japanese, who they believed were either entirely ignorant of the nation's war crimes or were actively committed to covering up the shameful past. Curiously, it was this facile popular perception of Japan as a nation of revisionists that also gave rise to a series of thoughtful, balanced treatments of the massacre by scholars in the United States. Seeking to test the correctness of public opinion, these historians produced an impressive body of work, with the result that the history of the massacre in the United States became richer than in any previous period.

"OKAY TO HATE": THE NEW JAPANESE "INVASION"

As the Berlin Wall was demolished and the perceived Soviet threat diminished in 1989, American concerns regarding foreign competition began to shift from the military arena to the economic. Many began to regard Japan's economic expansion into the United States as an unwelcome invasion. In 1989, Japanese companies bought such American icons as Columbia Pictures and Rockefeller Center in New York. In November 1991, the Gallup poll found that 77 percent of respondents answered that they considered Japan to be an economic threat.[1] In February 1992, only 47 percent replied that their opinions of Japan were very or mostly favorable, whereas 50 percent responded that their opinions were mostly or very unfavorable. Compared with the poll conducted in March 1989, favorable opinion of Japan declined by 22 percent.[2]

Public figures like television commentator Andy Rooney and the *Chicago Tribune*'s Mike Royko openly acknowledged their emotions against Japan.[3] Veterans viewed the flow of Japanese money to the United States as an economic invasion. Some concluded that Japan's goal was to dominate the world economy to avenge the defeat of 1945. In "Fear and Loathing of Japan," Lee Smith denounced these views as emotional and groundless and warned the public that thinking of Japan as an enemy engaged in economic warfare would damage national interests.[4] Charles Burress of *The San Francisco Chronicle* also cautioned against the public sentiment of anger toward Japan and challenged critics and scholars like James Fallows, who attacked the allegedly rapacious Japanese character.[5]

In May 1989, James Fallows wrote "Containing Japan," in which he argued that Japan was unable to restrain the one-sided and destructive expansion of its economic power, which he saw as potentially harmful to the rest of the world. Fallows criticized what he called the "unique Japanese character"—a character that seemed to him to respect few universal principles, basing its morality instead on intense personal loyalties. In his view, such character was at odds with principles like charity, democracy, and world brotherhood. Because he regarded Japan as America's single most valuable partner for the foreseeable future, Fallows did not suggest a severing of ties with Japan. Nevertheless, Fallows urged the containment of Japan to protect American and world economic interests.[6]

As Lee Smith suggested, "suddenly the Japanese [had] become the people it [was] okay to hate."[7] Imaginary and simplistic views of Japan and Japanese increased in the media in the early 1990s. Japanese takeovers of American companies and real estate rekindled public memories of Bataan and Pearl Harbor, as Americans again perceived themselves as victims of Japanese expansion.

THE *ENOLA GAY* CONTROVERSY AND
THE NANJING MASSACRE

In May 1995, Martin Harwit, director of the National Air and Space Museum (NASM), left the Smithsonian Institution after a nearly yearlong dispute over the exhibit of the restored *Enola Gay*.[8] Harwit and his staff originally planned to include artifacts intended to remind museum visitors of the tens of thousands who were killed or injured in Hiroshima and Nagasaki. However, this plan offended veterans and their supporters, and their outcries resulted in Harwit's resignation. In their reactions to the proposed exhibit, many commentators sought to justify their objections by referring to Japan's wartime atrocities, including the Nanjing Massacre, which, in their eyes, represented a moral and strategic counterweight to the bombings of Hiroshima and Nagasaki.

On September 5, 1994, for example, an essay by Mario Battista, former commander of American Legion Post 79, appeared in the *St. Petersburg Times* (Florida). Battista condemned "the revisionists at the Smithsonian" for distorting historical facts and discrediting, if not damaging, the United States in the eyes of the world. Because the planned exhibit stressed damage caused by the bomb rather than destruction inflicted in Asia by the Japanese forces, Battista urged the curators not to forget Japan's wartime savagery, which, in his eyes, was surpassed only by the Nazi Holocaust. Battista's examples of the Japanese brutalities were the atrocities in Nanjing, "where 40,000 unarmed Chinese men, women and children were sadistically butchered, set afire, raped and maimed"; "the unprovoked sneak attack on Pearl Harbor"; "the infamous Bataan Death March and Camp"; and "the documented brutality and inhuman treatment of prisoners of war."[9]

Veterans such as Mort Blumenfeld and Victor Tolley presented views similar to Battista's. To Blumenfeld, the American mission was "to finish what the enemy had started with Pearl Harbor, the Bataan Death March, the rape of Nanking and the beheading of some of Doolittle's Raiders." Blumenfeld expressed his gratitude for Truman's decision to drop atomic bombs, which, he argued, saved the lives of thousands of American soldiers, sailors, Marines, airmen, and nurses, and enabled them to resume their lives back in the United States.[10] In the eyes of Victor Tolley, the exhibit was not telling "the whole story." In order to tell the whole story of the war with Japan, Tolley urged, the exhibit should begin with Japan's invasion of Manchuria, followed by the Nanjing Massacre, Pearl Harbor, the Bataan Death March, Guadalcanal, Tarawa, Peleliu, Saipan, Iwo Jima, Okinawa, and Japanese suicide attacks on American ships. Representations of these events, he argued, would properly prepare museum visitors for a climactic end to the exhibit, which would "show the Enola Gay and her gallant crew of dedicated airmen carrying out their orders to drop the atomic bomb."[11]

The planned *Enola Gay* exhibit prompted journalists to refer to the Nanjing

Massacre as well. When the exhibit's original plan was abandoned, Pat Truly hailed the decision and argued that the exhibit should begin with the "Rape of Nanking, in which 300,000 Chinese civilians were killed by the Japanese army," followed by the oil embargo against Japan (1940), Pearl Harbor (1941), the suicide attacks (1944–45), the atomic bombings (1945), and the promulgation of Japan's Peace Constitution drafted by the United States (1946). Like the veterans mentioned above, Truly believed that Harwit and his staff had attempted to denigrate the United States by focusing on devastations caused by the bomb.[12] Similarly, Pat Buchanan hailed the cancellation of the "poisonous" plan, which he attributed to cultural elites with an "anti-Western bias." Buchanan argued:

> Americans should rightly debate the wisdom and necessity of using those terrible weapons on open cities. But, about who was the wartime aggressor in Asia, who behaved most barbarically toward prisoners and captive peoples, no contest. Bataan's butchers and the perpetrators of the Rape of Nanking deserved just what they got.[13]

Buchanan's remarks, which exclusively focused on ideals of national guilt and retribution, rested on the assumption that equated the populations of Hiroshima and Nagasaki with Japanese aggressors in Nanjing, Bataan, and Pearl Harbor, whose lives were deemed unworthy of sympathy.

Perhaps less predictably, the Nanjing Massacre also became a touchstone for those who either supported the Smithsonian's initial plan or were disappointed by the eventual watered-down exhibit of the *Enola Gay*. The curators of the initially proposed exhibit, such as Michael Neufeld, disagreed with the critics who urged that materials from Nanjing and other scenes of Japan's wartime misconduct should be exhibited alongside the *Enola Gay*, with no reference to the effects of the nuclear blast. Neufeld stressed that such display might carry a message that one atrocity or war crime deserved another and that Truman had dropped the bomb as revenge on Japan.[14]

Author Gar Alperovitz, on the one hand, conceded that nothing would be gained by downplaying Japan's responsibility for the Nanjing Massacre, the Bataan Death March, and slave labor in the prison camps. On the other hand, Alperovitz argued that the critics of the initial exhibit had exaggerated the number of lives allegedly saved by the atomic bomb and that they had ignored historical research, particularly regarding the alternatives available to American decision makers in 1945.[15]

John Whittier Treat, a professor of Japanese literature at the University of Washington, found the disputes over the *Enola Gay* exhibit reminiscent of similar disputes in Japan over the exhibits and conferences dealing with the Nanjing Massacre and medical experiments on prisoners of war. In Treat's view, the argument that the deaths in Hiroshima and Nagasaki were necessary to save a far greater number of lives was not persuasive. Rather, the underlying principle of the Americans who expressed this opinion was the same as that of those Japanese who claimed Japan had done no wrong during the war.[16] To Treat and others who objected to the revised exhibit, the lives of the residents in Hiroshima and Nagasaki counted as much as those of the residents in Nanjing, and it was impossible to ignore the human cost inflicted by the atomic blasts.

In late June 1995, the *Enola Gay* exhibit was opened to the public at the National Air and Space Museum in Washington. The exhibit showed the fuselage of the bomber with a panel explaining that the two atomic bombs dropped on Japan "destroyed much of the two cities and caused many tens of thousands of deaths. However, the use of the bombs led to the immediate surrender of Japan and made unnecessary the planned invasion of the Japanese home islands. Such an invasion, especially if undertaken for both main islands, would have led to very heavy casualties among American, Allied, and Japanese armed forces and Japanese civilians."[17]

Artifacts such as disintegrated clothes, a melted clock and lunch box, and various photographs of people bearing injuries inflicted by the two bombs—all of which the Smithsonian had initially planned to display—did not come to the museum. However, American University, which was organizing an atomic bomb exhibition at the same time as the Smithsonian, displayed these artifacts from July 8 until July 27.[18] Approximately 3,000 people visited this alternative exhibition during these weeks. Many of them expressed gratitude to the organizers for enlightening visitors as to the horrific effects of the bombs, such as: "Thank you for hosting the exhibits"; "Thanks for showing the courage that the Smithsonian lacked"; "Many more people should see this exhibit."[19]

However, other visitors emphasized Japan's wartime brutality and justified the droppings of the atomic bombs, which in their eyes had saved American and Chinese lives: "This exhibition should have displayed Japan's wartime atrocities, like the slaughter of massive numbers of civilians in China"; and "These artifacts present horrors of the war. Nevertheless, such destructions do not seem more cruel than Japanese destructions in Nanjing or Manila." In addition, a group of American University students who were frustrated with the atom bomb exhibit hosted a photographic presentation of Japan's wartime atrocities in Asia to apprise the visitors of how dreadful Japan's wartime atrocities were.[20]

Naono Akiko, an international student from Hiroshima who organized the official exhibit at the university, at first welcomed her fellow students' alternative exhibit. She hoped that, if everyone were given the opportunity to speak against the atrocities that most angered them, people of all opinions would have their minds opened to sufferings they had not previously acknowledged. Unfortunately, she was disappointed to discover that her expectation was too optimistic; those who criticized exhibits that denounced the use of the bomb were not willing to sympathize with the victims of Hiroshima.[21] The outraged veterans and students seemed able to think only in terms of national entities. To them, the Japanese who died on August 6 and 9, 1945, the casualties of radiation sickness, and their descendants who live with the fear of genetic mutation are disqualified as objects of sympathy because their nation was an aggressor.

The United States is the home not only of veterans who endured brutality in Japanese POW camps, but also of Asian immigrants who experienced Japanese wartime aggression firsthand or who heard of such events from parents and grandparents. In the eyes of such survivors and their descendants, the American media had never paid adequate attention to the wartime horrors caused by Imperial Japan compared with the extensive coverage devoted to Hiroshima and Nagasaki. Throughout the 1990s, the Nanjing Massacre and Hiroshima were often mentioned together in editorials and articles in major American newspapers. Directly and indirectly, Japanese were criticized for remembering Hiroshima but forgetting Nanjing.

On November 17, 1991, an editorial of *The New York Times* titled "Infamy Is Still Infamy" alleged that Japanese were attempting to evade their guilt for Pearl Harbor.[22] Writing in response to this editorial, Kin-Ming Liu stressed that Japan had been "eager to convince the world that it had been a victim and not the aggressor in the war." Liu argued that Japan constantly raised issues regarding Hiroshima and Nagasaki, while dismissing the Nanjing Massacre and Pearl Harbor. Liu, who was outraged by Ishihara Shintarō's denial of the massacre in November 1990, emphasized that the Japanese forces "embarked on atrocities and vandalism in which 340,000 Chinese were tortured and slaughtered" when Japan attacked Nanjing in December 1937.[23]

On February 2, 1992, Joanna Pitman wrote in the *San Diego Union-Tribune* of her meeting with Nagatomi Hiromichi, a member of the Group of Returnees from China (Chūgoku kikansha renrakukai). Nagatomi invited Pitman to his home and told her why he and other members of this group videotaped their confessions of atrocities in China, including the Nanjing Massacre, in which Nagatomi himself participated.[24] He expressed sentiments comparable to those of Liu, with a significant difference.[25] Whereas Liu spoke from the viewpoint of an outraged reader, Nagatomi, who had taken part in executing some 20 Chinese refugees, spoke as a remorseful perpetrator. In her article, Pitman wrote that, according to Nagatomi, the videotapes were intended "to prompt Japan to confront its own history. Since the war, younger generations have grown up in the belief that Japan was simply a victim of Allied aggression that culminated in the atomic bombing of Nagasaki and Hiroshima, bringing the brave Japanese to their knees."[26]

In August 1995, Jim Parsons of the *Star Tribune* reported on a grass-roots movement in Minnesota to commemorate Japan's invasion of China and mourn its victims. In order to remember what had been largely ignored in the United States, KaiMay Yuen Terry organized a public meeting, which included an orchestral work, testimonies of Chinese survivors of the war, and a presentation by a history professor.[27] The same month, Aurelio Rojas of the *San Francisco Chronicle* described another grass-roots movement to remember Japan's wartime atrocities and Chinese sufferings. The article discussed the psychological wounds of Chinese survivors and their descendants, wounds that remained unhealed 50 years after V-J Day. For example, Paul Hsu, at the age of 76, was still suffering from the trauma of losing his sister, who fell into the Yangtze River while attempting to escape from Japanese would-be rapists. Rojas wrote of the frustration of these people, who could not rest until Japan fully apologized for its wartime past and consented to "stop hiding the truth" from its nationals. Leland Yee told Rojas that he and his activist friends were urging other San Franciscans to educate their children about Japan's wartime crimes because the city's schools did not teach Japan's wartime atrocities such as the Nanjing Massacre.[28]

Judging from newspaper reports, many more Americans in the 1990s became aware of Japan's wartime atrocities in Asia, a subject formerly overshadowed by the Holocaust and Hiroshima. These articles often cited the Nanjing Massacre to illuminate the dreadful violence committed by Japan. But it was not until after 1997 that the "Rape of Nanking" was rediscovered and redefined in American public discourse.

HISTORY OR HYPERBOLE? *THE RAPE OF NANKING: THE FORGOTTEN HOLOCAUST OF WORLD WAR II*

In late 1997, Iris Chang published *The Rape of Nanking: The Forgotten Holocaust of World War II.*[29] The book, which received extensive coverage and favorable reviews, soon became a best-seller in the United States. On December 11, 1997, two days before the sixtieth anniversary of the Nanjing Massacre, Ken Ringle of the *Washington Post* favorably presented Chang's view of the massacre and Japanese remembrance of Nanjing in the postwar years. In the article, Chang told Ringle how stressful it had been to research the horrors of the massacre; during the writing process, her hair fell out, and her editor lost 10 pounds. Chang had been inspired to write her book when she attended a 1994 conference in Cupertino, California, organized by the Global Alliance for Preserving the History of World War II in Asia. At the conference, Chang came face-to-face with poster-size photographs of Japanese atrocities in Nanjing. Deeply moved, she remembered the dreadful stories of the massacre that she had heard from her parents and grandparents when she was a child.[30]

In the article, Chang emphasized that what she found during the research was "more horrible" than any stories or films she had ever encountered, including those of the Holocaust. In addition, she stressed that, unlike the Holocaust, school textbooks in the United States rarely discussed the Nanjing Massacre and that far more people were killed in Nanjing in eight weeks than in Hiroshima and Nagasaki combined. Chang, who had little knowledge of the Japanese historiography of the massacre, told Ringle that "the Japanese" had refused to see themselves as aggressors in the war and that the few courageous Japanese historians who had dared to study Japan's war responsibility had been compelled to live under death threats. Chang expressed to Ringle that she felt obliged to rescue the memory of the massacre from oblivion.[31]

On December 14, 1997, Orville Schell, dean of the Graduate School of Journalism at the University of California, Berkeley, wrote a rave review of Chang's work in the *New York Times*.[32] Fully accepting Chang's view, Schell wrote:

> During the two months after their entry into the Nationalist capital on Dec. 13, 1937, Japanese troops perpetrated a massacre that has virtually no parallel in recent history. Expert witnesses at the International Military Tribunal of the Far East . . . estimated that some 260,000 noncombatants were slaughtered in cold blood. Many experts now believe the number to be over 350,000. . . . The carnage was the result of a secret order sent to Japanese forces in China under the seal of Prince Asaka, uncle of Emperor Hirohito [Empress Nagako]: "Kill all captives." Soon competitions arose among soldiers to see who could kill most efficiently.[33]

Schell, who was aware of denials by Japanese politicians such as Ishihara Shintarō and Nagano Shigeto, concurred with Chang's demand that Japan and "the Japanese" face up to their "monstrous and protracted crime against humanity."[34]

For many ordinary Americans who had virtually no previous knowledge of the Nanjing Massacre, Chang's book immediately became an authoritative source. The shock created by its seeming revelations gave way to gratitude. The appreciation expressed by George Will, a political commentator, was representative:

> Something beautiful, an act of justice, is occurring in America today concerning something ugly that happened long ago and far away. . . . The rape of Nanking, a city of 1 million, by the Japanese army was perhaps the most appalling single episode of barbarism in a century replete with horrors. Yet it had been largely forgotten until Iris Chang made it her subject.[35]

While acknowledging wholesale Japanese atrocities in Nanjing, historians and critics who were familiar with the history of the massacre found Chang's book intellectually insufficient or seriously flawed. The light shed by the book had, perhaps, the power to illuminate, but it also had the capacity to distort. For example, in his review of *The Rape of Nanking*, David Kennedy, a professor of history at Stanford University, expressed skepticism that the atrocities in Nanjing deserved to be compared with the Holocaust or had been as thoroughly forgotten as Chang insisted. Although Kennedy agreed that Chang had achieved a shocking effect in her treatment of the disastrous horrors of Nanjing, he stressed that she did not conclusively explain the grounds on which the massacre was to be compared with the Holocaust. In the eyes of Kennedy, the latter was a systematic program based on Hitler's purposeful policy. By contrast, the massacre was an unfortunate incident of war, either an epidemic of individual cruelty or the result of the poor discipline among the Japanese soldiers, but not the product of a premeditated agenda. Noting that Chang depended solely on the author David Bergamini for her conclusion that formal political decisions at the highest levels had mandated the atrocities in Nanjing, Kennedy noted the problems with Bergamini's thesis discussed in critical reviews written by renowned historians a quarter of a century earlier.[36]

Moreover, Kennedy emphasized that, contrary to Chang's assertion, neither the United States nor Japan had ignored the Nanjing Massacre. He cited news reports and other documents of the massacre written by Americans and Europeans immediately after the incident and the ongoing work of the Japanese progressive left, which had preserved the history and memory of the massacre in Japan. To Kennedy, the keynote of Chang's book was accusation and outrage rather than analysis and understanding, and he found the project as a whole to be unsatisfactory as a scholarly work.[37]

Although recognizing that the book had good intentions, Joshua Fogel, a professor in history at the University of California, Santa Barbara, also found the book seriously flawed. Fogel was disturbed by Chang's repeated denunciations of an allegedly typical Japanese mentality. Although Chang at one point denied any intention to demonize the Japanese national character, this denial struck Fogel as unconvincing. Rather, it seemed to him that the style and structure of the book plainly identified and indicted a "Japanese" identity and perspective. In addition, Fogel condemned Chang's uncritical and unquestioning approach to the Chinese she interviewed and the documents she consulted, as well as her attempt to equate the massacre with the Holocaust. He urged Chang to consider how it was possible that "so many Chinese could be led to the slaughter when they so vastly outnumbered the Japanese invaders." He reminded her that, unlike the defenders of Nanjing, the European Jews neither possessed military force nor outnumbered their persecutors.[38]

Moreover, Fogel denounced Chang's discussion of postwar Japan as overly simplistic. Refuting Chang's claim that Japanese researchers addressed the massacre and other war crimes at grave risk to their careers and even their lives, Fogel referred to Japanese scholars such as Kasahara Tokushi and Yoshimi Yoshiaki, who had been studying these topics in safety for more than a decade. Pointing out that Chang herself had interviewed some of these historians, Fogel strongly criticized her for deliberately ignoring these voices in Japan and concluding that "the Japanese as a nation" were still trying to consign the victims of the massacre to historical oblivion.[39]

Although a number of historians and critics cautioned against accepting Chang's biased approach, her book seemed to have appeared at the right time for it to become an authoritative narrative of the massacre among many readers in the United States.[40] Chang's monochromatic view of Japanese society and memory acquired further credibility during the controversy over its publication in Japan.

KASHIWA SHOBŌ DISPUTE

In late February 1999, the American press reported that Kashiwa shobō, a commercial publisher that specializes in publishing translations of high-quality

Western titles and of collections of historical documents, had postponed the release of a Japanese translation of Iris Chang's *The Rape of Nanking*. These reports gave rise to contradictory speculations; some concluded that Kashiwa shobō had delayed the publication because it could not agree with the author regarding revisions of errors and inaccuracies in the book, while others spread rumors that the delay was a result of threats from extreme right-wing organizations. For example, the *Boston Globe* printed a brief account written by the Associated Press stating that Kashiwa shobō and Chang had reached an impasse regarding the revision of a portion of the book.[41] Jacob Heilbrunn of the *Los Angeles Times* assumed that nationalists were preventing Kashiwa shobō from publishing the translation.[42]

On May 17, 1999, Basic Books formally announced that it had agreed to terminate its contract with Kashiwa shobō for a Japanese edition of Chang's book. Two days later, Haga Hiraku, the chief editor and executive managing director of Kashiwa shobō, stressed at the Foreign Correspondents' Club of Japan in Tokyo that the publication was canceled not because of threats from right-wing extremists, but because of the disagreement with Chang regarding the proposed addition of notes, annotations, and commentary to the translated version.[43] Doreen Carvajal of the *New York Times* emphasized Chang's view that Kashiwa shobō had sought to add notes and commentary because of threats from ultranationalist organizations. Having talked to both Haga Hiraku and Iris Chang, Carvajal was convinced by Chang, who provided her with an e-mail correspondence sent by Haga to Chang on November 11, 1998, which included the following sentence: "As we have indicated before, our publishing company is subject to considerable attack and it's not an exaggeration to say that we have put ourselves in a life-threatening situation in publishing this book."[44]

Carvajal, however, did not present this sentence in its larger context. Immediately after the quoted passage, Haga's e-mail had continued:

> But as we stated in the beginning the entire company agreed that it was more important to publish your book for the purpose of exposing the Japanese people to the past war crimes that we are now striving to correct and bring to the consciousness of the Japanese people our responsibility as a nation in this matter.[45]

Thus, Haga was not expressing trepidation, but rather the publisher's strong determination to publish the translation regardless of any opposition from the right.

The publisher believed that the Japanese version required notes, annotations, and commentary in order to avoid unnecessary challenges from the right based on errors and inaccuracies in the original text. By late August 1998, Fujiwara Akira and Inoue Hisashi, historians who had long been members of the Research Committee on the Nanjing Incident and had been publishing books and articles on the massacre since the early 1980s, agreed to supervise the translation.[46] On October 19, 1998, more than three weeks before Haga sent his e-mail, Kashiwa shobō e-mailed a list of 62 proposed revisions to Chang. The publisher wished to insert bracketed material by Fujiwara and Inoue alongside portions of the original text, correcting factual errors and adding clarification to Chang's prose, words, and terms.[47]

In her reply to Kashiwa shobō, Iris Chang expressed her appreciation for the careful and diligent work of the two historians. Nevertheless, she declined to insert any brackets next to the original text or to authorize a separate footnote section, to be written by the historians. Regarding the 62 suggested corrections, she acknowledged that she had made 12 factual errors. As to these points, Chang demanded that they be corrected in the text itself, instead of being marked by brackets. Chang categorized 24 other proposed changes as additional details and comments about established facts, supplementary information that could be integrated seamlessly into the existing footnotes. Chang identified 15 suggestions as subjective or erroneous statements on the part of Inoue and Fujiwara, and these she rejected outright. As to the remaining 11 items, Chang offered no specific comment.[48]

On November 30, 1998, Kashiwa shobō e-mailed to Chang a translated draft of the commentary written by Inoue Hisashi, which the publisher was planning to include in the Japanese edition.[49] Titled "*The Rape of Nanking*: Its Significance and Its Problems" (*Za reipu obu Nankin no imi to mondaiten*), it first stressed the importance of the publication of the book. Since the study of the massacre had barely begun in the United States, Inoue appreciated that the book enlightened many people in English-speaking nations about the massacre. He urged Japanese readers to listen with open minds to Chang's view, which indicted Japanese both for committing the massacre and for burying its memory. While acknowledging the contribution of the book, Inoue also pointed out its weaknesses. He perceived the work as overly passionate, and its quality was further diminished in his eyes by more than a few misunderstandings and insufficient explanations.[50]

The following day, the Japanese publisher received a reply from Iris Chang, requesting that the publisher not include Inoue's commentary in the translation. Kashiwa shobō agreed with Chang and wrote that the Japanese edition would not include the commentary.[51] Anxious that its reputation as a serious academic publisher might be damaged if it released a book without accurate notes and commentary, Kashiwa shobō decided without consulting Chang to publish a separate anthology to coincide with the publication of *The Rape of Nanking*. This volume, while not expressly identified as a companion to Chang's book, was to include much of the information Chang did not wish to see inserted in the translation of her work, including Inoue's commentary, a brief history of the massacre by Fujiwara Akira, and critical reviews of *The Rape of Nanking* written by American historians and critics such as David Kennedy. Chang later learned from reporters that the anthology was about to be published and stressed that publishing any supplementary materials to her book would violate the contract agreement. On February 18, 1999, the publisher informed Japanese newspapers that it had been forced to postpone the release of both the translation and the anthology. Then, the publisher asked Chang to reconsider the inclusion of the notes and the commentary, but she again declined. Finally, in May, Kashiwa shobō and Basic Books terminated the contract.

Some American journalists, such as Sonni Efron of the *Los Angeles Times*, interpreted the breakdown between Kashiwa shobō and Iris Chang as an illustration of the complex issue of war and memory in Japan.[52] However, as Daqing Yang of George Washington University observed, many English-language newspapers attached a different significance to the dispute.[53] Uncritically taking Chang's side, these newspapers suggested that Kashiwa shobō's actions were evidence of a continuing reluctance on the part of Japanese to deal candidly with the massacre. Like Chang herself, portions of the American media failed to consider the history and memory of the massacre in Japan in its ambivalence and complexity.

LOOKING FOR LEVERAGE: THE JAPANESE REVISIONISTS' APPEAL TO THE UNITED STATES

While Chang's work was creating its stir in the media, Japanese revisionists attempted to influence American public opinion. Even to these revisionists who often claimed to be writing in the name of nationalism, the maintenance of friendly U.S.-Japanese relations seemed important. Few of these revisionists advocated that Japan should distance itself from the United States, nor did they argue in favor of isolationism. In 2000, Takemoto Tadao, a professor emeritus in French literature at Tsukuba University, and Ōhara Yasuo, a professor in Shintō studies at Kokugakuin University, published *The Alleged "Nanking Massacre": Japan's Rebuttal to China's Forged Claims*. Takemoto and Ōhara wrote their study in response to what they saw as the covert agenda of the PRC. They believed that Beijing was using the controversy over Nanjing to disrupt the U.S.-Japanese alliance and that once Japan had been estranged from the United States, China would exploit the ensuing power vacuum to achieve a hegemonic domination of East Asia.[54] In their eyes, the PRC was quietly sponsoring Chinese Americans, including Iris Chang, to remind Americans of Japanese wartime atrocities and thus to promote the desired isolation of Japan. As the Japanese government had made no effort to refute the claims of Iris Chang and other supposed dupes of the PRC, Takemoto and Ōhara decided to stand up for the nation to appeal to the American public in the name of Japanese justice. In their book, they argued, in the tradition of many other revisionists in Japan, that no slaughter of 300,000 Chinese had ever occurred in Nanjing and that the record kept by the burial organizations had been manipulated and substantially inflated.[55]

Similarly, in 2000, Sekai shuppan, a commercial publisher that is largely known for *Mangajin*, a monthly journal that features English translations of Japanese cartoons, published Tanaka Masaaki's *What Really Happened in Nan-*

king: The Refutation of a Common Myth. The volume was an abridgment of the English translation of his *Nanking jiken no sōkatsu: Gyakusatsu hitei 15 no ronkyo* (An Outline of the Nanjing Incident: Fifteen Grounds for the Denial of the Massacre), published in 1987, with a revised introduction by the author.[56] The publication of this book roughly coincided with the appearance of an organization called the Future Political Economy Research Institute. Actually, this institute seems to have existed in name only; it was merely an alter ego for a political organization that sponsored the publication of the volume. Nakajima Takao, CEO of the supposed institute, sent a copy of Tanaka's book to the members of the Association for Asian Studies.[57] In his accompanying cover letter, Nakajima, just like Takemoto and Ōhara, emphasized the PRC conspiracy theory and voiced his concerns that the American public might "have been deceived by the propaganda of Chinese government and their loyal envoy, Iris Chang, by twisting and fabricating the actions taken by our [Japanese] personnel."[58]

In his introduction, Tanaka insisted that Chang's volume had instigated the anti-Japanese campaigns in the United States and had succeeded in generating hatred toward Japan and the Japanese. Tanaka was convinced that the episode threatened to destabilize relations between Japan and the United States. Tanaka also expressed his disappointment that the Japanese government had failed to protest Chang's claim that 300,000 Chinese had been massacred in Nanjing. He urged Americans to read his book so they would realize that Chang's allegations were merely erroneous and groundless. In his introduction, Tanaka expressed his deep appreciation to Moteki Hiromichi, president of the publishing company and a member of Fujioka Nobukatsu's revisionist organization, for his encouragement and his effort to make Tanaka's work available to the American public.[59]

Tanaka and his supporters, however, miscalculated the impact of their work. For reasons that remain obscure, they evidently assumed that historians in the United States were drastically different from their counterparts in Japan and would therefore find the arguments denying the massacre more plausible. Since the revisionists had deeply distrusted the academic community in Japan for decades, it is strange that they expected a more receptive audience in America. Instead of raising suspicions about the reality of the massacre, the pleas of the revisionists incited concerned scholars in the United States to intensify their studies of Nanjing. Ironically, as with Chang's volume, a factually flawed and emotionally charged volume did more than the academically sounder work of the progressives to excite American scholarly interest in Nanjing.

THE FLOWERING OF NANJING SCHOLARSHIP IN AMERICA

The rediscovery of Nanjing and its aftermath in the 1990s undoubtedly contributed to the scholarship of the Nanjing Massacre in the United States. The last few years of the decade witnessed one international conference after another on the subject of the massacre, and Japanese historians were frequently invited to take part. Kasahara Tokushi, for example, participated in conferences held at Princeton University in November 1997 and at the University of California at Berkeley in April 1998.[60] Such conferences contributed to informing both members of the audience and the panelists and organizers themselves.[61]

The power of such conferences generated a new chapter of the study of Nanjing in the United States. In November 1999, Kajimoto Masato, a Japanese journalist studying at the Graduate School of Journalism at the University of Missouri at Columbia, went to an international conference held at Washington University. Kajimoto was inspired to compile a documentary website on the Nanjing Massacre, which included his interviews with scholars, critics, and activists in China, Japan, and the United States.[62] His online documentary provides rich oral, written, and visual materials to assist in learning about the Nanjing Massacre and the debate over history it has inspired. Unlike many emotional and one-sided Internet sources, Kajimoto gives visitors a chance to reach their own conclusions rather than telling them only what he wants them to believe.

Some of the international conferences have acquired second lives in print. The organizers of the Princeton conference later published *Nanking 1937: Memory and Healing*. The volume was not a mere collection of the papers presented at the conference. It included chapters written by authors who did not participate in the meeting and whose politics differ significantly. The article written by Sun Zhaiwei, vice director at the Institute of History at the Jiangsu Academy of Social Sciences, Nanjing, argued that the primary causes of the 300,000 deaths during the atrocities were the barbaric nature of the Japanese military and the strategic importance of Nanjing. To the contrary, Higashinakano Osamichi, a professor at Asia University, protested in his section that a massacre never occurred and discussed his definition of "massacre."[63] The wide spectrum of viewpoints presented in the volume not only illustrates why the topic is so controversial, but it also presses readers to decide which arguments they personally find most persuasive.

Analytical and historical materials pertaining to Nanjing appeared one after another during this most recent period. Daqing Yang's "Convergence or Divergence? Recent Historical Writings on the Rape of Nanjing" (1999) enlightened readers as to recent Japanese and Chinese scholarship on Nanjing.[64] Timothy Brook's *Documents on the Rape of Nanking* made primary sources on Nanjing widely available to American readers.[65] Bob Wakabayashi's "The Nanking One-Hundred-Man Killing Contest Debate: War Guilt Amid Fabricated Illusions, 1971–75" (2000) detailed the historical facts about the killing contest, and also discussed the historiography of the contest within Japan.[66] Joshua Fogel's *The Nanjing Massacre in History and Historiography* (2000) examined how perceptions of the Nanjing Massacre changed in China and Japan in the postwar period.[67] Yamamoto Masahiro's *Nanking: Anatomy of an Atrocity* (2000) discussed Nanjing in terms of military history.[68] David Askew's "The Nanjing Incident:

An Examination of the Civilian Population" (2001) estimated the civilian population in Nanjing at the time of the city's conquest.[69] Another article by Wakabayashi, "The Nanking Massacre: Now You See It, . . ." (2001) underscored the political subtexts of the controversy as well as problems encountered by Japanese revisionists who have recently published their volumes in English.[70] The reaction to Iris Chang's *The Rape of Nanking* has been one of those rare instances when the stream has risen above its source. Whereas Chang's book itself left much to be desired, the ensuing flowering of Nanjing scholarship in America would never have taken place without it.

CONCLUSION

In the 1990s, as a result of the public attention focused on the massacre, particularly after the publication of Iris Chang's *The Rape of Nanking*, many accounts of the massacre were published one after another in the United States. Both popular and scholarly works about the event became available to the public.[71] The results of this flood of information have been extremely mixed. On the one hand, the available popular accounts and the simplifications of the mass media have further entrenched the image of a monolithic "Japan" and have led many to believe that "the Japanese" were deliberately casting the nation's wartime crimes into oblivion while emphasizing their own victimization. On the other hand, many more scholarly works on Nanjing have lately appeared in the American market.

As in Japan and China, people in the United States have often viewed the Nanjing Massacre through the distorting filters of nationalism and ethnocentrism. To a number of Americans, Nanjing provided a *quid pro quo* before the fact for the civilian lives lost in Hiroshima and Nagasaki and other atrocities in the Pacific committed by the United States. To a number of Chinese Americans, the Nanjing Massacre became an icon of ethnic suffering and supplied a sense of ethnic identity that has transcended age, politics, or place of birth.

In the United States, the historiography of the Nanjing Massacre is still in its infancy. Although the volume of American scholarly materials on Nanjing significantly increased from the late 1990s on, popular reactions, often emotional and simplistic, also became extensively available to the public. As the study broadens, it should be guided by a spirit of scholarship, rather than a reflexive impulse to derogate "the Japanese" or to stir hostility among different ethnic groups in the United States. Ethnocentric narratives cast no light upon the causes of the Nanjing Massacre. They serve only to provoke hatred and conflicts because they encourage people to value human lives according to fictions of race and nationality.

Conclusion

I nterpretations of Nanjing have been contested ever since the atrocities occurred. From the 1970s on, the dispute over Nanjing has become more lively,
more globalized, and immeasurably more intense. The history and memory
of the Nanjing Massacre were no longer confined within one nation. Both domestic and international social and political contexts contributed to this internationalization. Unlike in the past decades, today those Japanese whose primary interest is to claim that the Nanjing Massacre was an illusion even
publish their work in English in order to persuade an international audience
and to confront not only Japanese progressives, but also foreign adversaries.

It is apparent that tens of thousands of Chinese were killed during and after
the battle of Nanjing. Why, then, do revisionists continue to deny the massacre
the status of a historical fact? They tend to believe that Imperial Japan and its
history have been unfairly demonized in the postwar period and that postwar
history education has deprived Japanese youth of national pride. The Nanjing
Massacre has been taught as one of the symbols of Japan's wartime evil in postwar Japan, and revisionists, responding to an impulse that they look upon as
patriotic pride, feel obliged to liberate the Japanese from the illusion fabricated
after the end of the war. They truly believe in their judgment, and their efforts
to revise the story of Nanjing will never cease until they silence their opposition, a highly unlikely possibility.[1]

As accounts of the Nanjing atrocities in English have begun to exert more influence on the master narrative of the history and memory of Nanjing, Japanese
revisionists have become more concerned with the publication of their accounts
in English and with the American scholarship of the Nanjing Massacre. *Annual
Report of Japan Association of "Nanjing" Studies 2003* included articles written by
Kitamura Minoru of Ritsumeikan University and Yamamoto Masahiro of the

University of Wyoming. Kitamura noted that his book *The Quest of the "Nanjing Incident"* will soon be translated into English and will be available to readers in English-speaking countries.[2] Yamamoto, author of *Nanking: Anatomy of an Atrocity*, investigated the current trend in studies of the Nanjing Massacre in the United States and complained that the studies had focused on the historiography of Nanjing rather than on the history of the Nanjing incident itself.[3]

Yamamoto's criticism certainly applies to this volume. By now readers may wonder which version of Nanjing is historically accurate. Should one believe, as the Chinese Nationalist government estimated during in February 1938, that Japanese troops slaughtered approximately 20,000 Chinese civilians during the Battle of Nanjing and its aftermath?[4] Or did they kill more than 200,000 Chinese civilians and POWs during the first six weeks of the Japanese occupation, as the Tokyo Trial determined?[5] Or did the figure approach 300,000 between December 12 and 21, 1937, as the military tribunal in Nationalist China concluded in 1947?[6] Are Fujioka Nobukatsu and Nishio Kanji correct in asserting that the great majority of the victims were combatants, rather than civilians, a claim that, if true, would greatly diminish the horror of the episode in the eyes of many?[7] Was the Nanjing Massacre a fabrication by China and the Allied Powers, as Tanaka Masaaki argued in *What Really Happened in Nanking* (2000)? Or was every single casualty in Nanjing the victim of a war crime, as Iris Chang implied in her book *The Rape of Nanking* (1997)? Above all, the ultimate question persists: How many Chinese were "massacred" in Nanjing?

The Research Committee on the Nanjing Incident, the organization of progressives that seemingly inspired the Japan Association for "Nanjing" Studies, has declined to endorse the highest available estimates of the death toll at Nanjing. In its *Thirteen Lies by the Deniers of the Nanjing Massacre* (1999), the committee members themselves stressed that they do not believe that the Japanese troops indiscriminately slaughtered 200,000–300,000 civilians in Nanjing. Kasahara Tokushi argued that group executions were more likely to have taken place in the vicinity of Nanjing than within the walled city itself. Nevertheless, he believed that between 100,000 and 200,000 Chinese civilians and soldiers in Nanjing and its six neighboring counties died at the hands of Japanese soldiers between early December 1937 and March 1938.[8]

Both the association and the research committee have supposedly been seeking for truth, and each organization includes academics. Why, then, have the two groups been unable to agree? The rifts between the two organizations have been enormously difficult, if not impossible, to overcome. The former excludes the killings of Chinese soldiers from their definition of "atrocities," while the latter regards these soldiers as victims.[9] Thus, the association never includes Chinese soldiers and plain-clothes guerrillas in its head count of the victims of Nanjing. In addition, though the latter defines "Nanjing" as the walled city and its six neighboring counties, an area in which the combined population exceeded 1 million, the former understands the term as the walled city and its immediate environs, a region with approximately 200,000 residents.[10]

Moreover, the two groups have adopted significantly different attitudes toward the official Chinese estimate of 300,000 deaths. For example, Kasahara stressed that the difference between his estimate and the Chinese one should not be regarded as important because both acknowledge wholesale atrocities in Nanjing on a scale of historical significance.[11] To Kasahara, every individual killed in and around the city had a name, siblings, parents, and relatives. What matters in his view is not a number, but rather the agony experienced by those who suffered violent deaths and the incalculable suffering in the heart and mind of every grieving survivor.[12] In contrast, Higashinakano focused on thoroughly refuting the death estimate, claiming it was a product of Chinese propaganda and must be discredited thoroughly. According to Higashinakano, this estimate propagates a fabrication in the minds of the Japanese and undermines healthy diplomatic relations between China and Japan.[13]

Considering how intractable the dispute has become even between two academic organizations, it is not surprising that arriving at a shared idea of truth across national boundaries has proved just as difficult. Since the early 1980s, the PRC government has promoted patriotic education, and Nanjing has become an indispensable part of this campaign. In today's China, the Nanjing Massacre stands as one of the national symbols of Japanese wartime atrocities. The PRC's version of the event treats every death as a consequence of Japanese atrocities and evinces no interest in researching whether victims were civilians or combatants, or whether they were killed legally or illegally according to the rules of war. To authors like Iris Chang, the atrocities in Nanjing were a forgotten holocaust, an argument that gains strength when one invokes the largest possible estimate.[14]

The lengthy dispute over the Nanjing Massacre has brought both benefits and detriments to the discipline of history. In Japan, China, and the United States, Nanjing has finally become a recognized symbol of the horrors of war and the human capacity for evil, worthy of being mentioned alongside the Holocaust and Hiroshima. Today many remember it as a dreadful event. Because of the dispute, new historical materials on Nanjing have continually been discovered and have enriched the history of the Nanjing atrocities. On the other hand, the public memory of Nanjing has also been occasionally tainted with overtones of nationalism and ethnocentrism. Too many people have responded to the massacre not from a basis of reason, but according to national or ethnic identities that they have been reflexively conditioned to love or hate. In its worst moments, the debate over Nanjing has served to fuel the same kinds of racial and cultural hatred that tend to lead to massacres in the first place.

The history of Nanjing has altered over time to meet the needs of changing societies in different sociopolitical contexts. Nanjing has been a mirror of larger attitudes and geopolitical imperatives. Understand the historiography of the massacre, and you will find that you possess a useful index to society and politics of each historical moment in the decades since 1937. It is no wonder that ethnocentric narratives of Nanjing prevailed at the time of the war, during which Japan, China, and the United States all found it necessary to promote mass killing in the name of the state and justice. It is understandable that news reports of the testimonies of Nanjing at the Tokyo Trial appalled many Japanese during the occupation, when the military was entirely discredited. It is no surprise that the authorized PRC accounts at the height of the Cold War blamed the United States for abetting Japanese atrocities in Nanjing. It is, finally, no wonder that the history of Nanjing was rediscovered in the United States in the post–Cold War period, just as the hitherto accepted history of the Pacific War had largely disregarded the perspectives of Chinese immigrants.

How will the history of Nanjing be told in Japan, China, and the United States 20 years from now? Will it be possible for all of these governments and peoples to share a single narrative of the Nanjing Massacre? I am afraid not. The various authors of Nanjing literature may never agree on a definition of truth, giving readers a wide range of narratives from which to choose their own preferred history of Nanjing. Nevertheless, it has already been possible for many individuals in all three nations to overcome the limitations of ethnocentrism and nationalism in their thinking about Nanjing. Motivated by the ideal of universal human rights, concerned persons may eventually be able to agree on an international history of the Nanjing Massacre whose objective will be to produce a more harmonious future. Such a history would seek neither to exploit, nor to exaggerate, nor to rationalize atrocity. Instead, it would articulate an understanding of events that values human life without regard to ethnicity, nationality, religion, or gender.

During the wars among nations that have already scarred the nascent twenty-first century, states still consider nationality and race when deciding who shall live and who shall die. Readers of this volume should question the purposes for which we need to remember Nanjing: whether we shall use it to construct a global society that respects dignity of all human beings or to privilege certain national or ethnic groups above those we perceive as alien and threatening. Perhaps the world will find a hopeful example in the paintings of the Marukis. After the end of the war, the Marukis became diehard peace activists and underscored the horrors of the war in their panels, including *The Rape of Nanking* (1975), which is printed on the front cover of this book and has been exhibited to receptive audiences around the world. Their panels did not aim to either praise or denigrate particular national or ethnic groups. Instead, their goal has been to use these events to urge a spirit of sympathy and kindness across national and ethnic boundaries. May the spirit of the Marukis prevail in the future literature of Nanjing.

NOTES

INTRODUCTION

1. Monbushō (Ministry of Education, Japan), *Shotōka kokushi* (Lower-Level National History), 1943, in *Nihon kyōkasho taikei kindai hen*, Vol. 20, pp. 369–370.

CHAPTER 1

1. "Keikakuteki no buryoku kō-Nichi rekizen" (Obviously Planned Anti-Japanese Armed Conflict), *Tōkyō asahi shinbun*, July 12, 1937, p. 2. For a more detailed historical analysis of the undeclared war between China and Japan, see James Morley et al., *The China Quagmire: Japan's Expansion on the Asian Continent, 1933–1941.*

2. "Fuhō shageki ni waga gun hangeki" (Our Army Fights Back against Illegal Shootings), *Tōkyō asahi shinbun*, July 9, 1937, p. 1. Also, see "Shinagun mata fuhō shageki" (Chinese Army Commits More Unlawful Shootings), *Tōkyō asahi shinbun*, July 20, 1937, p. 2; "Kōgun o jōmon ni irete totsujo mōsha o abisu, gekisen jitsuni san-jikan" (After Allowing Imperial Army inside Wall, [Chinese Army] Suddenly Begins Intense Shooting; Fight Lasts Three Hours), *Tōkyō asahi shinbun*, July 27, 1937, p. 2.

3. Shinbun taimusu sha, *Shina jihen senshi* (The History of the China Incident), Vol. 1, pp. 264–88. In this volume, the editor Miyai Kōtarō used only the reports of war correspondents to narrate the incident. In chapter 9, titled "Ā Tsūshū jiken" (Ah, the Tongzhou Incident), to which the editor devoted more than 20 pages, Chinese barbarism in Tongzhou was described as unimaginable and worse than the work of devils and beasts (*kichiku*).

4. "Sanagara jigoku emaki! Kichiku no zangyaku gengo ni zessu" (Just Like a Picture Scroll Illustrating Hell! Atrocities by Savages Are beyond Words), *Tōkyō asahi shinbun*, August 4, 1937, p. 1.

5. "Hoantai henjite kichiku, tsuminaki dōhō o gyakusatu" (Peace Preservation Force Turns into Savages; Innocent Countrymen Are Massacred), *Tōkyō asahi shinbun*, August 4, 1937, p. 1. Tanaka's first name is unknown. In these articles, "Japanese" subsumes not only people from Japanese islands but also from the Korean peninsula. Although survivors are categorized either as *naichijin* (those from Japanese islands) or *Chōsenjin* (those from the Korean peninsula), the dead seemed to have acquired an equal status. They were simply regarded as "Japanese."

6. "Bōrei! Kichiku no hoantai, taikyo hōi shite ransha" (Disgusting! Barbaric [Chinese] Peace Preservation Force; Troops Herded into a Mass, Then Shot at Random), *Tōkyō asahi shinbun*, August 10, 1937, p. 2.

7. See, for example, "Shanhai no wahei zetsubō" (No Hope for Peace in Shanghai), *Tōkyō asahi shinbun*, August 14, 1937, p. 2.

8. Itō's first name is unknown. See "Hyaku pāsento meichū" (Hit the Mark 100 Percent), *Tōkyō asahi shinbun*, August 14, 1937, p. 2.

9. "Chi ni ueta Shina ki bōgyaku no kagiri o tsukusu" (Bloodthirsty Chinese Fighters Indulge in Atrocities), *Tōkyō asahi shinbun*, August 15, 1937, p. 2.

10. *Jihen* literally connotes a more serious event that an "incident." Either "disturbance" or "conflict" would be more accurate. However, scholarly works in English, such as Louise Young's *Japan's Total Empire*, tend to render "jihen" as "incident," and this study conforms to that practice.

11. Kiyosawa Kiyoshi, "Kokusai pen kurabu kusen ki" (The Struggle at the International Association of Poets, Playwrights, Editors, Essayists, and Novelists), pp. 242, 245–46, 248.

12. Baba Tsunego, "Nihon ga susumu michi" (The Direction That Japan Should Take), 36–38.

13. Monbushō (Ministry of Education, Japan), *Jinjō shōgaku chiri sho* (Elementary School Geography), in *Nihon kyōkasho taikei kindai hen*, Vol. 16, p. 488. The textbook was revised in 1935 and was used by fifth-year elementary school students, beginning in 1936. This was the third revision since the first national geography textbook was published in 1903. The definition of Japan changed throughout that time: in the 1903 version, it did not include the Korean peninsula, though the Japanese islands were defined as Honshū, Shikoku, Kyūshū, Hokkaido, Taiwan, the Ryukyus, and the Kurils. From the 1910 version on, Korea was included in "Japan." Unlike *Asahi nenkan*, which excluded Taiwan from *naichi*, the textbook included Taiwan as one of the Japanese islands. Geography was taught in the fifth and sixth years during this period.

14. Monbushō (Ministry of Education, Japan), *Jinjō shōgaku chiri sho* (Vol. 2, 1936), p. 550.

15. Monbushō (Ministry of Education, Japan), *Jinjō shōgaku chiri sho* (Vol. 2, 1939), p. 644.

16. Monbushō (Ministry of Education, Japan), *Shōgaku kokushi* (Lower-Level National History), Vol. 2, in *Nihon kyōkasho taikei kindai hen*, Vol. 20, pp. 231–33. National history was taught in fifth (Vol. 1) and sixth grades (Vol. 2) in the six-year elementary school. The newly revised Vol. 1 was published in 1940, and Vol. 2 followed in 1941.

17. Monbushō (Ministry of Education, Japan), *Shōgaku kokugo tokuhon* (Vol. 1), in *Nihon kyōkasho taikei kindai hen*, Vol. 7, pp. 559–60. See also a chart of textbooks

used from 1904 through 1945, Nakamura Kikuji, *Kyōkasho no hensan, hakkō tō kyōkasho seido no hensen ni kansuru chōsa kenkyū* (A Study of the Changes of Compilation and Publishing of Textbooks), pp. 340–41.

18. Monbushō (Ministry of Education, Japan), *Shōgaku kokugo tokuhon* (Vol. 4), in *Nihon kyōkasho taikei kindai hen*, Vol. 7, pp. 633–35, 646–48. The second-year students used Vol. 3 in the first half, and Vol. 4 in the second half of the year.

19. Regarding Japanese readings as they existed prior to revision, see *Nihon kyōkasho taikei kindai hen*, Vol. 7, pp. 262–555. Readings in this period still included many stories that had nothing to do with the military. Previous textbooks had told many more stories of great non-Japanese people, including Europeans and Americans. By this time, however, although some Westerners, such as Alexander Graham Bell, continued to appear in the readings, others, like Abraham Lincoln, had been excised.

20. Monbushō (Ministry of Education, Japan), *Jinjō shōgaku shūshin sho* (Elementary School Ethics, Vol. 6), in *Nihon kyōkasho taikei kindai hen*, Vol. 3, pp. 328–58. This text consisted of 27 chapters. Three chapters are dedicated to the Imperial Rescript on Education, three chapters to obligations of the people, and two chapters to the development of the state.

21. Keigo Takiomi, *Nihon kyōkasho taikei kindai hen*, Vol. 3, pp. 216–358. Newly revised ethics texts for the first-year elementary school student were available in 1934; for the second year, in 1935; for the third year, in 1936; for the fourth year, in 1937; for the fifth year, in 1938; for the sixth year, in 1939 (Nakamura, *Kyōkasho no hensan*, p. 340). For discussions of Socrates, see pp. 297–98; Nogi Maresuke, pp. 298–99; Christopher Columbus, pp. 308–10; and Yoshida Shōin, pp. 320–21. The sixth-year textbook included only two non-Japanese: Benjamin Franklin was discussed in the section on public welfare (pp. 336–38), and Confucius was introduced in the section on virtue (pp. 346–47). However, the text still emphasized benevolence (pp. 347–48), courage (pp. 348–50), and international peace (pp. 345–46).

22. Kaigo, *Nihon kyōkasho taikei kindai hen*, Vol. 3, p. 327.

23. Ozaki Hotsuki, *Omoide no Shōnen kurabu jidai* (The Memorable Period of *Shōnen kurabu*), pp. 94–95.

24. Although "tonkatsu" in Japanese means "deep-fried pork cutlet," "tonkatsu" could mean "pig-victory."

25. Tagawa Suihō, *Norakuro sōkōgeki* (Norakuro's All-Out Attack), p. 160. For cartoon history, see Ishiko Jun, *Nihon manga shi* (History of Japanese Cartoons). For the representation of war in cartoons, see Ishiko Jun, *Manga ni miru sensō to heiwa 90 nen* (Peace and War in Cartoons during the Last Ninety Years). See also Akiyama Masami, *Maboroshi no sensō managa no sekai* (Wartime Cartoons Disappeared Like a Dream). This book discusses wartime cartoons published in the 1930s.

26. "Hyakunin giri kyōsō!, ryōshōi hayakumo 80 nin" (Contest to Cut Down One Hundred!; Two Second Lieutenants Already Up to Eighty), *Tōkyō nichi nichi shinbun*, November 30, 1937; "Kyūpitchi ni yakushin, hyakunin giri kyōsō no keika" (The Remarkable Progress of the Cut-Down Contest), *Tōkyō nichi nichi shinbun*, December 4, 1937; "'Hyakunin giri' dai sessen" (A Close Race in the "Contest to Cut Down One Hundred"), *Tōkyō nichi nichi shinbun*, December 6, 1937. For the translations of the first and third articles (which granted the two lieutenants anonymity),

see Honda Katsuichi, *The Nanjing Massacre*, pp. 125–26. Initial "M" indicates Mukai Toshiaki, while initial "N" indicates Noda Tsuyoshi. For Japanese texts, see Honda Katsuichi, *Nankin e no michi* (The Road to Nanjing), pp. 160–64; Nōmoa Nankin no kai (The No-More-Nanjing Association), Hōdō *ni miru Nankin 1937* (Newspaper Reports of Nanjing in 1937, reprinted in pamphlet form, 1997), p. 27. Mukai and Noda competed to cut down 100 Chinese on the way to Nanjing. As of December 5, 1937, Mukai had killed 89, while Noda had killed 78. By December 10, each had exceeded his goal of killing 100, but they were not sure who had reached 100 first. They therefore extended the contest so that the first to cut down 150 would be declared the victor. This contest will be analyzed in detail later in this study.

27. "Nankin wa me no shita da, warera no kokoro mo ichiban nori, hayaru kanki! Daishuga no saisoku! Jinsoku no kōgun, Shikinzan senryō no kaihō o ukete hayakumo ginza ni senshō kazari" (Nanjing Is Now under Our Eyes, in Our Minds We Are Already There, Joy Exceeds! A Great Celebration Awaits! Quick Advance of the Imperial Army, Banners Celebrating the Capture of the Zijin Mountain Appear along Ginza), *Yomiuri shinbun*, December 8, 1937.

28. Nihon Hōsō Kyōkai, *Shōwa 13 nen rajio nenkan*, pp. 122–23.

29. "Teki no kaitō tsuini kitarazu, kōgun danko kōryaku no hibuta, Nankin rakujō no unmei semaru" (The Enemy Does Not Respond; Imperial Army Opens Fire Resolutely; The Fall of Nanjing Expected Soon), *Tōkyō asahi shinbun*, December 11, 1937, p. 1.

30. The reporter obviously created this piece of news by distributing copies of the extra edition at a dance hall and provoking public excitement. "Odori dashita chōchin gyōretsu sakuya ame no teito no nigiwai" (Lantern Parades Burst into Tokyo Streets, Last Night's Great Commotion in the Rain), *Tōkyō asahi shinbun*, December 11, 1937, p. 6.

31. "Seki kitta hata no dotō, 'taiyō no machi' ni hanran, todoroku rokuman nin no banzai" (Flags Rush into "the City of Sun" Like Flood Water; Sixty Thousand People Give Cheers of Banzai), *Tōkyō asahi shinbun*, December 15, 1937, p. 2. "Tesei no hinomaru de keimusho demo banzai" (Celebration with Handmade Flags in the Prison), *Yomiuri shinbun*, December 15, 1937.

32. See, for example, articles about killing contests which appeared in *Tōkyō nichi nichi shinbun* on November 30, December 4, and December 6, 1937.

33. "Nankin ittai sōtō no senka, teki rokuman o horyo gekimetsu su, kōgun nao seisō o tsuzuku" (Achievement of the Mopping-up Operation in the Nanking Area; Sixty Thousand Captured or Annihilated; Imperial Army Continues Mopping-up Operation), *Tōkyō Asahi shinbun*, December 16, 1937, p. 1.

Regarding previous examples of victorious mopping-up operations, see, for example, "Teki niman tachimachi shikabane no yama" (Twenty Thousand Enemy Troops Immediately Reduced to Mountain of Dead Bodies), *Tōkyō asahi shinbun*, November 17, 1937, p. 2; "Taikyaku no teki o issei sōsha, waga bakugeki ni kaimetsu" (Wholesale Shooting against Retreating Enemy; Destroyed by Our Bombing), *Tōkyō asahi shinbun*, August 30, 1937.

34. "Teki shuto ni 'kimigayo,' takaku kakagu nisshōki" (National Anthem Sung in the Capital of the Enemy; Japanese Flag Flies High), *Tōkyō nichi nichi shinbun*, December 18, 1937, p. 1.

35. "Banzai no arashi, kyō Nankin nyūjōshiki no sōkan" (Storms of *Banzai*,

Spectacular Scenes of Entry into Nanjing Today), *Tōkyō asahi shinbun*, December 18, 1937, extra issue, p. 1.

36. Two examples of simple ultrapatriotic writings in which a heroic Japan punishes a villainous China are *Shina jihen chūyūdan, kangekidan* (Brave and Moving Stories of the China Incident) and Shinbun taimusu sha, *Shina jihen senshi* (The Military History of the China Incident). Both books include sections on the capture of Nanjing.

37. Kosaka Eiichi, "Nankin dai kōryakusen jūgun shiki" (A Private Narrative of the Great Capture of Nanjing), pp. 208–209.

38. Ibid., pp. 212–15.

39. Ōya Sōichi, "Honkon kara Nankin nyūjō" (From Hong Kong to the Entrance of Nanjing), p. 235.

40. Ibid., p. 241.

41. Ibid., pp. 236, 238–39, 242, 246.

42. Ibid., pp. 249–51.

43. See Awaya Kentarō and Nakazono Yutaka *Naimushō shinbunkiji sashitome shiryō shūsei* (Collection of Newspaper Articles Banned by the Ministry of Home Affairs), Vols. 6 and 7.

44. Restrictions on the press also applied to broadcasting. The NHK produced programs according to government regulations. On November 4, 1937, the Ministry of Communications notified the NHK to employ every means, including prior restraint, in order to prevent reports that might undermine the government's war efforts. See Nihon Hōsō Kyōkai, *Hōsō gojūnen shi* (The History of Fifty Years of Broadcasting), p. 118.

45. Hayashi Zensuke, "Shina jihenka ni okeru fuon kōdō to sono taisaku ni tsuite" (Alarming Activities and How They Were Dealt With at the Time of the China Incident), reprinted in *Shakai mondai sōsho* (Library of Social Problems), Ser. 1, Vol. 79, p. 8. The document was originally written in 1941. From January 1937 to October 1941, 3,148 people were arrested across the nation, and 1,229 of them were prosecuted under the Peace Preservation Law (p. 7).

46. Ibid., p. 12. From January 1937 to November 1941, 1,515 people were arrested for the alleged offense of spreading rumors; 427 of them were indicted on the charge of violating the military law.

47. Wada was sentenced on December 14, 1937. Nishigaya Tōru, "Shina jihen ni kansuru zōgen higo ni tsuite" (Regarding Lies and Rumors during the China Incident), reprinted in *Shakai mondai sōsho*, Ser. 1, Vol. 79, p. 142. Nishigaya was a district attorney in Tokyo. The report was originally written in December 1938.

48. Ozawa was sentenced on December 16, 1937. Ibid., p. 144.

49. Nishigaya, "Shina jihen ni kansuru zōgen higo ni tsuite," p. 23.

50. *Minzoku to heiwa* was published in June 1936. Yanaihara's "Kokka no risō" (Ideals of a Nation), published in *Chūō kōron* in September, also caused a controversy. See "Yanaihara teidai kyōju jihyō o teishutsu su" (Imperial University Professor Yanaihara Submits Resignation), *Tōkyō asahi shinbun*, December 2, 1937, p. 2.

51. "Saigo no kōgi ni otsu namida" (Tears at the Last Lecture), *Tōkyō asahi shinbun*, December 3, 1937, p. 2.

52. Naimushō keihokyoku hoanka (Home Ministry, Police Bureau, Peace Preservation Section), *Tokkō gaiji geppō shōwa jūninen jūnigatsu bun* (Monthly Gazette

on External Affairs of the Special Higher Police), (December 1937): 36. This monthly report was classified as an internal document.

53. Ibid.

54. *Asahi nenkan 1939*, p. 75. Here are the population totals reported for Japan and other areas:

Japanese islands	69,254,148
Korean peninsula	22,899,038
Taiwan	5,212,426
Kurils	331,943
Kwangtung province	1,656,726
South Sea islands	102,537

55. Hayashi, "Shina jihenka ni okeru fuon kōdō to sono taisaku ni tsuite," p. 140.

56. *Asahi nenkan 1939*, p. 82. Of these residents, 27,090 were from China, and 2,581 were from Manchukuo.

57. Ibid., p. 167.

58. Nishigaya, "Shina jihen ni kansuru zōgen higo ni tsuite," pp. 141 (Liu), 144 (Choe), 149 (Alexander). The list (pp. 139–209) gives detailed information about 193 cases of "lies and rumors."

59. Ishikawa Tatsuzō was a respected novelist, having won the first Akutagawa prize in September 1935. Nevertheless, the editor of *Chūō kōron*, the journal in which "Ikiteiru heitai" was published, exercised caution, eliminating what were seen as "dangerous sentences" from the manuscript. But this self-imposed censorship did no good. One day before the March issue of *Chūō kōron* was to reach the newsstands (February 18, 1938), the publisher received a notice prohibiting the publication of "Ikiteiru heitai." The journal, excluding Ishikawa's essay and another article, was published on February 23. In September 1938, Ishikawa was sentenced to four months in prison with a three-year stay of execution, and the editor of *Chūō kōron*, Makino Takeo, was fined 100 yen. See Chūō kōron sha, *Chūō kōron nanajūnen shi* (Seventy Year History of Chūō kōron sha), pp. 27–28; *Chūō kōron sha no hachijū nen* (Eighty Years of Chūō Kōron Company), pp. 281–84, 426–27. Also see Haruko Taya Cook, "The Many Lives of Living Soldiers," and Ishikawa Tatsuzō, *Soldiers Alive*.

60. Ishikawa Tatsuzō, *Bokei kazoku/Ikiteiru heitai* (The Maternal Family/Living Soldiers), pp. 7, 21–23, 27, 30, 50, 56, 61, 66.

61. Ibid., p. 21.

62. Ibid., pp. 48-49.

63. Ibid., p. 30.

64. Ibid., pp. 28–29.

65. Ishikawa's reprinted *Living Soldiers* was published by Kawade shobō in 1945, by Kaiguchi shoten in 1946, and by Yakumo shoten in 1948. The latest edition was published by Chūō kōron shinsha in 1999.

66. *Tokkō gaiji geppō* (November 1937), pp. 10–16. "Dear Japanese Soldiers!" (Shin'ai naru Nihon no heishi shokun!) read:

> About one month has passed since we began to fight on the battlefield. Whenever we fire our cannons at you, we feel unbearable pain. This is not because we are afraid to die, but because we feel that killing a brother is the most unfortunate thing a human being can do.

During this one month, as many as thirty thousand of your brothers [Japanese soldiers] were killed in Shanghai, and more than sixty airplanes, the fruit of your flesh and blood, were shot down.

And what did you get in return? . . . Massacring a mass of innocent civilians and trampling on Chinese culture passed down from our early civilization may have appeased the military clique for a moment, but internationally, it outraged human beings who now crave justice against Japan. And what did you get?

This war means death to you . . . [and] poverty to your family, doesn't it? Yet do you still insist on fighting for an "imperial state"?

All right. The "Manchurian incident" and "the first Shanghai incident" were also fought for the "imperial state," weren't they? And what did you get?

You and I are all children of our fathers and mothers. The pity we feel when we kill you is the same as you feel when you kill us. We volunteered to sacrifice ourselves for our mother land, but why must you suffer and bury yourself in a foreign land?

Dear friend, our bullets and shells are aimed at the Japanese military clique invading our mother land. Yet how unfortunate! Those who are hit are not the enemy we hate, but you whom we should shake hands with.

Between Chinese and Japanese peoples, no hatred has ever existed before, nor does any exist now.

The Japanese military clique is our common enemy. We soldiers protecting Chinese race appeal you in the name of brotherhood.

Soldiers of the Republic of China

67. *Tokkō gaiji geppō* (February 1938), pp. 12–13. The excerpts include (1) *Sanzen taru senryō chitai* (Occupied Area in the Depths of Misery) and (2) *Fassho no bōfū* (Storm of Fascism). The first number of the *Kyokutō sensō news* (October 25, 1937) is included in *Tokkō gaiji geppō* (December 1937), pp. 215–16. The publisher, Nyūsu sha, was located in Seattle, Washington. *Tokkō gaiji geppō* (December 1937) also included a two-page flyer, both in Japanese and English, titled "The Military-Fascists of Japan Stand Condemned!" and authored by the Japanese Commission of the Communist Party located in Seattle (the flyer's address, however, is different from that of Nyūsu sha).

68. Kaji's introduction was dated August 5, 1938. See Hora Tomio, *Nit-Chū sensō: Nankin daigyakusatsu jiken shiryōshū* (The Sino-Japanese War: A Collection of Historical Materials on the Nanjing Massacre), vol. 2, pp. 311–13.

69. Aoyama wrote his introduction in Hankou on July 24, 1938. Ibid., pp.314–17.

70. *Tokkō gaiji geppō* (February 1938), p. 12; *Tokkō gaiji geppō* (March 1938), p. 10; *Tokkō gaiji geppō* (June 1938), p. 14.

71. Hayashi, "Shina jihenka ni okeru fuon kōdō to sono taisaku ni tsuite," p. 185. Also in Tucker's possession were 13 copies of *Kōsen nijū ichi ka getsu go no Shina* (China: Twenty-One Months after the Anti-Japanese War), which, according to the police, stated that the Japanese military was creating not order, but disorder. It was also claimed that this publication exaggerated the killing of civilians in Canton. Tucker also had other materials published by the Chinese Information Committee (CIC), which was considered a Chinese intelligence agency. Hayashi suspected

that Tucker was trying to disturb order in Japan (p. 186). Luther Tucker was translit-
erated in katakana as Rūsā Takkā. The name, therefore, could be misspelled.

72. *Tokkō gaiji geppō* (May 1938), p. 35.

73. See *Amerasia* 2, no. 6 (August 1938) for translations of "An Announcement
to the Members of Japan's Various Political Parties," "Proclamation to the Tradesmen and Artisans of Japan," and "Proclamation to the Various Laborers." The pamphlet that urged support for the Kajis was similar to "Dear Japanese Soldiers!" (See
note 66.)

74. *Tokkō gaiji geppō* (May 1938), pp. 39–42. Kaji Wataru and his wife were considered traitors by Japanese authorities (see p. 37).

75. Ibid., pp. 34–36.

76. Ibid., p. 37.

77. Ono Kenji, Fujiwara Akira, and Honda Katsuichi, *Nankin dai gyakusatsu o
kiroku shita kōgun heishi tachi: Dai jūsan shidan Yamada shitai heishi no jinchū nikki* (Imperial Soldiers Who Recorded the Nanjing Massacre: The Field Diaries of the Yamada Unit of the Thirteenth Division). The book includes 19 field diaries. Descriptions of looting can be found quite frequently among all of the writers. As for the
killing of civilians, see, for example, pp. 63–64. On October 6, 1937, the anonymous
writer, named "Horikoshi Fumio," felt sorry for killed prisoners, including women
and children, but convinced himself that such misfortunes are inevitable in war
("Shinajin onna kodomo no toriko ari, jūsatsu su, mugotarashiki kana, kore tatakai
nari"). As for the killing of POWs at Wufu Mountain, see, for example, pp. 134 (Diaries on December 16 and 17, 1937, written by "Miyamoto Shōgo"), 147 (December
14, 1937, by "Sugiuchi Toshio"), 219 (December 16, 1937, by "Endō Takaaki"). All
but two of these diarists preferred to be anonymous.

78. Ibid., p. 36 (December 9, 1937). The girl was delighted, but her response
made him feel even more guilty. She reminded him of his children in Japan, a
thought that almost moved him to tears. On December 18, he wrote that he shot
prisoners at the coast of the Yangtze River without any particular emotion (p. 38).

79. Ibid., p. 133 (December 14, 1937).

80. Ibid., p. 319 (November 13, 1937).

81. Ibid., p. 367 (November 21, 1937).

82. Ibid., p. 361 (October 11 and 12, 1937); p. 368 (November 15, 1937).

83. Eguchi Keiichi and Shibahara Takuji, eds., *Nichtū sensō jūgun nikki* (Field
Diary from the Japan-China War). Ohara, born in 1910, wrote a diary of 11 volumes
from September 1, 1937, through August 7, 1938, and brought this journal back to
Japan with him. The transport corps was often looked down upon in the military because their primary mission was not to fight, but to carry military supplies. For general information about the transport corps, see Eguchi's commentary in the book,
pp. 479–99. Regarding his years as an elementary school teacher, see Shibahara's
foreword (pp. 3–17).

84. Ibid., p. 39 (October 1, 1937). When he visited a ruined village that had become a battlefield, he stated:

> How did the farmers who had lived peacefully feel about this? Unless they
> had been attacked by warlords, they could never have experienced such
> destruction. Floods, which are particular to this region, probably do not
> hurt the farmers as much as the war is doing. Because of the war, tran-

quility has disappeared overnight, and the farmers have run away from home and become homeless. They will come back home someday. Then, how much damage will such ruined homes cause in their minds? Righteous war must be carried out. Yet war damages must be avoided as much as possible. This may seem impossible. But for the happiness of the people, needless atrocities must be avoided. Imagine that someone destroyed our villages like this. Think if we were forced to be wanderers. Nothing is as cruel as war. It is the misfortune of human beings. While we are walking around the village, elderly people put their hands together in supplication. These farmers certainly do not understand why Japan and China are confronting each other. They might have lived without having any idea about Japan. What must the impression of Japan be for these farmers who have experienced this? I hope that so bad an impression will not be left behind. (p. 39)

See also October 2, 4, and 21, 1937.

85. Ibid., p. 130 (December 11, 1937). He was informed on December 11 that the city was captured. Although he expressed skepticism, he wished the news was true and wrote, "Nothing makes me feel happier than this."

86. Ibid., p. 143 (December 24, 1937). He witnessed hundreds or thousands of dead bodies at Zhongshan Wharf. Although he described his surprise, he recorded the scene in a relatively simple manner compared with his diary entries recording the guilt he felt for taking part in looting.

87. Hayashi, "Shina jihenka ni okeru fuon kōdō to sono taisaku ni tsuite," p. 98.

88. Ibid., p. 98.

89. Ibid., pp. 98, 100–10.

90. Hora Tomio, *Kindai senshi no nazo* (Riddles of Modern War History), pp. 1–2.

91. For reports of the "Contest to Cut Down a Hundred," see *Tōkyō nichi nichi shinbun* on November 30, 1937, and December 4, 1937. Quoted in Honda Katsuichi, *The Nanjing Massacre*, pp. 125–26. For a discussion of the annihilation of the enemy, see, for example, "Nankin ittai sōtō no senka, teki rokuman o horyo gekimetsu su, kōgun nao seisō o tsuzuku" (Achievement of the Mopping-Up Operation in the Nanking Area; Sixty Thousand Captured or Annihilated; The Imperial Army Continues Mopping-Up Operation), *Tōkyō Asahi shinbun*, December 16, 1937, p. 1.

CHAPTER 2

1. Those states represented on the council were: Belgium, Bolivia, the United Kingdom, China, Ecuador, France, Iran, Italy, Latvia, New Zealand, Peru, Poland, Romania, Sweden, and the Soviet Union. Secretary General M. J. Avenol also joined the meeting.

2. League of Nations, *Official Journal* 19, no. 2 (February 1938): 120. For Koo's speech at the Eighteenth Session of the assembly, see League of Nations, *Official Journal*, special supplement, no. 169: 47. The assembly was held from September 13 to October 6, 1937. Koo appealed to the assembly on September 15, 1937. The resolution, which recommended that members of the league refrain from taking any actions that would increase Chinese difficulties and that they extend aid to China, was adopted on October 6, 1937: "[The assembly] expresses its moral support for China, and recommends that Members of the League should refrain from taking any action

which might have the effect of weakening China's power of resistance and thus of increasing her difficulties in the present conflict, and should also consider how far they can individually extend aid to China" (p. 149).

3. League of Nations, *Official Journal* 19, no. 2 (February 1938): 121.

4. Ibid., pp. 121–22. At the time of the Manchurian Incident, Koo emphasized that the ultimate Japanese goal is to conquer the world, in accordance with the prophecies of the Tanaka Memorial. The Japanese representative challenged its authenticity, and a great many people, as Koo observed, expressed skepticism about its trustworthiness. See *Official Journal* (December 1932): 1882, 1892. For a useful analysis of the so-called Tanaka Memorial, see John Stephan, "The Tanaka Memorial (1927): Authentic or Spurious?"

5. League of Nations, *Official Journal* 19, nos. 5–6 (May–June 1938): 306–308, 378–80.

6. Ibid., p. 380.

7. League of Nations, *Official Journal*, special supplement, no. 183: 52.

8. *Wellington Koo Collection*, box 36, Rare Book and Manuscript Library, Columbia University.

9. League of Nations, *Official Journal* 19, nos. 8–9: 665–66.

10. Ibid., p. 666.

11. Ibid., pp. 668–69.

12. "Rinmei dai yonhyaku nijūichi gō" (Chief of the General Staff Order No. 421), issued on July 28, 1937; "Dairikushi dai hyakujū gō" (Chief of the General Staff Order No. 110), issued on April 11, 1938; "Dairikushi dai yonhyaku gojūni gō" (Chief of the General Staff Order No. 452), issued on May 13, 1939. All are reprinted in Yoshimi Yoshiaki and Matsuno Seiya, *Dokugasusen kankei shiryō II* (Historical Materials Concerning Chemical Warfare, Part 2), pp. 244, 253, 258.

13. "Hokyūyō danyaku chōsa hyō (HokuShina hōmengun, 1937.7.8–1938.11.10)," (Chart of Supplied Ammunition to the North China Army, July 8, 1937–November 10, 1938) and "Shamō danyaku chōsa hyō (HokuShina hōmengun, 1937.7.8–1938.10.31)," (Chart of Consumed Ammunition by the North China Army, July 8, 1937–October 31, 1938). Both are quoted in Yoshimi and Matsuno, *Dokugasusen kankei shiryō II*, pp. 396–97.

14. League of Nations, *Official Journal* 19, no. 11 (November 1938): 863–64.

15. League of Nations, *Official Journal* 19, no. 12 (December 1938): 1133.

16. Ibid., pp. 1133–34. See p. 1133 for the section 3. All figures except for the estimate of 20,000 deaths are taken from Lewis Smythe, *War Damage in the Nanking Area*, pp. 7–8.

17. League of Nations, *Official Journal* 19, no. 12: 1133. Also see Smythe, *War Damage*, p. 12, for figures on material losses. As to the statistics on rape, Smythe wrote that "8 percent of all females of 16–50 years" were raped, though he considered this figure seriously understated (p. 7 n. 2).

18. As regards activities of the International Committee for the Nanjing Safety Zone, see John Rabe, *The Good Man of Nanking*.

19. Smythe, *War Damage*, p. 1.

20. Nanking International Relief Committee, *Report of the Nanking International Relief Committee, November 1937 to April 30, 1939*, p. 32.

21. Smythe, *War Damage*, p. 8. An estimate that 20,000 civilians had been killed

was stated in "Some Recent Data" and probably came from the *Daily Telegraph and Morning Post* of January 28. See Koo's speech on February 2, 1938, at the sixth meeting at the 100th Session of the Council of the League of Nations.

According to Smythe's report of casualties within the walled city, 850 deaths had been caused by military operations; 2,400 deaths by soldiers' violence; 150 deaths by unknown causes. Fifty injuries had been inflicted by military operations; 3,050 injuries by soldiers' violence; 250 injuries by unknown causes; 4,200 people had been taken away, their fates unknown. (See Table 4.)

22. See Smythe, *War Damage*, p. 17 and Table 25 (page number unknown).

23. See Table 25. The total resident population of Kiangning, Kuyung, Lishui, Kiangpu, and Luho (only half of this latter county was surveyed) was 1.078 million; total deaths were estimated as 30,950 (this is the correct calculation, not 30,905 as written]: 22,490 males and 4,380 females were killed by violence, and 4,080 were killed by sickness.

24. Smythe, *War Damage*, p. 17. In the period of the survey, the Chinese dollar was steady at 3.40 Chinese dollars per U.S. dollar.

25. Ibid., p. 18.

26. The judgment of the International Military Tribunal for the Far East estimated the number killed during the six weeks after the fall of Nanjing at more than 200,000. See John Pritchard, *The Tokyo War Crimes Trial*, pp. 49, 604–605.

27. Miner Searle Bates, *Crop Investigation in the Nanking Area and Sundry Economic Data*; *The Nanking Population: Employment, Earnings, and Expenditures*.

28. Rabe, *Good Man of Nanking*, pp. 211–13.

29. *Wellington Koo Collection*, box 25, Rare Book and Manuscript Library, Columbia University.

30. Ibid.

31. *What War Means: Japanese Terror in China* (1938); *La Guerre Telle qu'elle Est: La Terreur Japonaise en Chine* (1939); *Waiguoren muduzhongzhi Rijun baoxin* (1938); *Gaikokujin no mita Nihongun no bōkō* (reprinted in 1972).

32. See Harold Timperley, *Japanese Terror in China*, pp. 20–45.

33. Ibid., p. 15.

34. Ibid., p. 71.

35. Shuhsi Hsu, *Documents of the Nanking Safety Zone*.

36. Shuhsi Hsu, *Japan and Shanghai*; *The War Conduct of the Japanese*; *Three Weeks of Canton Bombings*; *A Digest of Japanese War Conduct*; *A New Digest of Japanese War Conduct*.

37. *Wellington Koo Collection*, box 15, Rare Book and Manuscript Library, Columbia University. Telegram number 606.

38. *Wellington Koo Collection*, box 24, Rare Book and Manuscript Library, Columbia University. Telegram number 700. The *Times* story mentioned was probably by Tilman Durdin, "U.S. Naval Display Reported Likely unless Japan Guarantees Our Rights; Butchery Marked Capture of Nanking," *New York Times*, December 18, 1937, pp. 1, 10.

39. *Wellington Koo Collection*, box 29, Rare Book and Manuscript Library, Columbia University.

40. Hora Tomio, *Nit-Chū senso: Nankin daigyakusatsu jiken shiryōshū* (The Sino-Japanese War: A Collection of Historical Materials on the Nanjing Massacre), Vol. 2, pp. 311–13.

41. Kaji Wataru, *Chūgoku no jūnen* (Ten Years in China), pp. 4–7.

42. Kaji Wataru, *Shanhai sen'eki no naka* (During the Battle of Shanghai), pp. 68, 77. Xu Guangping (Mrs. Lu Xun), a friend of Kaji, asked Song Qingling (Mrs. Sun Yat-sen) whether Kaji could join the Nationalist government. Song told Xu to wait three days for an answer.

43. Among Kaji's friends were Chinese proletarian writers who had studied in Japan, such as Lu Xun, Hsia Yen, and Guo Moruo; Max and Grace Granich, editors of *Voice of China*, an English-language bimonthly magazine published by the Eastern Publishing Co.; and Rewi Alley, a New Zealand factory inspector of the Shanghai Municipal Council, who resigned his post in 1938 in order to help start the industrial cooperative movement in China. (See the document titled "Suggested Program for Three Week Visit to China," May 1945, *Indusco Collection*, box 60, Rare Book and Manuscript Library, Columbia University.)

44. Kaji, *Chūgoku no jūnen*, pp. 65–66.

45. Ibid., p. 69. Kaji Wataru, *Nihon heishi no hansen undō II* (Anti-War Movements by Japanese Soldiers, Part 2), p. 396.

46. Kaji, *Chūgoku no jūnen*, pp. 82–84.

47. Kaji Wataru, *Nihon heishi no hansen undō I* (Anti-War Movements by Japanese Soldiers, Part 1), pp. 79, 83–85; *Chūgoku no jūnen*, pp. 115–16.

48. Kaji, *Nihon heishi no hansen undō II*, pp. 237–38, 61. Sixteen members were transported to Zhenyuan, where some 500 Japanese soldiers were already imprisoned.

49. Hansen dōmei kiroku henshū iinkai (The Committee to Preserve the Records of the League of Anti-War Japanese), *Hansen heishi monogatari* (The Story of Anti-War Soldiers), pp. 1–9.

50. Kaji, *Chūgoku no jūnen*, p. 80.

51. Fujiwara Akira, " 'Sankō sakusen' to hoku-Shina hōmen gun 1" ("Three-Alls Operation" and the North China Army, Part 1), p. 23.

CHAPTER 3

1. Eleanor Tupper and George McReynolds, *Japan in American Public Opinion*, pp. 444–45.

2. See Nankin jiken chōsa kenkyūkai (The Research Committee on the Nanjing Incident), *Amerika kankei shiryō* (Historical Materials with Regard to the United States), Vol. 1 of *Nankin jiken shiryōshū* (A Collection of Historical Materials on the Nanjing Incident), pp. 380–554. The book contains numerous newspaper and periodical articles about Japanese atrocities in Nanjing and its neighboring areas. It also includes interviews with foreign correspondents Tilman Durdin and A. T. Steele (pp. 556–87).

3. Tilman Durdin, "U.S. Naval Display Reported Likely unless Japan Guarantees Our Rights; Butchery Marked Capture of Nanking," *New York Times*, December 18, 1937, pp. 1, 10. On December 19, 1937, his article about foreigners in Nanjing appeared in the paper. On the same day, Hallet Abend's article about the response of Japanese military commanders toward the massacre appeared in the *New York Times*. See Nankin jiken chōsa kenkyūkai, Vol. 1, pp. 422–26.

4. Tilman Durdin, "Japanese Atrocities Marked Fall of Nanking after Chinese

Command Fled," *New York Times*, January 9, 1938, p. 38. Durdin estimated that $20 million–$30 million worth of property in the neighboring areas of the city was destroyed by the Chinese military before the fall of Nanjing; however, destruction caused by the Japanese troops during and after the seizure of Nanjing accounted for the same amount, according to his estimates.

5. Ibid.

6. Nankin jiken chōsa kenkyūkai, Vol. 1, pp. 465–73. Archibald Steele, "Japanese Kill Thousands in Captured City," *Chicago Daily News*, December 15, 1937, p. 1; "War's Death Drama Pictured by Reporter," *Chicago Daily News*, December 17, 1937, p. 1; "Missionaries and Doctors Save Many Lives in Nanking Horror," *Chicago Daily News*, December 18, 1937, p. 1.

7. Steele, "War's Death Drama."

8. Durdin, "Japanese Atrocities"; Steele, "Japanese Kill Thousands."

9. Durdin, "Japanese Atrocities."

10. As for reviews, see, for example, Lillian Peffer's review of Timperley's book in *Amerasia* 11, no. 11 (January 1939): 553; Ward Perkins's review of Smythe's book in *Pacific Affairs* 12, no. 2 (June 1939): 220–22.

11. George Gallup, *The Gallup Poll, 1935–1971*, Vol. 1 (1935–48), pp. 69, 159. In 1937, the percentage of the respondents who favored "neither" Japan nor China was 55, whereas in 1939, 24 percent answered "neither."

12. Ibid.

13. See, for example, the Foreign Affairs Association of Japan (Nihon gaiji kyōkai), *What Happened at Tungchow?* (1937); *How the North China Affair Arose* (August 1937); *Why Japan Had to Fight in Shanghai* (September 1937); *The Sino-Japanese Conflict: A Short Survey* (October 1937). *The North China Incident* and *Japan's Case in the Shanghai Hostilities* were also published in 1937.

14. Foreign Affairs Association of Japan, *What Happened at Tungchow?*

15. Hino Ashihei, *Mugi to heitai* (Wheat and Soldiers). Translated by Lewis Bush and published by Kenkyusha under the title *Barley and Soldiers*, the book became available in English in 1939. Bush also translated Hino's *Tsuchi to heitai* (Mud and Soldiers) as well as *Hana to heitai* (Flower and Soldiers).

16. See, for example, Percy Noel, *When Japan Fights*; Shingoro Takaishi, *Japan Speaks Out*; Yakichiro Suma, *Where Japan Stands*.

17. A. F. Thomas, *I Speak for Japan*. Thomas received about 300 invitations while he was in the United States and England. Carl Crow's *I Speak for Chinese* appeared while Thomas was lecturing in England, hence the title.

18. For a detailed analysis of how American images of China in 1931–49 were being created, see Christopher Jespersen, *American Images of China, 1931–1949*. For discussions of the role of Time Inc. in rallying support for China, see his chapter 2 (pp. 24–44); for discussions of humanitarian organizations, see chapter 3 (45–58); for Song Meiling, see chapter 5 (82–107). The quoted figures in this paragraph are from *American Images of China*, pp. 12, 48, and 92.

19. Harold Timperley, *Japan: A World Problem*, pp. vii–viii.

20. Ibid., pp. vii, 107.

21. James Young, *Our Enemy*, p. 10. Young was jailed by the Japanese police because he wrote news "injurious" to Japan (p. 7).

22. Ibid., pp. 10–14, 101–103, 111.

23. Philip Jaffe, "Introduction," *Amerasia*, vol. 1 (no page number). Jaffe wrote the introduction in 1968 when the issues were reprinted. The founding editors were Frederick Field, Philip Jaffe, T. A. Bisson, Cyrus Peake, Ch'ao-Ting Chi, Robert Reischauer, Kenneth Colegrove, William Stone, and Owen Lattimore.

24. Smith was a professor of English at Rikkyō University from 1931 to 1936. He was a lecturer at Imperial University of Tokyo from 1934 to 1936. Between 1936 and 1940 he taught English at Columbia University. (See *Contemporary Authors Online*, http://www.galenet.com/servlet/BioRC.)

25. Bradford Smith, "Japan: Beauty and the Beast," pp. 86, 88. Smith also wrote "The Mind of Japan," in which he stressed that the Japanese concepts *shintō, kōdō,* and *bushido* had influenced the manner of thinking and behavior of the Japanese for centuries.

26. Smith, "Japan: Beauty and the Beast," p. 88.

27. Ibid., p. 94.

28. A. Grajdanzev, "Japan: Neither Beauty Nor Beast."

29. Ibid., p. 178.

30. Ibid., pp. 174–75.

31. William Holland, "The Common Man of Japan."

32. Ibid., p. 179.

33. Ibid., p. 180.

34. "Is There Another Japan?" pp. 35–42. The "other" Japan implied by *Amerasia* was a more peaceful, democratic Japan than was typically portrayed in American wartime media.

35. Ibid., p. 41. Embree was an anthropologist and the author of *Suye Mura*, a study of Japanese village life. He stressed that there was nothing mysteriously Oriental about Japanese and that Japanese thoughts and actions were, like those of other human beings, conditioned by early training and cultural environment (p. 1).

36. John Goette, *Japan Fights for Asia*; Sydney Greenbie, *Asia Unbound*. Goette, a journalist, insisted that the emperor, generals, junior officers, soldiers, civilian men, women, and children were all united, and he saw no hope of driving a wedge between the warlords and the people. Greenbie insisted that the real enemy was the Japanese people, who, in his eyes, were sentimental, hysterical, and inclined toward mysticism. (See "The Nature of Our Enemy, Japan," *Amerasia* 7, no. 12, pp. 390–91.)

37. "The Nature of Our Enemy, Japan," pp. 389–92. See Taro Yashima, *The New Sun*. Yashima, a proletarian artist, migrated to the United States in 1939 after being freed from prison. The book is Yashima's autobiography in pictures and words.

38. John Dower, *War Without Mercy*, pp. 53–54. Also see Hadley Cantril, *Public Opinion 1935–1946*, pp. 1118–19.

CHAPTER 4

1. Ariyama Teruo, *Senryōki mediashi kenkyū* (The Study of Media History during the Occupation), pp. 167–68.

2. Yamamoto Taketoshi, *Senryōki media bunseki*, pp. 48–53. See "Shintō kesseino kōsō" (Blueprint for a New Political Party), *Asahi shinbun*, September 15, 1945, p. 1; "'Hitō no bōkō' happyō e kokumin no koe" (Voices of Japanese Regarding "Atrocities in the Philippines"), *Asahi shinbun*, September 17, 1945, p. 1. The former article in-

cluded critical comments by Hatoyama Ichirō, a senior politician, regarding the American use of atomic bombs. The latter article alluded to public suspicions that the United States had fabricated stories of Japanese atrocities in the Philippines, of which the people had never heard and could hardly believe to have happened, in order to offset American crimes against Japanese civilians during the occupation. For the released information regarding Japanese atrocities in the Philippines, see " 'Hitō Nihonhei no bōjō' " (Atrocities by Japanese Soldiers in the Philippines), *Asahi shinbun*, September 16, 1945, p. 2.

3. Yamamoto, *Senryōki media bunseki*, p. 52.

4. "Tōjō gunbatsu no zaika" (Crimes of Military Leaders Led by Tōjō), *Asahi shinbun*, September 17, 1945, p. 1.

5. "Shinjuwan jiken no kuigo" (Regrets of Pearl Harbor Incident), *Asahi shinbun*, December 7, 1945, p. 1.

6. "Sensō hihan e no riron" (Toward a Theory of Criticism of the War), *Asahi shinbun*, December 14, 1945, p. 1.

7. U.S. Strategic Bombing Survey, *The Effects of Strategic Bombing on Japanese Morale*, no. 14 (June 1947): 150–52; 154–55. Fifty-four percent of participants stated that they were "better off than during war, but conditions [are] bad," and 18 percent said that they were "better off than during war, conditions [are] fairly satisfactory" (150). In addition, 70 percent said that they were satisfied with the occupation (154).

8. Ibid., 152–53. Twenty-two percent suggested that Japan should become a peaceful nation and abolish rule by militarists and military ideas, whereas 20 percent suggested making Japan more democratic (152). The percentage totals 106 because some people had more than one suggestion.

9. Tokutake Toshio, *Kyōkasho no sengo shi* (History of Postwar School Textbooks), pp. 41–43.

10. Ibid.

11. Kaigo Tokiomi, *Nihon kyōkasho taikei kindai hen*, Vol. 20, pp. 602–603.

12. Ibid.

13. Monbushō (Ministry of Education, Japan), "Kuni no Ayumi"(ge), *Nihon kyōkasho taikei kindai hen*, Vol. 20, p. 461.

14. Ibid., pp. 461–62.

15. Ibid., pp. 462–63.

16. Tawara Yoshifumi, *Kyōkasho kōgeki no shinsō* (The Intensity of Attacks on School Textbooks), p. 169.

17. On December 8, 1945, for example, the *Asahi* dedicated two full pages to "The History of the Pacific War." See "Taiheiyō sensō shi" (The History of the Pacific War), *Asahi shinbun*, December 8, 1945, pp. 2, 4. On the first day, the history covered the Manchurian Incident of 1931; domestic politics, specifically focused on February 26th Incident of 1936 and terrorism; the China Incident of 1937; and the war between Japan and the United States. See also "Taiheiyō sensō shi: senki no dai tenkan" (The History of the Pacific War: The Turning Point of the War), *Asahi shinbun*, December 9, 1945, p. 1; "Taiheiyō sensō shi: Rengōkoku no tainichi mōkō" (The History of the Pacific War: Fierce Attack against Japan by the Allied Forces), *Asahi shinbun*, December 10, 1945, p. 2; "Taiheiyō sensō shi: Hokyū o tatsu" (The History of the Pacific War: Cutting the Supply Lines), *Asahi shinbun*, December 11, 1945,

p. 2; "Taiheiyō sensō shi: Tōjō shushō no botsuraku" (The History of the Pacific War: The Fall of Premier Tōjō), *Asahi shinbun*, December 12, 1945, p. 4; "Taiheiyō sensō shi: Reite, Samāru no sensen" (The History of the Pacific War: The Battles of Leyte and Samar), *Asahi shinbun*, December 13, 1945, p. 2; "Taiheiyō sensō shi: Kanpai ni owatta Hitō sen" (The History of the Pacific War: The Complete Defeat at the Battle of the Philippines), *Asahi shinbun*, December 14, 1945, p. 2; "Taiheiyō sensō shi: Iōjima to Okinawa" (The History of the Pacific War: Iwo Jima and Okinawa), *Asahi shinbun*, December 15, 1945, p. 2; "Taiheiyō sensō shi: Soren kara mo hijitetsu" (The History of the Pacific War: Getting a Slap from the Soviet Union, Too), *Asahi shinbun*, December 16, 1945, p. 2; "Taiheiyō sensō shi: Tokyō wan jō ni chōin" (The History of the Pacific War: The Signing Ceremony in Tokyo Bay), *Asahi shinbun*, December 17, 1945, p. 2. See also Takeyama Akiko, "Senryōka no hōsō: Shinsō wa kōda" (Broadcasting during the Occupation), p. 113. Smith, a Quaker, was with the Office of War Information between 1942 and 1945. In 1946, he published "Experiment in Racial Concentration," pp. 214–18, in which he condemned the American government for its mistreatment of Japanese and Japanese Americans.

18. Nihon hōsō kyōkai, *Nihon hōsōshi* (The History of Broadcasting in Japan), bekkan, p. 80. See also Takeyama, "Senryōka no hōsō: Shinsō wa kōda," p. 140. The broadcast was aired from 8 to 8:30 PM on Sundays. The model of "Now It Can Be Told" was "The March of Time," which was broadcast by CBS beginning in March 1931 (Takeyama 141 n. 4).

19. "Taiheiyō sensō shi" (The History of the Pacific War), *Asahi shinbun*, December 8, 1945, p. 2.

20. On December 8, "The History of the Pacific War" stressed that military leaders suppressed truth and freedom of speech and that the surprise attack on Pearl Harbor was against the emperor's will. The December 12 installment condemned despotism by Tōjō and his supporters. See "Taiheiyō sensō shi" (The History of the Pacific War), *Asahi shinbun*, December 8, 1945, p. 2; "Taiheiyō sensō shi: Tōjō shushō no botsuraku" (The History of the Pacific War: The Fall of Premier Tōjō), *Asahi shinbun*, December 12, 1945, p. 4.

21. "Taiheiyō sensō shi" (The History of the Pacific War), *Asahi shinbun*, December 8, 1945, p. 4.

22. "Osanago ni mo bōkō; Wuiruson shi Nankin gyakusatsu o bakuro" (Children Also Brutalized; Dr. Wilson Discloses Nanjing Atrocities), *Asahi shinbun*, July 26, 1946, p. 2. "Onna kodomo mo higō no shi; Nankin no gyakusatsu o bakuro" (Women and Children Also Perished; Atrocities in Nanjing Revealed), *Yamanashi nichi nichi shinbun*, July 27, 1946, p. 1; "Miatari shidai shasatsu, Kyo Den'in shi shōgen, Nankin nyūjō no bankō" (Shoot to Kill If You See Them; Mr. Xu Chuanyin Testifies; Atrocities after Japanese Military's Entry into Nanjing), *Yamanashi nichi nichi shinbun*, July 27, 1946, p. 1. The headline of the *Asahi* on this day was "Akunaki bōkō sankagetsu; jinrui no higeki, Nankin no gyakusatsu" (Atrocities Continued for Three Months; Tragedy of Human Beings: The Nanjing Massacre; see *Asahi shinbun*, July 27, 1946, p. 2). For a general discussion of the Tokyo Trial, see John Dower, *Embracing Defeat*, 443–84.

23. See, for example, "Daigaku kōnai de renjitsu bōkō" (Atrocities on Campus Occurred Daily), *Asahi shinbun*, July 30, 1946, p. 2.

24. "Chūgokujin ni shai" (Gratitude to Chinese People), *Yomiuri shinbun*, July 31, 1946, p. 1.

25. "Nankin jiken" (The Nanjing Incident), *Asahi shinbun*, August 8, 1946, p. 2.

26. Radhabinod Pal, "The Dissenting Opinion of the Member for India," pp. 1098–99.

27. Ibid., p. 1098.

28. In addition to the testimony of Chen, Pal challenged testimonies offered by Xu Chuanyin and John Magee. See Pal, "Dissenting Opinion," pp. 1065–68.

29. John Pritchard, *The Tokyo War Crimes Trial*, Vol. 2: "Transcripts of the Proceedings in Open Session," pp. 2609–10.

30. Pal, "Dissenting Opinion," p. 1098.

31. Ibid., pp. 1098–99.

32. Ibid., p. 1069.

33. Tōkyō saiban kenkyūkai (The Research Committee on the Tokyo Trial), *Paru hanketsusho* (Pal's Judgment), Vol. 2, p. 130. In addition to Pal, Justices William Webb (Australia), B.V.A. Röling (the Netherlands), Delfin Jaranilla (the Philippines, and Henri Bernard (France) filed dissenting opinions. The defense's request was denied by Presiding Justice Webb.

34. "Indo hanji muzairon" (Indian Justice Votes Not Guilty), *Asahi shinbun*, November 13, 1948, p. 1.

35. John Pritchard, *Tokyo War Crimes Trial*, Vol. 20: "Judgment and Annexes," pp. 49606, 49608, 49610.

36. Tōkyō saiban kenkyūkai, p. 4.

37. As easy as it is to find public opinion supporting government war efforts in publications during the war, it is just as easy to find opinion that supports the Tokyo Trial in newspapers and periodicals. *Zoku hikiage engo no kiroku* (The Record of Assistance in Repatriation, Part 2) includes the summary of public opinions toward the trial. See *Zoku hikiage engo no kiroku*, pp. 152–53.

38. Tanaka Masaaki, *Sōyōshū: konomama dewa Nihon wa abunai* (Collected Essays: Japan Is Now in Peril), pp. 55–56.

39. Tanaka Masaaki, *Nihon muzairon: shinri no sabaki* (On Japan's Innocence: The Truth on Trial), pp. 2, 24–25, 30.

40. As Pal emphasized: "I am only dealing with the question of the alleged overall conspiracy. For this purpose, it is not at all necessary for me to consider whether or not Japan's actions in China were justified" ("Dissenting Opinion," p. 547).

41. Pal, "Dissenting Opinion," p. 1226.

42. Tanaka, *Nihon muzairon: shinri no sabaki*, p. 28.

43. Pal, "Dissenting Opinion," pp. 1065–68 (John Magee and Xu Chuanyin); 1098–99 (Chen Fubao).

44. Tanaka, *Nihon muzairon: shinri no sabaki*, p. 28. For the list of witnesses and statements submitted as evidence by the prosecution, see Hora Tomio, *Kyokutō kokusai gunji saiban kankei shiryō hen* (Historical Materials on the Tokyo War Crimes Trial), Vol. 1 of *Nit-Chū sensō: Nankin daigyakusatsu jiken shiryōshū* (The Sino-Japanese War: A Collection of Historical Materials on the Nanjing Massacre), pp. 417–20.

45. Tanaka, *Nihon muzairon: shinri no sabaki*, p. 8.

46. Akazawa Shirō et al., eds., *Tōkyō saiban handobukku* (Handbook of the Tokyo

Trial), p. 234; Miyata Eijirō, "Reddo pāgji" (Red Purge), in *Nihon kingendai shi jiten* (Encyclopedia of Modern Japanese History).

47. Sōrifu kokuritsu seron chōsajo (The Prime Minister's Office's National Research Institute of Public Opinion), *Kōshoku tsuihō ni tsuite no seron chōsa kekka hōkokusho* (The Report of Public Opinion Regarding Purges from Public Office), August 1952 (mimeograph copy), pp. 35–36. Between June and October 1951, SCAP lifted the purge of 177,261 wartime leaders; and the remaining 33,000 were allowed to return to public life in April 1952 (p. 1).

48. Nihon minshutō, "hajimeni" (Foreword), *Ureubeki kyōkasho no mondai* (Deplorable Problems in School Textbooks), pp. 18–19.

49. Ibid., pp. 26–27.

50. Ibid., pp. 27, 43.

51. Tawara, *Kyōkasho kōgeki no shinsō*, pp. 168–69. Kaikōdō continued to publish its junior high school history textbook, *Rekishi naiyō o shu to shita mono ge* (Discussion of Issues in History, Part 2), first published in 1954, until 1960. For contents of elementary and junior high school history textbooks in the 1950s and 1960s, see Ienaga soshōshien shimin no kai (The People's Group Supporting Ienaga's Case), *Taiheiyō sensō to kyōkasho* (The Pacific War and Textbooks).

52. Sōrifu kokuritsu seron chōsajo (The Prime Minister's Office's National Research Institute of Public Opinion), *Kyōiku ni kansuru seron chōsa* (Public Opinion Research Regarding Education), October 17, 1950, (mimeograph copy), pp. 3, 9.

53. For a general discussion of progressive intellectuals in the postwar period, see Carol Gluck, "The Past in the Present," pp. 64–95. As Gluck stresses, progressive intellectuals disagreed significantly among themselves and never coalesced into a single group or community. Throughout the postwar period, their primary concerns have not remained constant.

54. Daqing Yang's study briefly discusses the Nanjing Massacre in Japan in the 1950s and 1960s. Examples of writers who chose Nanjing as their topic of writing in the 1950s include Hotta Yoshie and Mishima Yukio. See Daqing Yang, "The Malleable and the Contested," pp. 55–58.

55. Masaki Hiroshi, *Chikakiyori* (Up Close), pp. 304–306, 313–15.

56. Hani Gorō, "Repaburikan Manifesuto" (Republican Manifesto), in *Hani Gorō chosaku shū* (The Postwar Works of Hani Gorō), pp. 78–79, 83, 86, 90–91.

57. In 1952, Takemoto Genji published a poem titled "My Students Died at War":

Students who will never come back,
My hands are smeared with your blood.
I held one end of the rope that choked you to death.
Ah! And I was a teacher.
How can I excuse myself by claiming that we were both deceived?
How can I atone for my sin?
You will never be alive again.
I now wipe tears from my eyes, wash my blood-soaked hands, and
    promise you,
"Never again!" (Tokutake 73–74)

58. Rekishi kyōikusha kyōgikai (Association for History Educators), *Rekishi kyōiku 50 nen no ayumi to kadai* (Fifty Years of History Education and Its Objectives), pp. 29–30.

59. Ibid., p. 3. The Historical Science Society of Japan (Rekken) had also supported similar doctrine. See Tōyama Shigeki, "Sengo no rekishigaku to rekishi ishiki" (Postwar Historical Study and Historical Consciousness), pp. 24, 28–29.

60. According to a survey conducted by the Prime Minister's Office in 1952, 74 percent of 1,000 persons polled expressed their anxiety that Japan might be dragged into a future war. See Sōrifu kokuritsu seron chōsajo (Prime Minister's Office's National Research Institute of Public Opinion), *Kōwa ni kansuru seron chōsa* (Public Opinion Survey Regarding the Japan-U.S. Peace Treaty), June 1952 (mimeograph copy), p. 30.

61. Nihon heiwa iinkai (Japan Peace Committee), *Heiwa undō 20 nen undō shi* (Twenty Years of the History of the Peace Movement), pp. 41–45; *Heiwa undō 20 nen shiryō shū* (A Collection of Materials Regarding 20 Years of the Peace Movement), p. 8.

62. Nihon heiwa iinkai, *Heiwa undō 20 nen undō shi*, pp. 96–101.

63. Tokutake, *Kyōkasho no sengo shi*, p. 71.

64. Nihon Chūgoku yūkō kyōkai zenkoku honbu (The Headquarters of the Japan China Friendship Association), *Nit-Chū yūkō undō shi* (The History of the Japan-China Friendship Movement), pp. 28, 30–31, 34–38. In 1954, Chinese members organized their own association in order to avoid being falsely accused of "interfering with domestic politics" (p. 34).

65. Akatsu Masuzō, *Hanaoka bōdō* (Uprising in Hanaoka), pp. 63, 66, 157–58. Akatsu later became a member of the Committee for Mourning the Dead Chinese Prisoners (Chūgokujin horyo junnansha irei jikkō iinkai).

66. Nihon Chūgoku yūkō kyōkai zenkoku honbu, p. 85; Chūgoku kikansha renrakukai (The Group of Returnees from China), *Sankō* (Three Alls), pp. 273–76.

67. Chūgoku kikansha renrakukai, *Shinryaku: Chūgoku ni okeru Nihon senpan no kiroku* (Invasion: Confessions of Japanese War Crimes in China).

68. Ibid. As for *Three Alls*, see its Chinese translation: Kanki Haruo, *Riben zhanfan de zibai*.

69. Suzuki Yoshio, "Hōka" (Arson).

70. Chūgoku kikansha renrakukai, *Shinryaku*, pp. 217–25.

71. The figure is taken from Kanda Fuhito, *Shōwashi nenpyō* (Chronology of the Showa Era), p. 76.

72. "Betonamu ni heiwa o!" shimin rengō kai (The Popular Alliance for Peace in Vietnam), *Shiryō "Beheiren" undō* (Historical Materials: The Movement of "Beheiren"), Vol. 1, pp. xii, 513–29.

73. Kyōkasho kentei soshō shien zenkoku renrakukai (The National Alliance for Supporting Lawsuit against Textbook Authorization), *Ienaga kyōkasho saiban* (Ienaga Textbook Trial), pp. iii–v; *Ienaga kyōkasho saiban jūnen shi* (The Ten-Year History of the Ienaga Textbook Case), p. 40. Tōyama Shigeki and Ōe Shinobu, *Ienaga Nihonshi no kentei* (The Authorization of Ienaga's History of Japan), pp. 12–14, 220–37.

74. The interview appeared in *Mainichi shinbun* on June 18, 1965, and is quoted in Kyōkasho kentei soshō shien zenkoku renrakukai, *Ienaga kyōkasho saiban jūnen shi*, pp. 42–43.

75. Ibid., pp. 314–64; Tōyama and Ōe, pp. 14–16.

76. See Ienaga Saburō, *Taiheiyō sensō* (The Pacific War), pp. iii–vii, 214–15. Although the title emphasized the conflict between Japan and the United States, Ienaga included a rich discussion of Japan's aggression in China.

77. Kumamoto heidan senshi hensan iinkai (The Editorial Committee for the Military History of Kumamoto Units), *Kumamoto heidan senshi, Shina jihen hen* (The Military History of Kumamoto Units: The China Incident), pp. 127, 129.

78. Gotō Kōsaku, *Nankin sakusen no shinsō: Kumamoto roku shidan senki* (The Truth about the Nanjing Operation: The Military History of the Kumamoto Sixth Division), pp. 104–105, 219–46, 249–51.

79. Hora Tomio, *Kindai senshi no nazo* (Riddles of Modern War History), pp. 13–52 ("The Marco Polo Bridge Incident"), 55–172 ("The Nanjing Incident"), 175–242 ("The Nomonhan Incident"), 245–320 ("The Korean War").

80. Ibid., pp. 1–3, 131, 140, 143.

CHAPTER 5

1. Chiang Kai-shek, *Statements and Speeches by Generalissimo Chiang Kai-shek (August-October, 1945)*, p. 3.

2. Masui Yasuichi, *Kankan saiban shi* (The Trials of the Chinese Collaborators), pp. 25–30.

3. The figures are taken from Meng Guoxiang and Cheng Tangfa, "Chengzhi hanjian gongzuo gaishu" (A General Account of Punishing Traitors), p. 110.

4. Masui, *Kankan saiban shi*, pp. 50–54, 60, 348–49.

5. Akazawa Shirō et al., eds., *Tōkyō saiban handobukku* (Handbook of the Tokyo War Crimes Trial), pp. 219, 225. The Nationalist government tried 883 individuals, as compared to 1,038 tried by the Dutch; 978 by the British; 949 by the Australians; and 1,453 by the Americans. Of these, 149 Japanese (including 8 Korean-born and 5 Taiwanese-born Japanese) were sentenced to death by the Guomindang government, whereas 236 were condemned by Dutch authorities, 223 (including 10 Korean-born and 6 Taiwanese-born Japanese) by British tribunals, 153 (including 7 Taiwanese-born Japanese) by Australian courts, and 143 (including one Korean-born and one Taiwanese-born Japanese) by the American judges.

6. Tani was arrested in Tokyo on February 2, 1946; Tanaka was arrested in Japan in May 1947; Noda was arrested in Japan on August 20, 1947; and Mukai was arrested in Japan on September 2, 1947. See Nankin jiken chōsa kenkyūkai, *Chūgoku kankei shiryō hen* (Historical Materials with Regard to China), Vol. 2 of *Nankin jiken shiryōshū*, pp. 290–291.

7. Tani Hisao, "Yuigonjo" (Testament), pp. 50–51.

8. Tanaka Gunkichi, "Isho" (Testament), pp. 82–83.

9. Mukai Toshiaki, "Jisei" (Last Words), p. 40; Noda Tsuyoshi, "Nisshi no kusabi to naran," p. 4.

10. Mukai, "Isho" (Testament), pp. 40–41.

11. Zhongguo dier lishi dang'anguan (Number Two China Historical Archives), et al., eds. *Qin-Hua Rijun Nanjing datusha dang'an* (Archival Materials on the Nanjing Massacre Committed by the Japanese Army of Invasion), pp. 604, 611.

12. Ibid., pp. 604, 608–11.

13. These statistics are presented in Akazawa et al., *Tōkyō saiban handobukku*, p. 225. Tani was shot to death on April 26, 1947, and the others shared the same fate on January 28, 1948.

14. Akazawa et al., *Tōkyō saiban handobukku*, p. 126.

15. "The Memoirs of Dr. V. K. Wellington Koo," *Wellington Koo Collection*, Columbia University Rare Book and Manuscript Library, p. D-61. The interview with Koo was conducted by Julie Lien-ying How, Te-kong Tong, Kai-fu Tsao, James Seymour, and Crystal Lorch Seidman. They began interviewing in 1958, and documents were unsealed in 1976.

16. "Yancheng zhanzheng zuifan" (To Discipline War Criminals Severely), *Jiefang Ribao*, translated in Nihon kokusai mondai kenkyūjo (Institute of International Affairs, Japan), *Shin Chūgoku shiryō shūsei* (Collection of Historical Materials on New China), Vol. 1, pp. 127–29.

17. "Zhongguo gongchandang zhongyangweiyuanhui '77' jinianri fabu duishiju kouhao" (Slogans of the Chinese Communist Party Central Committee Issued on Memorial Day, July 7), *Renmin ribao*, July 7, 1947, translated in *Shin Chūgoku shiryō shūsei*, Vol. 1, pp. 461–63.

18. "Jiefangjun zongbu fabu chengban zhanzheng zuifan mingling" (Order of the General Headquarters of the People's Liberation Army to Prosecute War Criminals), *Qunzhong* 2, no. 45: 13, translated in *Shin Chūgoku shiryō shūsei*, Vol. 2, pp. 323–24.

19. "Mao zhuxi zhongyao shengming" (Chairman Mao's Urgent Statement), *Qunzhong* 3, no. 4, pp. 2–3, translated in *Shin Chūgoku shiryō shūsei*, Vol. 2, pp. 400–403.

20. "Wu Xiuquan guanyu kongsu Meiguo qinlue Zhongguoan de fayangao" (Manuscript of Wu Xiuquan's Denunciation of the United States Invasion), *Zhongfuarenmingongheguo duiwaiguanxi wenjianji 1949–1950* (Collection of Materials on International Affairs of China 1949–50), pp. 221–39, translated in *Shin Chūgoku shiryō shūsei*, Vol. 3, pp. 216–18.

21. "Waijiaobuchang Zhou Enlai lai kangyi Meiguo zhengfu lianxu qinfan Zhongguo lingkong bing shiyong xijunwuqi tusha Zhongguorenmin de baoxing de shengming" (Zhou Enlai's Protest against American Violation of China's Air Space and Use of Biological Weapons), *Zhongfuarenmingongheguo duiwaiguanxi wenjianji 1951–1953* (Collection of Materials on International Affairs of China 1951–53), pp. 63–65, translated in *Shin Chūgoku shiryō shūsei*, Vol. 3, pp. 393, 395. The U.S. government repeatedly denied the allegation. See Sheldon Harris, *Factories of Death: Japanese Biological Warfare, 1932–45, and the American Cover-Up*, p. 231.

22. Arai Toshio, "Kyōjutsusho wa kōshite kakareta" (Testimonies Were Written as Such), pp.: 76–77. Most of the 1,108 Japanese were transferred from the Soviet Union in 1950. It is unknown how many of them were ethnic Korean or Taiwanese.

23. Ibid., pp. 74, 76–77.

24. Toyoda Masayuki, "Chūka jinmin kyōwakoku no senpan saiban" (War Crimes Trials in the People's Republic of China).

25. Daqing Yang, "A Sino-Japanese Controversy: The Nanjing Atrocity as History," p. 16.

26. "Zuiyi Rikou zai Nanjing datusha" (Recollections of the Great Japanese Massacre in Nanjing), which originally appeared on February 26, 1951.

27. Ibid., n.p.

28. Hora Tomio, *Nit-Chū sensō: Nankin daigyakusatsu jiken shiryōshū* (The Sino-Japanese War: A Collection of Historical Materials on the Nanjing Massacre), Vol. 2, p. 4.

29. "Tuanyixin, baowei heping" (Unite as One Heart, and Defend Peace), *Xinhua yuebao*, October 1952, pp. 55–58, translated in *Shin Chūgoku shiryō shūsei*, Vol. 3, p. 457.

30. Mei Ruao, "Shiyong yuanzidan he qingdan de baoxin buxu chongyan" (The Use of Atomic and Hydrogen Bombs: Never Again), *Renmin ribao*, August 7, 1955, p. 3.

31. Nihon heiwa iinkai (Japan Peace Committee), *Heiwa undō 20 nen undō shi* (Twenty Years of the History of the Peace Movement), pp. 100–101. The Soviet Union also sent delegates and donated the same amount. Fourteen countries sent a total of 52 delegates to the rally.

32. Xu Dunzhang, "Guangyu Ribenqiaoming he Ribenzhanfan wenti" (Concerning Japanese Residents and War Criminals), *Guangming ribao*, September 3, 1955, p. 4

33. Yang, "Sino-Japanese Controversy," pp. 16–17; Eykholt, "Aggression, Victimization, and Chinese Historiography of the Nanjing Massacre," p. 25.

34. Eykholt, "Aggression, Victimization," pp. 25–26.

35. Ibid., p. 26; Yang, "Sino-Japanese Controversy," pp. 16–17.

CHAPTER 6

1. Sheila Johnson, *American Attitudes toward Japan, 1941–1975*, p. 62.

2. "M'Arthur Sets Up Quotas for Press," *New York Times*, October 13, 1945, p. 4.

3. According to the Gallup poll conducted in December 1944, only 8 percent answered that a program of reeducation and rehabilitation of the Japanese people should be followed after the war; 28 percent preferred supervision and control of Japan; 33 percent favored the destruction of Japan as a political entity; and 13 percent wanted all Japanese killed. In contrast, 17 percent answered that a program of reeducation and rehabilitation of the German people should be followed after the war, and 44 percent called for the supervision and control of Germany. Revealingly, the genocide of all Germans was not presented as an option for the respondents. (See National Opinion Research Center, *Opinion News* 7: 10 [May 13, 1947], p. 5.)

The four-year trend of opinion regarding the Japanese people was as follows:

	Will always want war	Too easily misled	Potential good citizens
July 1942	54%	33%	13%
June 1943	62%	27%	11%
Dec. 1944	62%	27%	11%
July 1945	56%	31%	3%
Nov. 1945	49%	34%	17%
May 1946	37%	42%	21%

In comparison, the four-year trend of opinion regarding the German people is shown below:

	Will always want war	Too easily misled	Potential good citizens
July 1942	25%	44%	31%
June 1943	22%	46%	32%
Dec. 1944	37%	37%	26%
July 1945	41%	39%	20%
Nov. 1945	31%	43%	26%
May 1946	32%	46%	22%

(These figures are cited from NORC, *Opinion News* 7: 10 (May 13, 1947), p. 6.)

In addition, a *Fortune* survey released in December 1945 discussed the basic feelings among Americans toward Japanese and German people. The question was: "Do you regard the majority of the Japanese (German) people as being naturally cruel and brutal, if they have the chance, or do you think it is only a small part of the population that is like that?"

The finding is shown below:

Proportion Cruel and Brutal	Japanese	Germans
A majority	56%	39%
A small part	34%	54%
Don't know	10%	7%

(The figures are cited from NORC, *Opinion News* 7:10 (May 13, 1947), p. 7.)

4. "Only Temporary Surrender?" *New York Times*, August 14, 1945, p. 20.

5. The Gallup poll found in June 1945 that 54 percent of the respondents could identify the name of the emperor correctly. See George Gallup, *The Gallup Poll*, Vol. 1 (1935–48), pp. 511–12.

6. NORC, *Opinion News* 5: 4 (August 21, 1945), p. 3. The question reported in *Fortune* in April 1944 read:

Which of these comes closest to expressing your idea of the position of the Japanese Emperor?

He is the dictator.	16%
He is to Japan what the King is to England.	6%
He is only a figurehead (except in religion).	9%
He is the only Japanese god.	44%
Don't know.	15%

7. Frank Kluckhohn, "Hirohito in Interview Puts Blame on Tojo in Sneak Raid; Says He Now Opposes War," *New York Times*, September 25, 1945, pp. 1–2.

8. Ibid., p. 2.

9. Ibid., pp. 1–2.

10. "Hirohito Aide Says Japan Chose War," *New York Times*, September 25, 1945, p. 2.

11. "MacArthur Drops Japan's Censors," *New York Times*, September 29, 1945, pp. 1, 4. Ariyama Teruo, *Senryōki mediashi kenkyū* (The Study of Media History during the Occupation), p. 182.

12. Ibid. T. Urabe, secretary of the Japanese Board of Information, objected to Kluckhohn's report, arguing that the emperor never mentioned Tōjō by name in the written reply. According to Urabe, the emperor's answer was:

As to strategic details of the war such as disposition of military and naval forces and the time, place and manner of the attack, the Emperor was not generally consulted, these being decided almost exclusively by the High Command. At any rate it was His Majesty's intention to issue a formal declaration of war before the commencement of hostilities. ("MacArthur Drops Japan's Censors," p. 4)

On the other hand, Kluckhohn refuted Urabe, saying that the written and translated reply was: "His Majesty had no intention to have the war rescript used as General Tojo used it" ("Hirohito Did Assail Tojo," *New York Times*, October 2, 1945, p. 5).

13. Lindesay Parrott, "Tojo Faces Court as a War Criminal," *New York Times*, May 3, 1946, pp. 1, 10.

14. "War Crimes Trial to Start for 26 Japanese Leaders," *Christian Science Monitor*, May 2, 1946, p. 12. The *Monitor* forgot to include two additional prisoners—Itagaki Seishirō and Kimura Heitarō—who were scheduled to be repatriated on the following day.

15. Parrott, "Tojo Faces Court," pp. 1, 10.

16. "Japanese Leaders Plead Not Guilty," *New York Times*, May 6, 1946, p. 2; "Twenty-Seven Jap Leaders Plead Innocent in Allied Court," *Chicago Daily Tribune*, May 6, 1946, p. 1. Ōkawa received temporary media attention because of his dramatic slapping of Tōjō's head in articles such as "Court Startled by Lusty Slaps on Tōjō's Head," *Christian Science Monitor*, May 3, 1946, p. 5, and "He Who Gets Slapped," *Newsweek*, May 13, 1946, p. 50.

17. "Japanese Leaders Plead Not Guilty," p. 2; "Twenty-Seven Jap Leaders," p. 1.

18. "Tojo Condemned by Court to Hang; 24 Others Guilty," *New York Times*, November 12, 1948, pp. 1, 15; Lindesay Parrott, "Dooming of Tojo Impresses Japan," *New York Times*, November 13, 1948, pp. 1, 9.

19. "Text of the Tribunal's Verdict on Tojo," *New York Times*, November 13, 1948, p. 9. Such Tōjō-centered reportage was also the rule in other news reports. See, for example, Gordon Walker, "Tojo and Colleagues Given Sentences by Tokyo War Tribunal," *Christian Science Monitor*, November 12, 1948, pp. 1, 4; "Tojo's Private Death," *Newsweek*, December 6, 1948, p. 43.

20. "Tojo among Seven to Hang; None Freed," *Washington Post*, November 13, 1948, pp. 1, 3. On the previous day, the newspaper also reported the conviction of Tōjō and the other 24 defendants whom the court found guilty. See "Tojo and 24 Co-Defendants Found Guilty," *Washington Post*, November 12, 1948, pp. 1, 8.

21. "200,000 Killed in Nanking Rape, Professor Says," *Chicago Daily Tribune*, July 26, 1946, p. 9.

22. "Rape of Nanking Witness Recalls Forty Thousand Bodies," *Washington Post*, July 27, 1946, p. 5.

23. "These Are the Japanese," *New York Times Magazine*, August 26, 1945, pp. 6–7. The captions sometimes bear dubious relation to the photographs. For example, "school boy" is a young man wearing a cap with the word "college" across the front. "Housewife" is a elderly woman, seemingly in her seventies or eighties, who may well have been too old to do housework. "Business man" seems to be past the age of 60 and probably already retired. The *Times* was perhaps more interested in conveying a desired impression than in having the image fit reality.

24. Gallup, *Gallup Poll*, Vol. 1, pp. 521–22.

25. The United Press, "Tokyo Puts Toll of Atomic Bombs at 190,000 Killed and Wounded," *New York Times*, August 23, 1945, pp. 1, 5.

26. "Japanese Stress Hiroshima 'Horror,'" *New York Times*, August 25, 1945, p. 3.

27. The estimate was quoted in "From Hiroshima: A Report and a Question," *Time*, February 11, 1946, p. 27 n.

28. Ibid., pp. 26–27.

29. John Hersey, *Hiroshima*.

30. "Time from Laughter," *New York Times*, August 30, 1946, p. 16.

31. Charles Poore, "The Most Spectacular Explosion in the Time of Man."

32. The figure is based on Sheila Johnson's survey, included in her *American Attitudes toward Japan, 1941–1975*, p. 13.

33. According to the *New York Times* book review, the view that "we should never have used the bomb at all" was held only by a very small minority, no greater in number than the people who had already picked targets on which they wished the United States to drop another atomic bomb (Poore, "Most Spectacular Explosion," 56).

34. Johnson, *American Attitudes*, p. 38.

35. NORC, *Opinion News* 8, no. 10, May 13, 1947, p. 6.

36. Mark Gayn, *Japan Diary*, pp. 237–39.

CHAPTER 7

1. See Takashi Yoshida, "A Battle over History: The Nanjing Massacre in Japan," pp. 79–94.

2. Part 1 (nos. 1–11) was serialized on page 2 of the evening edition of *Asahi shinbun* from August 26, 1971, to September 14, 1971. The subsequent parts were also presented in serial form on page 2 of *Asahi shinbun* on the dates indicated in notes 3–5.

3. Part 2 (nos. 12–21) appeared from October 6, 1971, to October 19, 1971.

4. Part 3 (nos. 22–31) was printed between November 4 and November 16, 1971.

5. Part 4 (nos. 32–40) continued from December 13 to December 25, 1971.

6. Honda Katsuichi, "Chūgoku no tabi" (Travels in China), *Asahi shinbun*, evening ed., no. 24, November 6, 1971, p. 2; no. 25, November 8, 1971, p. 2; no. 26, November 9, 1971, p. 2; and no. 31, November 16, 1971, p. 2. Jiang found his missing brother in 1951 and his sister in 1956—after more than 18 years of separation.

7. Honda, "Chūgoku no tabi," *Asahi shinbun*, evening ed., no. 23, November 5, 1971, p. 2. What Jiang told Honda was likely an embellished version of the "Contest to Cut Down One Hundred" (*hyakuningiri kyōsō*) reported in *Tokyō nichi nichi shinbun* at the time. Between Wuxi and Jurong, Mukai killed 89, while Noda killed 78. The contest continued, and by the time they advanced toward Zijin Mountain, the former had killed 106, and the latter claimed 105. They were not sure which one achieved the goal first, so they decided to extend the contest; now the winner would be the first to kill 150. (As to the articles, see Honda Katsuichi, *The Nanjing Massacre*, pp. 125–27.)

8. According to an advertisement of the *Asahi*, circulation in November 1970 was 5,994,494 for the morning edition and 3,979,055 for the evening edition (the Japan Newspaper Publishers and Editors Association, *The Japanese Press 1971*, n.p.).

9. Honda, "Chūgoku no tabi," *Asahi shinbun*, evening ed., no. 12, October 6, 1971, p. 2.

10. Uno Shintarō, "Sensō sekinin o tsuku 'Chūgoku no tabi'" ("Travels in China" Pointed Out Japan's War Responsibility), *Asahi shinbun*, September 6, 1971, p. 5.

11. "Konshū no koe kara" (This Week's Excerpts from "Voice"), *Asahi shinbun*, September 16, 1971, p. 5.

12. Honda, "Chūgoku no tabi," *Asahi shinbun*, evening ed., no. 12 (October 6, 1971), p. 2.

13. Furukawa Mantarō, Nit-Chū sengo kankei shi nōto (Postwar Relations between Japan and China), pp. 266–74. The CCP and the Satō Eisaku administration had been hostile toward each other. For example, in November 1969, the CCP accused the Satō Eisaku administration of being responsible for the revival of Japan's militarism, and Satō responded by denouncing the CCP's nuclear policy as a threat to Japanese security (pp. 190, 195–97).

14. "Kotoshi no shūkei" (This Year in Abstract), Asahi shinbun, December 31, 1971, p. 5. Statements of opinion relating to the protection of plants and animals held first place; the Asahi received 2,201 letters on this issue. Letters regarding pollution marked the third (1,532), followed by miscellaneous contemporary issues (1,432), and college entrance and graduation (1,265).

15. As evidence of the fact that Honda was not motivated by changes in Sino-Japanese politics, it may be noted that Honda applied to the Chinese embassy for a visa at the end of 1970 and received permission in May 1971, more than one year before the normalization took place. (See "Chūgoku no tabi," Asahi shinbun, evening ed., no. 1, August 26, 1971, p. 2.).

16. Honda's serial article titled "Sensō to minshū" (War and People) ran between May and December 1967 in Asahi shinbun. Part 5, which received the most acclaim, was published as a book titled Senjō no mura (A Village in the Battlefield) in 1968. See Honda Katsuichi, Senjō no mura, pp. 21–50, 318.

17. Ibid., pp. 146–74, 222–23.

18. Honda Katsuichi, Sabakareta Nankin daigyakusastsu (The Nanjing Massacre on Trial), pp. 20–22.

19. Ben-Dasan's Nihonjin to Yudayajin (The Japanese and the Jewish), published in 1970, became a best-seller.

20. Isaiah Ben-Dasan, "Asahi shinbun no 'gomen nasai'" ("Apology" from Asahi shinbun).

21. Honda Katsuichi, "Izaya Bendasan shi e no kōkaijō" (An Open Letter to Mr. Isaiah Ben-Dasan), pp. 211, 217.

22. Ibid., pp. 212–17.

23. Isaiah Ben-Dasan, "Honda Katsuichi sama e no hensho" (Response to Mr. Honda Katsuichi), pp. 46, 53–55.

24. Ibid., pp. 46–51.

25. Honda Katsuichi, "Zatsuon de ijimerareru gawa no me" (From the Eyes of Those Who Were Forced to Suffer by the Unpleasant Noise), pp. 150–51, 160–65, 173–74.

26. Isaiah Ben-Dasan, "Honda Katsuichi sama e no tsuishin" (Postscript to Mr. Honda Katsuichi), pp. 132–43.

27. Suzuki Akira, "'Nankin daigyakusatsu' no maboroshi" (The Illusion of the "Nanjing Massacre"). See also Bob Wakabayashi, "The Nanking One-Hundred-Man Killing Contest Debate."

28. Suzuki, "'Nankin daigyakusatsu' no maboroshi," pp. 177–79.

29. Ibid., pp. 180, 185. See also Honda, "Chūgoku no tabi," Asahi shinbun, evening ed., no. 23 (November 5, 1971), p. 2.

30. Suzuki, "'Nankin daigyakusatsu' no maboroshi," pp. 180, 185.

31. Suzuki Akira, "Mukai shōi wa naze korosaretaka" (Why Was Second Lieutenant Mukai Executed?).

32. See, for example, Isaiah Ben-Dasan, "Kōzu shi no yongensoku to 'Chūgoku no tabi'" (The Four Principles of Mr. Kōzu and "Travels in China"); "'Hyakuningiri' to 'satsujin gēmu'" ("Cut Down One Hundred Contest" and "Killing Contests").

33. See, for example, Isaiah Ben-Dasan, *Nihonkyō ni tsuite* (About Japanism); Suzuki, *"Nankin daigyakusatsu" no maboroshi*.

34. Ishihara Shintarō and Kon Tōkō, "Kokunan koko ni kuru" (Facing a National Crisis), p. 86.

35. Tanaka Masaaki, *Nihon muzairon* (Thesis of Japan's Innocence), p. 82.

36. Honda, *Chūgoku no tabi*.

37. Honda Katsuichi, *Chūgoku no Nihongun* (The Japanese Army in China). The photographs were culled from exhibits at local museums in China.

38. "Henshū kōki" (From the Editors), *Shokun!* 4, no. 5 (May 1972): 256.

39. "Henshū kōki" (From the Editors), *Shokun!* 4, no. 4 (April 1972): 256. More than 150 letters responded to Yamamoto's "Honda Katsuichi sama e no hensho" (Response to Mr. Honda Katsuichi), a level of response unprecedented in the journal's history.

40. Hora Tomio, *Nit-Chū sensōshi shiryōshū 9: Nankin jiken* (A Collection of Historical Materials on the Japan-China War: The Nanjing Incident).

41. Hora Tomio, *Nankin daigyakusatsu: "maboroshi" ka kōsaku hihan* (The Nanjing Massacre: Criticism of the Making of an Illusion), p. ii.

42. Genbaku no zu Maruki bijutsukan (Maruki Gallery for the Hiroshima Panels Foundation), *Genbaku no zu* (The Hiroshima Panels), pp. 87–91, 102–105. The size of *Karasu* is approximately 6 by 24 feet, while *Nankin daigyakusatsu no zu* is approximately 13 by 27 feet. A turning point for the Marukis came in 1970, when they traveled to the United States and exhibited *The Hiroshima Panels*. One professor asked them what they would do if a Chinese artist opened an exhibition on the Nanjing Massacre. According to the Marukis, they had never questioned themselves about crimes that Japan had committed during the war, and the words of the professor opened their minds' eyes. (See "Kondo wa 'Nankin gyakusatsu no zu'" [Now the Panel of "The Rape of Nanking"], *Asahi shinbun*, evening ed., November 9, 1974, p. 8.)

43. As of 1994, the museum had approximately 4,500 supporting members. See Nishida Masaru, *Sekai no heiwa hakubutsukan* (Peace Museums in the World), pp. 91–92.

44. Oda Baku, "Jūgonen sonsō o dō oshieruka" (How to Teach the Fifteen-Year War), pp. 32–33.

45. Yoneda Shinji, "Kyōkasho ni okeru Chūgokuzō" (Images of China in Textbooks), pp. 19–20.

46. Tawara Yoshifumi, *Kyōkasho kōgeki no shinsō* (The Depth of Attacks on School Textbooks), pp. 158–70.

47. "Kyōkasho sarani 'senzen' fukken e" (Textbooks Return Further toward "Prewar" Position), *Asahi shinbun*, June 26, 1982, p. 1.

48. "Kō kawatta kōkō kyōkasho" (High School Textbooks Changed as Shown), *Asahi shinbun*, June 26, 1982, p. 22. Tokutake Toshio, *Kyōkasho no sengoshi*, pp. 201–202; Aoki Akira, "Kyōkasho 'gohō' o hiki okoshita shinbun no taishitsu" (Editorial Policies of Newspapers Causing Flawed Reports on Textbooks), p. 30.

49. "Chūgoku, kōshiki ni kōgi" (China Officially Protests), *Asahi shinbun*, July 27,

1982, p. 1. Also see "Chōgoku no mōshi ire naiyō" (The Texts of the Chinese Protest), *Asahi shinbun*, July 27, 1982, p. 3.

50. *Chūgoku geppō* translated an August 5, 1982, report of the Pacific News Service, a wire service similar to Associated Press. *Chūgoku geppō*, 286 (August 1982): 167.

51. "Nihonhin fubai undō o ketsugi" (Agreement to Boycott Japanese Products), *Asahi shinbun*, August 26, 1982, p. 3.

52. Tokutake, *Kyōkasho no sengoshi*, p. 203.

53. "Kokuren jinken'i demo hihan" (UN Subcommittee on Human Rights Criticized Too), *Asahi shinbun*, August 26, 1982, p. 3.

54. "Nihon seifu no kenkai, yōshi" (Summary: The Understanding of the Japanese Government), *Asahi shinbun*, July 29, 1982, p. 1.

55. "'Shinryaku' henkō yonkasho dake" ("Shinryaku" Altered Only in Four Passages), *Asahi shinbun*, July 29, 1982, p. 22.

56. "Kyōkasho kentei mondai no tōben" (Reply on the Issue of Textbook Authorization), *Asahi shinbun*, July 30, 1982, p. 4.

57. "'Shinryaku' yokusei, 30 nendai kara ikkan" (Suppression of "*shinryaku*" Has Gone on Constantly Since the Mid-1950s), *Asahi shinbun*, August 25, 1982, p. 3. According to Shuppan rōren, "*Nihonshi*" "*Sekaishi*" *kentei shiryōshū: Fukkatsu suru Nihon gunkoku shugi to rekishi kyōkasho* (Source Materials on Authorization of Textbooks on "Japanese History" and "World History"), the following chart reveals how some textbook descriptions of the Nanjing Massacre were revised in 1982 (pp. 23–24):

Before	*After*
Gakkō tosho's, *Nihonshi* (Japanese History):	
(In Text)	
"At this time [when the Japanese military occupied Nanjing] the Japanese military killed a great many (*obitadashii*) Chinese refugees, women, children, and unarmed soldiers who had already surrendered."	The sentence was relegated to a footnote.
Sanseidō's, *Shin sekaishi* (New World History):	
(In text)	(In text)
". . . the incident that killed a great many Chinese soldiers and civilians . . ."	". . . the incident that killed many Chinese soldiers and civilians . . ."
Sanseidō's, *Shin Nihonshi* (New Japanese History):	
(In footnote)	(In footnote)
"Immediately after the fall of Nanjing, the Japanese military killed many Chinese soldiers and civilians."	"While destroying fierce resistance by the Chinese military, the enraged Japanese military captured Nanjing and killed many Chinese soldiers and civilians."

Sanseidō's, *Kōkō Nihonshi* (High School Japanese History):

(In footnote)	(In footnote)
"The Japanese military that occupied Nanjing massacred (*gyakusatsu*) many non-combatants, prompting international protests."	"Infuriated by the fierce resistance by the Chinese military that had inflicted many casualties on the Japanese military, the army massacred many Chinese soldiers and civilians during the occupation of Nanjing."

58. "Seifu kenkai" (View of the Government), *Asahi shinbun*, August 27, 1982, p. 1.

59. Watanabe Shōichi, "Manken kyo ni hoeta kyōkasho mondai" (Ten Thousand Dogs Barked at the Textbook Controversy).

60. "'Shinryaku' henkō yonkasho dake," *Asahi shinbun*, July 30, 1982, p. 4.

61. For example, the *Sankei* reiterated this position on July 28, August 11, September 7, and September 8, 1982. See "Dokusha ni fukaku owabi shimasu" (Profound Apology to Readers), *Seiron* 112 (November 1982): 82–83; "Kyōkasho mondai Chūgoku kōgi no dodai yuragu" (Foundation of China's Claim in Textbook Controversy Shaken), *Seiron* 112 (November 1982): 84–85.

62. "Kyōkasho mondai Chūgoku kōgi no dodai yuragu," *Seiron*, p. 85.

63. Hidaka Rokurō, "'Hansei' towa nanika" (What Is "Reflection"?), pp. 46–48, 50, 52.

64. Ibid., pp. 53, 55.

65. Dai Guohui, "Nihon e no jogen" (Advice to Japan), pp. 72–74.

66. Kim Hak Hyon, "Kyōkasho mondai to 'yūkō' no kyokō" (Illusion of Friendship and the Textbook Controversy), pp. 77, 79–81.

67. Watanabe Shōichi, "Manken kyo ni hoeta kyōkasho mondai," p. 38.

68. Maeda Yūji, *Sensō no nagare no naka ni* (In the Course of the War), pp. 3–4, 122–24. Maeda's book was a memoir of his experience as a war correspondent during the war and covered not only Japan's attack on Nanjing, but also assaults on other places in China and Indochina.

69. Watanabe Shōichi, "Manken kyo ni hoeta kyōkasho mondai," p. 38.

70. Uno Seiichi, "Hyōki o aratameruna" (Do Not Alter Descriptions).

71. Mayuzumi Toshiro, "Kyōkasho mondai ni tsuite" (About the Textbook Controversy), pp. 174–76.

72. Honda, *Sabakareta Nankin daigyakusatsu*, p. 12.

73. Ienaga's second lawsuit passed through three levels of adjudication and a series of appeals. In July 1970, the local trial court ruled in his favor. The Tokyo High Court initially affirmed this judgment. However, in April 1982, the Supreme Court vacated the judgment of the high court and remanded the case to the high court for further consideration. The high court then reversed its earlier position and held against Ienaga. See "Dai sanji Ienaga kyōkasho soshō saikōsai hanketsu" (The Supreme Court Rules on Ienaga's Third Textbook Trial), *Asahi shinbun*, August 30, 1997, p. 11.

74. Honda, *Sabakareta Nankin daigyakusatsu*, p. 12.

75. "Dai sanji Ienaga kyōkasho soshō saikōsai hanketsu," p. 11.

76. Quoted in Kagami Mitsuyuki and Himeta Mitsuyoshi, *Shōgen Nankin daigyakusatsu* (Testimonies on the Nanjing Massacre), pp. 228–29.

77. Ibid., pp. 231–32.

78. "Nankin daigyakusatsu masshō o motome kyūgunjin ra teiso" (Veterans File Lawsuit Demanding Deletion of the Nanjing Massacre), *Asahi shinbun*, March 14, 1984, p. 22.

79. Tanaka Masaaki, *"Nankin gyakusatsu" no kyokō* (The Illusion of "the Nanjing Massacre"), pp. 353–54.

80. Ibid., pp. 357–58.

81. Ibid., pp. 26–27.

82. Watanabe Shōichi, " 'Nankin gyakusatsu' no kyokō ni yosete" (Contributing to *The Illusion of "the Nanjing Massacre"*), in *"Nankin gyakusatsu" no kyokō*, pp. 1–6.

83. Tanaka, *"Nankin gyakusatsu" no kyokō*, pp. 27–28, 355–56.

84. Ibid., pp. 42, 53–54, 325–30.

85. Hora Tomio et al., eds, *Nankin jiken o kangaeru* (Consideration of the Nanjing Incident), pp. 4–6; *Nankin daigyakusatsu no kenkyū* (Studies of the Nanjing Massacre), pp. 329–31.

86. Hora Tomio, *Nit-Chū sensō: Nankin daigyakusatsu jiken shiryōshū* (The Japan-China War: A Collection of Historical Materials on the Nanjing Massacre), 2 vols.

87. Hora Tomio, *Nankin daigyakusatsu no shōmei* (The Proof of the Nanjing Massacre), pp. 4–5.

88. Ibid., pp. 60, 64.

89. "Nankin gyakusatsu" shiryō ni kaizan" (Distortion in Nanjing Massacre Document), *Asahi shinbun*, November 24, 1985, p. 3.

90. Hora, *Nankin daigyakusatsu no shōmei*, pp. 24, 31–48, 59, 220–21.

91. Ibid., pp. 95, 127–153

92. Tanaka Masaaki, *Nankin jiken no sōkatsu: gyakusatsu hitei 15 no ronkyo* (An Outline of the Nanjing Incident: Fifteen Grounds for the Denial of the Massacre), pp. 340–42.

93. Kobori Keiichirō, "Susumeru kotoba" (A Word of Recommendation), *Nankin jiken no sōkatsu*, n.p. Tanaka's 1987 volume was translated into English and included in *What Really Happened in Nanking*, a collection of Tanaka's writings about the massacre. This collection also includes a more extensive foreword by Kobori, accusing the Tokyo Trial of inventing the Nanjing atrocities and praising Tanaka for his devoted work (vii–x).

94. Hora et al., *Nankin jiken o kangaeru*, pp. 55–68.

95. Hata Ikuhiko, *Nankin jiken* (The Nanjing Incident), pp. 73–75, 82–89, 102, 132–60, 227–29, 243–44.

96. Ibid., pp. 212–15.

97. Hora Tomio, *Nankin daigyakusatsu no shōmei* (The Proof of the Nanjing Massacre), p. 6.

98. Rekishi kyōikusha kyōgikai, *Rekishi kyōiku gojūnen no ayumi to kadai* (The History and Objectives of 50 Years of History Education), pp. 213–15, 255–56.

CHAPTER 8

1. "Zhonghua renmin gongheguo zhengfu, Ribenguo zhengfu lianhe shengming" (Joint Statement by the Chinese and Japanese Governments), *Renmin ribao*, September 30, 1972, p 1.

2. "Zhong-Ri Guanxi de xinpianzhang" (The New Chapter in Chinese-Japanese Relations), *Renmin ribao*, September 30, 1972, p. 2.

3. "Qingzhu Ribenguo tianhuang bixia shengri" (Japanese Emperor's Birthday Celebrated), *Renmin ribao*, April 29, 1973, p. 4.

4. In 1975, 1977–83, 1985, and 1987, Chinese media such as *Renmin ribao* reported that Chinese officials sent a congratulatory telegram and attended the party hosted by the embassy. See Gaimushō Ajiakyoku Chūgokuka (China Section, Asian Bureau, Ministry of Foreign Affairs, Japan), *Chūgoku geppō* (China Monthly) 174 (April 1973): 10; no.186 (April 1974): 14; no. 198 (April 1975): 4; no. 210 (April 1976): 7; no. 222 (April 1977): 6; no. 234 (April 1978): 7; no. 246 (April 1979): 6; no. 258 (April 1980): 11–12; no. 270 (April 1981): 2; no. 282 (April 1982): 9; no. 294 (April 1983): 8; no. 306 (April 1984): 8; no. 318 (April 1985): 3–4; no. 330 (April 1986): 7; no. 342 (April 1987): 6; no. 354 (April 1988): 7.

5. Allen S. Whiting, "Assertive Nationalism in Chinese Foreign Policy," p. 927.

6. "Yaoqiu Rifang jiuzheng wenbusheng cuangai qin-Hua lishi de cuowu" (Japanese Education Ministry Demanded to Correct Distortions of History of Chinese Invasion), *Renmin ribao*, July 28, 1982, p. 4.

7. "Riben baozhi yaojiu wenbusheng gaizheng jiaokeshu zhong de cuowu" (Japanese Newspapers Urge the Ministry of Education to Correct Textbook Errors), *Renmin ribao*, June 30, 1982, p.6.

8. "Zhongyan nier li yu xing" (Advice Hurts Ears, but Is Helpful to Behavior), *Renmin ribao*, July 30, 1982, p. 6.

9. Gaimushō Ajiakyoku Chūgokuka, *Chūgoku geppō*, no. 286 (August 1982): 9–25. Between August 1 and August 16, *Renmin ribao* included related articles every day. For the rest of the month, the newspaper carried related articles every other day (p. 9).

10. Ibid., pp. 10–11. For example, an interview with Wu Changde, who testified at the Tokyo Trial, was broadcast on August 6 and appeared in *Renmin ribao* on August 9, 1982.

11. Ibid., p. 10. For example, on August 3, *Renmin ribao* reported that, at its second annual meeting in Shenyang, the Chinese Association for Japanese Historical Studies condemned the revisions of the textbooks. Xinhua News Agency also reported protests by scholars in Shanghai (on August 11) and in Beijing (on August 12).

12. Ibid., p. 11. *Renmin ribao* ran a series of interviews with Japanese visitors, all of them critical of the textbook revisions. Interviews included: professors from Waseda University on August 4; Egami Namio, president of the Center for Cultural Exchanges in Asia (Ajia bunka koryū sentō), on August 5; Sugimoto Noriteru, the leader of an organization called, somewhat awkwardly, The Mourning of the Deaths of Chinese Slave Laborers during the Construction of the Dam at Sagami Lake (Nihon Sagamiko damu junnansha irei yūkō hōchūdan) on August 9; and Mitsuhashi Atsuko, a representative of the Japan Teachers Union (Nihon kyōshokuin kumiai) on August 10.

13. "Yiding yao ba zhenshi de lishi gaosusha yidai" (We Will Certainly Pass Down the True History), *Renmin ribao*, August 10, 1982, p. 4.

14. Gaimushō Ajiakyoku Chūgokuka, *Chūgoku geppō*, no. 286 (August 1982): 12–13.

15. Gaimushō Ajiakyoku Chūgokuka, *Chūgoku geppō*, no. 287 (September 1982): 21, 23–24.

16. "Xiwang Riben zhengfu yan bi xin, xing bi guo" (We Hope the Japanese Government's Actions Will Follow Its Words), *Renmin ribao*, September 10, 1982, p. 4.

17. "Relie qingzhu Zhong-Ribang jiao zhengchanghua shizhou nian" (Exciting Celebration of the Tenth Anniversary of the Diplomatic Normalization between China and Japan), *Renmin ribao*, September 29, 1982, p. 2. The translation is taken from Foreign Broadcast Information Service, "Renmin Ribao Greets Sino-Japanese Anniversary," *Daily Report: China*, September 30, 1982, D9–10.

18. Ibid.

19. For example, Xinhua News Agency reported on July 24, 1982, that *Zhongguo qingnian bao* was urging instructors to teach the youth about the war in order to maintain friendship between the two nations. See Gaimushō Ajiakyoku Chūgokuka, *Chūgoku geppō*, no. 285 (July 1982): 16.

20. Whiting, "Assertive Nationalism in Chinese Foreign Policy," p. 929.

21. "Guanyu jia qiang aiguo zhuyi xuanchuan jiaoyu de yijian" (Opinion on Strengthening and Propagating Patriotic Education), *Renmin ribao*, July 16, 1983, p. 2.

22. "Zhonggong zhongyang guanyu zhengdang de jueding" (Central Committee's Decision on Party Consolidation), *Renmin ribao*, October 13, 1983, p. 1.

23. For example, "Gaoju shehuizhuyi wenyi qizhi jianjue fangzhi he qingchu jingsheng wuran" (Raise the Flag of Socialism, Arts and Literature, Prevent Spiritual Pollution, Wipe It Out), *Renmin ribao*, October 31, 1983, p. 1. Xinhua News Agency reported on October 25, 1983, a weeklong symposium on Mao Zedong in Shandong Province and stressed the importance of Mao's thought in resisting the damaging effects of harmful thought whether internal or external in origin (*Chūgoku geppō*, no. 300 [October 1983]:126–28).

24. Gaimushō Ajiakyoku Chūgokuka, *Chūgoku geppō*, no. 321 (July 1985): 46–48.

25. Gaimushō Ajiakyoku Chūgokuka, *Chūgoku geppō*, no. 322 (August 1985): 38–39.

26 Ibid., pp. 39–40.

27. Ibid., pp. 44, 46.

28. Gaimushō Ajiakyoku Chūgokuka, *Chūgoku geppō*, no. 338 (December 1986): 82–83.

29. Gaimushō Ajiakyoku Chūgokuka, *Chūgoku geppō*, no 335 (September 1986): 150–51.

30. Zhongguo Renmin Kang-Ri Zhanzheng Jinianguan (The Museum of the War of Chinese People's Resistance against Japan), *Zhongguo renmin kang-Ri Zhanzheng jinianguan* (The Museum of the War of Chinese People's Resistance against Japan), n.p.

31. Zhongguo renmin zhengzhi xiesheng huiyi jiangsusheng Nanjingshi weiyuanhui wenshi ziliao yanjiu weiyuanhui (the Research Committee on Historical Materials of the City of Nanjing, Jiangsu Province, Chinese People's Political Consultative Conference), *Shiliao xuanji Qin-Hua Rijun Nanjing datusha shiliao zhuanji* (Historical Sources: Materials on the Nanjing Massacre Committed by the Japanese Army of Invasion), p. 85.

32. Ibid., p. 5.

33. Ibid., pp. 43–44.

34. See, for example, ibid., pp. 24–25.

35. Approximately the first two thirds of the book stressed the former point, while the rest emphasized the latter.

36. Nanjing datusha shiliao bianji weiyuanhui (Committee for the Compilation of Sources on the Nanjing Massacre), *Qin-Hua Rijun Nanjing datusha shiliao* (Historical Materials on the Nanjing Massacre Committed by the Japanese Army of Invasion).

37. Chapter 1 (pp. 1–155) detailed records written by Chinese people; chapter 2 (pp. 157–397) discussed records written by foreigners; and chapter 3 (pp. 399–487) recited survivors' narratives. See *Qin-Hua Rijun Nanjing datusha shiliao*.

38. Gao Xingzu, *Rijun qin-Hua baoxing: Nanjing datusha* (Japanese War Atrocities: The Nanjing Massacre).

39. Zhou Erfu, *Nanjing de xianluo* (The Fall of Nanjing); Zhongguo dier lishi dang'anguan (Number Two China Historical Archives) et al., eds, *Qin-Hua Rijun Nanjing datusha dang'an* (Archival Materials on the Nanjing Massacre Committed by the Japanese Army of Invasion). Xinhua News Agency reported the publication of the former on July 3, 1987, and the latter on July 13, 1987. See Gaimushō Ajiakyoku Chūgokuka, *Chūgoku geppō*, no. 345 (July 1987): 49–50.

40. See *Qin-Hua Rijun Nanjing datusha dang'an*, pp. 51–422, for documents on Japanese atrocities; pp. 423–60 for burial records; and pp. 589–622 for accounts regarding the proceedings of the military tribunal in Nanjing.

41. Mark Eykholt, "Aggression, Victimization, and Chinese Historiography of the Nanjing Massacre," p. 48.

42. Ibid., pp. 36–40.

43. Gaimushō Ajiakyoku Chūgokuka, *Chūgoku geppō*, no. 345 (July 1987): 42.

44. Gaimushō Ajiakyoku Chūgokuka, *Chūgoku geppō*, no. 331 (May 1986): 53.

45. Ibid., p. 10.

46. Ho Ying-chin's first speech was reported in *Zhongyang Ribao*, June 7, 1972. The translation is included in *Chūgoku geppō*, no. 164 (June 1972), p. 2.

47. The account of Ho Ying-chin's second speech appeared in *Zhongyang Ribao* from July 7 to July 9. The translation is included in *Chūgoku geppō*, no.165 (July 1972): 8. His *Who Actually Fought the Sino-Japanese War 1937–45?* was published in English by Lee Ming Company, Taipei, in 1979. This book was made available in the United States.

48. The Japanese translation of the editorial of *Zhongyang Ribao* on July 22, 1972, is included in *Chūgoku geppō*, no. 165 (July 1972): 4–5.

49. Guo's bibliographic information is taken from Nankin jiken chōsa kenkyūkai (The Research Committee on the Nanjing Incident), *Nankin jiken shiryōshū* (A Collection of Historical Materials on the Nanjing Incident), Vol. 2, p. 74.

50. Guo Qi, *Nanjing datusha* (The Nanjing Massacre), pp. 2–3, 8, 12, 16–19, 35, 118, 171, 222.

51. Li Yunhan, "Youguan 'Nanjing da tu sha' Zhongwai shiliao de pingshu" (In Regard to Chinese and Foreign Discussions of the Historical Materials on the Nanjing Massacre).

52. Zhongyang yanjiuyuan, *Kangzhan jianguoshi yantaohui lunwenji*, pp. 55–56, 96–97.

53. Hong Guiji, "Nanjing datusha" (The Nanjing Massacre), *Riben zai Hua baoxing lu* (Account of the Atrocities Committed by Japan in China), pp. 239–608. Zhongguo Guomindang dangshi weiyuanhui (Guomindang Party History Commission, China), *Rijun zai Hua baoxing : Nanjing datusha* (Atrocities Committed by the Japanese Army: The Nanjing Massacre), 2 vols.

54. See, for example, Hong, pp. 274–94 (Timperley), 414–518 (Guo), 579 (Hora), 585–87 (Honda); Guomingdang, v. 1, pp. 96–257 (Guo), 357–460 (Timperley), 461–553 (Smythe); v. 2, pp. 319–40 (Li).

55. For example, from September 3, 1978, to October 6, 1978, the Guomindang Party History Commission organized an exhibit at the Sun Yatsen Memorial Hall, opened in 1972, that celebrated the Nationalist victory in the war (see *Chūgoku geppō*, no. 239 (September 1978): 215); Ho Ying-chin organized the Fortieth Anniversary of Japan's Surrender on September 3, 1935. More than 2,500 representatives from various institutions and organizations took part in the ceremony. See *Chūgoku geppō*, no. 323 (September 1985): 161.

56. Fujio, Kishi, and 80 other active and retired LDP politicians visited Chiang Kaishek on his eighty-eighth birthday in 1974. They also expressed deepest regret about the discontinuation of the diplomatic relations between the Republic of China (Taiwan) and Japan (*Chūgoku geppō*, no. 192 [October 1974]: 107–108). In 1979, 52 LDP politicians, including Fujio, visited Taiwan to discuss current international affairs including the normalization between the PRC and the United States (*Chūgoku geppō*, no. 243 [January 1979]: 216–17). In October 1986, Fujio and six others visited Taiwan to celebrate the hundredth anniversary of Chiang's birth (*Chūgoku geppō*, no. 336: 149). In Japan, Kishi and two others organized a celebration of the same anniversary. They were joined by 6,500 individuals, including Taiwanese representatives (*Chūgoku geppō*, no. 335 [September 1986]: 170). When Ho Ying-chin died in 1987, Fujio and others expressed their condolences (*Chūgoku geppō*, no. 348 [October 1987]: 180).

57. *Chūgoku geppō* no. 350 (December 1987): 32.

CHAPTER 9

1. David Bergamini, *Japan's Imperial Conspiracy*, pp. xv–xvi.

2. Ibid., pp. xvi–xxi.

3. Ibid., pp. xxvii–xxviii, 335–37, 362–69, 395–99, 496–505.

4. Ibid., pp. 22–24. Bergamini erroneously identified Prince Asaka as Hirohito's uncle.

5. Ibid., pp. 23, 35, 42–43.

6. Ibid., pp. 81–82, 100–101, 113.

7. Herbert Bix, "Conspiracy That Failed"; Alvin Coox, review of *Japan's Imperial Conspiracy*; James Crowley, review of *Japan's Imperial Conspiracy*; *New York Times*, October 24, 1971, sec. 7, pp. 3, 66; Okamoto Shumpei, review of *Japan's Imperial Conspiracy*; Herschel Webb, review of *Japan's Imperial Conspiracy*; Richard Storry, "Imperial Conspiracy in Japan?"; Malcolm Kennedy, review of *Japan's Imperial Conspiracy*; Daniel Spencer, review of *Japan's Imperial Conspiracy*.

8. Crowley, pp. 3, 66; Okamoto, pp. 124–25.

9. Coox, pp. 1169–70.

10. Bix, "Conspiracy That Failed," p. 255.

11. Ibid., pp. 256–57.

12. Christopher Wren, "China Assails Japan's Books on 30's Invasion," *New York Times*, July 28, 1982, p. A6.

13. "Japanese Stands [sic] by Revisions in Texts That Irritate China," *New York Times*, August 11, 1982, p. A8.

14. "Transcript of President's News Conference on Foreign and Domestic Matters," *New York Times*, August 14, 1982, p. A4.

15. Henry Scott Stokes, "Tokyo Attempts to Placate Its Former Victims in Asia," *New York Times*, August 29, 1982, p. E4.

16. "Tokyo Text Change Protested," *New York Times*, September 19, 1982, p. A8.

17. John Burgess, "Japan Pursues Debate on 'Rape of Nanking'; Revisionists Challenge Postwar Accounts of Toll," *Washington Post*, January 25, 1985, p. A25.

18. Ibid.

19. James Reston Jr., "How Japan Teaches Its Own History," *New York Times*, October 27, 1985, sec. 6, pp. 52–60, 64–65.

20. Ibid., pp. 52, 54, 60.

21. Ibid., pp. 64–65.

22. James Bailey, "War Films Depict Japan as a Misunderstood Victim," *New York Times*, November 10, 1985, sec. 2, pp. 17, 19. The eight WWII films that Bailey discussed in the article were: *Dai-Nippon teikoku* (The Great Empire of Japan) (1982), *Mikan no taikyoku* (The Unfinished Game of Go) (1982), *Minami jūjisei* (Southern Cross) (1982), *Tokyō saiban* (The Tokyo War Crimes Trial) (1983), *Konoko o nokoshite* (Leaving This Child) (1984), *Shanhai Bansukingu* (Welcome to Shanghai) (1984), *Zero-sen Moyu* (The Burning of a Zero Fighter) (1984), and *Biruma no tategoto* (The Harp of Burma) (1985).

23. Susan Chira, "For Most Japanese, Pearl Harbor Is Just a Footnote," *New York Times*, December 7, 1985, p. A2.

24. A. J. Smith, "Who Attacked Who?" *San Diego Union-Tribune*, December 16, 1985, p. B12.

25. Frank Harrison Peters et al., eds., "The Bombings in Perspective," *San Diego Union-Tribune*, August 11, 1985, p. C3.

26. Stan Steenbock, "V-J Day: Why No Articles on the Fortieth Anniversary?" *Los Angeles Times*, August 24, 1985, part 2, p. 2.

27. Daniel Sneider, "Japan Encounters Fresh Flak in Battle over Its Textbook Accounts of WWII," *Christian Science Monitor*, June 23, 1986, p. 11. Kase was chairperson of the council (*gichō*), and Mayuzumi was management chief (*unei iinchō*).

28. Daniel Southerland, "China Claims Japanese Text Glosses Over World War II," *Washington Post*, June 5, 1986, p. A34.

29. Clyde Haberman, "Japanese Text Is Under Fire Once Again," *New York Times*, July 10, 1986, p. A13.

30. Clyde Haberman, "For Japan, Even the War Takes a Back Seat to Trade," *New York Times*, August 10, 1986, p. E26.

31. Ibid.

32. Clyde Haberman, "Japan's Education Chief Gets Lesson in Diplomacy," *New York Times*, September 10, 1986, p. A2.

33. Sam Jameson, "'Aggression' Disputed; Textbooks—Japan Splits on War Role," *Los Angeles Times*, September 10, 1986, p. 1.

34. Ibid.

35. Rekishi chiri kyōikusha kyōgikai (Association for History Educators), *Rekishi kyōiku gojūnen no ayumi to kadai* (The History and Objectives of Fifty Years of History Education), pp. 246–48. As to the statistics of the number of high schools in Japan, see Monbushō (Ministry of Education), *Monbu tōkei yōran shōwa 63-nen ban* (Details of Statistics Regarding Education, 1988), pp. 2–3.

36. *Rekishi kyōiku gojūnen no ayumi to kadai*, p. 247. For example, the association's Fukuoka branch published a special brochure titled "An Analysis of the Militaristic Textbook *New Edition of Japanese History*" (*Shinpen Nihonshi* o kiru) in October 1986. The branch also published 27 issues of newsletters between March 1987 and November 1991 aiming to raise public awareness and to prevent high school history teachers from using the council's textbook in the classroom (p. 247).

37. "1937 Invasion of China Is Focus of Art Exhibit," *New York Times*, December 20, 1987, p. A63. The exhibit was not reported by the *Washington Post*, the *Christian Science Monitor*, or the *Los Angeles Times*.

38. Joseph Policano, "The Rape of Nanking Must Be Remembered," *New York Times*, December 29, 1987, p. A18.

39. Clyde Haberman, "Japanese Cut 'Last Emperor,'" *New York Times*, January 21, 1988, p. C21. Serata Shinji, a spokesperson of Shōchiku, at first claimed that the film's producer in London, Jeremy Thomas, wondered in advance if the footage of the massacre would trouble Japanese viewers and that he asked Bertolucci to cut the scenes. However, Thomas and Bertolucci said they had no idea that the Nanjing footage would be deleted. The deleted footage was restored by the time of the opening.

40. Margaret Shapiro, "In Japan, the Edited 'Emperor'; Sensitive Footage from '37 Newsreel Deleted," *Washington Post*, January 20, 1988, p. C1.

41. "Playing with History," *Los Angeles Times*, January 21, 1988, part 2, p. 8.

42. See, for example, "A Japanese View of World War II Is Attacked," *New York Times*, April 27, 1988, p. A6; Margaret Shapiro, "Official Defends Japan's WWII Role; Remarks by Cabinet Member Spark Furor in China, S. Korea," *Washington Post*, April 27, 1988, p. A23.

43. "A Japanese View of World War II Is Attacked," p. A6.

44. See, for example, Clyde Haberman, "Japanese Official Fires New Furor on the War," *New York Times*, May 11, 1988, p. A14; Daniel Sneider, "History Controversy Again Stirs Japan," *Christian Science Monitor*, May 11, 1988, p. 9.

45. See, for example, Karl Schoenberger, "Japan Aide Quits Over Remark on WWII," *Los Angeles Times*, May 14, 1988, part 1, p. 6; Margaret Shapiro, "Minister Forced Out Over Defense of Japan's War Role," *Washington Post*, May 14, 1988, p. A28.

CHAPTER 10

1. "Tennōsei o kangaeru shinpo" (Symposium to Study the Emperor System), *Asahi shinbun*, (Kanagawa edition), October 5, 1988. Reprinted in Asahi shinbunsha, *Shōwa tennō hōdō* (Reports Regarding Emperor Shōwa), p. 281.

2. "Tennōsei kyōka ni hantai shimin gurūpu shūkai" (People Opposed to

Strengthening the Emperor System Organize Group Meeting), *Asahi shinbun*, (Kyōto edition), October 7, 1988. Reprinted in Asahi shinbunsha, *Shōwa tennō hōdō* (Reports Regarding Emperor Shōwa), p. 317.

3. "Tennōsei mondai de kōen shūkai" (Public Meeting Addresses Issues Regarding the Emperor System), *Asahi shinbun*, (Gunma Edition), October 8, 1988. Reprinted in Asahi shinbunsha, *Shōwa tennō hōdō* (Reports Regarding Emperor Shōwa), pp. 326–27.

4. "Jishuku no machi o aruku" (Wandering through the City in a Time of Voluntary Self-Restraint), *Asahi shinbun*, December 3, 1988.

5. "Kyōsan hatsugen de togikai funkyū" (Communist Outburst Disrupts the Metropolitan Assembly), *Asahi shinbun*, September 29, 1988.

6. Motoshima Hitoshi, *Nagasaki shichō no kotoba* (Statement of Mayor of Nagasaki), pp. 4–5.

7. Ibid., pp. 6–7.

8. Ibid., p. 14.

9. "Shimin ga shiji hyōmei" (City Residents Express Support), *Asahi shinbun* (Western ed.), December 15, 1988. Reprinted in Asahi shinbunsha, *Shōwa tennō hōdō* (Reports Regarding Emperor Shōwa), pp. 685–86.

10. Motoshima, *Nagasaki shichō no kotoba*, pp. 59–60.

11. "Shooting by Ultrarightist Has Japan Tense as Coronation Nears," *Asahi News Service*, January 19, 1990. Motoshima was shot on January 18, 1990.

12. Norma Field, *In the Realm of a Dying Emperor: Japan at Century's End*, pp. 270–71.

13. "'Jidai no kugiri' kakkai no koe" (Turning Point of the Era; Voices from Various Circles), *Asahi shinbun*, January 8, 1989, p. 5.

14. "Information," *Asahi jānaru* (February 24, 1989), p. 34.

15. Kōdansha, *Shōwa niman-nichi no zen kiroku* (The Entire Record of Twenty Thousand Days of the Shōwa), p. 103.

16. "Hosokawa shushō kisha kaiken no yōshi" (Summary of Prime Minister Hosokawa's Press Conference), *Asahi shinbun*, August 11, 1993, p. 5.

17. "Saki no sensō shinryaku sensō to meigen" (Recognition of the Last War as an "Aggressive War"), *Asahi shinbun*, August 11, 1993, p. 1.

18. "'Kagai' sekinin hajimete genkyū" ("Victimizer's" Responsibility Asserted for First Time), *Asahi shinbun*, August 16, 1993, evening ed., p. 1.

19. "Doi shūingichō no 'tsuitō no ji' yōshi" (Summary of Speaker Doi's Memorial Address), *Asahi shinbun*, August 16, 1993, evening ed., p. 1.

20. Hosokawa Morihiro, *The Time to Act Is Now*, pp. 118–19.

21. Yoshida Yutaka, "Sensō ninshiki o meguru kokkai rongi 1" (Debates in the Diet over the Understanding of the War, Part 1), pp. 71–72.

22. Ibid., pp. 74, 76.

23. Yoshida, "Sensō ninshiki o meguru kokkai rongi 2," pp. 68–69, 71.

24. The following is the complete text of the resolution:

> This Diet, in the fiftieth year since the war, offers its sincere tribute to the memory of the war dead throughout the world and to the victims who have suffered because of the war and other acts.
> Recalling the many instances of colonial rule and aggression-like acts [*shinryakuteki kōi*] in the modern history of the world, we recognize

those acts which our country carried out and the unbearable suffering inflicted on the peoples of other countries, particularly the nations of Asia, and express deep remorse.

Transcending differences in historical views of the past war [*saki no sensō*], we must humbly learn the lessons of history and build a peaceful international community.

This Diet joins hands with the countries of the world, under the doctrine of lasting peace enshrined in the Constitution of Japan, and expresses its determination to open up a future of coexistence for humankind.

We affirm the above.

See "Sengo gojūnen ketsugi (zenbun)" (The Text of the Diet Resolution Marking Fiftieth Anniversary of the War), *Asahi shinbun*, June 10, 1995, p. 1.

25. "Shinshintō no shūsei an" (Proposed Amendment of the New Frontier Party), *Asahi shinbun*, June 10, 1995, p. 7.

26. "'Dochira mo shinryaku gōrika'" ("Both Sides Are Rationalizing Aggression), *Asahi shinbun*, June 10, 1995, p. 3.

27. "Sengo ketsugi kessekisha no hitokoto" (Words of Those Absent from the Postwar Resolution Session), *Asahi shinbun*, June 10, 1995, p. 7.

28. "Sengo gojūnen shushō danwa" (Statement by Prime Minister), *Asahi shinbun*, August 15, 1995, evening ed., p. 2.

29. Ibid. The following is an excerpt of his speech:

During a time in the not too distant past, Japan, following a mistaken national policy, advanced along the road to war, only to ensnare the Japanese people in a fateful crisis, and through its colonial rule and aggression, caused tremendous damage and suffering to the people of many countries, particularly to those of Asian nations. In the hope that no such mistake be made in the future, I confront, in a spirit of humanity, these irrefutable facts of history and here express once again my feelings of deep remorse and state my heartfelt apology. Allow me also to express my feelings of profound condolence for all victims of that history both at home and abroad.

Building upon our deep remorse on this occasion of the fiftieth anniversary of the end of the war, Japan must eliminate self-righteous nationalism, promote international coordination as a responsible member of the international community, and thereby advance the principles of peace and democracy.

30. Aitani Kunio, "Sengo hoshō saiban no genjō to kadai" (The Present Condition and the Task of Postwar Compensation Trials), pp. 2–4.

31. Onodera Toshitaka, "Sengo hoshō saiban tōsō no kadai to tenbō" (Problems and Prospects in Postwar Legal Struggles over Compensation), pp. 13–14.

32. "Chūgokujin sensō higaisha no yōkyū o sasaeru kai dai nikai sōkai" (Report of the Second Annual Meeting of the Society to Support the Demands of Chinese War Victims), pp. 6–8; "Chūgokujin sensō higaisha no yōkyū o sasaeru kai dai sanka sōkai kettei" (Report of the Third Annual Meeting of the Society to Support the Demands of Chinese War Victims), pp. 7–8.

33. "Chūgokujin sensō higaisha no yōkyū o sasaeru kai dai sanka sōkai kettei" p. 8. The society's homepage address is: http://www.suopei.org/index-j.html.

34. Arai Shin'ichi, "Sōkan no ji" (Greetings to Our Readers on the Publication of Our First Issue), p. 3.

35. Titles of articles that have appeared in the past issues can be seen at: http://www.jca.apc.org/JWRC/index-j.html.

36. See Takashi Yoshida, "A Battle over History: The Nanjing Massacre in Japan," p. 127 n.124. There are more than 85 peace or war museums, both public and private, in Japan. See Rekishi kyōikusha kyōgikai (Association for History Educators), *Heiwa hakubutsukan, sensō shiryōkan gaido bukku* (Handbook for Peace and War Museums).

37. For example, Oka Masaharu Memorial Nagasaki Peace Museum focuses only on non-Japanese sufferings—military sex slavery, Korean atomic bomb victims, atrocities in China, and slave labor in Japan. Others addressed Japanese atrocities in connection with exhibits explaining why the Fifteen-Year War started in the first place as well as the Allies' justification for dropping conventional and atomic bombs on Japan.

38. Kamata Sadao, "Nagasaki genbaku shiryōkan no kagai tenji mondai" (Problems Regarding the Exhibition of Japan's Wartime Atrocities at the Nagasaki Atomic Bomb Museum), pp. 22–31. See also Nagasaki no genbaku tenji o tadasu shimin no kai (Citizen's Group That Seeks to Correct Atomic Exhibitions in Nagasaki), *Korede iinoka, Nagasaki genbaku shiryōkan* (This Isn't Right, Nagasaki Atomic Bomb Museum), pp. 18, 33–40.

39. Ritsumeikan daigaku kokusai heiwa myūjiamu (Kyoto Museum for World Peace), *Ritsumeikan daigaku kokusai heiwa myūjiamu dayori* (Newsletter from Kyoto Museum for World Peace, Ritsumeikan University), 1, no. 1 (May 19, 1993): 4.

40. *Ritsumeikan daigaku kokusai heiwa myūjiamu dayori*, 1, no. 2 (November 1, 1993): 2.

41. *Ritsumeikan daigaku kokusai heiwa myūjiamu dayori*, 2, no. 1 (January 20, 1995): 5–6. Other museums also hosted various lectures, symposia, and special exhibitions. See, generally, the newsletters published by these museums: Osaka International Peace Center's *Pīsu Ōsaka* (Peace Osaka); Oka Masaharu's Nagasaki Peace Museum's *Nishizaka dayori* (Newsletter from Nishizaka Town); Peace Museum of Saitama's *Saitama ken hewia shiryōkan dayori* (Newsletter from Peace Museum of Saitama).

42. 731 butaiten zenkoku jikkō iinkai (National Executive Committee for the Exhibition on Unit 731 Exhibition), pp. 112–13.

43. Ibid., pp. 9–101. Even after the national tour formally ended in December 1994, the panels and artifacts continued to travel around the nation. For example, in early December 1995, the objects were exhibited in Ebetsu, Hokkaido; between May 5 and 10, 1998, they were shown in Matsudo, Chiba; and from July 23 to July 28, 1998, they were displayed in Sagamihara, Kanagawa. See Rakunō gakuen shokuin kumiai 731 butaiten jikkō iinkai (Executive Committee for the Exhibition on Unit 731, Labor Union at Rakunō Gakuen University), *731 butaiten Ebetsu 1995 hōkokushū* (Report on Unit 731 Exhibition in Ebetsu); Tōkatsu sensōten jikkō iinkai (Executive Committee for the War Exhibition in the Tōkatsu Region), *Tōkatsu sensōten hōkokushū* (Report on the War Exhibition in the Tōkatsu Region); Sagamihara shimin no tsudoi 98 "731 butaiten" jikkō iinkai (Executive Committee on the

Unit 731 Exhibition, Citizen's Gathering in 1998), *731 butai to saikinsen* (Unit 731 and Biological Warfare).

44. "Gojukkaime no 8.15" (August 15: The Fiftieth Time), *Asahi shinbun*, August 15, 1995, evening ed., p. 11.

45. Nankin 1937 kaigaten jikkō iinkai, *The Nanking Massacre Art Exhibition in Tokyo.*

46. See, for example, Kanagawa-ken rekishi kyōikusha kyōgikai (Association for History Educators, Kanagawa), *Kanagawa-ken no sensō iseki* (The Scars of War in Kanagawa); Rekishi kyōikusha kyōgikai Tōhoku burokku (Association for History Educators in Tōhoku Region), *Tōhoku to jūgonen sensō* (Tōhoku and the Fifteen-Year War); Aichi heiwa no tameno sensōten jikkō iinkai (Executive Committee on the War Exhibition for Peace, Aichi), *Aichi no sensō iseki gaido* (Guidebook of War Memorial Sites in Aichi Prefecture); Chibaken Rekishi kyōikusha kyōgikai (Association for History Educators, Chiba), *Gakkō ga heisha ni natta toki* (When Schools Became Barracks); Tokyo Rekishi kyōikusha kyōgikai (Association for History Educators, Tokyo), *Fotogaido Tōkyō no sensō to heiwa o aruku* (A Pictorial Walking Tour of War and Peace in Tokyo); Shizuoka-ken chiikishi kyōiku kenkyūkai (Study Group on Local Historical Education in Shizuoka Prefecture), *Shizuoka-ken Minshū no rekishi o horu* (Examining People's History in Shizuoka Prefecture).

47. Gifu-ken Rekishi kyōikusha kyōgikai, *Machi mo mura mo senjō datta* (Cities and Towns, Too, Were "Battlefields"). The book discusses Chinese and Korean forced labor in the prefecture (pp. 54–60).

48. Ikeda Ichirō and Suzuki Tetsuya, *Kyōto no "sensō iseki" o meguru* (Visiting War Memorial Sites in Kyoto), pp. 52–54. The book examined Kyoto fire-bombing memorial sites and also sites commemorating Chinese and Korean forced labor (pp. 46–49, 56–57, 58–61).

49. Mie-ken Rekishi kyōikusha kyōgikai, *Mie no sensō iseki* (War Memorials in Mie), pp. 62–71.

50. Nankin jiken chōsa kenkyūkai (The Research Committee on the Nanjing Incident), *Nankin jiken shiryōshū* (A Collection of Historical Materials on the Nanjing Incident), Vol. 1.

51. Nankin jiken chōsa kenkyūkai, *Nankin jiken shiryōshū*, Vol. 2.

52. Yoshida Yutaka, "Kaisetsu" (Foreword), *Nankin jiken shiryōshū*, Vol. 1, pp. iii–iv.

53. Inoue Hisashi, "Kaisetsu" (Foreword), *Nankin jiken shiryōshū*, Vol. 2, p. 4.

54. Kasahara Tokushi, *Nankin nanminku no hyakunichi: gyakusatsu o mita gaikokujin* (One Hundred Days in the Nanjing Safety Zone: Foreigners Who Witnessed the Atrocities), pp. 41–46.

55. Ibid., p. 332.

56. Kasahara Tokushi, *Nankin jiken* (The Nanjing Incident), pp. 214–15.

57. Ibid., 218–28.

58. Ono Kenji, Fujiwara Akira, and Honda Katsuichi, *Nankin daigyakusatsu o kiroku shita kōgun heishi tachi* (The Imperial Soldiers Who Recorded the Nanjing Massacre).

59. See, for example, the diary of Horikoshi Fumio (pseudonym), pp. 58–85. Ono concealed the writer's identity to protect his privacy.

60. Ibid., pp. 74, 133, 233, 347, 350–51.

61. On December 17, 1937, Meguro Fukuharu (pseudonym) wrote that the Yamada Unit executed approximately 20,000 prisoners of war. See Ono, Fujiwara, and Honda, *Nankin daigyakusatsu o kiroku shita kōgun heishi tachi*, p. 373.

62. John Rabe, *The Diary of John Rabe: Nankin no shinjitsu* (The Truth about Nanjing).

63. Arai Shin'ichi, "Nankin jiken, Rābe hōkokusho" (The Nanjing Incident: Rabe's Report), p. 39.

64. Tawara Yoshifumi, *Kyōkasho kōgeki no shinsō*, p. 171. The textbook included a photograph of Japanese celebrating the fall of Nanjing. The caption read: "Victory of the Japanese military was reported widely, and the nation celebrated." For the market shares of the various 1997 junior high school textbooks, see Shuppan rōren (The Association for Labor Unions of the Publishing Industry), *Kyōkasho repōto 97* (Report of Textbooks in 1997), p. 64. The total sales of seven 1997 junior high school history textbooks were 1.5 million.

65. Tawara, *Kyōkasho kōgeki no shinsō*, p. 170–72. The share of the Ōsaka shoseki's text was 19.3 percent. (*Kyōkasho repōto 97*, p. 64.)

66. Tawara, *Kenshō 15 nen sensō to chūkō rekishi kyōkasho* (Examining the 15-Year War in Junior High and High School Textbooks), p. 47. Although the discussion of the Nanjing Massacre in the 1994 edition of *Shōsetsu Nihonshi* was nominal, its 1982 version had no mention at all about the event (p. 46).

67. Ibid., p. 41.

68. The former was authorized by the government in 1993, and the latter was approved in 1992.

69. Tawara, *Kenshō 15 nen sensō to chūkō rekishi kyōkasho*, p. 133.

70. Ibid., pp. 133, 136.

71. Tawara Yoshifumi, *Dokyumento "ianfu" mondai to kyōkasho kōgeki* (Documentary: The Issue of "Comfort Women" and Attacks on School Textbooks), p. 6.

72. Rekishi kentō iinkai, *Daitō-A sensō no sōkatsu* (An Outline of the Greater East Asian War), pp. 2–3.

73. Shūsen gojushūnen kokumin iinkai (National Committee for the Fiftieth Anniversary of the End of World War II), *Shūsen gojushūnen kokumin undō kirokushū* (Historical Record of the National Committee for the Fiftieth Anniversary of the End of World War II), p. 32. The author proudly stated that more than 70 percent of LDP members had joined the league.

74. Tawara, *Dokyumento "ianfu" mondai to kyōkasho kōgeki*, p. 7.

75. Ibid., p. 8. See, also, *Shūsen gojushūnen kokumin undō kirokushū*, p. 32.

76. Tawara, *Dokyumento "ianfu" mondai to kyōkasho kōgeki*, p. 9.

77. *Shūsen gojushūnen kokumin undō kirokushū*, pp. 26–27, 68–69.

78. National Committee for the Fiftieth Anniversary of the End of World War II, *A Tribute, Appreciation and Friendship: A Celebration of Asian Nations' Symbiosis*, pp. 1, 13–14, 16–17, 21–22, 26–27, 28–29, 31–32, 36.

79. Tawara, *Dokyumento "ianfu" mondai to kyōkasho kōgeki*, p. 48. See also Yoshida, "A Battle over History," p. 97. The Association for the Advancement of a Liberalist View of History is the official English name of Jiyūshugi shikan kenkyūkai.

80. Japanese Society for History Textbook Reform, *The Restoration of a National History*, pp. 3–4, 30–31.

81. "Playboy Interview: Shintaro Ishihara—candid conversation," pp. 59–70, 76, 84.

82. Ishihara Shintarō, Watanabe Shōichi, and Ogawa Kazuhisa, *Soredemo "No" to ieru Nihon* (The Japan That Can Still Say "No"), pp. 180, 184–85.

83. Azuma Shirō, *Waga Nankin puratōn: ichi shōshūhei no taiken shita Nankin daigyakusatsu* (My Platoon in Nanjing: A Conscript Soldier's Experience in the Nanjing Massacre).

84. Itakura Yoshiaki, "'Azuma nikki wa kyokō' to hanketsu" (Court Finds "Azuma's Diary" Is Fabrication), *Getsuyō hyōron*, May 15, 1996, pp. 2–3.

85. "Nagano hōshō no hatsugen yōshi" (A Summary of Justice Minister Nagano's Commentary), *Asahi shinbun*, May 7, 1994, p. 2.

86. "Hōshō hatsugen meguru kisha kaiken yōshi" (A Summary of Justice Minister Nagano's Press Conference), *Asahi shinbun*, May 7, 1994, p. 2.

87. Tanaka Masaaki, "'Nankin daigyakusatsu' no kyokō" (The Fabrication of the "Nanjing Massacre").

88. Ibid., pp. 268–71.

89. Itakura Yoshiaki, "'Nankin daigyakusatsu nijūman' setsu e no hanshō" (Refuting the Theory of Two Hundred Thousand Deaths in the "Nanjing Massacre"), pp. 71–79.

90. Fujioka Nobukatsu and Nishio Kanji, *Kokumin no yudan* (Negligence of the Nation), pp. 210–14.

91. Fukuda Kazuya, "Jon Rābe no nikki 'Nankin daigyakusatsu' o dō yomuka" (How to Read John Rabe's Diary), pp. 37–38, 45–46.

92. Kobayashi's *On War* sold more than a half million copies. See Fujioka Nobukatsu and Higashinakano Osamichi (Shūdō), *"Za reipu obu Nankin" no kenkyū: Chūgoku ni okeru 'jōhōsen' no teguchi to senryaku* (The Study of *The Rape of Nanking*: Methods and Strategies of Chinese Intelligence), p. 229.

93. Kobayashi Yoshinori, *Shin gōmanizumu sengen 5* (A Declaration of Arrogance, New Version, Vol. 5), pp. 141–48.

94. Fujioka and Higashinakano, *"Za reipu obu Nankin" no kenkyū*, pp. 2–3, 62–108, 208–19, 274–75.

95. Ishihara Shintarō applauded Fujioka and Higashinakano's book. Ishihara acclaimed the book as balanced, scholarly work (see promotional material on the inside cover of the cited edition). See also Kobayashi Yoshinori, *Shin gōmanizumu sengen 6* (A Declaration of Arrogance, New Version, Vol. 6), pp. 34–35.

96. See, for example, "Nihon no shazai to hoshō, Bei no gaiatsu nerau" (Seeking U.S. Diplomatic Pressure; Aiming at Japan's Apology and Compensation), *Sankei shinbun*, April 8, 1998; "Jijitsu gonin o eibun de shiteki" (Pointing Out Factual Errors in English), *Sankei shinbun*, April 13, 1998; "'Reipu obu Nankin' 2 nenmae dō taitoru shashinshū" (A Pictorial Book Also Titled *The Rape of Nanking* Published Two Years Ago), *Sankei shinbun*, May 25, 1998, evening ed.

97. "Bōryaku no 'Nankin daigyakusatsu' kyanpēn," pp. 6–26.

98. Matsuo Ichirō, "Nankin jiken nise shashin o seiryokuteki ni kenshō" (Rigorously Examining Fake Photographs of the Nanjing Incident), *Jiyū shugi shikan kenkyūkai kaihō* (Newsletter of the Association for the Advancement of a Liberalist View of History), p. 1.

99 Matsuo Ichirō, *Propaganda War, The "Nanjing Incident": The Truth of the "Nanjing Massacre" as Seen through Secret Photographs*, (Puropagandasen "Nankin jiken": Hiroku shashin de miru "Nankin daigyakusatsu no shinjitsu).

100. Higashinakano Osamichi *"Nankin gyakusatsu" no tettei kenshō* (Solid Examination of the "Nanjing Massacre").

101. Fujioka and Higashinakano, *"Za reipu obu Nankin" no kenkyū*, pp. 224, 226–30, 234, 257.

102. Suzuki Akira, *Shin "Nankin daigyakusatsu" no maboroshi* (The Illusion of the "Nanjing Massacre," rev. ed.).

103. Kitamura Minoru, "'Nankin daigyakusatsu' kenkyū josetsu" (An Introductory Study of the "Nanjing Massacre"), Parts 1–3. Kitamura's work was later published as a book, titled *The Quest for the "Nanjing Incident": The Search for the Reality* ("Nankin jiken" no tankyū: sono jitsuzō o motomente).

104. Kitamura Minoru, "'Nankin daigyakusatsu sanjūmannin setsu' no seiritsu: Timperley no sakubō o chūshin ni" (Timperley's Conspiracy: The Emergence of the Estimate of the 300,000 Deaths), pp. 43–44.

105. Nakamura's "Profile" is available on the home page of the *Isaribikai*. URL: http://www.isaribi.net.

106. Akazawa Shirō, "Eiga *Puraido* hihan" (Critique of the Film *Pride*), p. 50.

107. See, for example, Tanaka's *"Nankin gyakusatsu" no kyokō*, pp. 303–22. Itō Shunya, *Puraido: Unmei no toki* (Pride: The Moment of Destiny), videocassette.

108. Itō, *Puraido: Unmei no toki*.

109. Ibid.

110. Honda Katsuichi, "Baikokudo tachi ga tsukutta eiga" (A Film Made by Traitors), *Shūkan kinyōbi*, p. 57.

111. Akazawa Shirō, "Eiga *Puraido* hinan," pp. 50–54.

112. See Tawara Yoshifumi's home page: http://www.linkclub.or.jp/~teppei-y/tawara%20HP/kaisetu.html. Tawara has meticulously documented activities and meetings organized by the revisionists.

113. Nihon ronsōshi kenkyūkai (The Study Group on Debates in Japan), *Nippon no ronsō* (Debates in Japan), p. 82.

114. For additional discussion of *Don't Cry, Nanking*, including a plot summary, see chapter 11.

115. Nihon ronsōshi kenkyūkai, p. 82. On June 6, 1998, a man slashed the screen at a theater in Yokohama. Instead of closing the theater for repairs, the owner of the theater continued to show the film. See "Eiga 'Nankin 1937' ni hamono" (The Film *Don't Cry, Nanking* Slashed), *Asahi shinbun*, June 7, 1998, p. 31. Kimata Junji, a representative of the screening committee, estimates that as of March 1999, 50,000 people in Japan had either seen the film at public screenings or rented it on video (Kwan Weng Kin, "Fifty Thousand Japanese Have Seen 'Rape of Nanking,'" *Straits Times*, March 5, 1999, p. 24).

116. Nankin jiken chōsa kenkyūkai (The Research Committee on the Nanjing Incident), *Nankin daigyakusatsu hiteiron 13 no uso* (Thirteen Lies by the Deniers of the Nanjing Massacre), pp. 2–3.

117. Ibid., chaps. 1, 3, 4, 5, 9.

118. Ibid., pp. 14–19.

119. Ibid., pp. 42–48, 74–83.

120. Ibid., 60–71.

121. Higashinakano Osamichi, *Nihon "Nankin" gakkai nenpō: Nankin "gyaku-satsu" kenkyū no saizensen Heisei 14 nen ban* (Annual Report of Japan Association of Nanjing Studies: The Forefront of the Studies of the Nanjing "Massacre," 2002); Higashinakano Osamichi, *Nihon "Nankin" gakkai nenpō: Nankin "gyakusatsu" kenkyū no saizensen Heisei 15 nen ban* (Annual Report of Japan Association of Nanjing Studies: The Forefront of the Studies of the Nanjing "Massacre," 2003); *Nihon "Nankin" gakkai nenpō: Nankin "gyakusatsu" kenkyū no saizensen Heisei 16 nen ban* (Annual Report of Japan Association of Nanjing Studies: Forefront of the Studies of the Nanjing "Massacre," 2004); and *Nankin jiken "shōko shashin" o kenshō suru* (Examining the "Photographic Proof" of the Nanjing Incident).

122. Kasahara Tokushi, "Bunshun ga mata katsugidashita Nankin gyakusatsu hiteironja no osomatsuburi" (Bungei Shunjū Publisher Has Done It Again: Championing a Shabby Volume on the Nanjing Denial), pp. 66–67.

123. Matsumura Toshio, *"Nankin gyakusatsu" e no daigimon* (Serious Questions about the "Nanjing Massacre"), pp. 158–63, 359–63.

124. Watanabe Harumi, "The Meaning of 'Learning from History'" ("Rekishi kara manabu" koto no imi), p. 48.

125. Suzuki Chieko, "Trends and Issues Regarding the Nanjing Massacre" (Nankin daigyakusatsu o meguru dōkō to kadai), p. 34.

126. Ibid., pp. 34–35.

127. Nishio Kanji et al., eds, *Atarashii rekishi kyōkasho* (New History Textbook), pp. 270–71.

128. Shuppan rōren, *Kyōkasho repōto 2002* (Textbook Report 2002), no. 46 (February 2002), pp. 3, 66.

129. Ishiyama Hisao, "Chūgaku rekishi kyōkasho wa dō kakikaerareta ka" (How Were Junior High School History Textbooks Revised?), *Kyōkasho repōto 2002*, no. 46, pp. 17–18; Tawara, *Kyōkasho kōgeki no shinsō*, p. 162–66.

130. Nit-Chū-Kan sangoku kyōtsū rekishi kyōzai iinkai (The Committee for Sharing the Same Historical Material in Japan, China, and South Korea), *Mirai o hiraku rekishi: higashi Ajia sangoku no kingendaishi* (History That Opens the Future: The Modern History of Three East Asian Nations), pp. 126–27. The Chinese edition was published by the Social Science Academic Press, China (Zhongguo shehui kexue wenxian chubanshe), while the South Korean edition was published by the Hankyoreh Newspaper Press (Hangyeore Sinmunsa).

131. A list of these antirevisionist accounts is available on Tawara Yoshifumi's homepage: http://www.linkclub.or.jp/~teppei-y/tawara%20HP/tosyho%20osiryou.html

132. "Shimin undō an'naiban" (Bulleting Board on Grassroots Activism) in *Shūkan kinyōbi*, a weekly journal, contains schedules of meetings organized by activist organizations. The bulletin board usually appears at the very end of the journal. Various kinds of meetings are held daily, particularly in the Tokyo metropolitan area. These meetings are often devoted to WWII-related topics.

133. Nankin jiken chōsa kenkyūkai, *Nankin daigyakusatsu hiteiron 13 no uso*.

134. Some of the papers presented at the conference are included in Fujiwara Akira et al., *Nankin jiken o dō miruka* (How to View the Nanjing Massacre). Similar events were also held in Tokyo and Osaka.

CHAPTER 11

1. Reported by the Xinhua News Agency on April 20, 1989, translated in *Chūgoku geppō* (China Monthly), no. 366 (April 1989), p. 45. According to John Pomfret of the Associated Press, a crowd of about 3,000 gathered outside the compound, and 30 protesters were injured by the police. (John Pomfret, "Police Beat Pro-Democracy Protesters, Government Issues Warning," *Associated Press*, April 20, 1989.)

2. News reported by the Xinhua News Agency on April 22–25, 1989, translated in *Chūgoku geppō*, no. 366 (April 1989), pp. 45–47.

3. "Bixu qizhi xianmingdi fandui dongluan" (Take a Clear Stand against Upheavals), *Renmin ribao*, April 26, 1989, p. 1.

4. The Xinhua General Overseas News Service, "Li Peng's Speech at Beijing Cadre Meeting," May 19, 1989, Item no.: 0519173.

5. Information acquired from Beijing Radio, translated in *Chūgoku geppō*, no. 367 (May 1989), pp. 61–63.

6. "Jieyanbudui zhihuibu fayanren fabiao tanhua" (Public Statement by the Spokesman of Martial Law Enforcing Troops), *Renmin ribao*, June 5, 1989, p. 1. As to the Tienanmen Square Massacre, see for example, Subcommittee on International Relations, U.S. House of Representatives, *Was There a Tienanmen Massacre?* The document contains a summary concerning victims of the massacre provided by American and Chinese human rights activists and organizations such as Human Rights Watch, Asia.

7. Zheng Yanshi, "Baoluan pingxihou de chensi: Shixi shitai de fazhan weishema zouxiang qingnian xuesheng lianghao yuanwang de fanmian" (A post-rebellion reflection and attempt to analyze the question: Why did the situation develop in a way contrary to the students' good intentions?), *Renmin ribao*, June 21, 1989, p. 2.

8. Foreign Broadcast Information Service, "Commentator Urges Education in Patriotism," *Daily Report: China*, June 30, 1989, p. 27.

9. Foreign Broadcast Information Service, "In-Depth Education in Patriotism to be Conducted," *Daily Report: China*, April 9, 1990, p. 40.

10. Foreign Broadcast Information Service, "Hubei Colleges Conduct Education on Patriotism," *Daily Report: China*, May 28, 1990, p. 63.

11. Foreign Broadcast Information Service, "Education to Stress History, Patriotism," *Daily Report: China*, June 4, 1991, p. 35.

12. Foreign Broadcast Information Service, "Forum Discusses Education in Patriotism," *Daily Report: China*, May 4, 1993, p. 20.

13. Ibid. On October 9, 1993, *Renmin ribao* praised the decision by the Propaganda Department to utilize outstanding movies and television dramas in order to promote patriotism among youth. See "Aiguo zhuyi jiaoyu de hao xingshi" (A Good Way to Conduct Education in Patriotism), *Renmin ribao*, October 9, 1993, p. 1.

14. "Society for the Study of China's War against Japan Established," *BBC Summary of World Broadcasts*, Part 3: The Far East; B. International Affairs; 2. China; FE/0979/B2/ 1. Also, see *Chūgoku geppō*, no. 387 (January 1991), p. 126.

15. Ishii Akira, "Sengo Nit-Chū kankei no kiseki" (An Outline of Postwar Japan-China Relations), pp. 95–96.

16. Zhang Yijin, "Nanjing datusha shishi bulun fouren" (Nanjing Massacre: A Historical Fact That Brooks No Denial), *Renmin ribao*, November 18, 1990, p. 6.

17. Ibid.

18. See, for example, Foreign Broadcast Information Service, "Column Criticizes Japanese Minister's Remarks," *Daily Report: China*, May 12, 1994, p. 13; "Xinhua Commentary Accuses Japan of Historical 'Cover-Ups,'" *Daily Report: China*, July 21, 1996; "Absurd Views to Disrupt Sino-Japanese Ties," *Daily Report: China*, July 16,1997; "Xinhua Recounts Life of 'Japanese War Criminal' Tojo," *Daily Report: China*, May 11,1998; and "Commentary on Japanese Tokyo Court Verdict," *Daily Report: China*, December 25, 1998.

19. Foreign Broadcast Information Service, "'News Analysis' Views 'Ghost' of Japanese Militarism," *Daily Report: China*, August 14, 1996.

20. Foreign Broadcast Information Service, "Japanese 'Arrogance,' 'Militarism' Blamed on U.S. Policy," *Daily Report: China*, August 22, 1996.

21. Foreign Broadcast Information Service, "Commentary Views Japanese History of Military Aggression," *Daily Report: China*, September 17, 1996.

22. Foreign Broadcast Information Service, "Film on 'Nanjing Massacre' Nearing Completion," *Daily Report: China*, March 24, 1995, p. 26.

23. This summary has been adapted from "Nankin 1937" zenkoku jōei iinkai (The Committee to Tour *Nanjing 1937* Across Japan), *Nankin 1937: Don't Cry, Nanking* (1997), a pamphlet sold at theaters exhibiting the film, pp. 5, 8.

24. Kasahara Tokushi, *Nankin jiken*, pp. 114, 122, 128–36.

25. This estimate was mentioned by Wu Ziniu in his informal comments at a screening of the film at Columbia University on October 10, 2000.

26. Foreign Broadcast Information Service, "Mobile Exhibition on the Nanjing Massacre Opens," *Daily Report: China*, June 19, 1995, p. 19.

27. Foreign Broadcast Information Service, "Nanjing Massacre Exhibition Hosts 400,000 Guests," *Daily Report: China*, September 14, 1995, p.12.

28. Foreign Broadcast Information Service, "Jiangsu Produces Film on Nanjing 'Massacre,'" *Daily Report: China*, August 8, 1995, p. 60.

29. Foreign Broadcast Information Service, "Picture Album on Nanjing Massacre Published," *Daily Report: China*, July 17, 1995, p. 39.

30. Zhongyang dang'anguan (Central Historical Archives) et al., eds, *Nanjing datusha tuzheng* (Pictorial Evidence of the Nanjing Massacre).

31. Ibid., pp. 267–69, 272–78, 86, 89, 90. In the introduction, which has no page number, the editors described these revisionists not as *extremely* small in number (*jishaoshu*), but as a small number of (*shaoshu*) people in Japan.

32. The Foreign Broadcast Information Service, "Nanjing Commemorates 'Nanjing Massacre,'" *Daily Report: China*, December 13, 1996.

33. The Foreign Broadcast Information Service, "Spokesman on Japanese Envoy's Remarks on Nanjing," *Daily Report: China*, May 11, 1998.

34. The Foreign Broadcast Information Service, "More on PRC Spokesman on Japanese Court Verdict," *Daily Report: China*, December 24, 1998.

35. The Foreign Broadcast Information Service, "Commentary on Japanese Tokyo Court Verdict," *Daily Report: China*, December 25, 1998.

36. The Foreign Broadcast Information Service, "Radio Commentary on Sino-Japanese Relations," *Daily Report: China*, December 26, 1998.

37. The Foreign Broadcast Information Service, "Further on Tokyo Court Verdict Sokesman," *Daily Report: China*, December 28, 1998.

38. The Foreign Broadcast Information Service, "New Evidence Made Public on Nanjing Massacre," *Daily Report: China*, January 17, 1999.

39. Mizutani Naoko, "Watashi wa naze Azuma Shirō shi ni igi o tonaeru ka" (Why I Disagree with Mr. Azuma Shirō), pp. 220–21.

40. Mizutani's publications include "Moto 1644 butaiin no shōgen" (Testimony by a Former Member of Unit 1644) and "1644 butai no soshiki to katsudō" (Organizational Structure and Activities of Unit 1644). Unit 1644 was Japan's Chemical and Biological Unit located in Nanjing.

41. Mizutani, "Watashi wa naze Azuma Shirō shi ni igi o tonaeru ka," pp. 221–23.

42. Xu Zhigeng, *Nanjing datusha* (The Nanjing Massacre). Also see Xu Zhigeng, *Nanjing datusha*.

43. Hansheng zazhishe, *Muji kangzhan wushinian: 1895–1945 Zhong-Ri zhanzheng tulu* (Eyewitness to the Fifty-Year Resistance: A Pictorial History of the Sino-Japanese War of 1895–1945).

44. "Mainland, Taiwan Group to Make Film on Nanjing Massacre," *FBIS, China*, August 26, 1994.

45. Iris Chang, *Beiyi wang de datusha: 1937 Nanjing hao jie* (The Rape of Nanking: The Forgotten Holocaust of WWII).

46. Ibid., pp. 1–6.

47. See, for example, Zhu Chengshan, *Qin-Hua Rijun Nanjing datusha xinchunzhe zhengyanji* (Collection of Testimonies by Survivors of the Nanjing Massacre during the Japanese Army Invasion); Zhongguo dier lishi dang'anguan et al., *Nanjing datusha* (The Nanjing Massacre); Yin Jijun, *1937, Nanjing daqiuyuan: Xifangrenshi he Guojianquanqu* (The Great Rescue: Westerners and The International Safety Zone, 1937); Jiang Labei, *Labei riji* (The Diary of John Rabe); Zhu Chengshan et al., *Qin-Hua Rijun Nanjing datusha waijirenshi zhengyanji* (Collection of Testimonies by Non-Chinese About the Nanjing Massacre of the Japanese Army Invasion); Liu Huishu, *Nanjing datusha xinkao* (New Study of the Nanjing Massacre); Chen Anji, *Qin-Hua Rijun Nanjing datushashi guojixueshu yantaohui lunwenji* (Collection of Papers at the International Symposium on the History of the Nanjing Massacre of the Japanese Army Invasion); and Dong Shilang, *Dong Shilang ri ji* (The Diary of Azuma Shirō).

CHAPTER 12

1. George Gallup Jr., *The Gallup Poll: Public Opinion 1991*, pp. 240, 243.

2. George Gallup Jr., *The Gallup Poll: Public Opinion 1992*, p. 28.

3. Charles Burress, "The Dark Heart of Japan Bashing," *San Francisco Chronicle*, March 18, 1990, p. 7/Z.

4. Lee Smith, "Fear and Loathing of Japan," pp. 50–60.

5. Charles Burress, "The Dark Heart of Japan Bashing," p. 7/Z.

6. James Fallows, "Containing Japan," pp. 40–54.

7. Lee Smith, "Fear and Loathing of Japan," p. 51.

8. For a detailed discussion of the *Enola Gay* controversy, see Edward Linenthal and Tom Engelhardt, *History Wars: The Enola Gay and Other Battles for the American Past*.

9. Mario Battista, "What Was Crueler than 'Enola Gay'?: Japan at War," *St. Petersburg (Fla.) Times*, September 5, 1994, p. 2.

10. Mort Blumenfeld, "One Who Would Have Participated in Invasion of Japan Tells His Story," *San Diego Union-Tribune*, January 28, 1995, p. B7.

11. Victor Tolley, "Veterans Wanted the Whole Story Told," *San Francisco Chronicle*, February 12, 1995, p. 6.

12. Pat Truly, "Second-Guessing Is Not History," *Omaha World Herald*, February 3, 1995, p. 17.

13. Pat Buchanan, "Ignoring the Whole Story of Enola Gay," *Arizona Republic*, February 7, 1995, p. B5.

14. Edward Linenthal, "Anatomy of a Controversy," in *History Wars*, p. 47.

15. Gar Alperovitz, "Beyond the Smithsonian Flap: Historians' New Consensus," *Washington Post*, October 16, 1994, p. C3.

16. John Whittier Treat, "Remembering the Bomb," *New York Times*, June 25, 1995, Section 4, p. 15.

17. This report of the text of the wall panel is from Jeff Jacoby, "The Enola Gay Exhibit: Plane and Simple," *Boston Globe*, July 6, 1995, p. 11.

18. Philip Pan, "AU Offers a View of A-Bombs' Horrors; Exhibit Contains Items Rejected for Smithsonian's Enola Gay Display," *Washington Post*, July 9, 1995, p. B2.

19. Naono Akiko, *Hiroshima, America: Genbakuten o megutte* (Atomic Bomb Exhibit: Hiroshima in America), pp. 142–44.

20. Ibid., pp. 132–34, 140–41.

21. Ibid., pp. 132–35.

22. Leslie Gelb, "Infamy Is Still Infamy," *New York Times*, November 17, 1991, Section 4, p. 17.

23. Kin-Ming Liu, "Historical Forces Drove U.S. and Japan to War; Rape of Nanking," *New York Times*, December 2, 1991, p. A16.

24. Nagatomi visited Nanjing two weeks after the fall of Nanjing as a member of a patriotic students' expedition. See Noda Masaaki, *Sensō to zaiseki* (War and Responsibility), pp. 198–99.

25. Joanna Pitman, "Rape of Nanking: Legacy of Shame," *San Diego Union-Tribune*, February 9, 1992, p. C3. Nagatomi's given name was incorrectly reported as Hakudo. Although Pitman stated that Nagatomi had begun to confess his war crimes only recently, Nagatomi, a member of the Group of Returnees from China (Chūgoku kikansha renrakukai), had been a peace activist for decades and had long ago confessed to atrocities that he had committed. See Noda Masaaki, *Sensō to zaiseki* (War and Responsibility), pp. 214–15.

26. Pitman, "Rape of Nanking: Legacy of Shame," *San Diego Union-Tribune*, February 9, 1992, p. C3.

27. Jim Parsons, "A Culture Mourns Its Own; Program Marks Chinese Suffering," *Star Tribune*, August 11, 1995, p. 1B.

28. Aurelio Rojas, "Chinese Americans Call for Japanese Apology," *San Francisco Chronicle*, August 14, 1995, p. A13.

29. Iris Chang, *The Rape of Nanking: The Forgotten Holocaust of World War II*.

30. Ken Ringle, "The Forgotten Holocaust; Few Know What Took Place in 1937 Nanking, but It's Blazed in One Woman's Soul," *Washington Post*, December 11, 1997, p. C1.

31. Ibid.

32. Orville Schell, "Bearing Witness," *New York Times*, December 14, 1997, Section 7, p. 16.

33. Ibid. This citation contains errors and inaccuracies. Although the plaintiff insisted that 260,000 were killed, the tribunal ruled: "[T]he total number of civilians and prisoners of war murdered in Nanking and its vicinity during the first six weeks of the Japanese occupation was over 200,000" (Timothy Brook, *Documents on the Rape of Nanking*, p. 261). However, the sentence passed on Matsui Iwane, a Class A war criminal condemned for the atrocities, held him responsible for thousands of rapes and more than 100,000 murders committed by soldiers under his command (Ibid., p. 266)

As to the alleged secret order to "kill all captives" under the seal of Yasuhiko (Prince Asaka), the information provided by Chang seems to be hearsay rather than fact. David Bergamini claimed the existence of such an order, but he did not identify his source for this information (Bergamini, *Japan's Imperial Conspiracy*, p. 24). For reviews of Bergamini's book, see chapter 9.

Bergamini erroneously identified Prince Asaka as the emperor's uncle, not as the empress' uncle, and Chang copied this mistake from him. This error was perpetuated by Schell, quoting from Chang.

34. Schell, "Bearing Witness," *New York Times*, December 14, 1997, Section 7, p. 16.

35. George Will, "Breaking a Sinister Silence," *Washington Post*, February 19, 1998, p. A17.

36. David Kennedy, "The Horror," pp. 110, 113–14.

37. Ibid., pp. 114–16.

38. See Joshua Fogel, review of *The Rape of Nanking*, pp. 818–19.

39. *Ibid.*, p. 819.

40. As to other critiques of *The Rape of Nanking*, see, for example, Charles Burress, "Wars of Memory," *The San Francisco Chronicle*, July 26, 1998, p. 1/Z1; Daqing Yang, "Convergence or Divergence? Recent Historical Writings on the Rape of Nanjing," pp. 842–65.

41. "'Rape of Nanking' Book Delayed in Japan," *Boston Globe*, February 20, 1999, p. A12.

42. Jacob Heilbrunn, "Friendly Fire; In Japan, One of Few Growth Industries Is Anti-Americanism," *Los Angeles Times*, March 14, 1999, p. M1. The *Asahi Evening News* also stated on February 19, 1999, that threats from right-wing extremists prevented Kashiwa shobō from publishing the translation. See "Nanking Book Is Shelved," *Asahi Evening News*, February 19, 1999.

43. "Editor Explains Why Book Scrapped," *Asahi News Service*, May 21, 1999. I took part in the press conference held on May 20 in Tokyo (May 19 in the United States) as a translator for Haga Hiraku.

44. Doreen Carvajal, "History's Shadow Foils Nanking Chronicle," *New York Times*, May 20, 1999, p. E1.

45. Haga Hiraku to Iris Chang, November 11, 1998.

46. For a detailed discussion of the activities of the Research Committee, see chapter 7.

47. Yamazaki Takayasu to Iris Chang, October 19, 1998. The following selection

of changes suggested by Kashiwa shobō may provide some sense of the nature of the publisher's concerns:

(p.3) Abyssinia [Ethiopia]

(p.21) : he sent two [four] ships belching back smoke

(p. 23) . . . a Korean rebellion backed by Japanese ultranationalists. [This may refer to the Korean Kab-o peasants' uprising 1894 however this peasants' uprising was not backed by Japan or Japanese ultranationalists.]

48. Iris Chang to Yamazaki Takayasu, October 26, 1998.

49. Yamazaki Takayasu to Iris Chang, November 30, 1998.

50. Inoue presented his draft of the commentary in Japanese, at the Research Committee on the Nanjing Incident on February 13, 1999. My summary of the commentary is based on the draft circulated on this day.

51. Iris Chang to Yamazaki Takayasu, December 1, 1998; Yamazaki Takayasu to Iris Chang, December 2, 1998.

52. Sonni Efron, "War Again Is Raging over Japan's Role in 'Nanking'; History: Author Chang Attacked by Those Who Say Massacre Didn't Happen, And by Those Who Insist It Did But Say Book Hurts Their Cause," Los Angeles Times, June 6, 1999, p. A32.

53. Daqing Yang, "Convergence or Divergence?" p. 862 n. 100.

54. Takemoto Tadao and Ōhara Yasuo, The Alleged "Nanking Massacre": Japan's Rebuttal to China's Forged Claims, pp. 139–41. See also Wakabayashi, "The Nanking Massacre: Now You See It, . . . ," pp. 522–30.

55. Takemoto and Ōhara, The Alleged "Nanking Massacre," pp. 5–6, 32–45, 140–41.

56. Tanaka Masaaki, What Really Happened in Nanking: The Refutation of a Common Myth.

57. A person from Shūkan kinyōbi visited the address given for the institute but saw no indication of the organization's existence (See Kasahara, Nankin jiken to Nihonjin, p. 29 n. 5).

58. A letter from Nakajima Takao dated January 19, 2001. I, as a member of the association, also received a copy of the book.

59. Tanaka, What Really Happened in Nanking, pp. 1–6.

60. Kasahara Tokushi, Nankin jiken to sankō sakusen (The Nanjing Massacre and Three-Alls Operation), pp. 216–95.

61. See, for example, ibid., p. 321; Nozaki Yoshiko, "Gasshūkoku no daigakusei ga kangaeru Nihon no sensō hanzai" (Japan's War Crimes and College Students in the United States), p. 11.

62. For Kajimoto's online documentary, http://www.geocities.com/nankinga-trocities/

63. Fei Fei Li et al., Nanking 1937: Memory and Healing, pp. 35–46, 95–117.

64. Daqing Yang, "Convergence or Divergence?" pp. 842–65.

65. Brook, Documents on the Rape of Nanking.

66. Bob Wakabayashi, "The Nanking One-Hundred-Man Killing Contest Debate: War Guilt Amid Fabricated Illusions, 1971–75," pp. 307–40.

67. Joshua Fogel, The Nanjing Massacre in History and Historiography.

68. Masahiro Yamamoto, Nanking: Anatomy of an Atrocity.

69. David Askew, "The Nanjing Incident: An Examination of the Civilian Popu-

lation," pp. 2–20. Askew concludes that the closest estimate of the civilian population would be approximately 224,500 between December 24, 1937, and January 5, 1938.

70. Bob Wakabayashi, "The Nanking Massacre: Now You See It, . . . ," pp. 521–44.

71. See Brook, *Documents on the Rape of Nanking*; Yang, "Convergence or Divergence?" pp. 842–65; Fogel, *The Nanjing Massacre in History and Historiography*; Bob Wakabayashi, "The Nanking One-Hundred-Man Killing Contest Debate," pp. 307–40.

CONCLUSION

1. Takashi Yoshida, "Battle Over History," pp. 106–15.

2. Kitamura Minoru, "'Nankin daigyakusatsu sanjūmannin setsu' no seiritsu," p. 43.

3. Yamamoto Masahiro, "Amerika ni okeru 'Nankin' kenkyū no dōkō: Jēmuzu Bakku Other Losses o meguru giron to hikaku shite" (Trend in the Studies of "Nanking" in the United States: In Comparison with James Bacque's *Other Losses*).

4. League of Nations, *Official Journal*, vol. 19, no. 2 (February): 121.

5. John Pritchard, *The Tokyo War Crimes Trial*, vol. 20: "Judgment & Annexes," pp. 49606–49610.

6. Zhongguo dier lishi dang'anguan et al., eds. *Qin-Hua Rijun Nanjing datusha dang'an*, p. 604.

7. Fujioka Nobukatsu and Nishio Kanji, *Kokumin no yudan*, pp. 211–12.

8. Nankin jiken chōsa kenkyūkai, *Nankin daigyakusatsu hiteiron 13 no uso*, pp. 92–96.

9. See, for example, Higashinakano Osamichi, *Nihon "Nankin" gakkai nenpō* (2003), p. 292. Nankin jiken chōsa kenkyūkai, *Nankin daigyakusatsu hiteiron 13 no uso*, p. 95.

10. Nanking jiken chōsa kenkyūkai, *Nankin daigyakusatsu hiteiron 13 no uso*, pp. 92–93. Higashinakano, *Nihon "Nankin" gakkai nenpō* (2002), pp. 77–79.

11. Nankin jiken chōsa kenkyūkai, *Nankin daigyakusatsu hiteiron 13 no uso*, p. 96.

12. Ibid., p. 83.

13. Higashinakano, *Nihon "Nankin" gakkai nenpō* (2003), pp. 306–308.

14. Iris Chang, *The Rape of Nanking*, pp. 3–7.

BIBLIOGRAPHY

Aichi heiwa no tameno sensōten jikkō iinkai (Executive Committee on the War Exhibition for Peace, Aichi). *Aichi no sensō iseki gaido* (Guidebook of War Memorial Sites in Aichi Prefecture). Aichi: Aichi heiwa no tameno sensōten jikkō iinkai, 1998.

Aitani, Kunio. "Sengo hoshō saiban no genjō to kadai" (The Present Condition and the Task of Postwar Compensation Trials). *Kikan sensō sekinin kenkyū* (The Report on Japan's War Responsibility), no. 10 (winter 1995): 2–9.

Akatsu, Masuzō. *Hanaoka bōdō* (Uprising in Hanaoka). Tokyo: Sanseidō, 1973.

Akazawa, Shirō. "Eiga *Puraido* hihan," review of the film *Pride*. *Kikan sensō sekinin kenkyū*, no. 21 (fall 1998): 50–54.

Akazawa, Shirō, et al., eds. *Tōkyō saiban handobukku* (Handbook of the Tokyo Trial). Tokyo: Aoki shoten, 1989.

Akiyama, Masami. *Maboroshi no sensō managa no sekai* (Wartime Cartoons Disappeared Like a Dream). Tokyo: Natsume shobō, 1998.

"An Announcement to the Members of Japan's Various Political Parties." *Amerasia* 2, no. 6 (August 1938): 296.

Aoki, Akira. "Kyōkasho 'gohō' o hiki okoshita shinbun no taishitsu" (Editorial Policies of Newspapers Causing Flawed Reports on Textbooks). *Seiron* 112 (November 1982): 30–43.

Ara, Ken'ichi. *Kikigaki Nankin jiken* (Interviews on the Nanjing Incident). Tokyo: Tosho shuppansha, 1987.

Arai, Shin'ichi. "Nankin jiken, Rābe hōkokusho" (The Nanjing Incident: Rabe's Report). *Kikan sensō sekinin kenkyū*, no. 16 (summer 1997): 38–54.

———. "Sōkan no ji" (Greetings to Our Readers on the Publication of Our First Issue). *Kikan sensō sekinin kenkyū* (The Report on Japan's War Responsibility), no. 1 (autumn 1993): 2–3.

Arai, Toshio. "Kyōjutsusho wa kōshite kakareta" (Testimonies Were Written as Such). *Sekai* 648 (May 1998): 69–78.

Ariyama, Teruo. *Senryōki mediashi kenkyū* (The Study of Media History during the Occupation). Tokyo: Kashiwa shobō, 1996.

Asahi nenkan 1939 (Asahi Yearbook 1939). Osaka: Asahi shinbunsha, 1938.

Asahi shinbunsha. *Shōwa tennō hōdō* (Reports Regarding Emperor Shōwa). Tokyo: Asahi shinbunsha, 1989.

Askew, David. "The Nanjing Incident: An Examination of the Civilian Population." *Sino-Japanese Studies* 13, no. 2 (March 2001): 2–20.

———. "The Nanjing Incident: Recent Research and Trends." *Electronic Journal of Contemporary Japanese Studies* (accessed on April 4, 2002). Available at http://www.japanesestudies.org.uk/articles/Askew.html.

Awaya, Kentarō. *Shiryō Nihon gendaishi* (Historical Materials: Modern Japanese History). Vols. 2 and 3. Tokyo: Ōtsuki shoten, 1980–81.

Awaya, Kentarō, and Nakazono Yutaka. *Naimushō shinbunkiji sashitome shiryō shūsei* (Collection of Newspaper Articles Banned by the Ministry of Home Affairs). Vols. 6 and 7. Tokyo: Gendai shiryō shuppan, 1996.

Azuma, Shirō. *Waga Nankin puratōn: ichi shōshūhei no taiken shita Nankin daigyakusatsu* (My Platoon in Nanjing: A Conscript Soldier's Experience in the Nanjing Massacre). Tokyo: Aoki shoten, 1987.

Baba, Tsunego. "Nihon ga susumu michi" (The Direction That Japan Should Take). *Kaizō* 20, no. 1 (January 1938): 33–40.

Bates, Miner Searle. *Crop Investigation in the Nanking Area and Sundry Economic Data.* Shanghai: Mercury, 1938.

———. *The Nanking Population: Employment, Earnings, and Expenditures.* Shanghai: Mercury, 1939.

Ben-Dasan, Isaiah (Yamamoto Shichihei). "Asahi shinbun no 'gomen nasai'" ("Apology" from *Asahi shinbun*). *Shokun!* 4, no. 1 (January 1972): 166–79.

———. "Honda Katsuichi sama e no hensho" (Response to Mr. Honda Katsuichi). *Shokun!* 4, no. 3 (March 1972): 40–60.

———. "Honda Katsuichi sama e no tsuishin" (Postscript to Mr. Honda Katsuichi). *Shokun!* 4, no. 4 (April 1972): 132–43.

———. "'Hyakuningiri' to 'satsujin gēmu'" ("Cut Down One Hundred Contest" and "Killing Contests"). *Shokun!* 4, no. 6 (June 1972): 242–52.

———. "Kōzu shi no yongensoku to 'Chūgoku no tabi'" (The Four Principles of Mr. Kōzu and "Travels in China"). *Shokun!* 4, no. 5 (May 1972): 164–75.

———. *Nihonkyō ni tsuite* (About Japanism). Tokyo: Bungeishunjū, 1972.

Bergamini, David. *Japan's Imperial Conspiracy.* New York: William Morrow, 1971.

Bernstein, Joseph. "The Myth of National Unity in Japan." *Amerasia* 7, no. 3 (April 25, 1943): 66–72.

"Betonamu ni heiwa o!" shimin rengō kai (The Popular Alliance for Peace in Vietnam). *Shiryō "Beheiren" undō* (Historical Materials: The Movement of "Beheiren"). Vol. 1. Tokyo: Kawaide shobō, 1974.

Bix, Herbert. "Conspiracy That Failed." *Japan Interpreter* 8, no. 2 (spring 1973): 252–58.

"Bōryaku no 'Nankin daigyakusatsu' kyanpēn." *Sapio* 11, no. 12 (July 14, 1999): 6–13.

Brook, Timothy. *Documents on the Rape of Nanking.* Ann Arbor: University of Michigan Press, 1999.

"Byrnes Throws Bouquets to MacArthur." *Amerasia* 11, no. 1 (January 1947): 29.

"Candidates for Post-War Leadership in Japan: Ozaki and Okano." *Amerasia* 8, no. 15 (August 1944): 227–36.

Cantril, Hadley. *Public Opinion 1935–1946*. Princeton, N.J.: Princeton University Press, 1951.

Chang, Iris. *Beiyi wang de datusha: 1937 Nanjing hao jie* (The Rape of Nanking: The Forgotten Holocaust of WWII). Taipei: Tianxia wenhua chuban gufeng youxian gongsi, 1997.

———. *The Rape of Nanking: The Forgotten Holocaust of World War II*. New York: Basic Books, 1997.

Chen, Anji. *Qin-Hua Rijun Nanjing datushashi guojixueshu yantaohui lunwenji* (Collection of Papers at the International Symposium on the History of the Nanjing Massacre of the Japanese Army Invasion). Hefei: Anhui daxue chubanshe, 1998.

Chiang, Kai-shek. *Statements and Speeches by Generalissimo Chiang Kai-shek (August-October, 1945)*. Vol. 1. Shanghai: International, 1945.

Chibaken Rekishi kyōikusha kyōgikai (Association for History Educators, Chiba). *Gakkō ga heisha ni natta toki* (When Schools Became Barracks). Tokyo: Aoki shoten, 1996.

Chūgoku kikansha renrakukai (The Group of Returnees from China). *Sankō* (Three Alls). Tokyo: Banseisha, 1984.

———. *Shinryaku: Chūgoku ni okeru Nihon senpan no kiroku* (Invasion: Confessions of Japanese War Crimes in China). Tokyo: Shindokushosha, 1958.

"Chūgokujin sensō higaisha no yōkyū o sasaeru kai dai nikai sōkai" (Report of the Second Annual Meeting of the Society to Support the Demands of Chinese War Victims). *Suopei*, no. 8 (October 10, 1997): 6–8.

"Chūgokujin sensō higaisha no yōkyū o sasaeru kai dai sanka sōkai kettei" (Report of the Third Annual Meeting of the Society to Support the Demands of Chinese War Victims). *Suopei*, no. 14 (October 10, 1998): 7–8.

Chūō kōron sha. *Chūō kōron nanajūnen shi* (Seventy-Year History of Chūō kōron sha). Tokyo: Chūō kōron sha, 1955.

———. *Chūō kōron sha no hachijū nen* (Eighty Years of Chūō kōron Company). Tokyo: Chūō kōron sha, 1965.

Cook, Haruko T. "The Many Lives of Living Soldiers: Ishikawa Tatsuzō and Japan's War in Asia." In *War, Occupation, and Creativity: Japan and East Asia, 1920–1960*, edited by Marlene Mayo and Thomas Rimer, pp. 149–75. Honolulu: University of Hawaii Press, 2001.

Coox, Alvin. Review of *Japan's Imperial Conspiracy*, by David Bergamini. *American Historical Review* 77, no. 4 (October 1972): 1169–70.

Crow, Carl. *Japan's Dream of World Empire: The Tanaka Memorial*. New York: Harper, 1942.

Dai, Guohui. "Nihon e no jogen" (Advice to Japan). *Sekai* 443 (October 1982): 72–76.

"Dokusha ni fukaku owabi shimasu" (Profound Apology to Readers). *Seiron* 112 (November 1982): 82–83.

Dong, Shilang. *Dong Shilang ri ji* (The Diary of Azuma Shirō). Nanjing: Jiangsu jiaoyu chubanshe, 1999.

Dower, John. *War without Mercy: Race and Power in the Pacific War*. New York: Pantheon, 1986.

Eguchi, Keiichi, and Shibahara Takuji eds. *Nichtū sensō jūgun nikki* (Field Diary from the Japan-China War). Kyoto: Hōritsu bunka sha, 1989.

Embree, John. *The Japanese*. Washington D.C: Smithsonian Institution, 1943.

"Ersatz Democracy for Japan: U.S. Policy Shifts from Passive Tolerance to Active Support of the Old Guard." *Amerasia* 10, no. 4 (October 1946): 111–24.

Eykholt, Mark. "Aggression, Victimization, and Chinese Historiography of the Nanjing Massacre." In *The Nanjing Massacre in History and Historiography*, edited by Joshua Fogel, pp. 11–69. Berkeley: University of California Press, 2000).

Fallows, James. "Containing Japan." *Atlantic*, May 1989, pp. 40–54.

Field, Frederick. "Reply to Dr. Takeuchi." *Amerasia* 2, no. 4 (June 1938): 191–97.

Field, Norma. *In the Realm of a Dying Emperor: Japan at Century's End*. New York: Vintage, 1993.

Fogel, Joshua. Review of *The Rape of Nanking: The Forgotten Holocaust of World War II*, by Iris Chang. *Journal of Asian Studies* 57, no. 3 (August 1998): 818–20.

———. *The Nanjing Massacre in History and Historiography*. Berkeley: University of California Press, 2000.

Foreign Affairs Association of Japan (Nihon gaiji kyōkai). *How the North China Affair Arose*. Tokyo: Foreign Affairs Association of Japan, 1937.

———. *The Sino-Japanese Conflict: A Short Survey*. Tokyo: Foreign Affairs Association of Japan, 1937.

———. *What Happened at Tungchow?* Tokyo: Foreign Affairs Association of Japan, 1937.

———. *Why Japan Had to Fight in Shanghai*. Tokyo: Foreign Affairs Association of Japan, 1937.

———. *The North China Incident* and *Japan's Case in the Shanghai Hostilities*. Tokyo: Foreign Affairs Association of Japan, 1937.

"From Hiroshima: A Report and a Question," *Time*, February 11, 1946, pp. 26–27.

Fujioka Nobukatsu and Higashinakano, Osamichi (Shūdō). *"Za reipu obu Nankin" no kenkyū: Chūgoku ni okeru 'jōhōsen' no teguchi to senryaku* (The Study of *The Rape of Nanking*: Methods and Strategies of Chinese Intelligence). Tokyo: Shōdensha, 1999.

Fujioka, Nobukatsu, and Nishio Kanji. *Kokumin no yudan* (Negligence of the Nation). Tokyo: PHP kenkyūjo, 1996.

Fujitani, T, Geoffrey White, and Lisa Yoneyama. *Perilous Memories: The Asia-Pacific War(s)*. Durham, N.C.: Duke University Press, 2001.

Fujiwara, Akira. " 'Sankō sakusen' to hoku-Shina hōmen gun 1" ("Three-Alls Operation" and the North China Army, part 1). *Kikan sensō sekinin kenkyū*, vol. 20 (summer 1998): 21–29, 85.

Fujiwara, Akira, et al., eds. *Nankin jiken o dō miruka* (How to View the Nanjing Massacre). Tokyo: Aoki shoten, 1998.

Fukuda, Kazuya. "Jon Rābe no nikki 'Nankin daigyakusatsu' o dō yomuka." (How to Read John Rabe's Diary): *Shokun!* 29, no. 12 (December 1997): 34–46.

Furukawa, Mantarō. Nit-Chū sengo kankei shi nōto (Postwar Relations between Japan and China). Tokyo: Sanseidō, 1983.

Gaimushō (The Ministry of Foreign Affairs). *Shūsen shiroku 5* (The Historical Record of the End of the War). Tokyo: Gaimushō, 1978.

Gaimushō Ajiakyoku Chūgokuka (China Section, Asian Bureau, Ministry of Foreign Affairs, Japan). *Chūgoku geppō* (China Monthly), no. 164 (June 1972); no. 165 (July 1972); no. 174 (April 1973); no.186 (April 1974); no. 192 (October 1974); no. 198 (April 1975); no. 210 (April 1976); no. 222 (April 1977); no. 239 (September 1978); no. 234 (April 1978); no. 243 (January 1979); no. 246 (April 1979); no. 258 (April 1980); no. 270 (April 1981); no. 282 (April 1982); no. 285 (July 1982); no. 286 (August 1982); no. 287 (September 1982); no. 294 (April 1983); no. 300 (October 1983); no. 306 (April 1984); no. 318 (April 1985); no. 321 (July 1985); no. 322 (August 1985); no. 323 (September 1985); no. 330 (April 1986); no. 331 (May 1986); no 335 (September 1986); no. 336 (October 1986); no. 338 (December 1986); no. 342 (April 1987); no, 345 (July 1987); no. 350 (December 1987); no. 354 (April 1988); no. 366 (April 1989); no. 367 (May 1989); no.387 (January 1991).

Gallup, George. *The Gallup Poll, 1935–1971*. Vol. 1 (1935–48). New York: Random House, 1972.

Gallup, George Jr. *The Gallup Poll: Public Opinion 1991*. Wilmington, Del.: Scholarly Resources, 1992.

———. *The Gallup Poll: Public Opinion 1992*. Wilmington, Del.: Scholarly Resources, 1993.

Gao, Xingzu. *Rijun qin-Hua baoxing: Nanjing datusha* (Japanese War Atrocities: The Nanjing Massacre). Shanghai: Shanghai renmin chubanshe, 1985.

Gayn, Mark. *Japan Diary*. New York: William Sloane, 1948.

Genbaku no zu Maruki bijutsukan (Maruki Gallery for the Hiroshima Panels Foundation). *Genbaku no zu* (The Hiroshima Panels). Saitama: Maruki bijutsukan, 1996.

Gifu-ken Rekishi kyōikusha Kyōgikai (Association for History Educators, Gifu), *Machi: mo mura mo senjō datta* (Cities and Towns, Too, Were "Battlefields"). Gifu: Gifu-ken Rekishi Kyōikusha kyōgikai, 1995.

Gluck, Carol. "Kioku no sayō: Sekai no naka no 'ianfu'" (Operations of Memory: 'Comfort Women' and the World). In *Kanjō, kioku, sensō, 1935–1952, Koza kindai Nihon no bunkashi* (Emotion, Memory, and War, 1935–1952; Vol. 8 of Cultural History of Modern Japan), edited by Komori Yōichi et al., pp. 192–234. Tokyo: Iwanami shoten, 2002.

———. "The Past in the Present." In *Postwar Japan as History*, edited by Andrew Gordon, pp. 64–95. Berkeley: University of California Press, 1993.

Goette, John. *Japan Fights for Asia*. New York: Harcourt Brace, 1943.

Gotō, Kōsaku. *Nankin sakusen no shinsō: Kumamoto roku shidan senki* (The Truth about the Nanjing Operation: The Military History of the Kumamoto Sixth Division). Tokyo: Tokyō jōhōsha, 1965.

Grajdanzev, A. "Japan: Neither Beauty nor Beast." *Amerasia* 6, no. 4 (June 1942): 174–78.

Greenbie, Sydney. *Asia Unbound*. New York: Appleton Century, 1943.

Guo, Qi. *Nanjing da tu sha* (The Nanjing Massacre). Taipei: Zhongwai tushu chubanshe, 1979.

Hani, Gorō. *Hani Gorō chosaku shū* (The Postwar Works of Hani Gorō). Tokyo: Gendaishi shuppan kai, 1982.

Hanjungil Samguk Gongdong Yeoksa Pyeonchan Wiwonhoe (The Committee for Sharing the Same Historical Material, South Korea). *Miraereul Yeoneun Yeoksa* (History That Opens the Future). Seoul: Hangyeore Sinmunsa, 2005.

Hansen dōmei kiroku henshū iinkai (The Committee to Preserve the Records of the League of Anti-War Japanese). *Hansen heishi monogatari* (The Story of Anti-War Soldiers). Tokyo: Nihon kyōsantō, 1963.

Hansheng zazhishe. *Muji kangzhan wushinian: 1895–1945 Zhong-Ri zhanzheng tulu* (Eyewitness to the Fifty-Year Resistance: A Pictorial History of the Sino-Japanese War of 1895–1945). Taipei: Hansheng zazhishe, 1995.

Harris, Sheldon. *Factories of Death: Japanese Biological Warfare, 1932–45, and the American Cover-Up*. New York: Routledge, 1994.

Hata, Ikuhiko. *Nankin jiken: "gyakusatsu" no kōzō* (The Nanjing Incident: The Structure of the "Atrocities"). Tokyo: Chūkō shinsho, 1986.

Hayashi, Masaaki. "Futatsu no eiga ni miru ningen no hokori to rekishi ninshiki" (Pride of Human Beings and Historical Recognition in Two Films). *Shūkan kinyōbi*, no. 20 (May 29, 1998): 55–56.

Hayashi, Zensuke. "Shina jihenka ni okeru fuon kōdō to sono taisaku ni tsuite" (Alarming Activities and How They Were Dealt with at the Time of the China Incident), 1941. Reprinted in *Shakai mondai sōsho* (Library of Social Problems), Series 1, Vol. 79. Kyoto: Tōyō bunkasha, 1978.

"He Who Gets Slapped." *Newsweek*, May 13, 1946, p. 50.

"Henshū kōki" (From the Editors). *Shokun!* 4, no. 4 (April 1972): 256.

———. (From the Editors). *Shokun!* 4, no. 5 (May 1972): 256.

Hersey, John. *Hiroshima*. New York: Modern Library, 1946.

Hidaka, Rokurō. "'Hansei' towa nanika" (What Is "Reflection"?). *Sekai* 443 (October 1982): 46–55.

Higashinakano, Osamichi. *Nankin jiken "shōko shashin" o kenshō suru* (Examining the "Photographic Proof" of the Nanjing Incident). Tokyo: Sōshisha, 2005.

———. *"Nankin gyakusatsu" no tettei kenshō* (Solid Examination of the "Nanjing Massacre"). Tokyo: Tendensha, 1998.

———. *Nihon "Nankin" gakkai nenpō: Nankin "gyakusatsu" kenkyū no saizensen Heisei 14 nen ban* (Annual Report of Japan Association of Nanjing Studies: The Forefront of the Studies of the Nanjing "Massacre," 2002). Tokyo: Tendensha, 2002.

———. *Nihon "Nankin" gakkai nenpō: Nankin "gyakusatsu" kenkyū no saizensen Heisei 15 nen ban* (Annual Report of Japan Association of Nanjing Studies: The Forefront of the Studies of the Nanjing "Massacre," 2003). Tokyo: Tendensha, 2003.

———. *Nihon "Nankin" gakkai nenpō: Nankin "gyakusatsu" kenkyū no saizensen Heisei 16 nen ban* (Annual Report of Japan Association of Nanjing Studies: The Forefront of the Studies of the Nanjing "Massacre," 2004). Tokyo: Tendensha, 2005.

Hino, Ashihei. *Barley and Soldiers* (Mugi to heitai). Translated by Lewis Bush. Tokyo: Kenkyusha, 1939.

———. *Flower and Soldiers* (Hana to heitai). Translated by Lewis Bush. Tokyo: Kenkyusha, 1939.

———. *Mud and Soldiers*. (Tsuchi to heitai). Translated by Lewis Bush. Tokyo: Kenkyusha, 1939.

———. *Mugi to heitai* (Wheat and Soldiers). Tokyo: Kaizōsha, 1938.

Ho, Ying-chin. *Who Actually Fought the Sino-Japanese War 1937–45?* Taipei: Lee Ming, 1979.

Holland, William. "The Common Man of Japan." *Amerasia* 6, no. 4 (June 1942): 179–81.

Honda, Katsuichi. "Baikokudo tachi ga tsukutta eiga" (A Film Made by Traitors). *Shūkan kinyōbi*, no. 220 (May 29, 1998): 57.

———. *Chūgoku no Nihongun* (The Japanese Army in China). Tokyo: Sōjusha, 1972.

———. *Chūgoku no tabi* (Travels in China). Tokyo: Asahi shinbun sha, 1972.

———. "Izaya Bendasan shi e no kōkaijō" (An Open Letter to Mr. Isaiah Ben-Dasan). *Shokun!* 4, no. 2 (February 1972): 208–17.

———. *The Nanjing Massacre*. New York: M.E. Sharpe, 1999.

———. *Nankin e no michi* (The Road to Nanjing). Tokyo: Asahi shinbunsha, 1987.

———. *Sabakareta Nankin daigyakusastsu* (The Nanjing Massacre on Trial). Tokyo: Banseisha, 1989.

———. *Senjō no mura* (A Village in the Battlefield). Tokyo: Asahi bunko, 1981.

———. "Zatsuon de ijimerareru gawa no me" (From the Eyes of Those Who Were Forced to Suffer by the Unpleasant Noise). *Shokun!* 4, no. 4 (April 1972): 148–76.

Hong, Guiji. "Nanjing datusha" (The Nanjing Massacre). In *Riben zai Hua baoxing lu* (Account of the Atrocities Committed by Japan in China), pp. 239–608. Taipei: Guoshiguan, 1985.

Hora, Tomio. *Kindai senshi no nazo* (Riddles of Modern War History). Tokyo: Jinbutsu ōraisha, 1967.

———. *Nankin daigyakusatsu: "maboroshi" ka kōsaku hihan* (The Nanjing Massacre: Criticism of the Making of an Illusion). Tokyo: Gendaishi shuppankai, 1975.

———. *Nankin daigyakusatsu no kenkyū* (Studies of the Nanjing Massacre). Tokyo: Banseisha, 1992.

———. *Nankin daigyakusatsu no shōmei* (The Proof of the Nanjing Massacre). Tokyo: Asahi shinbunsha, 1986.

———. *Nit-Chū sensō: Nankin daigyakusatsu jiken shiryōshū* (The Sino-Japanese War: A Collection of Historical Materials on the Nanjing Massacre). 2 vols. Tokyo: Aoki shoten, 1985.

———. *Nit-Chū sensōshi shiryōshū 9: Nankin jiken* (A Collection of Historical Materials on the Japan-China War: The Nanjing Incident. Tokyo: Kawade shobō shinsha, 1973.

Hora, Tomio, et al., eds. *Nankin jiken o kangaeru* (Consideration of the Nanjing Incident). Tokyo: Ōtsuki shoten, 1987.

Hosokawa, Morihiro. *The Time to Act Is Now*. Tokyo: NTT Mediascope, 1993.

Hsu, Shuhsi. *A Digest of Japanese War Conduct*. Shanghai: Kelly & Walsh, 1939.

———. *A New Digest of Japanese War Conduct*. Shanghai: Kelly & Walsh, 1941.

———. *Japan and Shanghai*. Shanghai: Kelly & Walsh, 1938.

———. *Documents of the Nanking Safety Zone*. Shanghai: Kelly & Walsh, 1939.

———. *The War Conduct of the Japanese*. Shanghai: Kelly & Walsh, 1938.

———. *Three Weeks of Canton Bombings*. Shanghai: Kelly & Walsh, 1939.

Ienaga soshōshien shimin no kai (The People's Group Supporting Ienaga's Case). *Taiheiyō sensō to kyōkasho* (The Pacific War and Textbooks). Tokyo: Shisō no kagaku sha, 1970.

Ikeda, Ichirō, and Suzuki Tetsuya. *Kyōto no "sensō iseki" o meguru* (Visiting War Memorial Sites in Kyoto). Kyoto: Tsumugi shuppan, 1996.

Indusco Collection. Box 60. Rare Book and Manuscript Library, Columbia University.

Inoue, Hisashi. "Kaisetsu" (Foreword). In *Nankin jiken shiryōshū* (A Collection of Historical Materials on the Nanjing Incident), edited by Nankin jiken chōsa kenkyūkai (The Research Committee on the Nanjing Incident). Vol. 2, pp. 3–4. Tokyo: Aoki shoten, 1992.

"Is There Another Japan?" *Amerasia* 7, no. 2 (April 1, 1943): 35–42.

Ishihara, Shintarō, and Kon Tōkō. "Kokunan koko ni kuru" (Facing a National Crisis). *Shokun!* (January 1972): 84–92.

Ishihara, Shintarō, and Morita Akio. *"No" to ieru Nihon* (The Japan That Can Say "No"). Tokyo: Kōbunsha, 1989.

Ishihara, Shintarō, Watanabe Shōichi, and Ogawa Kazuhisa. *Soredemo "No" to ieru Nihon* (The Japan That Can Still Say "No"). Tokyo: Kōbunsha, 1990.

Ishii, Akira. "Sengo Nit-Chū kankei no kiseki" (An Outline of Postwar Japan-China Relations). *Gaikō fōramu* 10, special issue (1997): 94–107.

Ishijima, Noriyuki. "Kaidai" (Explanatory Notes). In *Nankin jiken shiryōshū* (A Collection of Historical Materials on the Nanjing Incident), edited by Nankin jiken chōsa kenkyūkai (The Research Committee on the Nanjing Incident). Vol. 2, pp. 6–9. Tokyo: Aoki shoten, 1992.

Ishikawa, Tatsuzō. *Bokei kazoku/ikiteiru heitatai* (The Maternal Family/Living Soldiers). Tokyo: Shinchōsha, 1957.

———. *Soldiers Alive.* Translated by Zeljko Cipris. Honolulu: University of Hawaii Press, 2003.

Ishiko, Jun. *Manga ni miru sensō to heiwa 90 nen* (Peace and War in Cartoons during the Last 90 Years. Tokyo: Porupu shuppan, 1983.

———. *Nihon manga shi* (History of Japanese Cartoons). Tokyo: Shakai shisōsha, 1988.

Ishiyama Hisao, "Chūgaku rekishi kyōkasho wa dō kakikaerareta ka" (How Were Junior High School History Textbooks Revised?). *Kyōkasho repōto 2002*, no. 46 (February 2002): 16–18.

Itakura, Yoshiaki. "'Nankin daigyakusatsu nijūman' setsu e no hanshō" (Refuting the Theory of Two Hundred Thousand Deaths in the "Nanjing Massacre"). *"Kingendaishi" no jugyō kaikaku*, no. 1 (September 1995): 71–79.

Itō, Shunya. *Puraido: Unmei no toki* (Pride: The Moment of Destiny). Videocassette. Tōei Video, 1998.

Jaffe, Philip. "China Can Win and Yet Lose: A Challenge to America and China." *Amerasia* 7, no. 7 (July 25, 1943): 195–205.

———. "Introduction." *Amerasia*, Vol. 1. New York: Greenwood Reprint, 1968.

The Japan Newspaper Publishers and Editors Association. *The Japanese Press 1971.* Tokyo: Japan Newspaper Publishers and Editors Association, 1972.

Japanese Society for History Textbook Reform. *The Restoration of a National History.* Tokyo: Japanese Society for History Textbook Reform, 1998.

Jespersen, Christopher. *American Images of China, 1931–1949.* Stanford, Calif.: Stanford University Press, 1996.

Johnson, Sheila. *American Attitudes toward Japan, 1941–1975.* Washington, D.C.: American Institute for Public Policy Research, 1975.

Kagami, Mitsuyuki, and Himeta Mitsuyoshi. *Shōgen Nankin daigyakusatsu* (Testimonies on the Nanjing Massacre). Tokyo: Aoki shoten, 1984.

Kaigo, Tokiomi. *Nihon kyōkasho taikei kindai hen* (The Systematic Study of School Textbooks in Modern Japan). Vols. 3, 7–9, 16, 20. Tokyo: Kodansha, 1962–65.

Kaji, Wataru. *Chūgoku no jūnen* (Ten Years in China). Tokyo: Jiji tsūshinsha, 1948.

———. *Nihon heishi no hansen undō* (Anti-War Movements by Japanese Soldiers). 2 vols. Tokyo: Dōseisha, 1962.

———. *Shanhai sen'eki no naka* (During the Battle of Shanghai). Tokyo: Tōhō shuppansha, 1975.

Kamata, Sadao. "Nagasaki genbaku shiryōkan no kagai tenji mondai" (Problems Regarding the Exhibition of Japan's Wartime Atrocities at the Nagasaki Atomic Bomb Museum). *Kikan sensō sekinin kenkyū* 14 (winter 1996): 22–31.

Kanagawa-ken rekishi kyōikusha kyōgikai (Association for History Educators, Kanagawa). *Kanagawa-ken no sensō iseki* (The Scars of War in Kanagawa). Tokyo: Ōtsuki shoten, 1996.

Kanda, Fuhito. *Shōwa shi nenpyō* (Chronology of the Showa Period). Tokyo: Shōgakkan, 1995.

Kanki, Haruo. *Riben zhanfan de zibai* (Confessions of Japanese War Criminals). Translated by Yuan Bai. Hong Kong: Shinxue shudian, 1957.

Kasahara, Tokushi. "Bunshun ga mata katsugidashita Nankin gyakusatsu hiteironja no osomatsuburi" (Bungei Shunjū Publisher Has Done It Again: Championing a Shabby Volume on the Nanjing Denial), *Shūkan kinyōbi*, no. 422 (2 August 2002): 66–67.

———. *Nankin jiken* (The Nanjing Incident). Tokyo: Iwanami shoten, 1997.

———. *Nankin jiken to Nihonjin* (The Nanjing Massacre and Japanese). Tokyo: Kashiwa shobō, 2002.

———. *Nankin jiken to sankō sakusen* (The Nanjing Massacre and Three All Operation). Tokyo: Ōtsuki shoten, 1999.

———. *Nankin nanminku no hyakunichi: gyakusatsu o mita gaikokujin* (One Hundred Days in the Nanjing Safety Zone: Foreigners Who Witnessed the Atrocities). Tokyo: Iwanami shoten, 1995.

Kennedy, David. "The Horror." *Atlantic*, April 1998, pp. 110–16.

Kennedy, Malcolm. Review of *Japan's Imperial Cosnpiracy*, by David Bergamini. *International Affairs* 48, no. 2 (April 1972): 367–68.

Kim, Hak Hyon. "Kyōkasho mondai to 'yūkō' no kyokō" (Illusion of Friendship and the Textbook Controversy). *Sekai* 443 (October 1982): 77–82.

Kitamura, Minoru. "'Nankin daigyakusatsu' kenkyū josetsu" (An Introductory Study of the "Nanjing Massacre," Parts 1–3). *Tōa*, no 388 (October 1999): 33–42; no. 390 (December 1999): 40–50; no. 391 (January 2000): 45–56.

———. "'Nankin daigyakusatsu sanjūmannin setsu' no seiritsu: Timperley no sakubō o chūshin ni" (Timperley's Conspiracy: The Emergence of the Estimate of the 300,000 Deaths). In *Nihon "Nankin" gakkai nenpō* (2003), edited by Higashinakano Osamichi, pp. 41–74. Tokyo: Tendensha, 2003.

———. *"Nankin Jiken" no tankyū: sono jitsuzō o motomete* (The Quest for the "Nanjing Incident": The Search for the Reality). Tokyo: Bungei shunjū, 2001.

Kiyosawa, Kiyoshi. "Kokusai pen kurabu kusen ki" (The Struggle at the International Association of Poets, Playwrights, Editors, Essayists, and Novelists). *Chūō kōron* 53, no. 1 (January 1938): 238–49.

Kobayashi, Yoshinori, *Sensōron* (On War). Tokyo: Gentōsha, 1998.

———. *Shin gōmanizumu sengen 5* (A Declaration of Arrogance, New Version, Vol. 5). Tokyo: Shōgakkan, 1998,

———. *Shin gōmanizumu sengen 6* (A Declaration of Arrogance, New Version, Vol. 6). Tokyo: Shōgakkan, 1999.

Kobori, Keiichirō. "Susumeru kotoba" (A Word of Recommendation). In *Nankin jiken no sōkatsu: gyakusatsu hitei 15 no ronkyo* (An Outline of the Nanjing Incident: Fifteen Grounds for the Denial of the Massacre), edited by Tanaka Masaaki, n.p. Tokyo: Kenkōsha, 1987.

Kōdansha, *Shōwa niman-nichi no zen kiroku* (The Entire Record of 20,000 Days of the Shōwa). Tokyo: Kōdansha, 1991.

Kosaka, Eiichi. "Nankin dai kōryakusen jūgun shiki" (A Private Narrative of the Great Capture of Nanjing). *Bungei shunjū* 16, no. 2 (January 1938): 208–17.

Kōseishō hikiage engokyoku (Repatriation relief Agency, Ministry of Health and Welfare). *Zoku hikiage engo no kiroku* (The Record of Assistance in Repatriation, Part 2). Tokyo: Kōseishō hikiage engokyoku, 1955.

Kumamoto heidan senshi hensan iinkai (The Editorial Committee for the Military History of Kumamoto Units). *Kumamoto heidan senshi, Shina jihen hen* (The Military History of Kumamoto Units: The China Incident). Kumamoto: Kumamoto nichi nichi shinbun, 1965.

Kyōkasho kentei soshō shien zenkoku renrakukai (The National Alliance for Supporting Lawsuit against Textbook Authorization). *Ienaga kyōkasho saiban* (Ienaga Textbook Trial). Tokyo: Sōgō tosho, 1967.

———. *Ienaga kyōkasho saiban jūnen shi* (The Ten-Year History of the Ienaga Textbook Case). Tokyo: Sōdo bunka, 1977.

"Kyōkasho mondai Chūgoku kōgi no dodai yuragu" (Foundation of China's Claim in Textbook Controversy Shaken). *Seiron* 112 (November 1982): 84–85.

League of Nations. *Official Journal*, Vol. 13, no. 12 (December 1932); Vol. 19, nos. 2 (February 1938), 5–6 (May–June 1938), 8–9 (August–September 1938), 11 (November 1938), 12 (December 1938); special supplement no. 169 (September 1937); special supplement no. 183 (September 1938).

Li, Fei Fei, Robert Sabella, and David Liu. *Nanking 1937: Memory and Healing*. New York: M.E. Sharpe, 2002.

Li, Yunhan. "Youguan 'Nanjing da tu sha' Zhongwai shiliao de pingshu" (In Regard to Chinese and Foreign Discussions of the Historical Materials on the Nanjing Massacre). In *Kang zhan jian guo shi yan tao hui lun wen ji* (Papers on the History of the War and Founding of the Nation), edited by Zhong yang yan jiu yuan, Jin dai shi yan jiu suo (The Institute of Modern History, Academia Sinica), Vol. 1, pp. 33–47. Taipei: Zhong yang yan jiu yuan, jin dai shi yan jiu suo, 1985.

Linenthal, Edward. "Anatomy of a Controversy." In *History Wars: The Enola Gay and Other Battles for the American Past*, edited by E. Linenthal, pp. 9–62. New York: Metropolitan, 1996.

Linenthal, Edward, and Tom Engelhardt. *History Wars: The Enola Gay and Other Battles for the American Past*. New York: Metropolitan Books, 1996.

Liu, Huishu. *Nanjing datusha xinkao* (New Study of the Nanjing Massacre). Shanghai: Shanghai sanlian shudian, 1998.

Maeda, Yūji. *Sensō no nagare no naka ni* (In the Course of the War). Tokyo: Zenponsha, 1982.

Manshūkoku shi hensan kankō iinkai (The Committee for Editing and Publishing the History of Manchukuo), *Manshūkoku shi* (The History of Manchukuo). Tokyo: Manmō dōhō engokai, 1970.

Masaki, Hiroshi. *Chikakiyori* (Up Close). Vol. 5. 1946. Reprint, Tokyo: Ōbunsha, 1979.

Masui, Yasuichi. *Kankan saiban shi* (The Trials of the Chinese Collaborators). Tokyo: Misuzu shobō, 1977.

Matsumura, Toshio. *"Nankin gyakusatsu" e no daigimon* (Serious Questions about the "Nanjing Massacre"). Tokyo: Tendensha 1998.

Matsuo, Ichirō. "Nankin jiken nise shashin o seiryokuteki ni kenshō" (Rigorously Examining Fake Photographs of the Nanjing Incident). *Jiyū shugi shikan kenkyūkai kaihō* (Newsletter of the Association for the Advancement of a Liberalist View of History), no. 25 (June 30, 1998), p. 1.

———. *Propaganda War, The "Nanjing Incident": The Truth of the "Nanjing Massacre" as Seen through Secret Photographs* (Puropaganda sen "Nankin jiken": Hiroku shashin de miru "Nankin daigyakusatsu" no shinjitsu), Tokyo: Kōjinsha, 2003.

Mayuzumi, Toshirō. "Kyōkasho mondai ni tsuite" (About the Textbook Controversy). *Seiron* 111 (October 1982): 174–77.

"The Memoirs of Dr. V. K. Wellington Koo." *Wellington Koo Collection*, Columbia University Rare Book and Manuscript Library.

Meng, Guoxiang, and Cheng Tangfa. "Chengzhi hanjian gongzuo gaishu" (A General Account of Punishing Traitors). *Minguo dang'an* 2 (1994): 105–12.

Mie-ken Rekishi kyōikusha kyōgikai (Association for History Educators, Mie). *Mie no sensō iseki* (War Memorials in Mie). Kyōto: Tsumugi shuppan, 1998.

Mitchell, Kate. "The Political Function of the Japanese Emperor." *Amerasia* 6, no. 9 (October 25, 1942): 382–90.

Miyadai, Shinji, et al. eds. *Sensōron mōsōron* (The Delusion of *On War*). Tokyo: Kyōiku shiryō shuppankai, 1999.

Miyata, Eijirō. "Reddo pagji" (Red Purge). in *Nihon kingendai shi jiten* (Encyclopedia of Modern Japanese History). Tokyo: Tōyō keizai shinpōsha, 1978.

Mizutani, Naoko. "1644 butai no soshiki to katsudō" (Organizational Structure and Activities of Unit 1644). *Kikan sensō sekinin kenkyu* 15 (spring 1997): 50–59.

———. "Moto 1644 butaiin no shōgen" (Testimony by a Former Member of Unit 1644). *Kikan sensō sekinin kenkyū* 10 (winter 1995): 56–65.

———. "Watashi wa naze Azuma Shirō shi ni igi o tonaeru ka" (Why I Disagree with Mr. Azuma Shirō). *Sekai* 664 (August 1998): 219–25.

Monbushō (Ministry of Education). *Jinjō shōgaku chiri sho* (Elementary School Geography). Vols. 1–2 (1936), Vol. 2 (1939). Reprinted in *Nihon kyōkasho taikei kindai hen* (The Systematic Study of School Textbooks in Japan), edited by Kaigo Tokiomi. Vol. 16, pp. 486–522, 523–73, 613–64. Tokyo: Kōdansha, 1965.

———. *Jinjō shōgaku shūshin sho* (Elementary School Ethics). Vol. 6. (1939). Reprinted in *Nihon kyōkasho taikei kindai hen* (The Systematic Study of School Textbooks in Japan), edited by Kaigo Tokiomi. Vol. 3, pp. 328–58.

———. *Kuni no Ayumi* (The Course of the Nation). Reprinted in *Nihon kyōkasho taikei kindai hen* (The Systematic Study of School Textbooks in Japan), edited by Kaigo Tokiomi. Vol. 20, pp. 423–64. Tokyo: Kōdansha, 1962.

———. *Monbu tōkei yōran shōwa 63-nen ban* (Details of Statistics Regarding Education). Tokyo: Dai-ichi hōki shuppansha, 1988.

———. *Shōgaku kokugo tokuhon* (Lower-Level Japanese Reader), Vol. 1 (1933). Reprinted in *Nihon kyōkasho taikei kindai hen* (The Systematic Study of School Textbooks in Japan), edited by Kaigo Tokiomi. Vol. 7, pp. 558–78. Kōdansha, 1963.

———. *Shotōka kokushi* (Lower-Level National History), Vol. 2 (1941). Reprinted in *Nihon kyōkasho taikei kindai hen* (The Systematic Study of School Textbooks in Japan), edited by Kaigo Tokiomi. Vol. 20, pp. 180–244. Tokyo: Kōdansha, 1962.

———. *Shotōka kokushi* (Lower-Level National History), Vol. 2 (1943). Reprinted in *Nihon kyōkasho taikei kindai hen* (The Systematic Study of School Textbooks in Japan), edited by Kaigo Tokiomi. Vol. 20, pp. 311–83. Tokyo: Kōdansha, 1962.

Morley, James, et al., eds. *The China Quagmire: Japan's Expansion on the Asian Continent, 1933–1941.* New York: Columbia University Press, 1983.

Motoshima, Hitoshi. *Nagasaki shichō no kotoba* (Statement of Mayor of Nagasaki). Iwanami bukkuretto no. 146. Tokyo: Iwanami shoten, 1989.

Mukai, Toshiaki. "Isho" (Testament). In *Seiki no isho* (Testaments of the Century), edited by Sugamo isho hensankai kankō jimusho (Sugamo: The Office of Editing and Publishing Testaments of the Century), pp. 40–42. Tokyo: Kōdansha, 1984.

Mukai, Toshiaki. "Jisei" (Last Words). In *Seiki no isho* (Testaments of the Century), edited by Sugamo isho hensankai kankō jimusho (Sugamo: The Office of Editing and Publishing Testaments of the Century), p. 40. Tokyo: Kōdansha, 1984.

Nagasaki no genbaku tenji o tadasu shimin no kai (Citizen's Group That Seeks to Correct Atomic Exhibitions in Nagasaki). *Korede iinoka, Nagasaki genbaku shiryōkan* (This Isn't Right, Nagasaki Atomic Bomb Museum). Nagasaki: Nagasaki no genbaku tenji o tadasu shimin no kai, 1996.

Naimushō keihokyoku hoanka (Home Ministry, Police Bureau, Peace Preservation Section). *Tokkō gaiji geppō* (Monthly Gazette on External Affairs of the Special Higher Police), December 1937–June 1938.

Nakamura, Kikuji. *Kyōkasho no hensan, hakkō tō kyōkasho seido no hensen ni kansuru chōsa kenkyū* (A Study of the Changes of Compilation and Publishing of Textbooks. Tokyo: Kyōkasho kenkyū sentā, 1997.

731 [nana-san-ichi] butaiten zenkoku jikkō iinkai (National Executive Committee for the Exhibition on Unit 731 Exhibition). *731 butaiten 1993.7–1994.12.* Tokyo: 731 butaiten zenkoku jikkō iinkai, 1995.

Nanjing datusha shiliao bianji weiyuanhui (the Committee for the Compilation of Sources on the Nanjing Massacre). *Qin-Hua Rijun Nanjing datusha shiliao* (Historical Materials on the Nanjing Massacre Committed by the Japanese Army of Invasion). Nanjing: Jiangsu guji chubanshe, 1985.

Nankin 1937 kaigaten jikkō iinkai (Executive Committee of the Nanjing Massacre Art Exhibition). *The Nanking Massacre Art Exhibition in Tokyo.* Tokyo: Nankin 1937 kaigaten jikkō iinkai, 1996.

"Nankin 1937" zenkoku jōei iinkai (The Committee to Tour *Nanjing 1937* Across

Japan). *Nankin 1937: Don't Cry, Nanking.* Aichi: Nankin 1937 zenkoku jōei iinkai, 1997.

Nankin jiken chōsa kenkyūkai (The Research Committee on the Nanjing Incident). *Nankin daigyakusatsu hiteiron 13 no uso* (Thirteen Lies by the Deniers of the Nanjing Massacre). Tokyo: Kashiwa shobō, 1999.

———. *Amerika kankei shiryō hen* (Historical Materials with Regard to the United States). Vol. 1 of *Nankin jiken shiryōshū* (A Collection of Historical Materials on the Nanjing Incident). Tokyo: Aoki shoten, 1992.

———. *Chūgoku kankei shiryō hen* (Historical Materials with Regard to China). Vol. 2. of *Nankin jiken shiryōshū* (A Collection of Historical Materials on the Nanjing Incident). Tokyo: Aoki shoten, 1992.

Nanking International Relief Committee. *Report of the Nanking International Relief Committee, November 1937 to April 30, 1939.* N.p, n.d.

Naono, Akiko. *Hiroshima, America: Genbakuten o megutte* (Atomic Bomb Exhibit: Hiroshima in America). Hiroshima: Keisuisha, 1997.

National Committee for the Fiftieth Anniversary of the End of World War II. *A Tribute, Appreciation, and Friendship: A Celebration of Asian Nations' Symbiosis.* Tokyo: National Committee for the Fiftieth Anniversary of the End of WWII, 1995.

"The Nature of Our Enemy, Japan." *Amerasia* 7, no. 12 (November 1943): pp. 389–92.

New York Times Magazine. "These Are the Japanese," August 26, 1945, pp. 6–7.

Nihon Chūgoku yūkō kyōkai zenkoku honbu (The Headquarters of the Japan China Friendship Association). *Nit-Chū yūkō undō shi* (The History of the Japan China Friendship Movement). Tokyo: Seinen shuppansha, 1975.

Nihon heiwa iinkai (Japan Peace Committee). *Heiwa undō 20 nen undō shi* (Twenty Years of the History of the Peace Movement). Tokyo: Ōtsuki shoten, 1969.

———. *Heiwa undō 20 nen shiryō shū* (A Collection of Materials Regarding Twenty Years of the Peace Movement). Tokyo: Ōtsuki shoten, 1969.

Nihon hōsō kyōkai. *Nihon hōsōshi* (The History of Broadcasting in Japan), bekkan (supplement). Tokyo: NHK, 1965.

———. *Hōsō gojūnen shi* (The History of Fifty Years of Broadcasting). Tokyo: NHK, 1977.

———. *Shōwa 13 nen rajio nenkan* (Radio Year Book, 1938). Tokyo: NHK, 1938.

Nihon kokusai mondai kenkyūjo (Institute of International Affairs, Japan). *Shin Chūgoku shiryō shūsei* (Collection of Historical Materials on New China). Vols. 1–3. Tokyo: Nihon kokusai mondai kenkyūjo, 1963.

Nihon kyōkasho taikei kindai hen (The Systematic Study of School Textbooks in Modern Japan). Vols. 3, 7–9, 16, 20. Tokyo: Kōdansha, 1962–65.

Nihon minshutō. *Ureubeki kyōkasho no mondai* (Deplorable Problems in School Textbooks). Tokyo: Nihon minshutō, 1955.

Nihon ronsōshi kenkyūkai (The Study Group on Debates in Japan). *Nippon no ronsō* (Debates in Japan. Tokyo: Natsume shobō, 1998.

Nishida, Masaru. *Sekai no heiwa hakubutsukan* (Peace Museums in the World). Tokyo: Nihon tosho sentā, 1995.

Nishigaya. Tōru. "Shina jihen ni kansuru zōgen higo ni tsuite" (Regarding Lies and Rumors during the China Incident), 1938. Reprinted in *Shakai mondai sōsho* (Library of Social Problems), Series 1, Vol. 79. Kyoto: Tōyō bunkasha, 1978.

Nishio, Kanji, et al., eds. *Atarashii rekishi kyōkasho* (New History Textbook). Tokyo: Fusōsha, 2001.

Nit-Chū-Kan sangoku kyōtsū rekishi kyōzai iinkai (The Committee for Sharing the Same Historical Material in Japan, China, and South Korea). *Mirai o hiraku rekishi: higashi Ajia sangoku no kingendaishi* (History That Opens the Future: The Modern History of Three East Asian Nations). Tokyo: Kōbunken, 2005.

Noda, Masaaki. *Sensō to zaiseki* (War and Responsibility). Tokyo: Iwanami, 1998.

Noda, Tsuyoshi. "Nisshi no Kusabi to naran" (Our Deaths Shall Become a Tie that Binds Japan and China Together). In *Seiki no isho* (Testaments of the Century), edited by Sugamo isho hensankai kankō jimusho (Sugamo: Office of Editing and Publishing Testaments of the Century), pp. 1–4. Tokyo: Kōdansha, 1984.

Noel, Percy. *When Japan Fights*. Tokyo: Hokuseido, 1938.

Nōmoa Nankin no kai (The No-More-Nanjing Association). *Hōdō ni miru Nankin 1937* (Newspaper Reports of Nanjing in 1937). Tokyo: Privately printed, 1997.

Nozaki, Yoshiko. "Gasshūkoku no daigakusei ga kangaeru Nihon no sensō hanzai" (Japan's War Crimes and College Students in the United States). *Let's* 28 (September 2000): 9–15.

Obinata, Sumio, et al., eds. *Kimitachi wa sensō de shineruka, Kobayashi Yoshinori "Sensōron" hihan* (Critique of Kobayashi Yoshinori's *On War*: Are You Willing to Die for the State?). Tokyo: Ōtsuki shoten, 1999.

Oda, Baku. "Jūgonen sensō o dō oshieruka" (How to Teach the Fifteen-Year War). *Rekishi chiri kyōiku* 219 (December 1973): 28–33.

Okamoto, Shumpei. Review of *Japan's Imperial Conspiracy*, by David Bergamini. *Journal of Asian Studies* 31, no. 2 (February 1972): 414–16.

Ono, Kenji, Fujiwara Akira, and Honda Katsuichi. *Nankin dai gyakusatsu o kiroku shita kōgun heishi tachi: Dai jūsan shidan Yamada shitai heishi no jinchū nikki* (Imperial Soldiers Who Recorded the Nanjing Massacre: The Field Diaries of the Yamada Unit of the Thirteenth Division). Tokyo: Ōtsuki shoten, 1996.

Onodera, Toshitaka. "Sengo hoshō saiban tōsō no kadai to tenbō" (Problems and Prospects in Postwar Legal Struggles over Compensation). *Hō to minshushugi* (Law and Democracy) no. 328 (May 1998): 12–15.

Ōya, Sōichi. "Honkon kara Nankin nyūjō" (From Hong Kong to the Entrance of Nanjing). *Kaizō* 20, no. 2 (February 1938): 226–51.

Ozaki, Hotsuki. *Omoide no Shōnen kurabu jidai* (The Memorable Period of *Shōnen kurabu*). Tokyo: Kōdansha, 1997.

Pal, Radhabinod. "The Dissenting Opinion of the Member for India." In *Separate Opinions*, Vol. 21 of *The Tokyo War Crimes Trial*, edited by John Pritchard. New York: Garland, 1981.

Peffer, Lillian. Review of *What War Means: Japanese Terror in China*, by Harold Timperley. *Pacific Affairs* 11, no. 11 (January 1939): 553.

Perkins, Ward. Review of *War Damage in the Nanking Area*, by Lewis Smythe. *Pacific Affairs* 12, no. 2 (June 1939): 220–22.

"Playboy Interview: Shintaro Ishihara—candid conversation," *Playboy* 37, no. 10 (October 1990), pp. 59–70, 76, 84.

Poore, Charles. "The Most Spectacular Explosion in the Time of Man." *New York Times Book Review*, November 10, 1946, pp. 7, 56.

Pritchard, John. *The Tokyo War Crimes Trial*. 22 vols. New York: Garland, 1981.

"Proclamation to the Tradesmen and Artisans of Japan." *Amerasia* 2, no. 6 (August 1938): 296–97.

"Proclamation to the Various Laborers." *Amerasia* 2, no. 6 (August 1938): 297.

Rabe, John. *The Diary of John Rabe: Nankin no shinjitsu* (The Diary of John Rabe: The Truth about Nanjing). Tokyo: Kōdansha, 1997.

———. *The Good Man of Nanking*. New York: Alfred A. Knopf, 1998.

———. *Labei riji* (The Diary of John Rabe). Nanjing: Jiangsu renmin chubanshe, 1997.

Rakunō gakuen shokuin kumiai 731 butaiten jikkō iinkai (Executive Committee for the Exhibition on Unit 731, Labor Union at Rakunō Gakuen University). *731 butaiten Ebetsu 1995 hōkokushū* (Report on Unit 731 Exhibition in Ebetsu). Rakunō gakuen shokuin kumiai 731 butaiten jikkō iinkai, 1996.

Rekishi kentō iinkai, *Daitō-A sensō no sōkatsu* (An Outline of the Greater East Asian War). Tokyo: Tendensha, 1995.

Rekishi kyōikusha kyōgikai (Association for History Educators). *Heiwa hakubutsukan, sensō shiryōkan gaido bukku* (Handbook for Peace and War Museums). Tokyo: Aoki shoten, 1995.

———. *Rekishi kyōiku 50 nen no ayumi to kadai* (Fifty Years of History Education and Its Objectives). Tokyo: Miraisha, 1997.

Rekishi kyōikusha kyōgikai Tōhoku burokku (Association for History Educators in Tōhoku Region). *Tōhoku to jūgonen sensō* (Tōhoku and the Fifteen-Year War). Tokyo: Sanseidō, 1997.

Ritsumeikan daigaku kokusai heiwa myūjiamu (Kyoto Museum for World Peace). *Ritsumeikan daigaku kokusai heiwa myūjiamu dayori* (Newsletter from Kyoto Museum for World Peace, Ritsumeikan University) 1, no. 1 (May 19, 1993); 1, no. 2 (November 1, 1993); 2, no. 1 (January 20, 1995).

Sagamihara shimin no tsudoi 98 "731 butaiten" jikkō iinkai (Executive Committee on the Unit 731 Exhibition, Citizen's Gathering in 1998). *731 butai to saikinsen* (Unit 731 and Biological Warfare). Kanagawa: Sagamihara shimin no tsudoi 98 "731 butaiten" jikkō iinkai, 1998.

"SCAP Censors Philip Murray." *Amerasia* 11, no. 2 (February 1947): 54.

Shina jihen chūyūdan, kangekidan (Brave and Moving Stories of the China Incident). Tokyo: Dai Nihon yūbenkai kōdansha, 1938.

Shinbun taimusu sha. *Shina jihen senshi* (The History of the China Incident). Vol. 1. Tokyo: Kōtoku hōsankai Shuppan, 1937.

Shizuoka-ken chiikishi kyōiku kenkyūkai (Study Group on Local Historical Education in Shizuoka Prefecture). *Shizuoka-ken Minshū no rekishi o horu* (Examining People's History in Shizuoka Prefecture). Shizuoka: Shizuoka shinbunsha, 1996.

Shuppan rōren (The Association for Labor Unions of the Publishing Industry). *Kyōkasho repōto 97* (Textbook Report 1997). Tokyo: Shuppan rōren, 1997.

———. *Kyōkasho repōto 2002* (Textbook Report 2002). Tokyo: Shuppan rōren, 2002.

———. *"Nihonshi" "Sekaishi" kentei shiryōshū: Fukkatsu suru Nihon gunkoku shugi to rekishi kyōkasho* (Source Materials on Authorization of Textbooks on "Japanese History" and "World History"). Tokyo: Shuppan rōren, 1982.

Shūsen gojushūnen kokumin iinkai (National Committee for the Fiftieth Anniversary of the End of World War II). *Shūsen gojushūnen kokumin undō kirokushū*

(Historical Record of the National Committee for the Fiftieth Anniversary of the End of World War II). Tokyo: Shūsen gojushūnen kokumin iinkai, 1996.

Smith, Bradford. "Experiment in Racial Concentration." *Far Eastern Survey* 15, no. 14 (July 17, 1946): 214–18.

———. "Japan: Beauty and the Beast." *Amerasia* 6, no. 2 (April 1942): 86–94.

———. "The Mind of Japan." *Amerasia* 6, no. 1 (March 1942): 7–14.

Smith, Lee. "Fear and Loathing of Japan." *Fortune*, February 26, 1990, pp. 50–60.

Smythe, Lewis. *War Damage in the Nanking Area*. Shanghai: Mercury, 1938.

"Society for the Study of China's War against Japan Established." *BBC Summary of World Broadcasts*, Part 3: The Far East; B. International Affairs; 2. China; FE/0979/B2/ 1.

Sōrifu kokuritsu seron chōsajo (The Prime Minister's Office's National Research Institute of Public Opinion). *Kōshoku tsuihō ni tsuite no seron chōsa kekka hōkokusho* (The Report of Public Opinion Regarding Purges from Public Office). August 1952 (mimeograph copy).

———. *Kōwa ni kansuru seron chōsa* (Public Opinion Survey Regarding The Japan-U.S. Peace Treaty). June 1952 (mimeograph copy).

———. *Kyōiku ni kansuru seron chōsa* (Public Opinion Research Regarding Education). October 17, 1950, (mimeograph copy).

Spencer, Daniel. Review of *Japan's Imperial Conspiracy*, by David Bergamini. *Perspective* 1, no. 1 (January 1972): 11.

Stephan, John. "The Tanaka Memorial (1927): Authentic or Spurious?" *Modern Asian Studies* 7, no. 4 (1973): 733–45.

Storry, Richard. "Imperial Conspiracy in Japan?" *Pacific Affairs* 45, no. 2 (summer 1972): 272–76.

Suma, Yakichiro. *Where Japan Stands*. Tokyo: Hokuseido, 1940.

Sun, Zhaiwei. "Cause of the Nanking Massacre." In *Nanking 1937: Memory and Healing*, edited by Fei Fei Li, Robert Sabella, and David Liu, pp. 35–46. New York: M.E. Sharpe, 2002.

Suzuki, Akira. "Mukai shōi wa naze korosaretaka" (Why Was Second Lieutenant Mukai Executed?). *Shokun!* 4, no. 8 (August 1972): 178–203.

———. " 'Nankin daigyakusatsu' no maboroshi" (The Illusion of the "Nanjing Massacre"). *Shokun!* 4, no. 4 (April 1972): 177–91.

———. *"Nankin daigyakusatsu" no maboroshi* (The Illusion of the "Nanjing Massacre"). Tokyo: Bungeishunjū, 1973.

———. *Shin "Nankin daigyakusatsu" no maboroshi* (The Illusion of the "Nanjing Massacre"). Revised ed. Tokyo: Asuka shinsha, 1999.

Suzuki, Chieko. "Nankin daigyakusatsu o meguru dōkō to kadai" (Trends and Issues Regarding the Nanjing Massacre). *Kikan sensō sekinin kenkyū*, no. 46 (winter 2004): 30–37.

Suzuki, Yoshio. "Hōka" (Arson). In *Shinryaku: Chūgoku ni okeru Nihon senpan no kiroku*, edited by Chūgoku kikansha renrakukai (The Group of Returnees from China), pp. 92–98. Tokyo: Shindokushosha, 1958.

Tagawa, Suihō. *Norakuro sōkōgeki* (Norakuro's All-Out Attack). Tokyo: Kōdansha, 1984.

Takaishi, Shingoro. *Japan Speaks Out*. Tokyo: Hokuseido, 1938.

Takakuwa, Kōkichi. *Makkāsā no shinbun kenetsu* (Censorship by MacArthur). Tokyo: Yomiuri shinbunsha, 1984.

Takemoto, Tadao, and Ōhara Yasuo, *The Alleged "Nanking Massacre": Japan's Rebuttal to China's Forged Claims* (Tokyo: Meiseisha, 2000)

Takeuchi, Tatsuji. "The Background of the Sino Japanese Crisis." *Amerasia* 2, no. 4 (June 1938): 183–91.

Takeyama, Akiko. "Senryōka no hōsō: Shinsō wa kōda" (Broadcasting during the Occupation). In *Zoku shōwa bunka* (Showa Culture Part 2), edited by Minami Hiroshi, pp. 105–44. Tokyo: Keisō shobō, 1990.

Tanaka, Gunkichi. "Isho" (Testament). In *Seiki no isho* (Testaments of the Century), edited by Sugamo isho hensankai kankō jimusho (Sugamo: The Office of Editing and Publishing Testaments of the Century), pp. 82–83. Tokyo: Kōdansha, 1984.

Tanaka, Masaaki. "'Nankin daigyakusatsu' no kyokō" (The Fabrication of the "Nanjing Massacre." In *Daitō-A sensō no sōkatsu* (An Outline of the Greater East Asian War), edited by Rekishi kentō iinkai, pp. 252–71. Tokyo: Tendensha, 1995.

———. *"Nankin gyakusatsu" no kyokō* (The Illusion of "the Nanjing Massacre"). Tokyo: Nihon kyōbunsha, 1984.

———. *Nankin jiken no sōkatsu: gyakusatsu hitei 15 no ronkyo* (An Outline of the Nanjing Incident: Fifteen Grounds for the Denial of the Massacre). Tokyo: Kenkōsha, 1987.

———. *Nihon muzairon: shinri no sabaki* (On Japan's Innocence: The Truth on Trial). Tokyo: Taiheiyō shuppansha, 1952.

———. *Nihon muzairon* (Thesis of Japan's Innocence). Tokyo: Nihon hyōronsha, 1972.

———. *Sōyōshū: konomama dewa Nihon wa abunai* (Collected Essays: Japan Is Now in Peril). Tokyo: Kokumin shinbun sha, 1994.

———. *What Really Happened in Nanking: The Refutation of a Common Myth*. Tokyo: Sekai shuppan, 2000.

The Tanaka Memorial: Japan's Dream of World Conquest. With a foreword by Upton Close. Seattle: Columbia Publishing, 1934.

Tani, Hisao. "Yuigonjō" (Testament). In *Seiki no isho* (Testaments of the Century), edited by Sugamo isho hensankai kankō jimusho (Sugamo: The Office of Editing and Publishing Testaments of the Century), pp. 50–51. Tokyo: Kōdansha, 1984.

Tawara, Yoshifumi. *Dokyumento "ianfu" mondai to kyōkasho kōgeki* (Documentary: The Issue of "Comfort Women" and Attacks on School Textbooks). Tokyo: Kōbunken, 1997.

———. *Kenshō 15 nen sensō to chūkō rekishi kyōkasho* (Examining the Fifteen–Year War in Junior High and High School Textbooks). Tokyo: Gakushū no tomo sha, 1994.

———. *Kyōkasho kōgeki no shinsō* (The Intensity of Attacks on School Textbooks). Tokyo: Gakushū no tomo sha, 1997.

Thomas, A. F. *I Speak for Japan*. Tokyo: Zushi shuppan, 1938.

Thomas, John. *The Institute of Pacific Relations: Asian Scholars and American Politics*. Seattle: University of Washington Press, 1974.

Timperley, Harold. *Gaikokujin no mita Nihongun no bōkō*. Tokyo: Ryūkeishosha, 1972.
———. *Japan: A World Problem*. New York: John Day, 1942.
———. *Japanese Terror in China*. New York: Modern Age, 1938.
———. *La Guerre Telle qu'elle Est: La Terreur Japonaise en Chine*. Paris: Editions A. Pedone, 1939.
———. *Waiguoren muduzhongzhi Rijun baoxin*. Hankou: Guomin chubanshe, 1938.
———. *What War Means: Japanese Terror in China*. London: V. Gollancz, 1938.
"Tojo's Private Death." *Newsweek*, December 6, 1948, p. 43.
Tōkatsu sensōten jikkō iinkai (Executive Committee for the War Exhibition in the Tōkatsu Region). *Tōkatsu sensōten hōkokushū* (Report on the War Exhibition in the Tōkatsu Region). Hokkaidō: Tōkatsu sensōten jikkō iinkai, 1998.
Tokutake, Toshio. *Kyōkasho no sengo shi* (History of Postwar School Textbooks). Tokyo: Shin Nihon shuppansha, 1995.
Tokyo Rekishi kyōikusha kyōgikai (Association for History Educators, Tokyo). *Fotogaido Tōkyō no sensō to heiwa o aruku* (A Pictorial Walking Tour of War and Peace in Tokyo). Tokyo: Heiwa bunka, 1995.
Tōkyō saiban kenkyūkai (The Research Committee on the Tokyo Trial). *Paru hanketsusho* (Pal's Judgment). 2 vols. Tokyo: Kōdansha gakujutsu bunko, 1984.
Tōyama, Shigeki. "Sengo no rekishigaku to rekishi ishiki" (Postwar Historical Study and Historical Consciousness). In *Tōyama Shigeki chosakushū* (The Works of Tōyama Shigeki), Vol. 8. Tokyo: Iwanami shoten, 1991.
Tōyama Shigeki and Ōe Shinobu. *Ienaga Nihonshi no kentei* (The Authorization of Ienaga's History of Japan). Tokyo: Sanseidō, 1976.
Toyoda, Masayuki. "Chūka jinmin kyōwakoku no senpan saiban" (War Crimes Trials in the People's Republic of China). Parts 1 and 2. *Kikan sensō sekinin kenkyū*, no. 17 (autumn 1997): 67–73; no. 18 (winter 1997): 46–53.
Tupper, Eleanor, and George McReynolds. *Japan in American Public Opinion*. New York: Macmillan, 1937.
Uno, Seiichi. "Hyōki o aratameruna" (Do Not Alter Descriptions). *Shokun!* 14, no. 10 (October 1982): 86–87.
U.S. Strategic Bombing Survey. *The Effects of Strategic Bombing on Japanese Morale*. Washington, D.C.: Government Printing Office, 1947.
U.S. Subcommittee on International Operations and Human Rights of the Committee on Internation Relations, House of Representatives. *Was There a Tienanmen Massacre? The Visit of General Chi*. Washington, D.C.: U.S. Government Printing Office, 1998.
Wakabayashi, Bob. "The Nanking Massacre: Now You See It, . . ." *Monumenta Nipponica* 56, no. 4 (winter 2001): 521–44.
———. "The Nanking One-Hundred-Man Killing Contest Debate: War Guilt Amid Fabricated Illusions, 1971–75." *Journal of Japanese Studies* 26, no. 2 (2000): 307–40.
Watanabe, Harumi. "'Rekishi kara manabu' koto no imi" (The Meaning of 'Learning from History'"). *Shūkan kinyōbi*, no. 488 (December 12, 2003): 48–49.
Watanabe, Kenji. *Heiwa no tame no sensōron* (The Thesis of War for the Purpose of Peace). Tokyo: Kyōiku shiryō shuppankai, 1999.
Watanabe, Shōichi. "Manken kyo ni hoeta kyōkasho mondai" (Ten Thousand Dogs

Barked at the Textbook Controversy). *Shokun!* 14, no. 10 (October 1982): 23–44.

———. " 'Nankin gyakusatsu' no kyokō ni yosete" (Contributing to *The Illusion of "the Nanjing Massacre"*). In *"Nankin gyakusatsu" no kyokō*, edited by Tanaka Masaaki, pp. 1–6. Tokyo: Nihon kyōbunsha, 1984.

Webb, Herschel. Review of *Japan's Imperial Conspiracy*, by David Bergamini. *Pacific Historical Review* 42, no. 1 (February 1973): 124–25.

Wellington Koo Collection. Boxes 15, 24, 25, 29, 54. Rare Book and Manuscript Library, Columbia University.

Whiting, Allen. "Assertive Nationalism in Chinese Foreign Policy." *Asian Survey* 23, no. 8 (August 1983): 913–33.

———. "Chinese Nationalism and Foreign Policy after Deng." *China Quarterly*, no. 142 (June 1995): 295–316.

Xu Zhigeng. *Nanjing datusha* (The Nanjing Massacre). Taipei: Shibao wenhua chuban qiye youxian gongsi, 1989.

———. *Nanjing datusha* (The Nanjing Massacre). Beijing: Kunlun chubanshe, 1987.

Yamamoto, Masahiro. "Amerika ni okeru 'Nankin" kenkyū no dōkō: Jēmuzu Bakk Other Losses o meguru giron to hikaku shite" (Trend in the Studies of "Nanking" in the United States: In Comparison with James Bacque's *Other Losses*). In *Nihon "Nankin" gakkai nenpō*, edited by Higashinakano Osamichi, pp. 143–92. Tokyo: Tendensha, 2003.

———. *Nanking: Anatomy of an Atrocity*. Westport: Praeger, 2000.

Yamamoto, Taketoshi. *Senryōki media bunseki* (The Analysis of Media during the Years of Occupation). Tokyo: Hōsei daigaku shuppan kyoku, 1996.

Yang, Daqing. "The Malleable and the Contested: The Nanjing Massacre in Postwar China and Japan." In *Perilous Memories*, edited by T. Fujitani, Geoffrey White, and Lisa Yoneyama, pp. 50–86. Durham, N.C.: Duke University Press, 2001.

———. "Convergence or Divergence?: Recent Historical Writings on the Rape of Nanjing." *American Historical Review* 104, no. 3 (June 1999): 842–65.

———. "A Sino-Japanese Controversy: The Nanjing Atrocity as History." *Sino-Japanese Studies* 3, no. 1 (November 1990): 14–35.

Yashima, Taro. *The New Sun*. New York: Henry Holt, 1943.

"Yijiubasan nian guonei shijian dashi" (Top Ten Important Domestic News Stories of 1983). *Banyuetan*, no. 24, December 25, 1983, p. 3.

Yin, Jijun. *1937, Nanjing daqiuyuan: Xifangrenshi he Guojianquanqu* (The Great Rescue: Westerners and The International Safety Zone, 1937). Shanghai: Wenhui chubanshe, 1997.

Yoneda, Shinji. "Kyōkasho ni okeru Chūgokuzō" (Images of China in Textbooks). *Rekishi chiri kyōiku* 216 (October 1973): 16–30.

Yoshida, Takashi. "A Battle Over History: The Nanjing Massacre in Japan." In *The Nanjing Massacre in History and Historiography*, edited by Joshua Fogel, pp. 70–132. Berkeley: University of California Press, 2000.

———. "I Will Live Strong." *Japanese American National Museum Quarterly* 13, no. 1 (summer 1998): 9–13.

Yoshida, Yutaka. "Kaisetsu" (Foreword). In *Nankin jiken shiryōshū* (A Collection of Historical Materials on the Nanjing Incident), edited by Nankin jiken chōsa kenkyūkai, Vol. 1, pp. iii–iv. Tokyo: Aoki shoten, 1992.

————. "Sensō ninshiki o meguru kokkai rongi" (Debates in the Diet over the Understanding of the War. Parts 1 and 2. *Kikan sensō sekinin kenkyū*, no. 10 (winter 1995): pp. 70–78; no. 12 (summer 1996): 65–71.

Yoshimi, Yoshiaki, and Matsuno Seiya. *Dokugasusen kankei shiryō II* (Historical Materials Concerning Chemical Warfare, Part 2). Tokyo: Fuji shuppan, 1997.

Young, James. *Our Enemy*. Philadelphia: David McKay, 1942.

Young, Louise. *Japan's Total Empire*. Berkeley: University of California Press, 1998.

Zhongguo dier lishi dang'anguan (Number Two China Historical Archives) et al., eds. *Qin-Hua Rijun Nanjing datusha dang'an* (Archival Materials on the Nanjing Massacre Committed by the Japanese Army of Invasion). Jiangsu: Jiangsu guji, chubanshe, 1987.

————. *Nanjing datusha* (The Nanjing Massacre). Beijing: Zhonghua shuju chuban, 1995.

————. *Qin-Hua Rijun Nanjing datusha dang'an* (Archival Materials on the Nanjing Massacre Committed by the Japanese Army of Invasion). Jiangsu: Jiangsu guji, chubanshe, 1987.

Zhongguo gongtong lishi jiaocai weiyuanhui (The Committee for Sharing the Same Historical Material, China). Dong-Ya jinxiandaishi (Modern East Asia). Beijing: Zhongguo shehui kexue wenxian chubanshe, 2005.

Zhongguo Guomindang dangshi weiyuanhui (Guomindang Party History Commission, China). *Rijun zai Hua baoxing: Nanjing datusha* (Atrocities Committed by the Japanese Army: The Nanjing Massacre). 2 vols. Taipei: Zhongyang wenwu gongyingshe, 1987.

Zhongguo Renmin Kang-Ri Zhanzheng Jinianguan (The Museum of the War of Chinese People's Resistance Against Japan). *Zhongguo renmin kang-Ri Zhanzheng jinianguan* (The Museum of the War of Chinese People's Resistance Against Japan). Beijing: Zhongguo heping chubanshe, 1998.

Zhongguo renmin zhengzhi xiesheng huiyi jiangsusheng Nanjingshi weiyuanhui wenshi zuliao yanjiu weiyuanhui (the Research Committee on Historical Materials of the City of Nanjing, Jiangsu Province, Chinese People's Political Consultative Conference). *Shiliao xuanji Qin-Hua Rijun Nanjing datusha shiliao zhuanji* (Historical Sources: Materials on the Nanjing Massacre Committed by the Japanese Army of Invasion). Nanjing: August 1983.

Zhongyang dang'anguan (Central Historical Archives) et al., eds. *Nanjing datusha tuzheng* (Pictorial Evidence of the Nanjing Massacre). Changchun: Jilin renmin chubanshe, 1995.

Zhongyang yanjiuyuan, Jindaishi yanjiusuo (The Institute of Modern History, Academia Sinica). *Kang zhan jian guo shi yan tao hui lun wen ji* (Papers on the History of the War and Founding of the Nation). Taipei: Zhong yang yan jiu yuan, jin dai shi yan jiu suo, 1985), 2 vols.

Zhou, Erfu. *Nanjing de xianluo* (The Fall of Nanjing). Beijing: Renmin wenxue chubanshe, 1987.

Zhu, Chengshan. *Qin-Hua Rijun Nanjing datusha xinchunzhe zhengyanji* (Collection of Testimonies by Survivors of the Nanjing Massacre during the Japanese Army Invasion). Nanjing: Nanjing daxue chubanshe, 1994.

Zhu, Chengshan, et al., eds. *Qin-Hua Rijun Nanjing datusha waijirenshi zhengyanji*

(Collection of Testimonies by Non-Chinese About the Nanjing Massacre of the Japanese Army Invasion). Nanjing: Jiangsu renmin chubanshe, 1998.

"Zuiyi Rikou zai Nanjing datusha" (Recollections of the Great Japanese Massacre in Nanjing), *Xinhua yuebao* 3 (1951): 988–91.

HOME PAGES

Chūgokujin sensō higaisha no yōkyū o sasaeru kai (the Society to Support the Demands of Chinese War Victims): http://www.suopei.org/index-j.html.

The Gale Group. *Contemporary Authors Online*: http://www.galenet.com/servlet/BioRC.

Isaribikai: http://www.isaribi.net.

Kajimoto Masato's online documentary: http://www.geocities.com/nanking-atrocities.

Sensō sekinin shiryō sentā (the Center for Research and Documentation on Japan's War Responsibility): http://www.jca.apc.org/JWRC/index-j.html.

Tawara Yoshifumi:

http://www.linkclub.or.jp/~teppei-y/tawara%20HP/tosyho%20siryou.html.

http://www.linkclub.or.jp/~teppei-y/tawara%20HP/kaisetu.html.

Zearizu entāpuraizu: http://theres.co.jp/index.html.

CORRESPONDENCE:

Haga Hiraku to Iris Chang, November 11, 1998.
Yamazaki Takayasu to Iris Chang, October 19, 1998.
Yamazaki Takayasu to Iris Chang, November 30, 1998.
Yamazaki Takayasu to Iris Chang, December 2, 1998.
Iris Chang to Yamazaki Takayasu, October 26, 1998.
Iris Chang to Yamazaki Takayasu, December 1, 1998.

INDEX

Akazawa Shirō (professor at Ritsumeikan University), 149
Amerasia, 40–41
American occupation of Japan, 7, 45,
60, 71, 141–42, 183
censorship, 45–46
interview of Hirohito, 72–73
and Nanjing Massacre, 48–49
progressives in, 54–56
and textbooks, 46–48
Tokyo Trial, 49–51
Alperovitz, Gar, 168
Aoki shoten, 143–44
Aoyama Kazuo, 23
apologies, 84–85, 129, 132–34, 144–45,
157, 171
Arai Shin'ichi, 135, 139
Askew, David, 178, 234n69
Association for the Advancement of
a Liberalist View of History
(Jiyūshugi shikan kenkyūkai), 142,
145, 225n79
Association for Japan-China Friendship
(Nit-Chūyukō kyōkai), 56
Association for History Educators
(Rekishi kyōikusha kyōgikai), 55,
88, 100, 123
Association for History Educators, Gifu
(Gifu-ken Rekishi kyōikusha
kyōgikai), 136

Association for History Educators, Mie
(Mie-ken Rekishi kyōikusha
kyōgikai), 136
Association for Preserving Peace,
Japan (Nihon heiwa o mamoru
kai), 55
Association for the Study of the
Anti-Japanese War (Kang-
Ri zhanzhengshi xuehui),
156
Association of Bereaved Families
(Nihon izokukai), 133, 142
Azuma Shirō, 143–44, 157, 160–62,
164

Baba Tsunego, 13
Bailey, James, 120
Basic Books, 174, 176
Bataan Death march, 48, 166–68
Bates, Miner Searle, 31, 49, 68
Ben-Dasan, Isaiah. *See* Yamamoto,
Shichihei
Bergamini, David, 115–17, 172
Bertolucci, Bernardo, 123, 220n39
Bix, Herbert, 116–17
Buchanan, Pat, 167
Bungei shunjū, 17, 98
Bungei shunjū, 87, 119
Burgess, John, 118–19
Burress, Charles, 166

259

Carvajal, Doreen, 174
Celebration of Asian Nations' Symbio-
    sis (Ajia kyōsei no saiten), 142
Center for Research and Documenta-
    tion on Japan's War Responsibility
    (Nihon no sensō sekinin shiryō
    sentā), 135, 139, 153
Chang, Iris, 146–47, 161, 163, 165,
    171–77, 179, 181–82
Chen Fubao (Ch'en Fu-pao), 50
Chen Gongbo, 63
Chen, Sam, 123
Chiang Kai-shek, 12, 15–16, 18, 26, 29,
    34–35, 39, 63, 65–67, 111, 145, 152
Chinese Alliance for Memorial and
    Justice, 114, 123
Chinese Communist regime
    Japanese diplomatic relations, 102–05
    and Japanese revisionists, 157–58
    Nanjing Massacre politicized by,
        105–10
    and Taiwan, 111, 156
    and war reparations, 102
Chinese patriotic education, 105–10,
    154–58, 164, 182
Chira, Susan, 120
Choe Wan-Seok, 20
Chūō kōron, 20, 190n59
Chūkyō shuppan, 91,
Civil Censorship Detachment (CCD), 46
Civil War, China
    CCP and Japanese war criminals,
        65–68
    CCP and Nanjing Massacre, 68–70
    GMD policy toward Japanese war
        criminals, 63–64
    GMD and Nanjing Massacre, 64–65
Cold War, 4–5, 45, 53, 60, 183
Committee to Examine History (Rekishi
    kentō iinkai), 141, 144
Coox, Alvin, 116
Counsel in the Case for Awarding Com-
    pensation to Chinese War Victims
    (Chūgokujin sensō higai baishō
    seikyū jiken bengodan), 134
Crowley, James, 116

Dai Guohui, 93
Deng Xiaoping, 105–06, 124
Diet Members for the Transmission of
    Correct History (Tadashii Rekishi

o tsutaeru kokkai giin renmei),
    141
Diet Members' League for the Fiftieth
    Anniversary of the End of War
    (Shūsen gojū shūnen kokkai giin
    renmei), 141
Doi Takako, 132
Don't Cry, Nanking, 149, 158–59, 163,
    227n115,
Durdin, Tilman, 38, 137

Efron, Sonni, 176
Embree, John, 41
Enola Gay, 165, 167–69
Etō Takami, 133, 141
Executive Committee of the Nanjing
    Massacre Art Exhibition (Nankin
    1937 kaigaten jikkō iinkai), 136
Eykholt, Mark, 70

Fallows, James, 166
Far-Eastern War News (Kyokutō sensō
    nyūsu), 23, 191n67
Fitch, George, 32, 98
Fogel, Joshua, 173, 178
Fujio Masayuki, 112–13, 122, 124,
    141
Fujioka Nobukatsu, 142–43, 145–47,
    149–50, 153, 177, 181
Fujiwara Akira, 97, 119, 134, 150,
    174–75
Fukuda Kazuya, 145–46
Fushun War Criminal Prison, 107
Future Political Economy Research
    Institute, 177

Gao Liang, 106–07
Gao Xingzu, 109
Gayn, Mark, 77
Global Alliance for Preserving the
    History of World War II in Asia,
    171
Gluck, Carol, 202n53
Gotō Kōsaku, 59–60, 96
Grajdanzev, A., 41
Group for Constitutional Study (Kenpō
    o manabu kai), 130
Group of Returnees from China
    (Chūgoku kikansha renrakukai),
    56–57, 88, 170
Guo Qi, 111–12

Guomindang (GMD)
    and Chinese traitors, 63–64
    and Japanese war crimes, 29, 63–65,
        204n5
    and Kaji Wataru, 23, 34–35
    and Nanjing Massacre, 64–65,
        111–13, 140
    Taiwan, 111–13
Guo Moruo, 34, 69, 196n43

Haberman, Clyde, 122–23
Haga Hiraku, 174
Hanaki Sankichi, 50
Hanaoka Incident, 56
Hani Gorō, 54–55
Harwit, Martin, 167–68
Hasegawa Michiko, 141
Hashimoto Mitsuji, 143–44
Hashimoto Ryūtarō, 132–33
Hata Ikuhiko, 99–100, 150
Hersey, John, 71, 75–77
Hidaka Rokurō, 53, 92–93
Higashinakano Osamichi, 146–47, 150,
    178, 182
Hino Ashihei, 39
Hirohito, Emperor, 45, 48, 85, 107,
    172
    and Chinese Communist Party, 66,
        103
    death, 129, 131
    SCAP, 71–73
    war responsibility of, 48, 66, 72–73,
        85, 115–17, 129–32
Hiroshima Panels, 88, 211n42.
    See also Maruki Iri and Maruki Toshi
Hiroshima Peace Memorial Museum,
    135
Historical Science Society of Japan
    (Rekishigaku kenkyūkai; Rekken),
    55, 131
"The History of the Pacific War"
    (Taiheiyō sensō shi), 48–49
History That Opens the Future (Mirai o
    hiraku rekishi), 151–52
Ho Ying-chin (He Yingchin), 111
Holland, William, 41
Honda Katsuichi, 88, 96–97, 112, 134,
    149, 15
    repercussions of "Travels in China,"
        84–87
    "Travels in China," 81–84

Hora Tomio, 20, 26, 60, 87, 96–100,
    112, 119, 160
Hosokawa Morihiro, 132–33, 141
Hsu Shuhsi, 33, 38
Hu Yaobang, 105–06, 154

Ienaga Saburō, 58–59, 95, 134
    See also trials
Inoue Hisashi, 137, 150, 174–75
Institute of Modern History, Academia
    Sinica, 112
international conferences on the Nan-
    jing Massacre, 177–78
International Military Tribunal for the
    Far East. See Tokyo Trial
International Committee for the Nan-
    jing Safety Zone, 30–33, 68
    See also Nanjing International Safety
    Zone
Iriye, Akira, 131
Ishihara Shintarō, 87, 133, 143, 146,
    157, 160, 170, 172
Ishikawa Tatsuzō, 20–22
Itakura Yoshiaki, 98, 144–45,
Itō Kazunaga, 135

Jameson, Sam, 122–24
Japan Association for "Nanjing"
    Studies (Nihon "Nankin" gakkai),
    150, 181
Japan Teachers Union (Nihon
    kyōshokuin kumiai; Nikkyōso), 53,
    56, 104, 118, 133
Japanese anti–U.S.-Japan Security
    Treaty movements, 57
Japanese denials of Nanjing, 5, 61, 99,
    121–24, 143–53, 157–58, 160–63,
    170, 172
    See also Fujioka Nobukatsu;
    Higashinakano Osamichi;
    Ishihara Shintarō; Itakura
    Yoshiaki; Kitamura Minoru;
    Suzuki Akira; Tanaka Masaaki;
    Watanabe Shōichi; Yamamoto
    Shichihei
Japanese education. See Ministry of
    Education, Japan
Japanese People's Antiwar Alliance
    (Nihonjin hansen dōmei), 27,
    34–35, 68
Japanese purges, 53, 55, 77

Japanese Society for History Textbook
Reform (Atarashii rekishi kyōkasho
o tsukuru kai), 142–43, 151–52
Japanese textbooks, 53, 89, 91, 95, 151
in the 1970s, 88–89
in the 1980s, 95–96
in the 1990s, 139–41
during occupation, 46–48
in the 2000s, 152
wartime, 3–4, 14
See also The Problem of Deplorable Textbooks; New History Textbook; textbook controversy of 1982;
trials
Jiang Genfu, 82, 85–86, 209nn6–7
Jiang Zemin, 160
Jiyūshobō, 95
Johnson, Sheila, 77

Kaji Wataru, 23–24, 27, 33–35, 56, 68
Kajimoto Masato, 178
Kasahara Tokushi, 97, 137–38, 140–41,
150–51, 164, 173, 178, 181–82
Kase Toshikazu, 122, 142, 219n27
Kashiwa shobō, 147, 173–76
Kawasaki Peace Museum (Kawasaki-shi
heiwakan), 135
Kaya Okinori, 93
Kennedy, David, 172–73, 175
Keenan, Joseph, 149
Kishi Nobusuke, 53, 57, 93, 112, 218n56
Kitamura Minoru, 147, 150, 180–81
Kiyosawa Kiyoshi, 13
killing contest, 16, 26, 64, 81–82,
85–87, 157, 178, 187n26
trial, 151
See also Honda Katsuichi; Jiang
Genfu; Suzuki Akira; Yamamoto
Shichihei
Kim Hak Hyon, 93
Kluckhohn, Frank, 72–73
Kobayashi Kunio, 119
Kobayashi Yoshinori, 142, 146, 153
Kobori Keiichirō, 99, 122, 141
Koo, Wellington, 28–30, 33, 65, 193n2,
194n4
Kosaka Eiichi, 17–18
Kumamoto Sixth Division, 59, 64
Kyōiku shuppan, 89
Kyoto Committee against Strengthen-
ing the Emperor System (Tennōsei

kyōka o yurusanai Kyōto jikkō
iinkai), 130
Kyoto Museum for World Peace, Ritsumeikan University (Ritsumeikan
daigaku kokusai heiwa myūjiamu),
135–36

The Last Emperor, 123–24
Li Peng, 155
Li Tenghui, 163
Living Soldiers (Ikiteiru heitai), 20–22
Li Yunhan, 112
Li Xiuying, 108–09, 139
trial, 151
Liberal Democratic Party (Jiyūmin-
shutō; LDP), 87, 93, 103, 112, 118,
121–22, 129–33, 141–42, 218n56
Liu Danian, 156
Liu Hanfu, 20

Maeda Yūji, 94, 96, 213n68
Magee, John, 32, 52, 98
MacArthur, Douglas, 47, 71–73, 121,
133
See also SCAP
Manchurian Incident (Sep. 18, 1931),
14, 23, 26, 29, 37, 46–47, 90, 93,
190n66, 194n4, 200n20
Mao Zdedong, 66, 103, 216n23
Maruki Iri and Maruki Toshi, 88, 183,
211n42
Masaki Hiroshi, 54–55
Matsui Iwane, 16–17, 51, 66, 74, 98–99,
116, 233n33
his field diary, 98–99
Matsumura Toshio, 151
Matsuo Ichirō, 147
Matsuoka Yōsuke, 74
Mayuzumi Toshirō, 94–95, 122, 142,
219n27
Meiji Gakuin University, 97
Memorial for Compatriot Victims of the
Japanese Military's Nanjing Mas-
sacre (Nanjing Massacre Memorial
Hall), 99, 107, 110, 113, 140, 157,
160
Ministry of Education, Japan, 3, 46, 48,
89–93, 95, 104, 117, 119, 122, 161
Miyazawa Kiichi, 91
Mizutani Naoko, 162
Morii Makoto, 130

Morita Akio, 143
Moteki Hiromichi, 177
Motoshima Hitoshi, 130–31, 135
Mukai Toshiaki, 64, 82, 86, 157,
    187n26, 204n6, 209n7
Murayama Tomiichi, 133–34, 156, 160
Museum of the War of Chinese People's
    Resistance against Japan, 106,
    163

Nagano Shigeto, 141, 144, 157, 172
Nagasaki Atomic Bomb Museum, 135,
    157
Nagatomi, Hiromichi, 170, 232n25
Nakamura Isao, 113, 227n105
Nakano Ryōko, 110
Nakasone Yasuhiro, 110, 119, 122
Nanjing Massacre Memorial Hall. See
    Memorial for Compatriot Victims
    of the Japanese Military's Nanjing
    Massacre
Nanjing Massacre's numbers of
    victims, 181–82
    and American historiography, 30, 38,
        168, 172, 176–78, 233n33
    and Chinese historiography, 28, 65,
        94, 112, 138, 157, 164
    and Japanese historiography, 49, 59,
        86, 97–98, 143, 145–47, 150
    and textbooks, 89, 95, 139–40, 152
    and Western eyewitness' estimates,
        31, 33, 194n21
Nanjing International Safety Zone, 21,
    68, 97, 158–59, 163
    See also International Committee for
    the Nanjing Safety Zone
Naono Akiko, 169
National Committee for the Fiftieth
    Anniversary of the End of World
    War II (Shūsen gojushūnen
    kokumin iinkai), 142
National People's Council to Defend
    Japan (Nihon o mamoru kokumin
    kaigi), 142–43
"Never Send Our Students to the Battle-
    field" (oshiego o futatabi senjō ni
    okuruna), 56
New Edition of Japanese History (Shinpen
    Nihonshi), 121–23, 152
New Frontier Party (Shinshintō), 133,
    141

New History Textbook (Atarashii rekishi
    kyōkasho), 151–52
Nihon shoseki, 89, 151
Nishi, Kanji, 142, 181
Noda, Tsuyoshi, 64, 82, 157, 187n26,
    204n6, 209n7
Nosaka Sanzō, 35
"Now It Can Be Told" (Shinsō wa kōda),
    48, 200n18
Number Two China Historical Archives,
    110, 159

Oda Baku, 88
Ogawa Heiji, 90
Ogawa Heishirō, 103
Ōhara Kōtarō, 25
Ōhara Yasuo, 176–77
Oka Masaharu Memorial Nagasaki
    Peace Museum (Oka Masaharu
    kinen Nagasaki heiwa shiryōkan),
    135, 223n37
Okamoto Shumpei, 116
Ōkawa Shūmei, 74, 148
Okuno Seisuke, 124, 133, 141–43
On Japan's Innocence: The Truth on Trial
    (Nihon muzai ron: shinri no
    sabaki), 51–52
    See also Tanaka Masaaki
Ono Kenji, 97
Onodera Toshitaka, 134
Osaka International Peace Center (Pīsu
    Ōsaka), 135
Ōsaka shoseki, 140, 225n65
Ōyama Isao, 12

Pal, Radhabinod, 50–52, 60, 148
Parsons, Jim, 170–71
patriotic education, China, 105–10,
    154–58, 164
Peace Museum of Saitama (Saitama-
    ken heiwa shiryōkan), 135
Pitman, Joanna, 170
Pride: The Moment of Destiny (Puraido:
    Unmei no toki), 148–49, 157
The Problem of Deplorable Textbooks
    (Ureubeki kyōkasho no mondai),
    53
Propaganda Department of the CCP
    Central Committee, 105–06, 156,
    229n13

The Rape of Nanking (Nankin
    daigyakusatsu no zu), 88, 183,
    211n42
Rabe, John, 31–32
    diary, 139, 145–46
Reagan, Ronald, 117–18
Red Purge, 53
Reischauer, Edwin, 123
Research Committee on the Nanjing
    Incident (Nankin jiken chōsa
    kenkyūkai)
Resolution to Renew Resolve for Peace
    Based on the Lessons of History
    (Rekishi o kyōkun ni heiwa e no
    ketsui o arata ni suru ketsugi), 133
Reston, James, Jr., 119–20
Ringle, Ken, 171–72
Rojas, Aurelio, 170–71
rōnōha (Labor-Farmer faction), 19
Rooney, Andy, 166
Royko, Mike, 166

Saitō Kunihiko, 161
Sankō. See *Three Alls*
Sanseidō (publisher), 95, 212n57
Satō Kazuo, 141
Schell, Orville, 172
Sekai shuppan, 176
Shapiro, Margaret, 124
Shimamura Yoshinobu, 141
"Shihua shishuo." *See* "To Tell the Truth"
Shimizu shuppan, 152
Smith, Bradford, 40–41, 48–49
Smith, Lee, 166
Smythe, Lewis, 30–31, 38, 60, 97–98,
    109, 112, 194n21
Sneider, Daniel, 121–22
Society to Support the Demands of
    Chinese War Victims (Chūgokujin
    sensō higaisha no yōkyū o sasaeru
    kai), 134
Song Meiling (Madame Chiang
    Kai-shek), 39
Special Higher Police (Tokkō), 18–19,
    23–24
Steele, Archibald T., 38, 137
Stockholm Appeal, 55
Stokes, Henry, 118
Study Group on Propaganda Photo-
    graphs (Puropaganda shashin
    kenkyūkai), 147

Sun Zhaiwei, 178
Supreme Commander for Allied Powers
    (SCAP), 45, 47–48, 51, 53, 71–73,
    76–77, 202n47
Suzuki Akira, 86–87, 94, 147
Suzuki Shun'ichi, 130
Suzuki Yoshio, 57
Suzuki Zenkō, 90, 104–05

Tagawa Suihō, 15
Takemoto Tadao, 176–77
Talbot, H., 29
Tanaka Giichi, 28
Tanaka Gunkichi, 64, 204n6
Tanaka Masaaki, 51–52, 54, 87,
    95–100, 112, 118–19, 122, 141,
    144, 148–49, 176–77, 181
Tanaka Memorial, 28–29, 194n4
Tang Shengzhi, 16, 38, 100, 159
Tani Hisao, 59–60, 64–65, 111, 204n6,
    204n13
Teikoku shoin, 91
"To Tell the Truth," 162
Teng Teng, 156
tennōsei (emperor system), 54–55, 61,
    85, 130–31
Tethler, Alexander, 20
textbook controversy of 1982
    and America, 117–19, 122, 124
    and China, 102–04, 113
    and Japan, 81, 89–93, 95, 100–01
Three Alls (Sankō), 56–57
"Three-Alls Operation" (burn all, kill
    all, and loot all), 35, 68, 82, 89
Tiananmen Massacre, 154–55
Timperley, Harold, 23, 32–33, 38–39,
    60, 112, 147
Tōjō Hideki, 46, 65, 71–74, 77, 148–49,
    157
Tokkō. *See* Special Higher Police
Tōkyō shoseki, 89, 95, 139
Tokyo Trial, 45, 49–51, 60, 69–70, 74–
    75, 77, 96–98, 115, 124, 140–41,
    148–50, 152, 181, 183
    and Japanese progressives, 54–55
trials
    Azuma Shirō, 143–44, 160–62
    Communist, 67–68
    compensation lawsuits, 134–35
    Guomindang, 59, 64–65, 70, 112,
        152, 157

Ienaga textbook lawsuits, 57–59, 95, 213n73
  killing contest, 151
  Li Xiuying, 151
Treat, John Whittier, 168–69
Tucker, Luther, 24, 191n71

Unemoto Masami, 95–97
Unit 731, 68, 107
  exhibition on Unit 731, 136
  Memorial Museum, 107, 136
United States Strategic Bombing Survey, 46
Uno Seiichi, 94
Uno Shintarō, 83
Up Close (Chikaki yori), 54

"victim consciousness," 55–56, 120, 135
"victimizer consciousness," 55, 82, 88–89, 100, 125, 132–34

Wakabayashi, Bob, 178–79
Wang Jingwei, 4
war crimes. See Tokyo Trial; trials
War Exhibition for Peace 1995
  (Heiwa no tame no sensōten 1995), 136

Watanabe Harumi, 97, 151
Watanabe Shōichi, 92, 94, 96, 143
Webb, Herschel, 116
Webb, William, 115–16, 149
What War Is (Sensō to wa), 23–24
Whiting, Allen, 103
Wilson, Robert, 49, 74
Wu Xiuquan, 67
Wu Ziniu, 149, 158–59, 230n25

Xiao Xiangqian, 103
Xinhua Yuebao, 68
Xu Chuanyin, 49, 52, 74

Yamada Unit, 25, 138
Yamakawa shuppan, 140
Yamamoto Masahiro, 178, 180–81
Yamamoto Shichihei, 84–85, 87, 89
Yanaihara Tadao, 19
Yang Daqing, 176, 178, 202n54
Yashima Tarō, 41
Yasuhiko, 115–16, 233n33
Yoshida Yutaka, 97, 137
Young, James, 40
Yu Shuning, 161

Zhou Enlai, 34, 67
Zhu Bangzao, 161

STUDIES OF THE WEATHERHEAD EAST ASIAN INSTITUTE

Columbia University

SELECTED TITLES

(Complete list at http://www.columbia.edu/cu/weai/studies-of-weatherhead.html)

The Merchants of Zigong: Industrial Entrepreneurship in Early Modern China, Madeleine Zelin. Columbia University Press, 2005

Science and the Building of a Modern Japan, Morris Low. Palgrave Macmillan, Ltd., 2005

Kinship, Contract, Community, and State: Anthropological Perspectives on China, Myron L. Cohen. Stanford University Press, 2005

Rearranging the Landscape of the Gods: The Politics of a Pilgrimage Site in Japan, 1573–1912, Sarah Thal. University of Chicago Press, 2005

Reluctant Pioneers: China's Expansion Northward, 1644–1937, James Reardon-Anderson. Stanford University Press, 2005

Contract and Property in Early Modern China, Madeleine Zelin, Jonathan K. Ocko, and Robert P. Gardella, eds. Stanford University Press, 2004

Gutenberg in Shanghai: Chinese Print Capitalism, 1876–1937, Christopher A. Reed. UBC Press, 2004

Japan's Colonization of Korea: Discourse and Power, Alexis Dudden. University of Hawai'i Press, 2004

Divorce in Japan: Family, Gender, and the State, 1600–2000, Harald Fuess. Stanford University Press, 2004

The Communist Takeover of Hangzhou: The Transformation of City and Cadre, 1949–1954, James Gao. University of Hawai'i Press, 2004

Taxation without Representation in Rural China, Thomas P. Bernstein and Xiaobo Lü. Modern China Series, Cambridge University Press, 2003

The Reluctant Dragon: Crisis Cycles in Chinese Foreign Economic Policy, Lawrence Christopher Reardon. University of Washington Press, 2002

Cadres and Corruption: The Organizational Involution of the Chinese Communist Party, Xiaobo Lü. Stanford University Press, 2000

Japan's Imperial Diplomacy: Consuls, Treaty Ports, and War with China, 1895–1938, Barbara Brooks. University of Hawai'i Press, 2000

China's Retreat from Equality: Income Distribution and Economic Transition, Carl Riskin, Zhao Renwei, and Li Shi, eds. M. E. Sharpe, 2000

Nation, Governance, and Modernity: Canton, 1900–1927, Michael T. W. Tsin. Stanford University Press, 1999

Assembled in Japan: Electrical Goods and the Making of the Japanese Consumer, Simon Partner. University of California Press, 1999

Civilization and Monsters: Spirits of Modernity in Meiji Japan, Gerald Figal. Duke University Press, 1999

The Logic of Japanese Politics: Leaders, Institutions, and the Limits of Change, Gerald L. Curtis. Columbia University Press, 1999

Contesting Citizenship in Urban China: Peasant Migrants, the State and Logic of the Market, Dorothy Solinger. University of California Press, 1999

Bicycle Citizens: The Political World of the Japanese Housewife, Robin LeBlanc. University of California Press, 1999

Alignment despite Antagonism: The United States, Japan, and Korea, Victor Cha. Stanford University Press, 1999